HUMAN RIGHTS & POLICING

SECOND REVISED EDITION

THE RAOUL WALLENBERG INSTITUTE
PROFESSIONAL GUIDES TO HUMAN RIGHTS
VOLUME 5

HUMAN RIGHTS AND POLICING

Second revised edition

By

Ralph Crawshaw
Stuart Cullen
Tom Williamson

THE RAOUL WALLENBERG INSTITUTE
PROFESSIONAL GUIDES TO HUMAN RIGHTS
VOLUME 5

MARTINUS NIJHOFF PUBLISHERS
LEIDEN/BOSTON
2007

A C.I.P. record for this book is available from the Library of Congress.

Printed on acid-free paper.

ISBN-13: 978 90 04 15437 7
ISBN-10: 90 04 15437 X

Printed and bound in The Netherlands.

Contents

PART III THE TREATMENT OF SUSPECTS – DECENCY AND DETENTION

PART IV INVESTIGATIVE INTERVIEWING: PROFESSIONALISM AND BEST PRACTICE

PART V POLICING CONFLICT, DISTURBANCE AND TENSION – PREVENTIVE AND REACTIVE RESPONSES

Contents

Preface

This is a second, thoroughly revised and expanded edition of a book that has four clear objectives: to provide a concise account and analysis of international human rights and humanitarian law standards relevant to policing; to set out arguments for compliance with those standards; to show how they may be met in two key areas of policing, interviewing suspects of crime, and policing in times of armed conflict, disturbance and tension; and to make practical recommendations on the management of police agencies. Good practice on interviewing suspects and on policing conflict is included because they are areas of policing where human rights are most at risk. Good management practice is included because intelligent management by enlightened leaders is necessary to secure effective, lawful and humane policing. For this edition, the three Parts dealing with international standards have been expanded and updated in a variety of ways. In particular, much more of the jurisprudence of courts and bodies established under international law to secure compliance with international human rights and humanitarian standards is included.

The account of international humanitarian law, or the laws of war, has been extended. The Part dealing with investigative interviewing includes a more comprehensive account of experimental and theoretical work behind the development of interviewing practices and techniques, including a critical social psychological analysis of the factors involved in human rights abuses and torture. A completely new Part, on policing in times of armed conflict, disturbance and tension, by a new co-author Stuart Cullen, has been added for this edition. The final Part, on strategies for management and change of police organisations, has been expanded with particular emphasis being given to practical aspects of police leadership. It was also written by Stuart Cullen as Barry Devlin, who wrote this Part in the first edition, was unable to contribute to the second edition.

Whilst the book was in the final stages of its preparation, the Human Rights Council was established by the General Assembly of the United Nations in its resolution 60/251 of 15 March 2006. This replaces the Commission on Human Rights, described in chapter 1 of Part 1 herein, which was formally abolished on 16 June 2006.

This book is produced as one of a series of four on the theme of human rights and policing. Also available, from the same publisher, are *Police and Human Rights - a Manual for Teachers, Resource Persons and Participants in Human Rights Programmes*, May 1999, by Ralph Crawshaw; *Essential Texts on Human Rights for the Police*, March 2001, by Ralph Crawshaw and Leif Holmstrom (eds) (a compilation of international human rights instruments with introductions); and *Essential Cases on Human Rights for the Police*, published in 2006, by Ralph Crawshaw and Leif Holmstrom (reviews and summaries of cases essential to police practice and to the development of policy, strategy and tactics from international human rights courts and bodies). Each book can be used independently, and the series is a comprehensive source of reference for the subject area of human rights and policing.

The books are written for police officials (especially those with command responsibilities), lawyers, prosecutors, human rights workers with an interest in human rights and policing, and resource persons and teachers responsible for the education of police officials.

The authors wish to acknowledge the diligent and careful work of Carin Laurin of the Raoul Wallenberg Institute in the editing of this book. The preparation and dissemination of the present publication have been generously supported by the Foreign and Commonwealth Office of the United Kingdom, and by the Swedish International Development Cooperation Agency (Sida).

Ralph Crawshaw, Tom Williamson and Stuart Cullen

Introduction

All states are bound under international law, to varying degrees, to protect the human rights of people living within their jurisdiction. The extent to which they meet or fail to meet some of their most important legal obligations in this respect depends crucially on all of the processes of law enforcement, and particularly on those executed by police agencies. However whilst it can be assumed that police officials are aware of national law governing the exercise of their powers and protecting human rights, it is demonstrably clear that they are largely unaware of international legal provisions on those matters and of international instruments directly addressed to police officials. It is also clear that police officials have little understanding of international humanitarian law also known as the laws of war.

The importance of police in protecting rights and meeting standards as required by international law, is one substantial reason for advocating that the international dimension to human rights protection should form part of the body of knowledge of all police officials and, certainly, of police leaders and those responsible for educating and training police. Another substantial reason is that it is important to introduce or reinforce a human rights culture within police agencies as a means of securing good behaviour by police.

In times of armed conflict international humanitarian law regulates the conduct of hostilities, the permissible means and methods of warfare, and protects victims of armed conflict. As police officials become involved in international armed conflicts in a variety of ways, and as they are one of the means by which states respond to internal conflicts or civil war, it is clearly important that police, especially police leaders, should understand relevant principles and provisions of this branch of law. They need to do so as a matter of good professional practice, in order that they may behave correctly, benefit from the forms of protection to which they are entitled, promote the protection of others, and enforce or encourage correct behaviour on the part of others. Furthermore, the application of international humanitarian law, even in those conflict situations that fall below the threshold of armed conflict and where this branch of law may not be legally applicable, amounts simply to good practice.

It is absolutely essential that both branches of law inform police responses to terrorism, which may or may not occur in the context of armed conflict. Acts of terrorism are murderous assaults on individuals and on humankind generally, and subversive of civilised values common to all cultures and societies. However, when police or other state officials react by violating the great principles of justice and humanity embodied in human rights law and international humanitarian law, they further erode those same values which it is their function to protect. Law breaking by law enforcers for the purposes of law enforcement, and acts of inhumanity by protectors of humankind for the purposes of restoring humanity are matters of monumental absurdity and folly.

To focus on human rights and good behaviour in policing is not only important as an end in itself, it is also important as a means of securing effective policing in times of peace and in times of conflict. The support of the community, essential to effective policing in a democracy, is dependent upon police respecting the rule of law, and respecting the human rights of groups and individuals within that community. Furthermore the success of any police action, and hence its effectiveness, cannot be judged independently of the means adopted to achieve it. Any police action in which unlawful or inhumane methods are adopted is a failure of policing, regardless of any other results the action may have achieved.

This book provides a concise account and analysis of international human rights and humanitarian law standards relevant to policing. It then shows how these standards may be met in two key areas of policing, interviewing suspects and policing conflict, areas in which human rights are most at risk. Finally it makes practical recommendations on the management of police agencies.

Part I of the book deals with the democratic framework for policing. The international system for the protection of human rights is described, and the relationship between human rights and policing considered, as is the relationship between human rights and democracy. Finally, in the context of a discussion on police ethics, two international codes of behaviour for police are analysed.

Part II of the book deals with the international standards governing police responses to armed conflict, disorder and tension, and those regulating the use of force by police. International humanitarian law and human rights law are compared and contrasted, and elements of international humanitarian law especially relevant to police are introduced. Reference is made to terrorism, as a form of conflict, in the context of international human rights law, international humanitarian law, and other responses of the international community to that phenomenon. The right to life and the means for its protection under international human rights law are considered, and international standards addressed to police on the use of force and firearms are closely analysed.

Part III of the book deals with the treatment of suspects who are detainees in police custody. The phenomenon of torture is examined as is the extent of its prohibition (total and absolute) under international law. Torture and abuse of terrorist suspects is discussed. The rights of detainees under international human rights law, and specific standards concerning the interviewing of suspects are considered.

Part IV provides an example of best practice for interviewing suspects of crime and witnesses to crime in accordance with international standards described in Part III. In the context of a professional approach to police investigations, it sets out theoretical bases for investigative interviewing, describes the practice of investigative interviewing in relation to suspects and witnesses, and includes some methods to secure best practice through supervision, monitoring and training. Specific standards concerning the regulation of interviewing of suspects are considered, together with examples of international best practice norms.

Part V shows how police responses to armed conflict, disturbance and tension can be conducted in compliance with the standards discussed in Parts I to III, and especially those described in Part II dealing with international humanitarian law and with the use of force. It sets out strategies for conflict prevention, and discusses command, planning and operations in conflict situations and strategies for peace and security in post conflict situations.

Part VI deals with management, and specifically the management of change, within police organisations. It discusses democratisation and reform in police agencies, considers the management of people, managing the process of change, and police ethics and corruption, and it examines the nature of the effective organisation.

Whilst there are many highly competent and dedicated police officials and many well managed and well resourced agencies, some of which have undergone radical transformation processes, it remains true to say that no police agency is meeting in full its obligations to respect human rights in the processes of law enforcement. No police agency is meeting in full its duty actively to protect human rights. These shortcomings mean that no police agency is operating as effectively, lawfully and humanely as it could be. It is hoped that this book will inform, enlighten, support and encourage all those seeking to improve the craft and profession of policing.

PART I

THE DEMOCRATIC FRAMEWORK
– LAW AND ETHICS

Chapter 1. The International System for the Protection of Human Rights

(A) THE NATURE OF HUMAN RIGHTS

The present international system for the protection of human rights, in existence since the middle of the last century, has protected the physical and mental integrity of countless numbers of people, and granted remedy and redress to many victims of human rights violations. In spite of the fact that this system is imperfect, as are all human systems; in site of the fact that it is cynically manipulated and ignored by some and disparaged by others; in spite of the brutality and lawlessness of some of those vested with power it is one of the greatest achievements of humankind. International human rights standards have been agreed and promulgated; means to secure compliance by states with their obligations to secure human rights have been established; and international tribunals hold individuals to account for their criminal abuse of power. Nevertheless, in the graphic language of the Preamble to the Universal Declaration of Human Rights,[1] disregard and contempt for human rights continue to result in barbarous acts that outrage the conscience of mankind.

Police agencies and police officials are uniquely placed to prevent the barbarity of gross abuse of power; to protect the mental and physical integrity of vulnerable people; to alleviate the suffering of victims of human rights violations; and to bring to justice those responsible for such violations. The purposes of this book are to indicate to police officials the centrality of human rights to their craft and profession, and to show them why and how they should use their power, authority, skills and resources to secure respect for and protection of human rights.

Whilst human rights have a history that precedes the establishment of the United Nations in 1945, for our present purposes they are most usefully understood as those rights enshrined in international instruments promulgated by the United Nations and regional bodies subsequent to that date. These instruments include, for example, the Universal Declaration of Human Rights, the International Covenant on Economic, Social and Cultural Rights, the International Covenant on Civil and Political Rights,[2] regional human rights treaties, and instruments dealing with specific aspects of human rights protection such as the prohibition of torture. These international treaties and agreements represent commitments entered into by States towards people living within their jurisdiction. Under this protection regime, human rights are said to derive from the inherent dignity and worth of the human person and they are universal, indivisible and interdependent.

Human rights concern the relationship between individuals and the state. They control and regulate the exercise of state power over individuals, endow individuals

---

[1] Adopted under General Assembly resolution 217 A (III) of 10 December 1948.
[2] Both Covenants were adopted under General Assembly resolution 2200 A (XXI) of 16 December 1966.

3

with freedoms in relation to the state, and place requirements on states to satisfy basic human needs of individuals within their jurisdiction.

These characteristics of human rights are an indication that there are different categories of human rights, and some of these categories are apparent in the names of the two International Covenants referred to above. Economic and social rights (such as the right to work, the right to social security, the right to a standard of living adequate for health and well-being, and the right to education) amount to requirements on states to meet those basic needs. Civil rights (such as the right to life, the prohibition of arbitrary deprivation of liberty, and the prohibition of torture) protect individuals against abuse of power by states. Political rights, and rights essential to the political process, (such as the right to participate in government, the right to freedom of peaceful assembly and association, and the right to freedom of opinion and expression) secure specific rights and freedoms for individuals in relation to the state. They constitute the basic democratic rights and freedoms.

Other categories of rights have emerged in recent years (for example collective rights such as the right to development) but the focus in this book is on civil and political rights, and, to a lesser extent, economic, social and cultural rights. In any event it should be remembered that, in addition to having universal application, all human rights, whatever their category, are indivisible and interdependent.

(B) THE OBLIGATION OF STATES TO PROTECT AND PROMOTE HUMAN RIGHTS

The Universal Declaration of Human Rights, which embodies civil, political, economic, social and cultural rights, is proclaimed as a common standard of achievement for all peoples and all nations. The preambular paragraphs of the two International Covenants recognise that the ideal of free human beings enjoying freedom from fear and want can only be achieved if conditions are created whereby everyone may enjoy his economic, social and cultural rights, as well as his civil and political rights. Furthermore, all Member States of the United Nations are bound under the Charter of the United Nations to promote universal respect for, and observance of human rights and fundamental freedoms for all without distinction as to race, sex, language, or religion.

This requirement of the United Nations Charter is one of the ways in which States are bound as a matter of international law to secure observance of human rights. States are also bound, under the various human rights treaties to which they are parties, to ensure respect for and protection of the rights of individuals within their jurisdiction according to the terms of those treaties. For example, article 2 of the Covenant on Economic, Social and Cultural Rights requires States to take steps, to the maximum of their available resources, to achieve progressively the full realisation of the rights recognised in the Covenant, whereas article 2 of the Covenant on Civil and Political Rights requires States parties to respect and to ensure to all individuals within their jurisdiction the rights recognised in that Covenant. The immediacy of the obligation in the latter Covenant should be compared with the incremental nature of the obligation in the former. Each Covenant requires the rights to be exercised or ensured without distinction on a number of grounds, which include race, colour sex, language or religion.

The regional human rights treaties, the African Charter on Human and Peoples' Rights[3] and the American and European Conventions on Human Rights,[4] contain similar obligations. Furthermore, the Covenant on Civil and Political Rights and the European Convention on Human Rights create the right to effective remedy for violation of the rights they guarantee; the African Charter creates the right to remedy for violation of rights guaranteed by conventions, laws, regulations and customs; and the American Convention creates the right to effective remedy for violations of rights it guarantees as well as rights guaranteed by national constitutions or laws. This right to effective remedy before national authorities, courts or tribunals is an important element of the protection of human rights, and of the obligations on States to secure observance of human rights.

In the first instance these requirements mean that the constitutional and legal arrangements of States must be in conformity with their international legal obligations. However, for the protection of human rights to be meaningful, constitutional and legal provisions must be respected and human rights observed or delivered. That responsibility rests, initially, on governments and it engages almost the entire range of governmental activity at one time or another. In addition to basic political functions of law making and resource allocation, also involved are formulation of policies and practices and the establishment of structures and systems throughout the machinery of government For example, in relation to policing, the explicit and implicit requirements arising out of international human rights law to secure political accountability and judicial supervision of police, and lawful and humane policing generally, have a bearing upon detailed aspects of command, management and administration of police organisations.

---

[3] Adopted by the Assembly of Heads of State and Government of the Organisation of African Unity, at Nairobi, on 27 June 1981.
[4] The American Convention on Human Rights was signed by Member States of the Organisation of American States, at San José, Costa Rica, on 22 November 1969. The Convention for the Protection of Human Rights and Fundamental Freedoms (European Convention on Human Rights) was signed by Member States of the Council of Europe, at Rome, on 4 November 1950.

I:1

Traditionally international law only regulated relations between states, and up to the time of the Second World War it would have been inconceivable for international law to have exercised such a degree of influence over the legal and political systems of states. However the political excesses and the gross violations of human rights which occurred during that conflict, and the decade which preceded it, provided a clear indication of the need to protect the individual against abuse of state power. Henceforth international law became a means to regulate relationships between individuals and governments.

(C) INTERNATIONAL HUMAN RIGHTS INSTRUMENTS

On a global level the United Nations initiated the processes leading to the adoption of the three instruments that form the international bill of human rights. The first of these, the Universal Declaration of Human Rights, was adopted by U.N. General Assembly resolution in 1948. The rights it enshrines were then given legal force in the two International Covenants that came into force in 1976. These are the two instruments referred to above, protecting economic, social and cultural rights, and civil and political rights that, together with the Universal Declaration, constitute the international bill of human rights.

Regional systems for the protection of human rights were also developed, leading to the promulgation of regional human rights treaties, the Convention for the Protection of Human Rights and Fundamental Freedoms (commonly referred to as the European Convention on Human Rights), the American Convention on Human Rights, and the African Charter on Human and Peoples' Rights which came into force in 1953, 1969 and 1986 respectively. Typically, a State within a region to which one of these treaties applies is a party to the global treaties as well as to the treaty of its region.

A state may also be a party to subject specific treaties, for example the Convention on the Prevention and Punishment of the Crime of Genocide[5] the International Convention on the Elimination of All Forms of Racial Discrimination,[6] the Convention on the Elimination of All Forms of Discrimination against Women,[7] the Convention against Torture and Other Cruel, Inhuman or Degrading Treatment or Punishment,[8] and the Convention on the Rights of the Child.[9]

---

[5] Approved by General Assembly resolution 260 A (III) of 9 December 1948.
[6] Adopted by General Assembly resolution 2106 A (XX) of 21 December 1965.
[7] Adopted by General Assembly resolution 34/180 of 18 December 1979.
[8] Adopted by General Assembly resolution 39/46 of 10 December 1984.
[9] Adopted by General Assembly resolution 44/25 of 20 November 1989.

In this way a state may be bound by a variety of international human rights treaties, each treaty requiring compliance with its provisions by the State party and thus imposing obligations on its legislature, executive and judiciary, and necessitating specific responses from those officials with the responsibility for running State agencies or organisations.

All of the rights and freedoms expressed in the International Covenant on Economic, Social and Cultural Rights, the International Covenant on Civil and Political Rights, and the three regional human rights treaties may be affected, for good or for ill, by policing. Furthermore, they all should influence the objectives of policing and the ways in which policing is carried out, although some rights and freedoms, such as the right to life, the prohibition of arbitrary arrest, and the right to humane treatment as a detainee are clearly more affected by police activity and have a greater impact on the exercise of police powers than some other rights.

Some subject specific human rights treaties, such as those referred to above, also have direct relevance to policing, as does yet another type of international instrument. These are non-treaty instruments, some of which are addressed specifically to police agencies and police officials. All of the instruments identified so far, apart from the Universal Declaration of Human Rights, are treaties, legally binding on parties to them. Non-treaty texts do not have legal force in themselves but they do have great moral and political force, and they typically re-state rights and freedoms that are protected in legally binding treaties. Furthermore, the provisions of such instruments encourage, promote and require compliance with important human rights expressed in treaties.

The moral and political force of non-treaty instruments derives from their adoption by UN bodies or regional human rights institutions. For example the UN General Assembly adopted a Code of Conduct for Law Enforcement Officials.[10] Two further instruments of this nature exemplify the ways in which non-treaty texts re-state, and reinforce protection of, rights enshrined in legally binding treaties. The Basic Principles on the Use of Force and Firearms by Law Enforcement Officials[11] express standards on good police practice in the use of force and firearms, thereby promoting and protecting the right to life. The Body of Principles for the Protection of All Persons under Any form of Detention or Imprisonment,[12] which embodies detailed measures to prevent arbitrary arrest and detention and to secure humane treatment of detainees, reiterates the prohibition on torture and the right to humane

---

[10] Adopted by General Assembly resolution 34/169 of 17 December 1979.
[11] Adopted by the Eighth United Nations Congress on the Prevention of Crime and the Treatment of Offenders, Havana, Cuba, 27 August to 7 September 1990.
[12] Approved by General Assembly resolution 43/173 of 9 December 1988.

treatment as a detainee. An example of a regional non-treaty instrument is the European Code of Police Ethics.[13]

(D) INTERNATIONAL MEANS OF SUPERVISION AND ENFORCEMENT

The establishment of international standards on human rights was an important step, but insufficient in itself to secure respect for and observance of human rights. The means of supervision and enforcement referred to here are, largely, those means developed to secure compliance by states with the standards, and they fall within two broad categories: Charter based institutions and procedures and treaty based institutions and procedures. Charter based institutions have also been established to hold individuals to account for crimes that constitute violations of human rights, and violations of international humanitarian law. Outside these categories another institution, the Freedom of Association Committee of the Governing Body of the International Labour Organization, is also relevant to the purposes of this book and is described below.

(a) Charter Based Institutions and Procedures

Charter based institutions and procedures are those that have been established under the authority granted by the Charter of the United Nations to the Economic and Social Council (ECOSOC) and, through it, to its subsidiary Commission on Human Rights and the Sub-Commission on the Promotion and Protection of Human Rights (formerly known as the Sub-Commission on Prevention of Discrimination and Protection of Minorities).[14]

(i)   Commission on Human Rights and Sub-Commission on the Promotion and Protection of Human Rights

The Commission on Human Rights, composed of 53 representatives of Member States of the United Nations, is the main body dealing with human rights issues. It drafts international human rights instruments, promotes human rights, and responds to allegations of violations of human rights. In this latter respect the Commission is authorised, under resolution 1235 (XLII) of the Economic and Social Council, to examine information concerning gross violations of human rights and fundamental freedoms, and to make a thorough study of situations that reveal a consistent pattern of violations of human rights. Resolution 1503 (XLVIII) of the Council authorises

---

[13] Recommendation Rec. (2001) 10, adopted by the Committee of Ministers of the Council of Europe on 19 September 2001.

[14] The Human Rights Council, established by the General Assembly in its resolution 60/251 of 15 March 2006, replaces the Commission on Human Rights, which was formally abolished on 16 June 2006.

the Commission to respond to complaints from individuals and non-governmental organisations that appear to reveal a consistent pattern of gross and reliably attested violations of human rights.

The Sub-Commission, which the Commission established, is composed of 26 experts selected by the Commission to serve in their individual capacity. It undertakes studies in light of the Universal Declaration of Human Rights, makes recommendations to the Commission and reports to the Commission.

Under the authority granted to it by resolution 1235 (XLII) the Commission has developed 'country specific' and 'thematic' practices. For country specific procedures, the Commission has appointed rapporteurs or working groups to collect and analyse information on human rights violations in particular countries. For thematic procedures the Commission has appointed rapporteurs or working groups to collate information on human rights violations of a specific nature in any country, in order to identify issues or practices that violate human rights, and to seek to resolve them. For example the Special Rapporteur on Torture reports to the Commission on the crime of torture in general, and the Working Group on Enforced or Involuntary Disappearances follows the phenomenon whereby people are 'disappeared', having been forcibly abducted. The Working Group processes complaints by channelling information between governments and families concerned. There have also been appointed a Special Rapporteur on Extra-Legal Executions; a Special Rapporteur on Religious Intolerance; and a Working Group on Arbitrary Detention. This latter body is the only UN Charter based mechanism whose mandate provides for consideration of individual complaints. Its actions are based on the right of petition of individuals anywhere in the world, regardless of whether or not a State named in a petition is a party to any particular human rights treaty.

(ii) International Criminal Tribunals

International Criminal Tribunal for the former Yugoslavia and International Criminal Tribunal for Rwanda
Two international institutions have been established by Security Council resolutions when the Council invoked its mandatory powers to preserve peace under Chapter VII of the UN Charter. Their focus is on individuals, holding them to account for crimes arising out of conflicts, rather than on States.

The International Criminal Tribunal for the former Yugoslavia was established by Security Council resolution 827 of 25 May 1993, in response to the serious violations of international humanitarian law committed in the territory of the former Yugoslavia since 1991, and to the threat to international peace and security posed by those serious violations. The ICTY functions in accordance with the provisions of the Statute of the International Criminal Tribunal for the former Yugoslavia. It is located in The Hague, The Netherlands. The ICTY's mission is to bring to justice those allegedly responsible for violations of international humanitarian law; to render justice to the victims; to deter further crimes; and to contribute to the restoration of peace by promoting reconciliation in the former Yugoslavia.

The International Criminal Tribunal for Rwanda was established by Security Council resolution 955 of 8 November 1994 for the prosecution of persons responsible for genocide and serious violations of international humanitarian law committed in the territory of Rwanda between 1 January 1994 and 31 December 1994. The Statute of the International Criminal Tribunal for Rwanda governs the Tribunal. It is located in Arusha, Tanzania. The purpose of the Tribunal is to contribute to the process of national reconciliation in Rwanda and to the maintenance of peace in the region. It may also deal with the prosecution of Rwandan citizens responsible for genocide and other such violations of international law committed in the territory of neighbouring States during the same period.

Special Court for Sierra Leone
A third *ad hoc* tribunal, the Special Court for Sierra Leone, was established by an agreement signed by the UN and the government of Sierra Leone in January 2002, pursuant to Security Council resolution 1315 (2000) of 14 August 2000. The purpose of this tribunal is, *inter alia*, to prosecute people charged with crimes arising out of the conflict in that country and it, too, is governed by its own Statute.

International Criminal Court
Finally, and most importantly, in 1998 the United Nations Diplomatic Conference of Plenipotentiaries on the Establishment of an International Criminal Court adopted the Rome Statue of the International Criminal Court. This Court has jurisdiction with respect to the crime of genocide, crimes against humanity, war crimes and the crime of aggression. The Statute entered into force on 1 July 2002, and the Chief Prosecutor took office on 16 June 2003. This is the first ever permanent, treaty based, international criminal court established to promote the rule of law and ensure that the gravest international crimes do not go unpunished.

(b) Treaty Based Institutions and Procedures

The principal human rights treaties contain provisions on the establishment and functioning of institutions and procedures to oversee their implementation.

(i) Human Rights Committee

The Human Rights Committee operates under the International Covenant on Civil and Political Rights together with the first Optional Protocol,[15] which sets out a procedure for individual complaints, and the Second Optional Protocol,[16] which aims at the abolition of the death penalty. The Committee is established under article 28 of the Covenant, and is composed of 18 human rights experts who, although nominated by the State party of which they are nationals, serve in their personal capacity.

The Committee has two main functions – 'supervision' and 'applications'. Supervision is conducted through a reporting procedure whereby States parties to the Covenant submit periodic reports on the measures they have adopted which give effect to the rights recognised in the Covenant and on the progress made in the enjoyment of those rights. Applications involve communications (complaints) from individuals who are alleging violations of their rights protected under the Covenant, and from States parties to the Covenant in relation to the conduct of other States parties.

Article 4 of the International Covenant on Civil and Political Rights stipulates that the Human Rights Committee shall transmit to the States parties such General Comments as it may consider appropriate. The purposes of the General Comments are, *inter alia*, to make the Committee's experience available for the benefit of all States parties in order to promote the further implementation of the Covenant; and to stimulate the activities of those States and international organisations in the promotion and protection of human rights.

(ii) Committee on Economic, Social and Cultural Rights

The Committee on Economic, Social and Cultural Rights was established by the Economic and Social Council to monitor the implementation by States parties of the International Covenant on Economic, Social and Cultural Rights. The Committee consists of 18 members elected by the Council and serving in their personal capacity. Whilst there is a system of periodic reporting by States parties to this Covenant, there is no procedure for considering individual complaints, although an Optional Protocol that would introduce such a procedure is presently being drafted.

---

[15] Adopted by General Assembly resolution 2200 A (XXI) of 16 December 1966.
[16] Adopted by General Assembly resolution 44/128 of 15 December 1989.

I:1

(iii) Committee on the Elimination of Racial Discrimination

The Committee on the Elimination of Racial Discrimination is established under article 8 of the International Convention on the Elimination of All Forms of Racial Discrimination. The Committee consists of 18 members elected by the States parties and serving in their personal capacity.

This Committee receives periodic reports from States parties to the Convention. It may also receive communications from States parties in relation to the conduct of other States parties, and from individuals or groups of individuals within their jurisdiction who are alleging violations of any of the Convention rights if the State party has recognised the competence of the Committee to do so.

(iv) Committee on the Elimination of Discrimination against Women

The Committee on the Elimination of Discrimination against Women is established under article 17 of the Convention on the Elimination of All Forms of Discrimination against Women. The Committee consists of 23 experts of high moral standing and competence in the field covered by the Convention. They are elected by States parties but serve in their personal capacity.

Whereas the Convention established a system of State party reporting, there was no system for the communication of individual complaints until the UN General Assembly adopted the Optional Protocol to the Convention in October 1999. Under the Protocol, which entered into force in December 2000, State parties to the Protocol recognise the competence of the Committee to receive and consider communications submitted by or on behalf of individuals or groups of individuals, under the jurisdiction of a State party, claiming to be victims of a violation of any of the Convention rights by that State party.

(v) Committee against Torture

The Committee against Torture was established under Article 17 of the Convention against Torture and Other Cruel, Inhuman or Degrading Treatment or Punishment. It consists of ten experts of high moral standing and recognised competence in the field of human rights and, although they are appointed by States parties, they serve in their personal capacity.

This Committee receives periodic reports from States Parties to the Convention, and examines information that appears to contain well-founded indications that torture is being systematically practised within the territory of a State Party. It may also receive communications from States Parties to the Convention in relation to the conduct of other States Parties, and from individuals who are alleging violations of their Convention rights.

On 18 December 2002, the UN General Assembly adopted the Optional Protocol to the Convention against Torture and Other Cruel, Inhuman or Degrading Treatment or Punishment. Any State that has ratified or acceded to the Convention may become a party to the Optional Protocol. It will enter into force when twenty States have ratified or acceded to it.

The purpose of the Optional Protocol is to establish a system of regular visits undertaken by independent international and national bodies to places where people are deprived of their liberty, in order to prevent torture and other cruel, inhuman or degrading treatment or punishment. For that purpose, the States parties will elect a Subcommittee on Prevention of Torture and Other Cruel, Inhuman or Degrading Treatment or Punishment of the Committee against Torture. Each State party also undertakes to maintain, designate or establish one or several independent national preventive mechanisms for the prevention of torture at the domestic level.

A similar system is already functioning at the European level but, unlike the UN mechanism which is a Sub-Committee of the Committee against Torture, the European Committee for the Prevention of Torture and Inhuman or Degrading Treatment or Punishment is not directly linked to, nor derived from, other human rights institutions.

(vi) Committee on the Rights of the Child

The Committee on the Rights of the Child is established under article 43 of the Convention on the Rights of the Child. It consists of ten experts of high moral standing and recognised competence in the field covered by the Convention. The members of the Committee are elected by States parties but serve in their personal capacity. A system of State party reporting was established under the Convention, but there is no system for the communication of individual complaints. However, the Convention includes civil and political rights protected in the International Covenant and regional treaties and, where appropriate, the procedures under those treaties may be invoked.

(vii) European Court of Human Rights

Article 19 of the European Convention on Human Rights prescribes the setting up of the European Court of Human Rights to ensure the observance of the engagements undertaken by the High Contracting Parties to the Convention.

I:1

Member States of the Council of Europe signed this Convention in 1950, and it entered into force in 1953. The Council of Europe was established by the Statute of the Council of Europe signed in London in 1949. The policy-making and executive organ of the Council of Europe is the Committee of Ministers of the Council of Europe, which is comprised of all Foreign Ministers of Member States of the Council.

The European Court of Human Rights consists of a number of judges equal to that of the High Contracting Parties to the Convention and is located in Strasbourg, France. The judges, who sit on the Court in their individual capacity, must be of high moral character and must either possess the qualifications required for appointment to high judicial office or be jurisconsults of recognised competence.

The jurisdiction of the Court extends to all matters concerning the interpretation and application of the Convention and its Protocols. Any High Contracting Party may refer to the Court any alleged breach of the provisions of the Convention and Protocols by another High Contracting Party. The Court may also receive applications from any person, non-governmental organisation or group of individuals claiming to be a victim of a violation by one of the High Contracting Parties of the rights set forth in the Convention or the Protocols. This means that, unlike the Inter-American Court, there is compulsory jurisdiction in respect of both categories of complaints.

The Committee of Ministers of the Council of Europe monitors the enforcement of the Court's judgements.

Until November 1998, the task of ensuring observance of the provisions of the Convention was shared by two part-time bodies, the European Commission on Human Rights and the European Court of Human Rights. Protocol 11 to the European Convention introduced the full time Court described above, and the Commission was abolished.

(viii)   Inter-American Court of Human Rights

The inter-American human rights system was established with the adoption of the American Declaration of the Rights and Duties of Man in Bogota, Colombia in April 1948 at the Ninth International American Conference. The Charter of the Organisation of American States (OAS) was adopted at that same conference.

The Inter-American Commission on Human Rights was created in 1959 and is located in Washington, DC, USA. It has seven members elected in a personal capacity. The Commission is an autonomous organ of the OAS, and its mandate is found in the OAS Charter and the American Convention on Human Rights. The Commission has powers regarding all Member States of the Organisation of American States, and not only regarding those that are parties to the Convention.

The American Convention on Human Rights was signed in 1969 at San José, Costa Rica by Member States of the OAS, and entered into force in 1978.

The Inter-American Court of Human Rights was established by the American Convention on Human Rights, and consists of seven judges elected in an individual capacity who must be persons of high moral authority and recognised competence in the field of human rights. It is located in Costa Rica. The jurisdiction of the Court comprises all cases concerning the interpretation and application of the provisions of the Convention that are submitted to it, provided that the States parties to the case recognise such jurisdiction.

Under the Convention any person, group of persons, or non-governmental organisation legally recognised in one or more of the OAS States, may submit petitions to the Commission alleging violations of the Convention by a State party. There is also a right of inter-State complaint (by way of communications to the Commission), but this is subject to a prior declaration regarding the competence of the Commission in this respect. This means that whereas the right of individual complaint is automatic, the right of inter-State complaint is not. For those States that are not parties to the Convention, the Commission applies the American Declaration.

(ix) African Commission on Human and Peoples' Rights

Article 30 of the African Charter on Human and Peoples' Rights establishes the African Commission on Human and Peoples' Rights within the Organisation of African Unity, to promote human and people's rights and ensure their protection in Africa.

The African Charter on Human and Peoples' Rights was adopted in 1981 by the Eighteenth Assembly of Heads of State and Government of the Organisation of African Unity. It entered into force on 21 October 1986. There were two bodies responsible for ensuring the promotion and protection of human and peoples' rights, the Commission, and the Assembly of Heads of State and Government of the Organisation of African Unity (OAU). However, the OAU was replaced by the African Union in July 2002, following the adoption of the Constitutive Act of the African Union in July 2000.

I:1

A Protocol to the African Charter establishing an African Court on Human and Peoples' Rights entered into force on 25 January 2004. When it is established the Court will consider cases of human rights violations referred to it by the African Commission on Human and Peoples' Rights and States parties to the Protocol and, where a State party accepts such a jurisdiction, by individuals and non-governmental organisations. The Court will have authority to issue legally binding and enforceable decisions on cases brought before it.

The Commission on Human and Peoples' Rights is composed of eleven members elected by secret ballot by the Assembly of the Heads of State and Government for a six year renewable term. Members, who serve in their personal capacity, are chosen from among African personalities reputed for their high morality, integrity, impartiality and competence in matters of human and peoples' rights. The Commission has its headquarters in Banjul, The Gambia.

The Commission has three major functions: the promotion of human and peoples' rights, the protection of human and peoples' rights, and the interpretation of the African Charter on Human and Peoples' Rights. The African Charter provides for inter-State complaints and individual communications, both procedures being mandatory to the States parties.

After studying the complaint and exhausting all means to reach an amicable solution to the matter, the Commission submits a report together with such recommendations as it deems useful to the Assembly of Heads of State and Government, which takes the final decision.

(c) A Body Established by a UN Specialized Agency

The International Labour Organization (ILO) is a specialised agency of the United Nations that seeks to promote social justice and internationally recognised human and labour rights. Its Constitution states that its purpose is to promote universal and lasting peace based on social justice, and it has adopted international labour legislation in the form of Conventions and Recommendations to improve the situation of working people.

The fundamental human rights standards of the ILO cover four basic subjects: freedom of association and protection of the right to organise, and freedom from forced labour, child labour and discrimination. Whilst standards in these areas are expressed in many ILO instruments, eight Conventions are generally considered to embody the core principles of the ILO on these matters.[17]

Freedom of Association Committee of the Governing Body of the ILO
The Special Procedures for supervising the application of ILO standards on the right to freedom of association are the responsibility of two bodies, the Fact-Finding and Conciliation Commission on Freedom of Association, and the Freedom of Association Committee of the Governing Body of the ILO. The mandate of the former is to examine any complaint concerning alleged infringements of trade union rights referred to it by the Governing Body of the ILO but, in practice, very few cases have been dealt with by the Commission.

The Freedom of Association Committee is a tripartite body composed of nine members from the government, workers' and employers' groups of the Governing Body. The mandate of the Committee is to determine whether any given legislation or practice complies with the principles of freedom of association and collective bargaining laid down in the relevant Conventions.[18] It is empowered to examine the extent to which the exercise of trade union rights may be affected in cases of infringements of civil liberties.

Having carried out preliminary examinations of complaints submitted to it under the Special Procedure, the Committee makes its recommendations to the Governing Body. In a number of its recommendations the Committee has reinforced an important principle on police involvement in labour disputes, that the primary purpose of any police action in a dispute between employers and employees is to maintain order so that the dispute can be resolved within the appropriate legal and administrative framework. The police are not the servants of any of the parties to such a dispute, and should carry out their duties impartially and strictly within the law. On most occasions, of course, these disputes are settled without the need for police intervention.

(E) HUMAN RIGHTS AND POLICING

The purpose of this opening Chapter has been to provide basic introductory information about the nature of human rights and the international system for

---

[17] Freedom of Association and Protection of the Right to Organise, 1948 (No. 87); Right to Organise and Collective Bargaining, 1949 (No. 98); Forced Labour, 1930 (No. 29); Abolition of Forced Labour, 1957 (No. 105); Equal Remuneration, 1950 (No. 100); Discrimination (Employment and Occupation), 1958 (No. 111); Minimum Age, 1973 (No. 138); Worst Forms of Child Labour, 1999 (No. 182).
[18] The Freedom of Association and Protection of the Right to Organise Convention, 1948 (No. 87), and the Right to Organise and Collective Bargaining Convention, 1949 (No. 98).

securing their protection. More detailed accounts of these matters can be found in some of the texts set out under 'source Materials and Recommended Reading' at the end of this book.

As human rights concern the relationship between individuals and the state, controlling and regulating the exercise of state power over individuals, and as police exercise power on behalf of the state, it is now necessary to consider the nexus between human rights and policing. This connection is explored principally in the next Chapter, and then specific aspects of it are considered in Chapters 3 and 4.

Chapter 2. Human Rights and Policing

(A) POLICING OR LAW ENFORCEMENT?

Policing is one of the means by which states meet or fail to meet their obligations under international law to secure respect for and observance of the human rights of people within their jurisdiction. The extent to which some of these obligations are met depends, therefore, on the attitudes and behaviour of police officials towards those individuals and groups with whom they interact at a personal level and on a daily basis in the processes of policing.

Many of the interactions between police and the public they serve take place in the context of extremely difficult and challenging situations. Furthermore, for the greater part, there is no direct supervision of those interactions. These considerations, and the crucial role of policing in relation to a state's international legal obligations, are an indication of the nature and importance of the task facing police leaders in securing protection of and respect for human rights. Given this task it is important to explore the nexus between human rights and policing, and to do so within the terms of international human rights instruments, especially those considered in the previous Chapter and in more detail in subsequent Chapters.

A significant feature of those instruments, and especially those addressed to police, is that police are referred to as 'law enforcement officials'. This is an unsatisfactory term for officials carrying out the whole range of policing functions. It is also unsatisfactory in terms of an examination of the nexus between human rights and policing.

It is generally recognised that the principle police functions are to prevent and detect crime, to maintain and, where necessary, restore order, and to provide aid and assistance in emergencies. Police do enforce law, and in order to carry out these functions they may invoke the law, but 'law enforcement' is not the only or even the main thing that police do. In fact, apart from officials in specialised crime detection agencies, most operational police officials engaged in routine, day to day policing probably spend most of their time on the last function referred to above, assisting people who are experiencing some kind of personal emergency. This latter observation is expressed by the social scientist Egon Bittner in developing his thesis that "police are empowered and required to impose or, as the case may be, coerce a provisional solution upon emergent problems without having to brook or defer to opposition of any kind, and that further, their competence to intervene extends to every kind of emergency, without any exceptions whatever".[19] Interestingly, in an earlier study another social scientist, Jean-Louis Loubet Del-Blayle, defined the police function as that of ensuring the internal organisation of a society and obedience to the rules by recourse to coercive methods including, eventually, the use

---

[19] E. Bittner, *Aspects of Police Work* (Northeastern University Press, Boston, 1990).

I:2

of force.[20] The emphasis that these scholars place on coercion and force, and the close connection they make between that and police functions, underscores the importance of the standards on the right to life and the use of force by police discussed in Part II of this book.

In examining the nexus between human rights and policing, it is important to take into account the relationship between the various policing functions, and to consider that nexus across the entire range of police activity and not only in relation to law enforcement.

Whilst policing functions can be seen as distinct forms of activity, there is also a sense in which they amount to a single, seamless policing function. For example, by maintaining social order and providing assistance in times of emergency the police serve the community in ways that might prevent some forms of criminality or even alleviate some of the social or economic conditions that are at the root of criminality or disorder. Furthermore, police involvement with, and assistance to, the community may also promote public cooperation in the detection of crime. The detection of some crimes may, in turn, prevent other forms of criminality or serve to reduce social tension or militate against outbreaks of disorder.

Those situations, in all their diversity and complexity, which require, or get, a policing response are not readily separated into distinct categories corresponding to differentiated policing functions. If the relationship between those functions is ignored and one function receives priority to the detriment of the other functions, it is highly likely that, in the long term, overall police effectiveness will be reduced. Furthermore the capacity of police to act as a positive force in the protection of the different categories of human rights will be diminished.

Whilst police are referred to as law enforcement officials in international human rights instruments, the wider policing functions are acknowledged in provisions of those instruments. For example article 1 of the United Nations Code of Conduct for Law Enforcement Officials requires such officials to serve the community as well as to protect all persons from illegal acts. Paragraph (c) of the commentary to the article states that service to the community "is intended to include particularly the rendition of services of assistance to those members of the community who by reason of personal, economic, social or other emergencies are in need of immediate aid".[21] Another example can be found in the opening paragraph of the United Nations Basic Principles on the Use of Force and Firearms by Law Enforcement

---

[20] J.L. Loubet Del Blayle, *La Police dans le Systeme Politique* (*Centre d'Études et de Recherches sur la Police*, Toulouse, 1981).
[21] Code of Conduct for Law Enforcement Officials, *supra* note 10.

Officials, which recognises that the work of police officials "is a social service of great importance".

(B) POLICING AS A POSITIVE FACTOR IN THE PROTECTION OF HUMAN RIGHTS

The wider policing functions and the protection of the different categories of rights by and through policing are also implicit in the provisions of article 28 of the Universal Declaration of Human Rights: "Everyone is entitled to a social and international order in which the rights and freedoms set forth in this Declaration can be fully realised."

The reference in this article to an international order is the source from which the right to development has been drawn by the international community, but it also includes the idea of a social order meaning the quality of life experienced at a national level.

Clearly human rights cannot be realised without social order, and social order, as characterised by tolerable levels of criminality and low levels of social tension or civil unrest, is dependent, in part, upon effective policing. In this sense policing, through the performance of all of its functions, can be seen as a positive factor in the protection of human rights and, specifically, all of the rights set forth in the Universal Declaration of Human Rights which enshrines civil, political, economic, social and cultural rights.

In addition to assisting in the realisation of all human rights through its contribution to the maintenance of social order generally, policing can be a positive factor in the protection of specific human rights in very particular ways. For example, the right to life as expressed in the International Covenant on Civil and Political Rights and regional human rights treaties requires the right to life to be protected by law. This means, *inter alia*, that States have to enact laws that create offences of murder and other types of unlawful killing, and the prevention and detection of such crimes is a police task. In a similar way police action in preventing and detecting the crime of theft contributes to the fulfilment of the right to own property and the prohibition of arbitrary deprivation of property as set out in article 17 of the Universal Declaration of Human Rights. The right to life is a civil right, and similar examples can be found for the protection of political rights and economic, social or cultural rights.

Where there are laws prohibiting discrimination on grounds of religion or belief, or prohibiting manifestations of religious intolerance, the effective prevention and detection of breaches of those laws is directly supportive of the political rights to freedom of thought, conscience and religion, and to freedom of opinion and

I:2

expression. Where police functions include attending and reporting on industrial accidents, effective prevention and detection of offences under law designed to secure safety at work is directly supportive of the social right to just and favourable conditions of work.

Another extremely important aspect of human rights protection, of which police should be acutely aware, is protection against discrimination on grounds of race. The preamble to the International Convention on the Elimination of All Forms of Racial Discrimination reaffirms that discrimination between human beings on grounds of race, colour or ethnic origin is capable of disturbing peace and security among peoples, and the harmony of persons living side by side even within one and the same State. These are compelling reasons for police to act against discrimination on grounds of race, especially when they have at their disposal measures under their national laws that prohibit words or deeds intended to, or likely to, stir up racial hatred.

These examples of the ways in which police protect specific human rights and freedoms arise out of their prevention and detection functions, and when the other functions of policing are taken into account, similar examples can be found. In providing effective social or emergency services for people who, because of various emergencies, are in need of immediate aid police may protect their right to life. In performing this function police may also protect the right to equal enjoyment of rights, enshrined in article 2 of the Universal Declaration of Human Rights, and they may promote delivery of some economic and social rights by bringing to notice the plight of people deprived of rights.

This account of the ways in which policing can be a positive factor in the protection of human rights is by no means exhaustive but it does indicate how effective policing is essential to that process. However, the notion that policing assists in the realisation of human rights through its part in maintaining social order requires further consideration.

Policing can respond, with greater or lesser effectiveness, to manifestations of criminality, social tension and civil unrest but, whilst it might prevent some forms of criminality or even alleviate some of the social or economic conditions that are at the root of tension or disorder, it cannot remove their underlying causes. When those underlying causes are not satisfactorily addressed policing can assist in maintaining a form of social order characterised mainly by a relative lack of civil unrest. However it will be a social order dependent upon repression and injustice rather than on consent, respect for democratic values, and delivery of social justice.

Such a form of social order, because of its unresolved, underlying tensions is not stable, and it is not one in which human rights and freedoms are fully realised.

(C) POLICING AS A NEGATIVE FACTOR IN THE PROTECTION OF HUMAN RIGHTS

Just as article 28 of the Universal Declaration of Human Rights can be used as the basis for an examination of policing as a positive factor in the protection of human rights, so article 29(2) of the Declaration can be used as the basis for an examination of policing as a negative factor in their protection. The second paragraph of article 29 reads:

> "In the exercise of his rights and freedoms, everyone shall be subject only to such limitations as are determined by law solely for the purposes of securing due recognition and respect for the rights and freedoms of others and of meeting the just requirements of morality, public order and the general welfare in a democratic society."

The legal protection of human rights derives not only from the fact that the various rights find expression in legally binding texts, both international and national, but also from the fact that any limitations on them are also expressed in such texts.

The paragraph from article 29 of the Universal Declaration of Human Rights quoted above is important and interesting for a number of reasons. Firstly, it is the general source of the specific limitation clauses to be found in articles in the International Covenant on Civil and Political Rights – for example articles 18, 19 and 21 protecting the rights to freedom of thought, conscience and religion, freedom of opinion and expression, and freedom of peaceful assembly respectively. Similar limitation clauses are to be found in regional human rights treaties.

Whilst the language of each of these limitation clauses varies slightly, they all require any limitations on the rights protected in the respective articles to be specified by law, and to be necessary in a democratic society in the interests of public safety, for the protection of public order, health or morals, or for the protection of the rights or freedoms of others. In other words they identify similar grounds to the Universal Declaration of Human Rights for justifying restrictions on the exercise by individuals of human rights and freedoms they protect.

Secondly, the permissible reasons for limiting rights can also be seen as an expression of basic policing functions, for securing recognition and respect for rights and freedoms of others, and meeting the just requirements of morality, public order and general welfare are all benefits of living in a democratic society which can be achieved, in part at least, through policing. When police enforce law by seeking to prevent and detect crime, they secure due recognition for the rights and freedoms of others, such as the right to life. In the same way, police meet the just requirements of morality when those requirements have been given legal force. The just requirements of public order are met directly when police maintain or restore order, and the general welfare is safeguarded when police provide emergency assistance to people in need of immediate aid.

The third and final reason for focussing particularly on this provision of the Universal Declaration of Human Rights is the most important. In stipulating the sole purposes for which rights and freedoms may be limited, the Declaration is setting limits on police powers. Police may not be given powers under the law to restrict rights and freedoms for any other purposes. In stipulating that rights and freedoms are to be subject only to such limitations as are determined by law, the Declaration is stating a fundamental rule of police behaviour. Police may not exceed their lawful powers.

The fact that the terms of this article of the Declaration can also be seen as an expression of police functions indicates a significant link between the actual fulfilment of those functions and the ways in which they are fulfilled. It accentuates the connection between police effectiveness and police behaviour, challenging the argument that compliance with rules of good behaviour lessens police effectiveness, and exposing the seriously flawed notion of effectiveness implicit in that argument.

Unfortunately even though human rights are protected by law, and any limitations which can be placed on rights and freedoms are set in law, police officials, who are described as law enforcement officials, break the law designed to protect human rights when enforcing other law. This situation exists because a readiness to violate human rights law persists as part of a powerful police sub-culture that regards human rights, which are inalienable and inherent in every human being, as incompatible with the process of policing.

Furthermore some human rights violations, for example violations of the right to life and of the absolute prohibition of torture, are very serious crimes and, in committing such acts in order to 'fight crime', police are not reducing criminality, they are adding to it. In many instances, the crime of torture will be more serious than the crime being investigated. Those human rights violations that do not amount to criminal acts are enshrined in international law and the laws of states, and encoded as principles of good police practice. It cannot be said that policing that adds to criminality or that violates the professional values of policing is effective.

Clearly, breaking the law in order to enforce the law and committing crime in order to fight crime are absurdities.

There is a debate about the nature and extent of the tension that exists between order and liberty, but very little of that debate can be carried through to the debate about policing and human rights, for almost all of the tension has been removed by law. Under law, human rights and freedoms are clear, the limitations on those rights and freedoms are clear, and police powers, which mirror those limitations, are clear. Police, whose legitimacy is based on law, must comply with that law absolutely.

The areas of policing where that tension has not been removed by law are, largely, those areas where police officials are required, or able, to exercise discretion in the course of their duties, and this issue is connected with the great autonomy of action enjoyed by many police officials. Whilst the extent and nature of discretion exercised by police officials varies from jurisdiction to jurisdiction, all police officials at different levels in police hierarchies exercise discretion to some extent. This is because it is neither possible nor desirable for all laws to be consistently and rigorously enforced. Questions of resources and deployment of those resources arise, and choices have to be made about which laws are to be enforced and to what extent. Individual police officials, at the lowest levels of the police hierarchy, have it in their power to ignore breaches of law and to decide, correctly or incorrectly, not to enforce the law in respect of specific instances of law breaking.

The exercise of discretion by police officials is connected with their varying degrees of autonomy, and both are an indication of the extent to which much police work is unsupervised and unsupervisable. A great deal of supervision and control within police agencies is supervision and control after the event. Information is fed into the system at ground level, and subordinates are able to control the nature and quality of that information. Supervisors receive edited and partial accounts of incidents dealt with by their subordinates, and of their subordinates' responses to those incidents.

Where no legal provisions are in place to regulate or define what police action should be in particular circumstances, and where no other rules or guidelines have been developed, the great legal and humanitarian principles of respect for the inherent dignity and of the equal and inalienable rights of all members of the human family remain to prompt and inform police action. Indeed these principles, and the specific provisions of human rights law that derive from them, provide a sound basis for codes of behaviour and other texts designed to secure ethical standards in the profession and craft of policing. These and other related matters are considered in Chapter 4 of this part (Human Rights and Police Ethics).

I:2

At a theoretical level there is no tension between human rights and policing. The fact that such a tension exists in practice is inimical to effective policing and human rights, and it is subversive of the rule of law. A short term 'victory' in dealing with a particular manifestation of criminality may be applauded by a public eager to see wrongdoing punished and to live in a secure and peaceful society. However, when such a 'victory' is found to have been secured through unlawful and unethical means the applause of the public becomes a little uneasy and less enthusiastic. When unlawful and unethical police practices lead to miscarriages of justice and the punishment of innocent people, as they inevitably do, the applause ceases, public confidence and trust in the police is damaged, people are less inclined to co-operate with and assist police, and courts are reluctant to accept the testimony of police as witnesses. The 'victory' has become a defeat.

Policing should not be a negative factor in the protection of human rights, and one of the great tasks of police leaders is to develop and sustain a human rights culture within police organisations.

(D) HUMAN RIGHTS AND POLICE – RESPECT, PROTECT, INVESTIGATE AND ENTITLEMENT

In a publication of this nature, it is important and relevant to examine the relationship between human rights and policing within the terms of international human rights instruments, and in particular within the terms of articles 28 and 29(2) of the Universal Declaration of Human Rights. From this examination it can be seen that the relationship can be characterised by the terms protect and respect. It can also, helpfully, be characterised by the terms investigate, and entitlement. The latter term refers to the entitlement of police officials to human rights.

(a) Protect and Respect

Police are expected to protect human rights in the performance of their functions. Indeed, the protection of human rights is a police function, although one that is rarely made explicit. It is argued above that this is one of the positive aspects of the relationship between human rights and policing, and examples of ways in which policing assists in the realisation of all human rights and in the protection of specific human rights in very specific ways have already been considered. If this aspect of policing were made more explicit, and acknowledged to a greater extent, this positive aspect of the relationship could be one means of developing a human rights culture within police agencies.

The point is also made above that police may not exceed their lawful powers. That is to say, police are required to respect human rights in the exercise of their powers.

This aspect of the relationship is the most commonly addressed, because one of the primary purposes of human rights is to protect people from abuse of power by the state. Human rights limit police powers, exercised on behalf of the state, to use force, to deprive people of their liberty, and to carry out search and surveillance activities or operations. They require humane treatment of detainees. Equally, the lawful and reasonable exercise of police powers may legitimately limit human rights. Most of the jurisprudence of human rights institutions concerning police acts or omissions arises from this aspect of the relationship.

(b) Investigate

Police have a duty to investigate human rights violations because some violations, as indicated above, are very serious crimes. Furthermore, human rights instruments[22] and the jurisprudence of human rights institutions[23] require that alleged or suspected violations of human rights should be investigated. Whilst it has not been specified that police should carry out these investigations, indeed in some cases it would not be appropriate for them to do so, in many cases it is inevitable that police will investigate. Prompt, impartial and effective investigation of human rights abuse reinforces other measures to ensure respect for and protection of human rights, including human rights of police.

(c) Entitlement

It is important to secure the human rights of police officials as a desirable end in itself, and as another means of developing a human rights culture within police agencies. It will be recalled from the previous chapter that human rights are inclusive, and that they apply to all members of the human family. Everyone is entitled to human rights, including police officials. States are required to secure the human rights of all within their jurisdiction without discrimination and, when they fail to do so, they have to provide an effective remedy for the violation. When they fail to do that, providing certain other conditions are fulfilled, an individual can have recourse to an international institution, for example the Human Rights Committee or

---

[22] *See e.g.*, article 12 of the Convention against Torture and Other Cruel, Inhuman or Degrading Treatment or Punishment, which requires that each State Party shall ensure that its competent authorities proceed to a prompt and impartial investigation wherever there is reasonable ground to believe that an act of torture has been committed in any territory under its jurisdiction.

[23] *See e.g.*, *McCann and Others* v. *the United Kingdom, Publications of the European Court of Human Rights*, Series A: *Judgments and Decisions*, vol. 324 (1996), application No. 18984/91, judgment of 27 September 1995, in which the European Court of Human Rights held that there should be some form of effective official investigation when individuals have been killed as a result of the use of force by the State.

I:2

one of the institutions established under regional human rights treaties, to secure remedy and redress.

Under the heading 'Rights of Police Personnel', article 31 of the European Code of Police Ethics states:

> "Police staff shall as a rule enjoy the same civil and political rights as other citizens. Restrictions to these rights may only be made when they are necessary for the exercise of the functions of the police in a democratic society, in accordance with the law, and in conformity with the European Convention on Human Rights."

The commentary to article 31 refers, *inter alia*, to the overall principle that police in an open democratic society should have the same rights as other citizens, to the fullest possible extent. This is an important element of the rule of law and of making the police part of the society it serves. The commentary emphasises that Member States shall not deprive their police staff of any civil and political rights, unless there are legitimate reasons directly connected to the proper performance of police duties in a democratic State governed by the rule of law.

Although it is not a common occurrence, police officials have had recourse to international institutions in order to secure their rights. For example, in *Halford* v. *the United Kingdom*,[24] the applicant, a senior police official, claimed that calls made from her home and her office telephones were intercepted for the purposes of obtaining information to use against her in proceedings she was bringing at an Industrial Tribunal. She had instituted those proceedings alleging that she had been discriminated against on grounds of sex. The European Court of Human Rights concluded that the conversations held by Ms Halford on her office telephones fell within the scope of the notions of 'private life' and 'correspondence'. The Court found that there had been a violation of article 8 of the European Convention on Human Rights, which protects the right to private and family life, in relation to the interception of calls made on the applicant's office telephones, but felt that there was insufficient evidence to suggest that calls made from her home telephone were being intercepted.

In *Munoz Hermoza* v. *Peru*[25] the author of the communication was an ex-sergeant of the Guardia Civil (police). He alleged that he had been temporarily suspended from

---

[24] European Court of Human Rights, *Reports of Judgments and Decisions*, 1997-III, p. 1004, judgment of 25 June 1997.
[25] United Nations, *Official Records of the General Assembly, Forty-fourth Session, Supplement No. 40* (A/44/40), annex X, sect. D, communication No. 203/1986, views adopted on 4 November 1988.

the Guardia Civil on 25 September 1978 on false accusations of having insulted a superior but, when he was brought before a judge on 28 September 1978 on that charge, he was immediately released for lack of evidence. Nevertheless, by administrative decision dated 30 January 1984, he was discharged from service. The author claimed that after having served in the Guardia Civil for over 20 years he had been arbitrarily deprived of his livelihood and of his acquired rights, including accrued retirement rights, thus leaving him in a state of destitution, particularly considering that he had eight children to feed and clothe. He then spent 10 years going through numerous and diverse domestic administrative and judicial instances seeking reinstatement in the Guardia Civil, without success.

In considering the merits of this case, the Human Rights Committee noted that the concept of a fair hearing, as set out in article 14(1) of the International Covenant on Civil and Political Rights, necessarily entails that justice be rendered without undue delay. It reviewed the multifarious domestic procedures followed by the author, observing in particular that an administrative review kept pending for seven years constituted an unreasonable delay, and concluded that such a seemingly endless sequence of instances and the repeated failure to implement decisions were incompatible with the principle of a fair hearing.

The Committee was of the view that the events of this case disclosed a violation of article 14, paragraph 1, of the International Covenant on Civil and Political Rights. The State party was under an obligation, in accordance with the provisions of article 2 of the Covenant, to take effective measures to remedy the violations suffered by Rubén Toribio Muñoz Hermoza, including payment of adequate compensation for the loss suffered.

(E) THE SPECIFIC NATURE OF THE POLICE ENTITLEMENT TO HUMAN RIGHTS

It is a fundamental principle of human rights protection that human rights apply equally to all members of the human family, and this principle should not be lost in distinguishing between the differing needs and entitlements of various social groups. However, it is recognised that special provisions have to be made to secure the human rights of vulnerable categories of people, for example women and children.[26] Moreover, it is evident that some groups, for example occupational groups, will regard some human rights as more important than others; that different conditions need to be fulfilled in order to secure the human rights of different groups; and that states have differing types of obligations to secure rights for the various groups. For

---

[26] *See e.g.*, Convention on the Elimination of All Forms of Discrimination against Women, *supra* note 7, and Convention on the Rights of the Child, *supra* note 9.

I:2

example, it is to be expected that the right to freedom of opinion and expression[27] will be regarded as extremely important by journalists, whereas police officials may consider that the right to equal access to public service[28] has great importance because unfair criteria for appointments to public service could prevent some applicants from following their chosen profession.

Regarding the conditions that need to be fulfilled to secure human rights for different occupational groups, and differing obligations on states in this respect, it is instructive to consider the requirement on states to protect the right to life. The conditions to be fulfilled in order to protect the right to life of a journalist or a delegate of the International Committee of the Red Cross working in a war zone are different to those to be fulfilled in order to protect the right to life of a police official. They each require information and skills, hence training and briefing, and they each require equipment. However, because the nature of their tasks and the conditions under which they carry them out differ, their training needs and equipment differ. Furthermore, as police officials are state officials there is a direct obligation on the state to train and equip them, whereas the state has no such direct obligation in relation to the journalist or the ICRC delegate.

In order to illustrate the nature and extent of the obligation on the state to protect the right to life of police, and how it may happen that a state fails to meet this obligation, the author recalls a situation that arose during a human rights programme for police he was conducting in a country making the transition to democracy. During a discussion on the right to life, the participants explained that a large number of police officials had been killed in the course of their duties during the previous year. They gave a figure for police deaths that seemed excessively high, even though the incidence of violent crime in that country was also high. In spite of the large number of murders of police, the participants claimed that not one of the incidents had been analysed with a view to taking preventive and protective action in the future. Hence no changes had been made in selecting, training, equipping, briefing and deploying police officials in response to the killings. If their account was accurate then, clearly, there had been a gross failure on the part of the police leadership and the government, and the state had not met its obligation to protect the right to life of its police officials. These shortcomings were brought to the notice of the senior officials organising the programme.

International standards for police on equipment, including protective equipment, and on selection, training, and counselling, are set out in the Basic Principles on the Use

---

[27] *See e.g.*, article 19 of the Universal Declaration of Human Rights, and equivalent articles in the regional human rights treaties.
[28] *See e.g.*, article 21(2) of the Universal Declaration of Human Rights.

of Force and Firearms by Law Enforcement Officials. These principles express professional, practical standards on the use of force and firearms by police, and on the personal safety of police officials. Whilst not legally binding, they indicate some of the conditions that need to be fulfilled by States in order that they may meet their treaty obligations to protect the right to life of all those involved, including police, in operations where force or firearms may be used by police.

It is not the purpose of this chapter to examine the full range of human rights from the point of view of police entitlements, but some economic social and cultural rights clearly have great significance for police. For example, the right to just and favourable remuneration ensuring an existence worthy of human dignity is important for police officials everywhere, and for the communities they serve.[29] Governments need to ensure that police pay and conditions of service are sufficient to maintain the human dignity of police officials, and to provide a bulwark against corruption.

In respect of this category of rights, article 32 of the European Code of Police Ethics states:

> "Police staff shall enjoy social and economic rights, as public servants, to the fullest extent possible. In particular, staff shall have the right to organise or to participate in representative organisations, to receive an appropriate remuneration and social security, and to be provided with special health and security measures; taking into account the particular character of police work."

The Commentary to article 32 points out, *inter alia*, that social and economic rights may be limited for reasons of the special character of police work, and that the list of social and economic rights in the article highlights a few crucial rights but it is not exhaustive.[30] The Commentary also states that the rights to appropriate remuneration and social security, as well as special health and security measures have been highlighted in the recommendation because of the special character of police work. This refers, for example, to the unpredictable tasks that police personnel are facing every day, to the risks and dangers inherent in police work and to the irregular working hours. Moreover, these rights of police personnel are also crucial conditions for making the police profession attractive. This aspect is extremely important, considering the need for highly qualified staff to be recruited to, and retained within, the police. Furthermore, well remunerated police personnel are more likely not to be involved in undesired activities, such as corruption.

---

[29] *See e.g.*, article 23(3) of the Universal Declaration of Human Rights, and article 7 of the International Covenant on Economic, Social and Cultural Rights.
[30] European Code of Police Ethics, *supra* note 13.

(F) INTERNATIONAL HUMAN RIGHTS STANDARDS OF PARTICULAR RELEVANCE TO POLICING

Whilst all human rights and freedoms may be affected by policing, given the nature and purposes of police activity it is inevitable that the most fundamental human rights are of particular relevance to policing. Some of these rights and freedoms, the treaties that embody them, and non-treaty instruments designed to give greater effect to treaty provisions and to set good professional standards for policing are referred to briefly in the previous chapter. In order to examine further the nexus between human rights and policing it is useful to consider, in a little more detail, those international human rights standards that, between them, have great significance for every aspect of the theory and practice of policing.

In this chapter provisions of international human rights instruments affecting the exercise of police powers to use force and to deprive people of their liberty are outlined, as are those relevant to the investigation of crime and the policing of armed conflict and internal disturbances and tension. In the latter case reference is also made to international humanitarian law. Finally, other international standards relevant to policing are referred to. These concern the protection of particular categories of people, measures to counteract various kinds of intolerance and discrimination, and the prevention of crime. In the next two chapters, respectively, international standards having particular relevance to policing in a democracy and to police ethics are considered. Where it is applicable, the Universal Declaration of Human Rights is the initial point of reference in each case.

(a) Use of Force

The right to life is the right most affected by the use of force. It is protected under article 3 of the Universal Declaration of Human Rights. Some of the obligations placed on states to secure this right and the ways in which it may be protected through policing, have already been referred to. The treaty provisions expressing this right, for example the International Covenant on Civil and Political Rights and regional human rights treaties, prohibit arbitrary deprivation of life, although the European Convention does not use that term. Instead, it lists three sets of circumstances under which deprivation of life will not be regarded as being in contravention of the Convention when resulting from the use of force that is no more than absolutely necessary. That list is exhaustive.

Two instruments have been promulgated to protect people from arbitrary deprivation of life and to give guidance to police on the use of force. The exact purposes of the Principles on the Effective Prevention and Investigation of Extra-legal, Arbitrary and Summary Executions are apparent in the title of the instrument.[31] The existence of these Principles is a reflection of the international community's concern about extra-legal executions and of their prevalence. In short they are designed to prevent unlawful killings by agents of the State, sometimes operating in groups known as death squads, and to secure proper investigation of such killings.

The Basic Principles on the Use of Force and Firearms by Law Enforcement Officials is a very detailed and practical instrument designed to secure compliance with the principles of necessity and proportionality in the use of force by police. It requires, *inter alia*, rules and regulations to be adopted on the use of force and firearms by police; the issue to police of proper defensive equipment and equipment to allow for a differentiated use of force and firearms; firearms to be used against persons only as a defence against imminent threat of death or serious injury; proper reporting and review procedures when force or firearms are used by police; very high standards of selection and training of police; and proper accountability of senior officials and their subordinates.

Neither instrument has legal force but compliance with their provisions is an essential element in the protection of the right to life. The power to use force is an essential police power, and the Basic Principles on force and firearms lay down internationally recognised standards of good practice on this matter and provide a very useful basis for the development or review of national standards.

A more complete account of the right to life and the use of force, and an analysis of the international standards on the use of force by police are set out in Chapters 3 and 4 of Part II herein.

(b) **Deprivation of Liberty**

The power to arrest and to detain is also an essential police power, and the right most affected by the exercise of that power is the fundamental right to liberty of person protected by article 3 of the Universal Declaration of Human Rights. Article 9 of the Universal Declaration prohibits arbitrary arrest and detention, and all of these rights are given legal force in the International Covenant on Civil and Political Rights and the regional treaties.

People in detention are vulnerable to ill-treatment and to torture. The right to humane treatment as a detainee is protected in the International Covenant and in the

---

[31] Recommended by Economic and Social Council resolution 1989/65 of 24 May 1989. The UN General Assembly endorsed these Principles in its resolution 44/162 of 1 December 1989.

I:2

regional human rights treaties. The prohibition of torture, expressed in article 5 of the Universal Declaration of Human Rights, is repeated in the treaties.

The crime of torture is an extremely serious human rights violation. The prohibition of torture is absolute, and there are no circumstances whatsoever under which torture may be practised lawfully or is in any way justifiable. However it remains widely practised throughout the world and, for this reason, the prohibition of torture referred to above has been reinforced by the adoption of two instruments dealing specifically with that atrocity. These instruments are the Declaration on the Protection of All Persons from Being Subjected to Torture and Other Cruel, Inhuman or Degrading Treatment or Punishment, and the Convention against Torture and Other Cruel, Inhuman or Degrading Treatment or Punishment. The latter instrument is legally binding on parties to it.

Both instruments define torture and they each require, *inter alia*, training of police to take full account of the prohibition of torture, the prohibition to be included in rules or instructions issued to police officials responsible for custody of detainees, and States to keep interrogation methods and practices under systematic review.

Explicit provisions for the protection of detainees are set out in the Body of Principles for the Protection of All Persons under Any Form of Detention or Imprisonment, which was adopted by U.N. General Assembly resolution.[32] This instrument repeats the prohibition of arbitrary arrest and detention, the prohibition of torture, and the right of detainees to receive humane treatment. It then sets out detailed and practical measures by which, if followed, those ends may be secured. As with the Basic Principles on Force and Firearms, the Body of Principles on Detainees lays down internationally agreed standards of good practice and provides a useful basis for the development, or review, of national standards.

More complete accounts of the prohibition of torture under international law, and the rights of detainees are set out in Chapters 2 and 3 of Part III herein

(c) Investigation of Crime

The rights principally affected by the investigation of crime are the right to a fair trial and the presumption of innocence, which are protected under articles 10 and 11 of the Universal Declaration of Human Rights. Both rights are protected in the International Covenant on Civil and Political Rights and in the regional treaties.

---

[32] Body of Principles for the Protection of All Persons under Any Form of Detention or Imprisonment, *supra* note 12.

A lawful and ethical investigation of crime can protect the right to a fair trial whereas an unlawful or unethical investigation can subvert that right even before the trial has commenced. Some of the minimum guarantees to which a person is entitled under the fair trial provisions have important implications for police investigations: the rights to be tried without undue delay, to examine or have examined witnesses against him, and not to be compelled to testify against himself or to confess guilt for example. The right to be presumed innocent until proved guilty by law should inform the attitude and the behaviour of police investigators towards people suspected of crime and subject to investigation.

The prohibition of arbitrary interference with privacy, embodied in article 12 of the Universal Declaration of Human Rights and also included in human rights treaties, is a limiting factor on police powers to search, especially individuals and their homes, and to intercept correspondence, telephone conversations and other forms of communication. These powers are necessary for the investigation of crime, and indeed other policing functions, but they should be exercised strictly in accordance with domestic law and guidelines.

The rights of victims of crime are an especially important consideration. Their basic rights to be treated with compassion and respect, to be informed of their role in the proceedings and of the disposition of cases, to have their views represented and considered, and to have their privacy and safety protected are set out in the Declaration of Basic Principles of Justice for Victims of Crime and Abuse of Power.[33]

Apart from this Declaration there are no instruments setting out standards of good practice on the aspects of criminal investigation referred to here, or indeed on other aspects. For example there are no instruments giving detailed technical guidance on such matters as interviewing suspects or witnesses, or on covert areas of policing that are equivalent to those on the use of force and firearms, and this is regrettable.

There are very significant and succinctly expressed international standards on the treatment of suspects in the interview process, and these are analysed in Chapter 4 of Part III herein. In order to meet, in part, the deficiency in international standards referred to above, Part IV of this Book is devoted entirely to 'Investigative Interviewing – Professionalism and Best Practice'.

---

[33] Adopted by General Assembly resolution 40/34 of 29 November 1985.

I:2

(d) **Policing in Times of Armed Conflict and Internal Disturbance and Tension**

In times of armed conflict, disturbance and tension the human rights most vulnerable are the fundamental rights to life, liberty and security of person. Tragically and regrettably arbitrary killings, torture and arbitrary arrest and detention are common features of armed conflicts, and of states' responses to acts of terrorism and internal disturbances and tensions. This is in spite of the fact that such crimes and atrocities are prohibited by international humanitarian law, international human rights law and the domestic law of states. In some cases these means are adopted by states under the cruel and mistaken belief that they are the only or the most effective way of responding to such situations. In other cases they may not be explicitly adopted by states, but members of police and security forces believe that they are required or entitled to use such means. The fact that they are allowed to violate fundamental human rights with impunity reinforces their belief.

The provisions of human rights treaties that allow for derogation are relevant to policing in situations considered under this sub-heading. In times of officially proclaimed emergency which threaten the life of the nation States parties to the International Covenant on Civil and Political Rights, and to the American and European Conventions on Human Rights, may take measures derogating from some of their obligations under those treaties. The nature and extent of such measures varies, but all of the treaties are consistent in the fact that there may be no derogation from the provisions protecting the right to life or prohibiting torture and ill-treatment. The African Charter on Human and Peoples' Rights contains no specific derogation article but many of the articles in the instrument contain 'claw back' clauses that, in effect, entitle a State to restrict the rights to the extent permitted by domestic law. Treaty provisions on derogation are described in more detail in Chapter 1 of Part II herein.

Some provisions of the Basic Principles on the Use of Force and Firearms have particular relevance to the policing of internal disturbances. These include the requirements to avoid using force, or to use minimum force, in dispersing unlawful but non-violent assemblies; to use firearms only when less dangerous means are not practicable in dispersing violent assemblies, and then only in defence against imminent threat of death or serious injury; and to train police in alternatives to the use of force and firearms, in the understanding of crowd behaviour, and in methods of persuasion, negotiation and mediation. There are also two provisions in this instrument that are derived from principles of international humanitarian law. These are the requirements to minimise damage and injury and to respect and preserve human life; and to provide assistance and medical aid to injured or affected persons.

(G) INTERNATIONAL HUMANITARIAN LAW AND POLICE – RESPECT, PROTECT, INVESTIGATE AND ENTITLEMENT

International humanitarian law, like international human rights law, is a branch of public international law. Its purposes are to regulate the conduct of hostilities and to protect victims of armed conflicts, and it only comes into force in times of armed conflict. An account of aspects of international humanitarian law relevant to police is set out in Chapters 1 and 2 of Part II herein. It is important for police to be aware of the fundamental principles on which its provisions are based, and to know how some terms and concepts are defined, especially those of 'combatant' and 'civilian', and how police fit within those categories. Furthermore, this branch of law is legally applicable to police operations in both international and non-international armed conflicts, and some of its principles and provisions are relevant to policing conflict just below the threshold of armed conflict, and to policing other less serious or less durable forms of social disorder, even though they are not legally applicable in such circumstances

The relationship between police and international humanitarian law can be characterised in much the same terms as those used in characterising the relationship between police and human rights. Police officials are required to comply with its provisions, and to protect victims of armed conflict and the civilian population. They may be called upon to investigate crimes arising out of armed conflict, and they can benefit from various forms of protection available under international humanitarian law.

There are benefits arising for police officials when this branch of law is complied with, just as there is when human rights law is complied with and, whilst these matters are dealt with in Chapters 1 and 2 of Part II, it is appropriate to introduce them at this stage. For example, in an international armed conflict, some members of armed law enforcement agencies that have been incorporated into the armed forces of a party to a conflict have combatant status. This means that they have some forms of protection on the battlefield, and are entitled to treatment as prisoners of war in the event of capture by the adverse party. However, the majority of police, as members of civilian police agencies, would have civilian and not combatant status in the event of such a conflict. This means that they would be entitled to the protection afforded to the civilian population set out in 1949 Geneva Convention IV and 1977 Additional Protocol I.[34]

---

[34] Geneva Convention IV Relative to the Protection of Civilian Persons in Time of War was adopted on 12 August 1949. Additional Protocol I to the Geneva Conventions of 12 August 1949, and Relating to the Protection of Victims of International Armed Conflicts was adopted on 8 June 1977.

I:2

1949 Geneva Convention IV requires any civilian, military, police or other authorities who in time of war assume responsibilities in respect of protected persons, to possess the text of the Convention and be specially instructed as to its provisions.[35] 1977 Additional Protocol I requires any military or civilian authorities who, in time of armed conflict, assume responsibilities in respect of the application of the Conventions and the Protocol, to be fully acquainted with the text thereof.[36] Perhaps these obligations on High Contracting Parties could also be regarded as rights of police officials?

(H) OTHER INTERNATIONAL STANDARDS RELEVANT TO POLICING

Other standards embodied in international instruments that are relevant to policing concern the protection of children and the protection of refugees, measures against various forms of intolerance and discrimination, and the prevention of crime, particularly through international co-operation.

There is a wide range of international instruments dealing with children. These instruments are mainly directed at preventing exploitation of children, securing proper and humane treatment of children who have been detained, and setting standards on juvenile justice. The Convention on the Rights of the Child, which is a legally binding treaty, is the most important and the most recent of these instruments, but it was preceded by a large number of detailed sets of rules and guidelines.

The international standards designed to protect refugees are embodied in the Convention relating to the Status of Refugees[37] and the later Protocol relating to the Status of Refugees.[38] The key elements of the term refugee, as defined in the Convention, are a person who "owing to well-founded fear of being persecuted for reasons of race, religion, nationality, membership of a particular social group or political opinion, is outside the country of his nationality". Depending on their functions and the situation in their particular country, the standards in the Convention could be of direct relevance to the work of some police officials.

The significance to police of measures to combat discrimination on grounds of race, and intolerance and discrimination based on religion or belief has already been

---

[35] 1949 Geneva Convention IV, article 144.

[36] 1977 Additional Protocol I, article 83(2).

[37] Signed by Member States of the United Nations and other States invited, at Geneva, on 28 July 1951.

[38] Signed by the President of the General Assembly and the Secretary General of the United Nations, at New York, on 31 January 1967.

referred to above. These, and measures to deal with discrimination against women, also significant to police, are embodied in various Declarations, Conventions and Protocols, some of which have been referred to in the previous chapter. They are important instruments, for the principle of non-discrimination is one of the bases of human rights protection, and discrimination and intolerance are causes of social tension and social disorder. Furthermore, many states have created offences under their criminal law prohibiting discrimination and intolerance on such grounds as race, sex, and religion or belief.

Finally there is a wide ranging set of instruments establishing standards on the prevention of crime that are largely directed at securing international co-operation in the prevention of crime, and encouraging national crime prevention initiatives by Member States of the United Nations.[39] These instruments have been developed through the work of the United Nations Congresses on the Prevention of Crime and the Treatment of Offenders. The Congresses have brought together representatives of the world's national governments, specialists in crime prevention and criminal justice, scholars, and members of non-governmental organisations.

---

[39] *See e.g.*, Recommendations on international co-operation for crime prevention and criminal justice in the context of development, adopted under United Nations General Assembly resolution 45/107 of 14 December 1990.

Chapter 3. Human Rights, Democracy and Policing

(A) UNITED NATIONS GENERAL ASSEMBLY RESOLUTION 34/169

On 17 December 1979 the General Assembly of the United Nations adopted a Code of Conduct for Law Enforcement Officials. The Code of Conduct is considered in the next Chapter of this book. General Assembly resolution 34/169 by which the Code of Conduct was adopted includes the following precept:

> "That, like all agencies of the criminal justice system, every law enforcement agency should be representative of and responsive and accountable to the community as a whole…"

The General Assembly resolution, consisting of 14 short paragraphs, is brief and concise but it makes a number of fundamental statements about law enforcement, law enforcement officials and law enforcement agencies. Arguably, the paragraph quoted above is the most fundamental of those statements. Indeed it could be considered to be more important than the Code of Conduct adopted under the resolution.

General Assembly resolutions are only recommendatory and have no legal force unless they express an already existing rule of international law. However, this particular resolution does reflect practice already followed in many States, and it does reflect democratic principles expressed in articles of the Universal Declaration of Human Rights and in human rights treaties. These are all powerful reasons for arguing that the recommendations it embodies should be followed by all States.

(B) POLICE ORGANISATIONS, POLITICAL SYSTEMS AND COMMUNITIES

In stating that law enforcement agencies should be representative of and responsive and accountable to the community as a whole, the General Assembly resolution established fundamental standards on the nature of law enforcement agencies, and their relationships with the political systems within which they function and the communities they serve. It set standards for democratic policing.

The importance of these standards derives mainly from the fact that, in a fundamental sense, policing is a highly political activity. The need for a policing function arises at an early stage in the development of a society and, indeed, is one of the indicators of the politicisation of a society. Furthermore, because police contribute to a number of essential processes in the political functioning of a society, the police role is closely tied to the political organisation of that society.

For example, police enforce laws enacted by the legislature and, moreover, modify the effect of those laws through the exercise of discretion in their enforcement; police maintain peace and security in society so that the political processes can be conducted constitutionally; and police are involved in the political socialisation

I:3

process. In meeting police, citizens come into direct contact with the state. The impressions they gain from this type of encounter influence their view of the political culture in which they find themselves. An authoritarian, violent and arbitrary police gives rise to fear, and favours the development of a political culture of subjection. A less interventionist, less violent, more law-abiding police promotes a participatory culture.

Due to the nature of police organisations and their functional relationships to political systems and the larger society, the standards expressed in General Assembly resolution 34/169 will be met largely through the political and legal institutions of a State, but they may also be met through arrangements made directly between police and the community. This is because police organisations, as one of the executive arms of government, are state agencies. Nevertheless they remain, to varying degrees, deeply embedded in society and in contact with all strata of society. The deep insertion of many police organisations in social systems distinguishes them from other administrations in political systems.[40]

The essentially political nature of policing and the necessity, in a democratic political system, of attempting to sustain non-partisan, politically neutral policing betoken a dilemma that is probably impossible to resolve completely. The extent to which it is resolved within any political system, the extent to which democratic policing is achieved, is an indication of the nature and quality of democracy within that system. United Nations General Assembly resolution 34/169 requires policing to be carried out in accordance with three principles essential for democratic policing. Indeed the three principles it expresses are essential for democracy to prevail within a political system.

(C) HUMAN RIGHTS AND DEMOCRACY

Other standards expressed in international human rights instruments also make requirements on police that are essential for democratic policing. Furthermore, international instruments express principles and standards that require political systems to function according to democratic principles. The second preambular paragraph of the Universal Declaration of Human Rights links freedoms essential to democracy with freedoms fundamental to human existence when it asserts:

> "the advent of a world in which human beings shall enjoy freedom of speech and belief and freedom from fear and want has been proclaimed as the highest aspiration of the common people..."

---

[40] These observations on the relationship between police and the political system are expressed in Loubet Del Blayle, *supra* note 20.

The third preambular paragraph refers to the antithesis to democracy, raises the prospect of rebellion against that and identifies other elements essential to democracy when it asserts:

> "it is essential, if man is not to be compelled to have recourse, as a last resort, to rebellion against tyranny and oppression, that human rights should be protected by the rule of law…"

The fifth preambular paragraph refers to the affirmation of the peoples of the United Nations in the Charter of the United Nations to, *inter alia*, promote social progress and better standards of life in larger freedom.

The Universal Declaration of Human Rights, under article 21, then expresses a fundamental principle of democracy, that "the will of the people shall be the basis of the authority of government", and sets out a number of rights establishing standards for democratic forms of government. These include the right of everyone to take part in the government of his country, directly or through freely chosen representatives; the right to periodic and genuine elections; the right to universal and equal suffrage; and the right to secret vote or equivalent free voting procedures.

A number of other rights essential for democracy are also expressed in the Universal Declaration of Human Rights. These include the right to freedom of thought, conscience and religion (article 18); the right to freedom of opinion and expression (article 19); and the right to freedom of peaceful assembly and association (article 20).

It is partly through the expression of democratic principles and of rights essential for democratic government in the Universal Declaration of Human Rights and human rights treaties that it can now be argued that representative democracy has become a standard for political legitimacy for all regimes of the world.[41] Furthermore the mutual dependence of democracy and of human rights is made apparent. A number of human rights are essential for democracy to prevail but, at the same time, human rights are more likely to be respected and protected under representative, responsive and accountable forms of government.

---

[41] *See e.g.*, International Covenant on Civil and Political Rights, articles 18, 19, 21 and 22; African Charter on Human and Peoples' Rights, articles 8, 9, 10, 11 and 13; the American Convention on Human Rights, articles 12, 13, 15, 16 and 23; the European Convention for the Protection of Human Rights and Fundamental Freedoms, articles 9, 10, and 11; and the Protocol 1 to the European Convention, article 3.

I:3

(D) REPRESENTATIVE, RESPONSIVE AND ACCOUNTABLE

An essential element of representative government is an assembly of representatives, elected from the community, to perform the basic functions of a legislature and to scrutinise the exercise of power by government, to make it responsive and accountable. Responsiveness and accountability are necessary to secure popular control over political decision-making, as are widespread participation by the population in political processes and respect for the rule of law. Representativeness is one of the elements necessary to secure political equality in the exercise of that control.

A police official is not a 'representative of the community' in the same sense as a member of an elected assembly, which is one of the reasons why police officials are not normally elected from the community. Whilst, in a democracy, effective policing is dependent upon the consent and cooperation of the community, it would be difficult, if not impossible, for an individual police official to exercise his or her powers independently and impartially if his or her position in a police agency were dependent upon popular support. The rule of law and the proper administration of justice would be seriously jeopardised if police officials were to be driven by the same impulses that cause politicians, sometimes, to respond to crime and terrorism in populist but simplistic and counterproductive ways in the belief that it wins them votes.

For a police agency to be representative of the community as a whole its membership must be representative of that community according to such criteria as race, colour, sex, language and religion. Minority groups must be adequately represented, and individuals from those groups must be able to pursue their careers fairly and without discrimination. Very few, if any, police agencies are representative of the community in this sense, especially in so far as the recruitment of women is concerned.

For a police agency to be responsive to the community, police leaders, in the first instance, must be aware of public concerns and expectations in relation to matters that can be addressed by policing, and in relation to police methods and performance. The extent to which their awareness is informed by information transmitted from the community to the police via the political institutions of the state is a measure of the effectiveness of the constitutional means to secure popular control over political decision making.

The extent to which such concerns, needs and expectations are reflected in police policy, strategy and action is a further measure of the effectiveness of those means. It is also a measure of the willingness of police leaders to police with the consent and cooperation of the community, and of their ability to translate their willingness into action.

For a police agency to be accountable there must be legal accountability and political accountability. A police agency must be accountable to the law, and to the community it serves through the political institutions of the state. Legal accountability includes the personal accountability of individual police officials to the law for their own acts or omissions. Political accountability includes the ability to ensure that a police agency is accountable for the ways in which it uses the resources that have been allocated to it. This type of accountability enables public scrutiny of the entire management and administration of a police agency as well as of its operational practices.

Article 5 of the European Code of Police Ethics requires that police personnel shall be subject to the same legislation as ordinary citizens, and stipulates that exceptions may only be justified for reasons of the proper performance of police work in a democratic society. The Commentary to the article explains that the article expresses a cardinal principle of the rule of law. Articles 16 and 17 of the Code also express standards on the legal accountability of police. The former article states that police personnel, at all levels, shall be personally responsible and accountable for their own actions or omissions or for orders to subordinates. The latter article requires police organisations to provide for a clear chain of command within the police, and that it should always be possible to determine which superior is ultimately responsible for the acts or omissions of police personnel.

The nature of police accountability is expressed in articles 13 and 15 of the Code. These require, respectively, that the police, when performing police duties in civil society, shall be under the responsibility of civilian authorities; and that the police force shall enjoy sufficient operational independence from other State bodies in carrying out its given police tasks, for which it should be fully accountable.

Accountability and control of the police generally is dealt with in later articles of the Code in ways that reinforce and expand upon the standards expressed in UN General Assembly resolution 34/169. Article 59 requires that the police shall be accountable to the State, the citizens and their representatives, and that they shall be subject to efficient external control. Articles 60 and 62 require, respectively, that State control of the police shall be divided between the legislative, the executive and the judicial powers; and that accountability mechanisms, based on communication and mutual understanding between the public and the police, shall be promoted.

In their jurisprudence, human rights institutions have required states to conduct investigations and bring to account individuals responsible for human rights

I:3

violations. For example, in concluding that a State was directly responsible for the disappearance and subsequent assassination of one of its citizens, the Human Rights Committee not only stressed the duty of that State to investigate thoroughly alleged violations of human rights, and in particular forced disappearances of persons and violations of the right to life, it insisted that it should prosecute criminally, try and punish those held responsible for such violations.[42]

It has been the usual practice of the Inter-American Court of Human Rights to decide that where a State has been found in violation of its obligations under the American Convention on Human Rights, the State should conduct an investigation to determine the persons responsible for the human rights violations referred to in its judgments and punish them.[43]

In a number of its judgements the European Court of Human Rights has ruled that the obligation to protect life under article 2 of the European Convention, read in conjunction with the State's general duty under article 1 to secure to everyone within its jurisdiction the rights and freedoms defined in the Convention, required by implication that there should be some form of effective official investigation when individuals had been killed as a result of the use of force by agents of the State.[44]

One noteworthy case concerning accountability of police officials for crimes arising out of human rights violations is *Selmouni* v. *France*.[45] In this case the European Court of Human Rights examined the investigation proceedings of the French authorities into allegations of torture made against police officials by the victim. Ultimately four police officials were sentenced to terms of imprisonment after conviction on assault and wounding charges. The judgement of the Court records the observations of the domestic court that passed the sentences. This court stated, *inter alia*, that the defendants were guilty of offences being exceptionally serious, to be regarded as instances of particularly degrading treatment. Having been committed by senior officials responsible for enforcing the laws of the Republic, they had to be punished firmly. Such conduct could not be justified, irrespective of the personality of the offenders in their charge and the degree of their corruption and

---

[42] *Bautista de Arellana* v. *Colombia*, United Nations, *Official Records of the General Assembly, Fifty-first Session, Supplement No. 40* (A/51/40), vol. II, annex VIII, sect. S, communication No. 563/1993, views adopted on 27 October 1995.

[43] *See e.g., Villagrán Morales et al.* v. *Guatemala* (the "*Street Children*" case), Inter-American Court of Human Rights, Series C: *Decisions and Judgments*, No. 63 (2000), petition No. 11383, judgment of 19 November 1999.

[44] *See e.g., Kaya* v. *Turkey*, European Court of Human Rights, *Reports of Judgments and Decisions*, 2000-III, p. 149, application No. 22535/93, judgment of 28 March 2000.

[45] European Court of Human Rights, *Reports of Judgments and Decisions*, 1999-V, p. 149, judgment of 28 July 1999.

dangerousness. The European Court of Human Rights was satisfied that the physical and mental violence, considered as a whole, committed against the victim caused severe pain and suffering and was particularly serious and cruel. Such conduct must be regarded as acts of torture for the purposes of article 3 of the Convention. It concluded, therefore, that there had been a violation of this provision.

As indicated above, because of the relationships of police agencies to the political system within which they function and to the communities they serve, the fundamental standards of representativeness, responsiveness and accountability may be met not only through the political institutions of the state but also through various formal and informal links with the community.

(E) HUMAN RIGHTS, DEMOCRACY AND THE RULE OF LAW

The dependence of democracy and human rights upon each other is clear. One powerful reason for considering the nature of this dependence, and for considering the elements of democratic policing, is so that the right to democratic government at all levels of government, and especially at the subordinate levels, can be given due emphasis.

It is critically important for officials exercising state power at subordinate levels of government to appreciate fully that this right, and indeed all human rights, are entitlements, and not privileges granted by government. It is important that a human rights culture should be developed within agencies of the state so that human rights can be properly regarded as inalienable, and inherent in every human being, and not as a series of obstacles that somehow have to be overcome, circumvented or ignored in the exercise of power.

One very significant reason why police officials should not seek to overcome, circumvent or ignore human rights is that they are protected by the rule of law, and it is particularly inappropriate for officials required to enforce law to undermine the rule of law. In fact the rule of law is the third and final factor in an equation that expresses the factors necessary to prevent abuse of power. The other two factors are democracy and human rights, and all three are dependent upon each other.

The third preambular paragraph of the Universal Declaration of Human Rights, referred to above, asserts that it is essential that human rights be protected by the rule of law. This assertion is an acknowledgement by those drafting the Declaration, and by the U.N. General Assembly when adopting it, that if human rights are not so protected any formulation of rights would exist only as a catalogue of unenforceable and unattainable aspirations.

I:3

Furthermore, a number of rights that are supportive of and essential to the rule of law are expressed in the Universal Declaration of Human Rights, and indeed in other human rights instruments. For example, article 7 of the Universal Declaration protects the right to equality before the law and to equal protection of the law, and Article 10 protects the right to a fair trial by an independent and impartial tribunal. The rule of law does not prevail if it is not applied equally, and it cannot prevail without an independent judiciary.

The interdependence of democracy and the rule of law is also readily apparent because unaccountable government is unlikely to make itself subject to the rule of law, and the rule of law is unlikely to prevail in a state where democratic government is not practised. The rule of law has been identified above as one element necessary to secure popular control over political decision-making.

Respect for the rule of law by police is not only necessary because police enforce law; it is also necessary because social order is dependent upon a number of conditions, one of which is that the rule of law of law should prevail. Unlawful and arbitrary policing undermines the rule of law and it is a very serious form of social disorder. It is a form of 'tyranny and oppression' that may, in its turn, provoke disorder by those against whom it is practised.

One of the ways in which police maintain and restore social order is to secure respect for the rule of law. This is done not only by enforcing law but also by requiring respect for the rule of law in other ways, for example by removing immunity where this exists, and by insisting on the application of due process where this is absent. The rule of law is reinforced when people, previously immune because of power or influence, are made accountable to the law, and when legal or administrative procedures, previously ignored or eroded, are complied with.

In respect of this latter point it is not only police who may be culpable as far as, for example, unlawful arrests and searches, and unauthorised seizures of property are concerned. Judicial authorities can be careless or compliant in these matters, and political authorities can ignore or even encourage malpractice on grounds of expediency. Police do not have to, and should not, exploit such failings or collaborate with other authorities in abuse of power.

Where police should collaborate with political and legal authorities is in the effective operation of those means designed to secure accountability of police to the community through the democratic institutions of government, and to secure accountability of police to the law. They should also collaborate with those authorities in the development and implementation of effective policies in the domain of law enforcement and policing generally.

In a democracy, effective policies are those that can be developed and implemented in a manner acceptable to those affected by them. In order for this to happen there needs to be informed debate within the community. Police contributions to such debates need to be tempered by an awareness of the tendency of some politicians on some occasions to exploit public concern about 'law and order' and criminal justice issues in order to gain popular approval or to further some other political agenda. This is especially the case when they invoke, for example, a 'war on terror' in seeking to limit hard won civil and political rights and, in doing so, undermine the very values under attack from terrorists, which they themselves have a duty to protect. When this occurs the possibilities for informed debate are diminished and the likelihood of the formulation of bad law and ineffective policies correspondingly increased. By making objective, rational and reasonable contributions to public debate on policing matters, police promote democratic principles and contribute to effective policy making.

(F) PROTECTION OF RIGHTS TO DEMOCRATIC FREEDOMS

Informed public debate is also dependent upon the exercise by individuals and groups of rights essential to democratic political processes such as the rights to freedom of thought, conscience and religion, to freedom of opinion and expression, and to peaceful assembly and association.

In a general, but very necessary sense, police contribute to the protection of these rights through the part they play in maintaining social order so that the rights may be enjoyed. In fact the entitlement to such a social order as expressed in article 28 of the Universal Declaration of Human Rights, and the part police play in protecting it, are referred to in Chapter 2. However, the fact that rights of this nature may conflict with each other, with other human rights, and with other public and private ends of a desirable nature is recognised in the articles of treaties that protect them. For example, article 21 of the International Covenant on Civil and Political Rights, which protects the right to peaceful assembly, states that no restrictions may be placed on the exercise of the right:

> "other than those imposed in conformity with the law and which are necessary in a democratic society in the interests of national security or public safety, public order (ordre public), the protection of public health or morals or the protection of the rights and freedoms of others."

Similar clauses in articles 18 and 19 of the Covenant, that protect the right to freedom of thought conscience and religion and the right to freedom of opinion and expression respectively, prohibit restrictions on those rights except as provided by

I:3

the law for such purposes as the protection of the rights of others and public order or public morals. Articles in the American and European Conventions protecting these rights, and the right to freedom of peaceful assembly and association, also embody limitation clauses.

The relationship of these clauses to police functions and to police powers is considered in Chapter 2, where similar provisions in article 29(2) of the Universal Declaration of Human Rights are discussed. The exercise of legal powers to limit rights of this nature imposes immense responsibilities on police, either because they exercise the powers or because they report or make recommendations to another authority who does so.

Not only does the enjoyment of important human rights have to be balanced against the enjoyment of other rights or such desirable ends as public order, the effects of repressing freedoms such as the right to opinion and expression or to peaceful assembly have to be taken into account, as do the effects of failing to enforce the rule of law. In the shorter term prohibiting a public assembly may prevent disorder, but in the longer term it may contribute to an increase in tension in society, which, in turn, could lead to greater public disorder. On the other hand, failing to enforce the rule of law by allowing an assembly that has been lawfully and properly prohibited may create other tensions that are equally conducive to disorder. Denial of political rights or of rights essential to political processes, and failure to enforce the rule of law can each be underlying causes of long term and intractable tension and disorder in a society. To make these points is to acknowledge the extremely difficult dilemmas that sometimes confront police leaders.

Article 43 of the European Code of Police Ethics states that the police, in carrying out their activities, shall always bear in mind everyone's fundamental rights. It then refers, *inter alia*, to freedom of thought, conscience, religion, expression and peaceful assembly. The Commentary to the article points out that the police play a major part in safeguarding these rights - without which democracy becomes an empty notion without any basis in reality - either directly, through safeguarding democratic arrangements, or indirectly, through their general responsibility for upholding the rule of law.

Jurisprudence of human rights institutions reinforces the importance of democratic rights and rights essential for democratic government. Violations of the right to freedom of opinion and expression have led to findings and pronouncements by a variety of international human rights institutions in cases of which police leaders should be aware.

For example, the Human Rights Committee has observed that the freedoms of information and of expression are cornerstones in any free and democratic society. It is in the essence of such societies that citizens must be allowed to inform themselves about alternatives to the political system/parties in power, and that they may criticise or openly and publicly evaluate their Governments without fear of interference or punishment, within the limits set by article 19 paragraph 3.[46]

The Inter-American Court of Human Rights, citing an earlier Advisory Opinion, linked public order in a democratic society with the guarantee of the widest possible circulation of news, ideas and opinions, as well as the widest access to information by society as a whole. It pointed out that freedom of expression constitutes the primary and basic element of the public order of a democratic society, which is not conceivable without free debate and the possibility that dissenting voices be fully heard.[47]

The European Court of Human Rights, reiterating the fundamental principles that emerged from its judgments relating to article 10 of the European Convention, observed that freedom of expression constituted one of the essential foundations of a democratic society and one of the basic conditions for its progress and for each individual's self-fulfilment. Subject to paragraph 2 of that article, it was applicable not only to information or ideas that were favourably received or regarded as inoffensive or as a matter of indifference, but also to those that offended, shocked or disturbed. Such were the demands of that pluralism, tolerance and broadmindedness without which there was no democratic society. As set forth in article 10, this freedom was subject to exceptions, which had, however, to be construed strictly, and the need for any restrictions had to be established convincingly.[48]

In a case on the freedom of thought, conscience and religion, the same Court pronounced that this freedom was one of the foundations of a democratic society within the meaning of the Convention.[49] It was, in its religious dimension, one of the most vital elements that go to make up the identity of believers and their conception of life, but it was also a precious asset for atheists, agnostics, sceptics and the

---

[46] *Aduayom, Diasso and Dobou* v. *Togo Ibidem, Fifty-first Session, Supplement No. 40* (A/51/40), vol. II, annex VIII, sect. C, communications No. 422/1990, No. 423/1990 and No. 424/1990, views adopted on 12 July 1996.

[47] The *Ivcher Bronstein* case (*Peru*), Inter-American Court of Human Rights, Series C: *Decisions and Judgments,* No. 74 (2002), petition No. 11762, judgment of 6 February 2001.

[48] *Zana* v. *Turkey*, European Court of Human Rights, *Reports of Judgments and Decisions*, 1997-VII, p. 2533, application No. 18954/91, judgment of 25 November 1997.

[49] *Kokkinakis* v. *Greece, Publications of the European Court of Human Rights*, Series A: *Judgments and Decisions*, vol. 260-A (1993), application No. 14307/88, judgment of 24 June 1993.

I:3

unconcerned. The pluralism indissociable from a democratic society, which had been dearly won over the centuries, depended on it.

Principally because of their function to maintain order, police are uniquely placed to avoid and to prevent violations of the right to peaceful assembly and association, and to protect the right.

The duty on States to protect the right to peaceful assembly was expressed very clearly by the European Court of Human Rights when it pronounced that genuine and effective freedom of peaceful assembly could not be reduced to a mere duty on the part of the State not to interfere.[50] A purely negative conception would not be compatible with the object and purpose of article 11 of the Convention. Like article 8, article 11 sometimes required positive measures to be taken, even in the sphere of relations between individuals, if need be.

The right to freedom of peaceful assembly and association in an area that requires particularly sensitive policing, that of labour disputes and industrial relations, has resulted in some important and interesting cases being considered by the Freedom of Association Committee of the Governing Body of the International Labour Office.[51] Clearly this right and the activities it protects are essential to trade unionists and employers, and fundamental to democracy. The primary purpose of any police action in labour disputes is to maintain order so that they may be resolved within the appropriate framework. On most occasions, of course, such disputes are settled without the need for police intervention. The Committee, whilst recognising the need to maintain public order, has insisted that an authority's response has to be proportionate to the situation faced.

This approach is reflected in a report on Case No. 1014 (*Dominican Republic*), in which the Committee recalled that freedom from government interference in the

---

[50] *Plattform "Ärzte für das Leben"* v. *Austria, Publications of the European Court of Human Rights*, Series A: *Judgments and Decisions*, vol. 139 (1988), application No. 10126/82, judgment of 21 June 1988.

[51] The Freedom of Association Committee of the Governing Body of the International Labour Organisation (ILO) is one of two bodies responsible for supervising the application of ILO standards on freedom of association. The ILO is a specialised agency of the United Nations that seeks the promotion of social justice and internationally recognised human and labour rights. The mandate of the Freedom of Association Committee is to determine whether any given legislation or practice complies with the principles of freedom of association and collective bargaining laid down in the relevant Conventions (Freedom of Association and Protection of the Right to Organise, 1948 (No. 87); Right to Organise and Collective Bargaining, 1949 (No. 98)). It is empowered to examine the extent to which the exercise of trade union rights may be affected in cases of infringements of civil liberties.

holding and proceedings of trade union meetings constituted an essential element of trade union rights.[52] It insisted that the public authorities should refrain from any interference which would restrict this right or impede its exercise, unless public order was disturbed thereby or its maintenance seriously and imminently endangered.

The report on Case No.1285 (*Chile*), included an objection to a law punishing any person who, without permission, promoted or called for collective public acts in streets, squares and other places in public use and who promoted or incited demonstrations of any other kind that allowed or facilitated a breach of the public peace.[53] In response to this objection, the Committee pointed out that the requirement of administrative permission to hold public meetings and demonstrations was not objectionable *per se* from the standpoint of the principles of freedom of association. The maintenance of public order was not incompatible with the right to hold demonstrations so long as the authorities responsible for public order reached agreement with the organisers of a demonstration concerning the place where it would be held and the manner in which it would take place.

A report on Case No. 1598 (*Peru*), included allegations of a violent intervention by the police at a trade union meeting that resulted in a death and injuries to workers, and of the violent repression of a march by police.[54] The Committee brought to the attention of the Government the fact that the authorities should resort to the use of force only in situations where law and order was seriously threatened. It also expressed the opinion that the intervention of the forces of law and order should be in due proportion to the danger to law and order it was attempting to control. Governments should take measures to ensure that the competent authorities received adequate instructions so as to eliminate the danger entailed by the use of excessive violence when controlling demonstrations that might result in a disturbance of the peace.

A report on Case No. 2189 (*China*) indicates how the Committee attaches great importance to the principle that responses of authorities to demonstrations and other events arising out of labour disputes should be in due proportion to the danger to law and order that the authorities were attempting to control.[55] It requested the Government to consider preparing relevant instructions for the forces of law and order aimed at eliminating the danger of resorting to the use of excessive violence

---

[52] International Labour Office, *Official Bulletin*, vol. LXIV, Series B, No. 3 (1981), p. 130, interim report of 13 November 1981.
[53] *Ibid.*, vol. LXVIII, Series B, No. 3 (1985), p. 115, definitive report of 7 November 1985.
[54] *Ibid.*, vol. LXXVIII, Series B, No. 1 (1995), p. 38, request report of 27 March 1995.
[55] *Ibid.*, vol. LXXXVI, Series B, No. 1 (2003), p. 101, interim report of 21 March 2003.

I:3

when controlling demonstrations. It is interesting to note that the Committee took into account the context to this case, that of an economy in transition, and the Government's determination to achieve simultaneous development in economic and social fields. The Committee pointed out that it was precisely within that context that the only durable solution to the apparently increasing social conflict experienced in the country was through full respect for the right of workers to establish independent organisations of their own choosing.

These and other cases considered by the Committee are of great relevance and importance to police leaders determined to ensure that their agencies operate under the rule of law and in accordance with democratic principles. Police leaders must ensure that interventions in the affairs of workers' or employers' organisations and in labour disputes are appropriate and justifiable in policing terms. Furthermore, when an intervention is so justified, it should be lawful and proportionate to the threat to law and order. Respect for and protection of the rights of all individuals and groups within society is a prerequisite for a social order based on, and derived from, the rule of law.

(G) ENLIGHTENED POLICING IN A DEMOCRACY

Enlightened policing, policing imbued with democratic principles and informed by an awareness of the relationship of the police role to the political organisation of the society within which it is carried out, can enhance the accountability and the effectiveness of government at the primary level, and at the subordinate level at which police function.

It is a function of police to enable democratic political debate and other democratic political activity in accordance with the requirements of representative and accountable government. It is a function of police to play a part in ensuring that the processes of social or political change are constitutional, legal and peaceful. All of this means that when a community, or a section of a community, articulates demands on the political system police are to facilitate the transmission of those demands and not to suppress them; it means that when opponents of a regime or government seek to achieve their ends through violence or intimidation, or otherwise illegally, police should frustrate them; it means that when the means or ends of government are at odds with accountable government or the rule of law, police are not to serve those means or ends. In this sense police can act as a 'conscience of constitutionality'.

This may be a statement of an ideal which is, perhaps, only attainable within an extremely sophisticated and advanced democracy by an extremely sophisticated and advanced police organisation. It is, nevertheless, an ideal embodied in United

Nations General Assembly resolution 34/169, which requires every law enforcement agency to be representative of, and responsive and accountable to the community as a whole. Perhaps one of the difficulties with the resolution is that it takes insufficient account of the fact that police are an arm of government exercising power on behalf of the State, particularly the power to use force. It begs the question 'who or what do the police serve?' Most of the time, under favourable conditions in a democratic state, there may be no conflict between serving the community and exercising power on behalf of the state. Nevertheless, occasions do arise when the interests of at least some sections of a community conflict with those of the state as perceived by a particular government faced with a particular challenge. Sometimes such conflict reflects a genuine dilemma that a government must resolve, and the interests of one part of the community have to take precedence over those of another part. Sometimes, however, conflict arises because of unjust treatment of one part of the community by another, or by the government, or both. In such cases, police action, particularly when it involves the use of force, directed against that part of the community being victimised, can be an abuse of power. Injustice can be compounded by police action.

The requirements of General Assembly resolution 34/169 are of enormous relevance to leaders of police organisations for they set out some of the most significant principles by which policing is to be conducted, and some of the most significant criteria by which a police organisation is to be judged. Furthermore, in the management of change within a police organisation, they indicate fundamental ideals to be achieved or reinforced through that change.

The fundamental question the resolution raises, 'who or what do the police serve?' is also of great relevance to police leaders because that question points at an acute and very real dilemma for police in a democracy governed by the rule of law. For a police agency to aspire to the level of sophistication required to meet the ideal referred to above, to be able to resolve the dilemma raised by the fundamental question requires an enlightened police, led by women and men who have the capacity for independent and critical thought, and the courage to maintain principles of good policing when under pressure to act otherwise. Police officials, and particularly police leaders, need to be aware of the political and social context within which they operate. All states of the category to which I am referring have, to varying degrees, constitutional and legal arrangements that allow police a measure of operational independence. That independence should be exploited to the full, in recognition of the facts that the state can only operate through its officials, and that the nature of the state is influenced to a great extent by the nature of its police.

I:3

The challenge of human rights for police leaders, and the management of change within police organisations are two matters that are examined in Part VI of this Book, 'Police Organisations – Strategy for Management and Change'.

Chapter 4. Human Rights and Police Ethics

(A) PREDICAMENTS OF POLICING

Policing can be extremely difficult and demanding – emotionally, intellectually and physically. In practising their craft and profession police can experience personal danger and discomfort, and severe trauma and anxiety. Furthermore, the sheer moral complexity of life itself is reflected in, and perhaps magnified by, the nature of police work, the demands that it makes on police officials and the costs to them of undertaking it.

Police are required to respond with restraint to physical attacks on their persons; they are required to respond dispassionately and compassionately to the immediate effects of serious criminality on victims; they experience the frustrations of being unable to deliver to justice the authors of shocking crimes; and they are subject to pressure from society, the news media, and from politicians to obtain results. In the case of really atrocious crimes, or where there is serious public concern about levels of criminality, or where 'law and order' has become or has been made an issue of party politics this pressure can be such that police feel they are entitled, or perhaps even required, to adopt unlawful and inhumane methods. Furthermore people engaged in organised crime, or certain types of financial criminality, have at their disposal vast sums of money that can be, and at times is, used to corrupt police.

These are some of the factors that combine to confront individual police officials with a variety of ethical problems and dilemmas. They are factors that create or reinforce a sub-culture that can be inimical to human rights and the rule of law, a sub-culture that can be comfortable with the absurd and sinister notion of 'noble cause corruption'- law breaking for the purposes of law enforcement. They derive from the nature of the police task, and the nature of police organisations and their relationship to political systems and the societies within which they function, all matters referred to in the preceding two chapters.

Almost all of the ethical problems and ethical dilemmas that confront police can be resolved by reference to the legal rules and administrative guidelines applicable in a given situation, and by complying with those rules and guidelines. However given the factors referred to above, and these are by no means all of the significant factors, it is unsurprising that police do not, as a matter of course, respect the law. Moreover, the law can be unclear and it can be silent on some of the most intractable problems with which police are required to deal.

What is required then, is a means of reinforcing the law, a means of encouraging police to respect the law even when the reasons for not doing so appear to be very strong indeed. What is also required is a source of reference for police to consult when the law is inadequate or silent, or when they are required to exercise discretion in the course of their duties, or, conversely, when they have no choice but to carry out their professional duty.

I:4

This latter point is of great significance in policing, for police are probably more aware than practitioners of other crafts or professions that sometimes in doing their professional duty they have no choice, except perhaps in their attitude and in the method they adopt, but to carry out their duty.

Consider, for example, the situation of police required to respond to crime and disorder in a society where they feel, with some justification, that over-reliance is being placed on oppression and repression, and that other necessary measures in the realms of social and penal policy are not being taken. They may feel compelled to call for a more complete range of responses to crime and social tension but this would almost certainly put at risk their efforts to remain non-partisan and politically neutral. They may be able to implement some preventive strategies that take into account the wider causes of crime and disorder, but these would remain relatively ineffective within the prevailing social and political context.

Whatever they may feel about the situation within which they are required to operate, the duty of the police is to deal with criminality and disorder regardless of its causes, and in spite of any unsound or misconceived government policies that may be introduced. In such a situation the obligation on police to act lawfully and humanely is very high indeed if social injustice is not to be compounded by judicial and penal injustice.

(B) THE ETHICS OF POLICING

Reflections of this nature, wherever else they may lead, steer us to the discipline of moral philosophy, that branch of philosophy concerned with ethics. Primarily this is the study of morals in human conduct but it also, more specifically, addresses the rules of conduct appropriate to a particular profession or area of life. It is interesting to note, in this respect, that the Explanatory Memorandum to the European Code of Police Ethics states that, in the context of the Code, the word ethics "refers to that body of principled requirements and prescriptions that is deemed fit to regulate the conduct of the occupation. It is important to note that ethics in this sense represents an attempt to apply everyday ethics to the specialist demands and dilemmas of public organisations. It is in this sense that 'ethics' is used in 'The European Code of Police Ethics'." The study and development of ethical theory and the difficult process of applying it to practical work are the functions of philosophers. The ethics of policing is expertly and cogently elucidated in other publications by philosophical scholars.[56]

---

[56] *See e.g.*, J. Kleinig, *The Ethics of Policing* (Cambridge University Press, Cambridge, 1996).

Whilst the focus of this book is on the legal nature of human rights, it can be argued that human rights are pre-eminently a moral concept. Indeed one type of moral theory centres on rights. However, the reasons for referring to the ethics of policing here are that both human rights and ethics deal with behavioural aspects of policing; ethical theory and its practical application generally reinforce human rights and humanitarian law standards; international human rights instruments require attention to be given to issues of police ethics;[57] and some such instruments are proclaimed as ethical codes or codes of conduct. Two of these are considered below. Most importantly, however, the subject is addressed here for two further reasons. Firstly, to acknowledge that situations do arise where police have to make ethical choices, and secondly, to insist that these can almost never be convincingly proposed as reasons for law breaking and human rights abuse.

Where the law is clear, where police powers and the limitations on those powers are clear, the idea that it is acceptable for individual police officials to exceed or abuse their powers in order to achieve some 'higher good' and then attempt to 'justify' their decisions to do so on ethical grounds, is very dubious indeed. Police powers are defined and qualified by lawmakers, and policing is to be carried out within that framework. When it is, policing is lawful and consistent. When it is not, policing is unlawful and arbitrary. There can be no ethical justification for the latter. Attempts to justify law breaking by law enforcers on ethical grounds are, in effect, attempts to justify corrupt policing, brutal policing, inept policing or, quite simply, lazy policing.

It is true that, extremely rarely, a police official is faced with a genuinely terrible choice, and that whichever decision he or she takes will have unwanted or tragic consequences. To fail to acknowledge this would be morally frivolous. However, such situations are so uncommon that most police officials do not encounter them in the course of their entire careers. They are so uncommon that it is unrealistic to legislate for them and, in any event, it would be very difficult if not impossible to frame law that would resolve the dilemmas they raise. In such situations a decision based on sound ethical principles and measured consideration of all of the issues, and taken in full awareness of all of the consequences, would be much easier to defend, even if it did entail law breaking.

Apart from discounting, on grounds of improbability, attempts to justify law breaking and abuse of power on ethical grounds in almost all of the cases where they are made, this is an argument for the education of police to include the ethics of policing. Such an educational process provides, among other benefits, a vocabulary

---

[57] *See e.g.*, principle 1 of the Basic Principles on the Use of Force and Firearms by Law Enforcement Officials.

and set of concepts more likely to result in a justifiable decision than one arrived at through 'common sense' or legal reasoning. However, given that not all police officials could benefit from this type of education, and given the extreme rarity of situations involving truly terrible choices, the best hope for ethical, lawful and humane policing lies in clear law and guidelines, police leadership that ensures command and control of police officials and police operations, and personal accountability of police officials to the law.

Education of police officials in police ethics would also help them to confront those less extreme, more mundane situations where they are faced with ethical dilemmas because the law is unclear or silent. This may arise because it is badly drafted or because not all situations to which police have to respond can be neatly encompassed by law. Such situations are likely to arise when an investigator is deciding, for example, whether or not it would be ethically and tactically sound to use deception or entrapment in order to detect the author of a crime.

It is through the identification and promulgation of ethical principles appropriate to the craft and profession of policing within a democratic polity governed by the rule of law that police can be encouraged to respect the law; that police can be provided with a source of reference for the occasions when the law does not or cannot direct them; that police can be guided in the exercise of discretion, or in their conduct when they have little or no discretion; and that efforts to corrupt police financially can be counteracted.

Reference has already been made, in Chapter 2, to the way in which the great legal and humanitarian principles of international human rights law can be used to prompt and inform police action, and to the fact that these principles, and specific provisions derived from them, have been used as a basis for codes of behaviour for police. Given that human rights law is concerned with relationships between individuals and the state, that it seeks to regulate and control the exercise of state power *vis-à-vis* individuals and groups of people, the relevance of human rights to police ethics and to the content of ethical codes for police is readily apparent.

(a) Codes of Behaviour for Police

Professional codes of behaviour, or ethical codes, are intended to elicit a set of desired attitudes and responses in each member of the group to which they are addressed. As guides to action they serve to remind members of the group what is expected of them, they provide a common vocabulary for the discussion of difficult cases, they establish and reinforce shared values, and they militate against adverse aspects of the occupational culture and malign external influences.

Codes of behaviour for police, adopted by the General Assembly of the United Nations and the Committee of Ministers of the Council of Europe respectively, are considered below. Police codes of this nature, often based on either or both of these international codes, have subsequently been developed by a number of national police agencies. This is because it is being increasingly recognised that the promulgation of codes of behaviour is one of a number of means whereby an ethos conducive to lawful and ethical behaviour, humanity and high standards of professional competence can be fostered within police agencies.

For example, debates around this issue have become intensified on some occasions when police officials have been found guilty of serious criminal offences, especially those concerning the administration of justice. Colleagues and supervisors have asked what can be done to prevent otherwise seemingly idealistic and honest individuals from deciding to commit perjury or to pervert the course of justice. In seeking answers to that question they have focussed on means to bolster an individual's sense of propriety in the face of powerful provocations and inducements to behave improperly. One such means is a code of behaviour or an ethical code for police.

(i) Code of Conduct for Law Enforcement Officials

The United Nations Code of Conduct for Law Enforcement Officials was adopted by resolution 34/169 of the United Nations General Assembly on 17 December 1979. Resolution 34/169 is referred to at the beginning of the preceding chapter with regard to its requirement that law enforcement agencies should be representative of and responsive and accountable to the community as a whole.

In the same resolution the General Assembly recognised that the establishment of a code of conduct is only one of several important measures for providing the citizenry served by law enforcement officials with protection of all their rights and interests. Other measures include securing accountability of police to the law, and accountability to the community through democratic political processes; and securing good leadership of police through enlightened, competent and vigilant command, management and supervision.

The Code of Conduct has eight articles, each with an explanatory commentary. In adopting the Code, the General Assembly decided to transmit it to governments with the recommendation that favourable consideration should be given to its use within the framework of national legislation or practice as a body of principles for observance by law enforcement officials.

I:4

Article 1 requires all law enforcement officials to fulfil the duty imposed on them by law, by serving the community and by protecting all persons against illegal acts, consistent with the high degree of responsibility required by their profession. In this way it places emphasis on duty and responsibility, and acknowledges that policing is more than law enforcement, especially in its reference to serving the community. The definition of that term, as set out in paragraph (c) of the Commentary, is referred to in Chapter 2 above.

The term 'law enforcement official' is defined in paragraph (a) of the Commentary as "all officers of the law, whether appointed or elected, who exercise police powers, especially the powers of arrest or detention". It is important that law enforcement officials should be defined in terms of the exercise of police powers for it means that, for example, the Code applies to military personnel vested with police powers and deployed in policing situations as well as to members of civil police agencies.

Article 2 endorses the notion that, in addition to respecting human rights when carrying out their duties, police are enjoined to protect human rights as a substantive function of policing. It requires all law enforcement officials to respect and protect human dignity and maintain and uphold human rights. The Commentary lists various international human rights instruments relevant to law enforcement.

Article 3 sets out basic principles as well as explicit provisions on the use of force and firearms by police. For example the article stipulates that law enforcement officials may use force only when strictly necessary and to the extent required for the performance of their duty, whilst paragraph (c) of the Commentary includes a requirement that firearms should not be used "except when a suspected offender offers armed resistance or otherwise jeopardises the lives of others and less extreme measures are not sufficient to restrain or apprehend the suspected offender". In expressing such real and detailed norms of conduct this article can be seen as a model for articles in codes of this nature.

Article 4 is less explicit. In dealing with confidentiality, it merely requires that matters of a confidential nature in the possession of law enforcement officials be kept confidential, unless the performance of duty or the needs of justice strictly require otherwise. Its lack of detail and failure to identify real situations to which the norm of behaviour it expresses can be applied are likely to reduce its impact on attitudes and responses, and to diminish its efficacy as a guide to action.

Article 5 reiterates the prohibition of torture. It is comparable to article 3 in that it expresses principles and detailed provisions, and embodies detailed norms of behaviour. The article and Commentary together amount to a complete statement about the absolute nature of the prohibition of torture, and make it perfectly clear that there are no circumstances whatsoever which could justify its practice.

Article 6 requires law enforcement officials to ensure the full protection of the health of persons detained in custody. This is clearly an important provision, but it would have had greater utility if it had also embodied specific requirements on other matters concerning humane treatment of detainees and their health. For example, personal hygiene, sleep, food and the regulation of the temperature to which detainees are exposed are all relevant in this context.

Article 7 deals with corruption. The Commentary acknowledges that the definition of corruption must be subject to national law but it does, nevertheless, offer its own brief definition. Whilst the article requires law enforcement officials to 'rigorously oppose and combat' corruption and paragraph (a) to the Commentary requires the law to be enforced fully with respect to any official who commits an act of corruption, the article could have been more specific by requiring law enforcement officials to report such acts.

Article 8 requires law enforcement officials to respect the law and the Code of Conduct and, to the best of their ability, prevent and rigorously oppose any violations of them. Law enforcement officials are further required to report any violations of the Code, which they have reason to believe have occurred or are about to occur, to superior authorities or other authorities with reviewing or remedial power.

In making these requirements article 8 does not provide clear guidance to law enforcement officials in respect of unlawful orders from senior officers, and specifically in respect of unlawful orders that would lead to violations of basic human rights and freedoms. The requirements to respect the law and the Code and to oppose violations of them may be interpreted as a requirement to disobey unlawful orders; and the requirement for a law enforcement official to report his or her belief that a violation of the Code has occurred or is about to occur may have the same effect as disobeying unlawful orders. However in the absence of a clearly and strongly stated obligation to disobey unlawful orders, a law enforcement official who has received an order, even though unlawful, from a senior officer is likely to experience considerable difficulty in disobeying it.

Clearly one of the difficulties facing the drafters of the Code was that referred to in paragraph (b) of the Commentary of article 8 – the requirement "to preserve the balance between the need for internal discipline of the agency on which public safety is largely dependent, on the one hand, and the need for dealing with violations of basic human rights, on the other". Paragraph (b) seeks to preserve that balance by

I:4

requiring law enforcement officials to report violations within the chain of command and to take lawful action outside that chain "only when no other remedies are available or effective".

The last sentence of paragraph (b) provides some support to officials who report violations of the Code when it stipulates that officials making such reports shall not suffer administrative or other penalties. Furthermore, paragraph (e) states that law enforcement officials who comply with the provisions of the Code (and hence those requiring violations to be reported) deserve the respect, support and cooperation of the community and of the law enforcement agency in which they serve, as well as the law enforcement profession. However these provisions would provide little or no support to a police official faced with the immediate difficulty of deciding whether or not to obey or disobey an unlawful order.

Another, perhaps greater, deficiency is the lack of any provision expressing the principle that senior officials are vicariously responsible for the acts or omissions of their subordinates. Whilst all police officials, whatever their rank, are personally responsible and accountable for the results of their own conduct, those with command and supervisory responsibilities have a clear duty to ensure that their subordinates fulfil their duties in accordance with the rules.

Both unlawful orders and command responsibility, specifically in relation to the use of force and firearms, are dealt with in another United Nations instrument, the Basic Principles on the Use of Force and Firearms for Law Enforcement Officials. However, whilst these principles provide clear guidance on command responsibility, they do not include a categorical requirement to disobey unlawful orders. These principles are considered in Chapter 4 of Part II herein.

On 24 May 1989 the United Nations Economic and Social Council, in resolution 1989/62, adopted Guidelines for the Effective Implementation of the Code of Conduct for Law Enforcement Officials. These require, *inter alia*, the principles embodied in the Code to be reflected in national legislation and practice; the provisions of national legislation connected with the Code to be included in training programmes of law enforcement officials; the Code to be made available to all law enforcement officials; and the Code and domestic laws giving effect to it to be disseminated to the public in general. Governments are required to inform the Secretary General of the United Nations at appropriate intervals of at least five years on the extent of the implementation of the Code.

(ii) European Code of Police Ethics

The European Code of Police Ethics was adopted by the Committee of Ministers of the Council of Europe in 2001 at the 765[58] meeting of the Ministers' Deputies.[58] It consists of 66 articles in seven parts, and is accompanied by a comprehensive Explanatory Memorandum that includes Commentaries on each of the articles of the Code. This Code is, therefore, much more detailed and comprehensive than the UN Code of Conduct, to which it refers in the Recommendation under which it was adopted.

The Parts deal, respectively, with objectives of the police; legal basis of the police under the rule of law; the police and the criminal justice system; organisational structures of the police; guidelines for police action/intervention; accountability and control of the police; and research and international co-operation. Some of its provisions, dealing with various aspects of police accountability, are cited in the preceding chapter herein.

The Code applies to traditional public police forces or police services, or to other publicly authorised and/or controlled bodies with the primary objectives of maintaining law and order in civil society, and who are empowered by the State to use force and/or special powers for these purposes.

Article 1 states that the main purposes of the police in a democratic society governed by the rule of law are to maintain public tranquillity and law and order in society; to protect and respect the individual's fundamental rights and freedoms as enshrined, in particular, in the European Convention on Human Rights; to prevent and combat crime; to detect crime; to provide assistance and service functions to the public. In effect, it encompasses the main points of articles 1 and 2 of the UN Code of Conduct.

Article 4, in Part II dealing with the legal basis of the police under the rule of law, requires that legislation guiding the police shall be accessible to the public and sufficiently clear and precise, and, if need be, supported by clear regulations equally accessible to the public and clear. The necessity for clear law and guidelines to secure good behaviour of police is stressed under the subheading 'The Ethics of Policing' above.

Article 8, in Part III dealing with the police and the criminal justice system, requires, *inter alia*, that it must always be possible to challenge any act, decision or omission affecting individual rights by the police before the judicial authorities.

---

[58] European Code of Police Ethics, *supra* note 13.

In contrast to the UN Code of Conduct, the European Code does refer to the responsibility of senior officials for the acts or omissions of their subordinates. However, it does so in the context of 'responsibility for orders'. Article 16, in Part IV dealing with organisational structures of the police, states that police personnel, at all levels, shall be personally responsible and accountable for their own actions or omissions or for orders to subordinates. Article 17 requires that the police organisation shall provide for a clear chain of command within the police, and that it should always be possible to determine which superior is ultimately responsible for the acts or omissions of police personnel.

The term "which superior is responsible for the acts or omissions of police personnel" seems to indicate a wider responsibility than that set out in article 16 (i.e. for orders), however the Commentary to article 17 clarifies this point as follows:

> "This Article, which is complementary to Article 16, concerns the responsibility for orders within the police. The fact that all police personnel are responsible for their own actions, does not exclude that superiors may also be held responsible, for having given the order. The superior may be held responsible side by side with the "implementing" official, or alone in cases where the latter person followed orders in "good faith". (See also Article 38.) Through an established *chain of command*, ultimate responsibility for police action can be traced in an effective way."

Article 26, in the same Part, requires that police training, which shall be based on the fundamental values of democracy, the rule of law and the protection of human rights, shall be developed in accordance with the objectives of the police.

Articles 31 to 34, also in Part IV, include a welcome and innovative reference to the rights of police officials, requiring, *inter alia*, that police staff shall as a rule enjoy the same civil and political rights as other citizens, and that restrictions to these rights may only be made when they are necessary for the exercise of the functions of the police in a democratic society, in accordance with the law, and in conformity with the European Convention on Human Rights. Furthermore, police staff are to enjoy social and economic rights, as public servants, to the fullest extent possible. In particular, staff shall have the right to organise or to participate in representative organisations, to receive an appropriate remuneration and social security, and to be provided with special health and security measures, taking into account the particular character of police work.

Articles in Part V, guidelines for police action/intervention, require respect for the right to life; reiterate the prohibition of torture or inhuman or degrading treatment or punishment; stipulate that the police shall interfere with an individual's right to privacy only when strictly necessary and only to obtain a legitimate objective; and require the police, in carrying out their activities, always to bear in mind everyone's fundamental rights, such as freedom of thought, conscience, religion, expression, peaceful assembly, movement and the peaceful enjoyment of possessions. In this way, they are more explicit about a wider range of rights than articles in the UN Code of Conduct.

The European Code then goes further than the UN Code in three very important ways. In article 38 it reinforces the rule of law by requiring police always to verify the lawfulness of their intended actions, reminding police that they should always act within the law. In article 39 it states that, whilst police personnel shall carry out orders properly issued by their superiors, they shall have a duty to refrain from carrying out orders that are clearly illegal and to report such orders, without fear of sanction. In article 46 it requires police personnel to oppose all forms of corruption within the police, and to inform superiors and other appropriate bodies of corruption within the police. The UN Code is not sufficiently specific on the requirement to report corruption, nor is it sufficiently clear on the question of unlawful orders.

Regarding interviews, not dealt with in the UN Code but addressed in other UN instruments,[59] article 50 states that guidelines for the proper conduct and integrity of police interviews shall be established, which shall, in particular, provide for a fair interview during which those interviewed are made aware of the reasons for the interview as well as other relevant information. The article also requires systematic records of police interviews to be kept.

The same can be said of witnesses and victims of crime, again included in another UN instrument[60] but not in the UN Code. Article 51 of the European Code states that the police shall be aware of the special needs of witnesses, and shall be guided by rules for their protection and support during investigation, in particular where there is a risk of intimidation of witnesses. Article 52 requires the police to provide the necessary support, assistance and information to victims of crime, without discrimination.

The European Code, again, is more specific than the UN Code concerning the health of detainees. Article 56 states that the police shall provide for the safety, health,

---

[59] *See e.g.*, article 11 of the Convention against Torture and Other Cruel, Inhuman or Degrading Treatment or Punishment, and principle 21 of the Body of Principles for the Protection of All Persons under Any Form of Detention or Imprisonment.
[60] *See* the Declaration of Basic Principles of Justice for Victims of Crime and Abuse of Power, *supra* note 33.

I:4

hygiene and appropriate nourishment of persons in the course of their custody. Police cells shall be of a reasonable size, have adequate lighting and ventilation and be equipped with suitable means of rest. Of course, there are a variety of UN instruments that embody very detailed provisions of this nature for the protection of detainees.[61]

Finally, in the European Code, article 63 states that codes of ethics of the police, based on the principles set out in the present recommendation, shall be developed in Member States and overseen by appropriate bodies.

(b) The Responsibilities of Police Leaders

Police leaders are acutely aware that police officials need guidance and support in order to cope with the various conflicting pressures they face. Police officials need to understand, without any doubt whatsoever, that neither the community, nor their colleagues, nor their senior officers, nor political leaders expect or require them to break the law or to violate human rights in order to do their job.

Support for, and insistence on, lawful and ethical policing must come from all of those sources and especially from senior police officers. They have a particularly heavy responsibility to establish and maintain high ethical standards within police organisations. In particular, police leaders need to consider the example they set by their own behaviour; the ways in which they respond to the unlawful and unethical behaviour of colleagues or subordinates; the ways in which they can protect subordinates from external pressures to act improperly; and the totality of measures they can adopt to maintain high ethical standards within police organisations.

The promulgation of a code of behaviour within a police organisation is only one such measure, which, if adopted, must amount to more than mere window dressing. A code of behaviour must be developed according to a process that enables the expression of realistic, explicit and detailed norms of behaviour that have a high degree of acceptance and ownership throughout the organisation. Once its contents have been agreed it must be disseminated widely, and constantly reinforced by example and insistence on the good practices it embodies.

The crucial task of police leaders is to command and manage police organisations so that they become and remain driven by an ethos of excellence; an ethos that is conducive to lawful and ethical behaviour, humanity, and to high standards of

---

[61] *See* the Standard Minimum Rules for the Treatment of Prisoners, adopted by the First United Nations Congress on the Prevention of Crime and the Treatment of Offenders held at Geneva in 1955, approved by the Economic and Social Council by its resolution 663 C (XXIV) of 31 July 1957 and 2076 (LXII) of 13 May 1977.

professional competence; an ethos that is hostile to the notion of 'noble cause corruption'.

This form of corruption sustains and justifies human rights violations by police, the breaking of law to enforce law, by reference to a higher 'noble cause' recognised not by the law but by the consciences of those who invoke it. The practice of policing based on an ethic of noble cause corruption is intolerable, and has no place in a democratic polity where the rule of law prevails. The 'noble cause' espoused is no more and no less than the subversion of the criminal justice system, and the 'corruption' which is practised consists of some of the most serious criminal offences. Apart from the fact that it is unlawful, it is objectionable because it is arbitrary as a process and random in its effects.

Part VI of this book is devoted to an account of the measures necessary for police leaders to introduce and sustain the ethos of excellence, referred to above, within the organisations for which they are responsible.

PART II

POLICING CONFLICT:
HUMANITY AND FORCE

Chapter 1. The Law of Rights and the Law of Conflict

(A) PURPOSES AND REASONS

This Part of the book has two purposes. The first is to promote international standards relevant to policing in times of conflict. The international standards referred to are those of international human rights law, and international humanitarian law sometimes referred to as the international law of armed conflict or the laws of war. There are two aspects to the laws of war, *jus ad bellum*, the rules governing resort to armed conflict, and *jus in bello*, the rules governing the conduct of armed conflict. This book deals with the latter.

The forms of conflict are international armed conflict, non-international armed conflict, and internal disturbances and tensions. These terms are defined in the next chapter, where examples of rules of behaviour applicable in the various types of conflict are discussed in relation to policing. Reference is also made in that chapter to terrorism, as a form of conflict, in the context of international human rights law, international humanitarian law, and other responses of the international community to that phenomenon.

The second purpose is to consider the right to life as it relates to the use of force by police, and to discuss the very specific international human rights standards on police use of force. These standards apply to any situation whatsoever in which police exercise their power to use force in the performance of their normal, civil policing functions. Where, untypically, police officials are engaged in an international armed conflict as combatants, the standards on the use of force are those embodied in the law of armed conflict. This is also the case where, again untypically, police officials are deployed in military style engagements with armed insurgents in the context of a non-international armed conflict. The status of police, combatant or otherwise, is considered in the next chapter. International human rights standards protecting the right to life and regulating the use of force by police are considered in Chapters 3 and 4 respectively of this part of the book.

The reasons for seeking to disseminate standards of good behaviour and best practice on these aspects of policing are that police officials can become involved in international armed conflicts in a variety of ways; police are one of the means by which states respond to internal conflicts or civil wars; it is a fundamental function of police to maintain or restore social order, whatever its scale; the use of force is an essential police power, if not the primary power; and these are all aspects of policing in which human rights and humanitarian standards are vulnerable.

II:1

Furthermore, police officials need to understand and apply international humanitarian law as a matter of good professional practice, in order that they may behave correctly, benefit from the forms of protection to which they are entitled, promote the protection of others, and enforce or encourage correct behaviour on the part of others (where this is possible and appropriate).

Finally, the application of international humanitarian law, even in those situations where this branch of law may not be legally applicable, amounts simply to good practice because of police duties to protect life and property, and to restore and maintain peace and social order. For this reason some of its principles should form an important element in the strategy and tactics of policing civil disturbances, especially when those disturbances are serious in terms of scale or intensity of violence.

In spite of all of the above, it remains true that police officials are generally insufficiently aware of those aspects of international humanitarian law that are legally applicable to police operations in times of armed conflict, and relevant to policing internal disturbances or tensions. This lack of awareness should be remedied.

(B) INTERNATIONAL HUMAN RIGHTS LAW AND INTERNATIONAL HUMANITARIAN LAW

International human rights law and international humanitarian law are each branches of public international law. The fact that they are distinct systems of law is evidenced by their different historical developments and fields of application, but they are both concerned with securing minimum standards of behaviour and treatment in various situations, and they are both concerned with the protection of individuals. In contrast to human rights law, international humanitarian law is not generally expressed in terms of rights, but in terms of obligations it imposes on parties to armed conflicts.

(a) International Human Rights Law

Human rights can be considered as those rights that are fundamental to the human condition and as fundamental principles of justice. For these reasons human rights, or values on which they are based, find almost universal expression in the world's religious, moral and ethical belief systems. The first preambular paragraph of the Universal Declaration of Human Rights designates them as "the equal and inalienable rights of all members of the human family".

As indicated in Chapter 1 of Part I herein, where the international system for the protection of human rights is described, international human rights law has developed largely since the end of the Second World War although, as with international humanitarian law, its origins can be traced to earlier historical periods. For example, during the nineteenth century international legal measures were adopted against the slave trade, and during the first part of the twentieth century measures for the protection of workers' rights were introduced on the creation of the International Labour Organisation.

(b) International Humanitarian Law

Although this branch of international law, in its present form, developed relatively recently it has its origins in antiquity when, for example, military leaders would sometimes order captured enemy fighters to be spared and the enemy civilian population to be treated humanely. Practices of this kind gradually developed into a body of customary principles and rules which parties to a conflict are legally bound to respect.

The fundamental customary principle is that the right of belligerents to adopt means of injuring the enemy is not unlimited. This principle affects, for example, the use of weapons, prohibiting belligerents from using weapons that give rise to unnecessary suffering or superfluous injury. Two further principles derive from this, the principles of proportionality and discrimination. The principle of proportionality is intended to limit the use of force by, for example, requiring proportionate responses to an adversary's actions. The principle of discrimination is about care in the selection of methods, of weaponry and of targets.

The laws of war as they now stand consist of two sets of treaty law ('Hague Law' and 'Geneva Law') plus a number of customary rules based on the principles already described. The codification of principles and rules into legal texts, which began to occur in the second half of the nineteenth century, did not displace customary law. Indeed the development of international humanitarian law can be seen as the gradual elaboration of these principles and rules in greater and more specific detail in response to changes in means and methods of warfare; power relations between states; and greater awareness of and sensitivity towards humanitarian considerations.

The two strands of treaty law are distinguished in that 'Hague Law' governs the conduct of hostilities, the permissible means and methods of warfare, whereas 'Geneva Law' is concerned with the protection of victims of war. In fact the distinction now is not quite so marked, as the two strands are merging to some

II:1

extent through later treaty provisions, for example the two Protocols of 1977 Additional to the Geneva Conventions.

The laws of war, both customary and conventional, were developed in full cognisance of the realities of warfare and military requirements, which means that, except where specific rules allow military considerations to be taken into account, military necessity cannot be pleaded as a reason for disregarding those laws.

(i)   Hague Law

The more immediate origins of the law of Hague lie in a set of instructions devised during the course of the American Civil War (Instructions for the Government of Armies of the United States in the Field – prepared by a lawyer, Francis Lieber, and promulgated by the President of the United States of America), and an international treaty, the St. Petersburg Declaration of 1868.

There then followed a series of conferences at The Hague, and at the first of these, in 1899, the text of a Convention with annexed regulations on the conduct of land warfare was adopted. The provisions of these regulations were revised and embodied in a treaty which remains in force today – the 1907 Hague Convention IV Respecting the Laws and Customs of War on Land. Since they first entered into force many of the 'Hague Regulations' have been developed or superseded by the Geneva Conventions and their Additional Protocols.

(ii)   Geneva Law

It was the Battle of Solferino (1859) in northern Italy that provided the impetus for the development of 'Geneva Law'. Here a citizen of Geneva, J. Henry Dunant, witnessed the condition of thousands of wounded French and Austrian soldiers. Their plight moved him to publish a book in 1862, *Un Souvenir de Solferino*, and to involve himself in activities that led to the formation of the International Committee of the Red Cross and the conclusion of a treaty between states. In fact in 1864 a diplomatic conference in Geneva adopted the Convention for the Amelioration of the Condition of the Wounded in Armies in the Field.

The law of Geneva then went through a variety of stages before the horrific events of the Spanish Civil War and the Second World War provided the incentive for further revision and development of the then existent treaties, and the promulgation of the present four Geneva Conventions of 1949.[62] These treaties make provision for

---

[62] The four Geneva Conventions were adopted on 12 August 1949, and entered into force on 21 October 1950. They are: 1949 Geneva Convention I for the Amelioration of the Condition of Wounded and Sick in Armed forces in the Field; 1949 Geneva Convention II for the

combatants who become victims of war - either as sick, wounded or shipwrecked casualties, or prisoners of war (in the first, second and third Conventions), and for the protection of civilians in the power of an opposing belligerent (in the very long and detailed fourth Convention). Apart from article 3 common to all four Conventions, all of the Conventions' provisions concern the protection of victims of international armed conflicts.

The imperatives of contemporary warfare, and the continuing determination of the United Nations Organisation, some states, and the International Committee of the Red Cross to remedy long recognised defects in both 'Hague' and 'Geneva' law then resulted in the adoption, in 1977, of the two Protocols Additional to the Geneva Conventions of 1949.[63] The First Additional Protocol updates and elaborates existing rules of combat as well as rules for the protection of war victims, bringing about the partial fusion of 'Hague' and 'Geneva' law referred to above. The Second Additional Protocol supplements the provisions of article 3 common to the 1949 Geneva Conventions, which contains a number of obligations binding on the parties to non-international armed conflicts. Both Additional Protocols take into account current developments in the international protection of human rights, applying these to the protection of victims of armed conflicts.

(C) FIELDS OF APPLICATION OF INTERNATIONAL HUMAN RIGHTS LAW AND INTERNATIONAL HUMANITARIAN LAW

The purpose of international human rights law is to secure the lawful rights and freedoms of individuals. In order to achieve this it imposes obligations on governments in relation to individuals and groups within the functional jurisdiction of the states they govern. It limits and controls the exercise of power by states in relation to individuals and groups. Human rights law applies in all places and at all times, in times of peace and in times of conflict. Its scope and effectiveness may be diminished through measures taken by governments during periods of national emergency to derogate from some provisions of human rights treaties, but it remains

---

Amelioration of the Condition of Wounded, Sick and Shipwrecked Members of Armed Forces at Sea; 1949 Geneva Convention III Relative to the Treatment of Prisoners of War; 1949 Geneva Convention IV Relative to the Protection of Civilian Persons in Time of War.
[63] The two Additional Protocols were adopted on 8 June 1977, and entered into force on 7 December 1978. They are: 1977 Geneva Additional Protocol I to the Geneva Conventions of 12 August 1949, and Relating to the Protection of Victims of International Armed Conflicts; 1977 Geneva Additional Protocol II to the Geneva Conventions of 12 August 1949, and Relating to the Protection of Victims of Non-international Armed Conflicts. Additional Protocol III Relating to the Adoption of an Additional Distinctive Emblem was adopted on 8 December 2005.

applicable. In any event, provisions protecting some human rights, such as the prohibition of torture, are non-derogable.

The purposes of international humanitarian law are to regulate the conduct of hostilities and to protect victims of armed conflicts. It imposes obligations on parties to armed conflicts and comes into force only when armed conflict occurs. The great bulk of the provisions of international humanitarian law apply to international armed conflicts or to situations that have been specifically included within that category. Only article 3 common to the Geneva Conventions and the Second Additional Protocol apply to non-international armed conflicts. As indicated above, provisions of international humanitarian law that are legally applicable to police operations in times of armed conflict, and relevant to policing internal disturbances or tensions are considered in the following chapter.

These differences in fields of application mean that the two systems of law are essentially complementary. For example human rights law can be seen as operating in the normal state of society and then merging, via measures of derogation, with humanitarian law as social order becomes disrupted or breaks down. Even when war breaks out the human rights regime, although diminished, does not become inoperative. It remains ready to return to full effect as the normal state of society is restored.

The two international Covenants (on Economic, Social and Cultural Rights, and Civil and Political Rights) apply in times of peace and times of war and to the full range of conflicts, international or non-international. This same concept also applies to other human rights treaties including the regional treaties.

(D) THE PROTECTION OF CHILDREN IN TIMES OF ARMED CONFLICT

There are specific provisions of international humanitarian law for the protection of children. For example, article 24 of 1949 Geneva Convention IV requires parties to the conflict to, *inter alia*, take the necessary measures to ensure that children under fifteen, who are orphaned or separated from their families as a result of war, are not left to their own resources, and that their maintenance, the exercise of their religion and their education are facilitated in all circumstances.

International humanitarian law provisions are reinforced by article 38 of the Convention on the Rights of the Child. This requires States parties to undertake to respect and to ensure respect for rules of international humanitarian law applicable to them in armed conflicts that are relevant to the child. States parties are to take all feasible measures to ensure that persons under fifteen years do not take a direct part in hostilities, and shall refrain from recruiting any person who has not attained the age of fifteen years into their armed forces. In recruiting among those persons who have attained the age of fifteen years but who have not attained the age of eighteen years, States parties are to endeavour to give priority to those who are oldest. Finally, in accordance with their obligations under international humanitarian law to protect the civilian population in armed conflicts, States parties are to take all feasible measures to ensure protection and care of children who are affected by an armed conflict.

(E) DEROGATION FROM HUMAN RIGHTS OBLIGATIONS IN TIMES OF EMERGENCY

The necessity of impinging upon human rights to secure the survival of the nation is acknowledged and allowed for under human rights treaties. For example, article 4 of the International Covenant on Civil and Political Rights states that during an officially proclaimed public emergency that threatens the life of the nation, States parties to the Covenant may take measures derogating from their obligations under the Covenant.

Such measures must be strictly required by the exigencies of the situation; they must not be inconsistent with other obligations under international law; and they must not be discriminatory on grounds of race, colour, sex, language, religion or social origin. No derogation is permitted from a number of articles including those protecting the right to life, and prohibiting torture or cruel, inhuman or degrading treatment or punishment (articles 6 and 7 respectively).

Other States parties to the Covenant, through the intermediary of the Secretary General of the United Nations, are to be advised of the details of the derogation and, eventually, of its termination.

In order to assist States parties to meet the requirements of article 4, the Human Rights Committee adopted General Comment No.29 (72).[64] As part of the general guidance it offers, this General Comment makes specific reference to situations of armed conflict and to international humanitarian law.

In paragraph one the Committee emphasises the paramount importance of article 4 for the protection of human rights under the Covenant allowing, as it does, for a State party unilaterally temporarily to derogate from a part of its obligations under the Covenant whilst subjecting both the measure of derogation, as well as its

---

[64] Adopted by the Human Rights Committee, at its 1950th meeting (72nd session), on 24 July 2001.

II:1

material consequences, to a specific regime of safeguards. In the same paragraph the Committee insists that the restoration of a state of normalcy where full respect for the Covenant can again be secured must be the predominant objective of a State party derogating from the Covenant.

The exceptional and temporary nature of measures of derogation is emphasised in paragraph two. Before a State moves to invoke article 4, two fundamental conditions must be met: the situation must amount to a public emergency that threatens the life of the nation, and the State party must have officially proclaimed a state of emergency. The latter requirement is essential for the maintenance of the principles of legality and rule of law at times when they are most needed. When proclaiming a state of emergency with consequences that could entail derogation from any provision of the Covenant, States must act within their constitutional and other provisions of law that govern such proclamation and the exercise of emergency powers. It is the task of the Committee to monitor that the laws in question enable and secure compliance with article 4.

The emphasis the Committee places on legality and the rule of law in this paragraph is hugely important for police when they are given extended powers under emergency legislation. In many respects it is by and through the exercise of police powers that States endeavour to deal with emergencies. The Committee insists that States, and hence police exercising State power, "must act within their constitutional and other provisions of law". The granting of extended powers is not a licence to go beyond those already extended powers, nor is it licence to violate non-derogable rights. Neither extended powers of detention nor the difficulties faced by security forces in dealing with an emergency can be justifications of torture or ill-treatment of detainees.

The first reference to armed conflict is made in paragraph three of the General Comment, in which the Committee points out that not every disturbance or catastrophe qualifies as a public emergency which threatens the life of the nation as required by paragraph one of the article. During armed conflict, whether international or non-international, rules of international humanitarian law become applicable and help, in addition to the provisions of article 4 and article 5, paragraph 1, of the Covenant, to prevent the abuse of a State's emergency powers.[65] The Covenant requires that even during an armed conflict, measures derogating from the

---

[65] Article 5, paragraph 1 of the Covenant states that nothing in Covenant may be interpreted as implying for any State, group or person any right to engage in any activity or perform any act aimed at the destruction of any of the rights and freedoms recognised in the Covenant or at their limitation to a greater extent than is provided for in the Covenant.

Covenant are allowed only if and to the extent that the situation constitutes a threat to the life of the nation.

Here, again, the Committee is stressing the importance of legality not only in complying with articles of the Covenant but also with international humanitarian law. This branch of law is cited again in paragraph 9 of the General Comment which states that article 4, paragraph 1, requires that no measure derogating from the provisions of the Covenant may be inconsistent with the State party's other obligations under international law, particularly the rules of international humanitarian law. Article 4 of the Covenant cannot be read as justification for derogation from the Covenant if such derogation would entail a breach of a State's other international obligations, whether based on treaty or general international law.

In paragraph 12 the Committee points out that in assessing the scope of legitimate derogation from the Covenant, one criterion can be found in the definition of certain human rights violations as crimes against humanity. If action conducted under the authority of a State constitutes a basis for individual criminal responsibility for a crime against humanity by the persons involved in that action, article 4 of the Covenant cannot be used as a justification that a state of emergency exempted the State in question from its responsibility in relation to the same conduct. Therefore, the Committee concludes in paragraph 12, the recent codification of crimes against humanity, for jurisdictional purposes, in the Statute of the International Criminal Court is of relevance in the interpretation of article 4 of the Covenant. Some articles of the Statute of the Court, appropriate to this chapter, are considered below under the heading Action against Individuals.

A footnote clarifying and expanding upon the above paragraph cites articles 6 (genocide) and 7 (crimes against humanity) of the Statute of the International Criminal Court, and states that while many of the specific forms of conduct listed in article 7 of the Statute are directly linked to violations against those human rights that are enlisted as non-derogable provisions of article 4, paragraph 2, of the Covenant, the category of crimes against humanity as defined in that provision also covers violations of some provisions of the Covenant that have not been mentioned in the said provision of the Covenant. For example, certain grave breaches of article 27 of the Covenant may at the same time constitute genocide under article 6 of the ICC Statute, and article 7 of the Rome Statute, in turn, covers practices that are related to, besides articles 6, 7 and 8 of the Covenant, also articles 9, 12, 26 and 27.[66]

---

[66] Article 27 of the Covenant prohibits persons belonging to ethnic, religious or linguistic minorities from being denied the right to enjoy their own culture, to profess and practice their own religion, or to use their own language; article 6 protects the right to life; article 7 embodies the prohibition of torture and ill-treatment; article 8 prohibits slavery; article 9

II:1

The Committee identifies, in paragraph 13 of the General Comment, elements that, in the Committee's opinion, cannot be made subject to lawful derogation even though they are not listed in article 4, paragraph 2. Illustrative examples of these include the right to humane treatment as a detainee set out in article 10 of the Covenant; the prohibitions against hostage taking, abduction or unacknowledged detention, considered to be norms of general international law; elements of the international protection of the rights of persons belonging to minorities, this being reflected in the prohibition against genocide, the inclusion of a non-discrimination clause in article 4 itself, and the non-derogable nature of article 18; deportation or forcible transfer of population without grounds permitted under international law, in the form of forced displacement by expulsion or other coercive means from the area in which the persons concerned are lawfully present, and which constitutes a crime against humanity; and engaging in propaganda for war or advocating national, racial or religious hatred constituting incitement to discrimination, hostility or violence contrary to article 20 of the Covenant.

International humanitarian law is cited again in paragraph 16 of the General Comment where the Committee points out that as certain elements of the right to a fair trial are explicitly guaranteed under that branch of law during armed conflict, it finds no justification for derogation from these guarantees during other emergency situations. It is the Committee's opinion that the principles of legality and the rule of law require that fundamental requirements of fair trial must be respected during a state of emergency. Only a court of law may try and convict a person for a criminal offence. The presumption of innocence must be respected. In order to protect non-derogable rights, the right to take proceedings before a court to enable the court to decide without delay on the lawfulness of detention, must not be diminished by a State party's decision to derogate from the Covenant.

Both the American Convention on Human Rights and the European Convention on Human Rights embody similar derogation provisions (in articles 27 and 15 respectively) and, although there is some variation between the three instruments on the complete lists of rights protected from derogation, all of them prohibit derogation from articles protecting the right to life and prohibiting torture or ill-treatment. The African Charter on Human and Peoples' Rights contains no specific article entitling a State to derogate from any of its obligations. However many of the

---

protects the right to liberty and security of person, and prohibits arbitrary arrest or detention; article 12 protects the right to liberty of movement of people lawfully within the territory of a state; and article 26 embodies the right to equality before the law, and to equal protection of the law.

articles contain 'claw back' clauses entitling a State to restrict the rights they embody to the extent permitted by domestic law.

It is important for police officials to understand and accept the point made by the Human Rights Committee in its General Comment No. 29, that not every situation of conflict, disorder or tension is of sufficient gravity to justify derogation from the provisions of human rights treaties, and when conditions for derogation are not met the entire range of human rights applies and States remain bound by their treaty obligations to respect those rights. However, impairment of some rights may still occur through a wider application of the limitation clauses that are attached to some articles of human rights treaties. For example it may be felt that the right to peaceful assembly, protected under article 21 of the Covenant, should be lawfully restricted in the interests of national security or public order. Even when conditions for derogation do exist, derogation to the fullest possible extent is not necessarily justifiable and governments have to exercise judgment as to which rights people within their jurisdiction will be denied during a public emergency.

It must also be recognised that measures of derogation can be a seriously limiting factor on human rights protection, their effect extending beyond those rights subject to derogation and affecting non-derogable rights. For example those safeguards designed to secure judicial supervision of detainees following arrest or detention on criminal charges may be diminished following derogation from article 9 of the International Covenant on Civil and Political Rights. Torture or ill-treatment of detainees, and even unlawful killings, can occur as a consequence of the limitation of this form of supervision. However these dangers can be reduced by proper scrutiny of the effects of emergency legislation by treaty bodies when they have cause to consider measures of derogation in particular cases, thereby ensuring that such safeguards are retained to some extent.

In respect of the prohibition of torture and the prohibition of arbitrary killing (which are non-derogable) it should be recalled that article 2 of the Convention against Torture and Other Cruel, Inhuman or Degrading Treatment or Punishment states that no exceptional circumstances whatsoever, whether a state of war or a threat of war, internal political instability or any other public emergency, may be invoked as a justification of torture. The Principles on the Effective Prevention and Investigation of Extra-Legal, Arbitrary and Summary Executions (principle 1), and the Declaration on the Protection of All Persons from Enforced Disappearances (article 7) contain similar provisions in respect of extra-judicial killings and enforced disappearances respectively.

II:1

(F) INTERNATIONAL HUMAN RIGHTS LAW AND INTERNATIONAL HUMANITARIAN LAW – MEANS TO SECURE COMPLIANCE WITH OBLIGATIONS

(a) International Human Rights Law

The various means to secure compliance with international human rights law are largely directed at encouraging states to create and sustain the constitutional and legal arrangements necessary for them to be able to meet their international legal obligations to protect human rights. States are then required to secure compliance with their own constitutions and laws by administrative and other means and, when these are breached, to provide effective remedies to victims of human rights violations.

International mechanisms fall within two broad categories – Charter based institutions and procedures and treaty based institutions and procedures, and these are described in Chapter 1 of Part I under the heading 'International Means of Supervision and Enforcement'.

(b) International Humanitarian Law

The means for securing implementation of, and compliance with, international humanitarian law are fewer and probably less effective than those for securing compliance with international human rights law. There is a pessimistic view, supported by the number of terrible war crimes committed during the last century and at the dawn of this one, that international humanitarian law is virtually ineffective. Political and military leaders have taken deliberate decisions not to comply with it, and in the terror and confusion of battle fighters have ignored its provisions, whilst others were unaware of them. However, breaches of international humanitarian law have legal, political, economic and military consequences. Furthermore, for reasons of reciprocity and self-preservation, it is in the interests of fighters and their political and military leaders to comply. Violations committed against combatants or the civilian population of one party to a conflict can lead to retaliatory violations,[67] this effect being enhanced by widespread publicity given to

---

[67] Reprisals, actions that would otherwise be illegal, taken as a response to a violation of the law by an adverse party and intended to secure a return to legality by the adverse party are permitted. However, acts of reprisal against certain categories of protected person or certain objects are expressly prohibited. *See e.g.,* articles 46, 47, 13 and 33 of 1949 Geneva Conventions I – IV respectively, which prohibit reprisals against protected persons and objects, and articles 52 – 56 of 1977 Additional Protocol 1, which prohibit reprisals against civilian objects generally and against certain specified civilian objects (for example, cultural

the more egregious abuses. Political and military leaders, and fighters have been convicted and punished for breaches, and some of the guilty have suffered severe psychological disturbances because of their crimes. For these, and other, reasons international humanitarian law has secured the good behaviour of politicians and military, it has protected people who would otherwise have been killed or brutalised, and it has been a positive force in the spread of humanitarian ideals generally.

In the first instance, responsibility for complying with international humanitarian law lies with parties to a conflict, that is to say states or insurgent parties as the case may be. The four Geneva Conventions and Additional Protocol I each include measures to secure the execution of their provisions. For example, Additional Protocol I requires High Contracting Parties and Parties to the conflict to take all necessary measures, without delay, for the execution of their obligations under the Conventions and the Protocol. They are to give orders and instructions to ensure observance of the Conventions and the Protocol, and to supervise their execution. Parties to the conflict are to grant the International Committee of the Red Cross all facilities within their power so as to enable it to carry out humanitarian functions assigned to it by the Conventions and the Protocol in order to ensure protection and assistance to the victims of conflicts. High Contracting Parties and Parties to the conflict are to ensure that legal advisers are available, when necessary, to advise military commanders at the appropriate level on the application of the Conventions and the Protocol and on the appropriate instruction to be given to the armed forces on this subject. Furthermore, the High Contracting Parties undertake, in time of peace as in time of armed conflict, to disseminate the Conventions and the Protocol as widely as possible in their respective countries.[68]

There are also provisions for the repression of grave breaches of the Conventions and Additional Protocol I, and of acts contrary to their provisions other than grave breaches. For example, High Contracting Parties are to enact any legislation necessary to provide effective penal sanctions for persons committing, or ordering to be committed, grave breaches of the Conventions or the Additional Protocol I. They are then under an obligation to search for persons alleged to have committed, or to have ordered to be committed, grave breaches and to bring such persons, regardless of their nationality, before their own courts. Such persons may also be handed over for trial to another High Contracting Party concerned.[69] Grave breaches include such acts as wilful killing, torture or inhumane treatment of protected persons, wilfully

---

objects and places of worship, and objects indispensable to the survival of the civilian population). In fact, the scope for reprisals is now severely limited.

[68] 1977 Additional Protocol I, articles 80, 81, 82 and 83.

[69] Articles 49, 50, 129 and 146 of the four 1949 Geneva Conventions respectively. *See also* articles 85 and 86 of the 1977 Additional Protocol I.

II:1

causing them great suffering or serious injury to body or health, their unlawful deportation, and the taking of hostages. The Additional Protocol contains a provision requiring High Contracting Parties to afford one another the greatest measure of assistance in connection with criminal proceedings brought in respect of grave breaches of the Conventions or the Additional Protocol.[70] Clearly police officials could be required to investigate crimes of this nature, to search for suspected offenders and to assist police of other states in their investigations.

Article 3 common to the four Geneva Conventions and 1977 Additional Protocol II, regulating the conduct of non-international armed conflict, are weak in terms of means to secure compliance with their provisions. Article 19 of Additional Protocol II merely requires the Protocol to be disseminated as widely as possible, and the only form of international monitoring allowed for is the provision in common article 3 which stipulates that an impartial humanitarian body may offer its services to parties to the conflict. Furthermore, there are no provisions on individual or collective responsibility in either text. However the penal enforcement provision at the end of each of the Geneva Conventions, obliging High Contracting Parties to take measures necessary for the suppression of all acts contrary to their provisions other than grave breaches (which are dealt with separately), applies to common article 3.

Finally, within the terms of its mandate, the International Committee of the Red Cross has been an effective and important factor in securing compliance with international humanitarian law by parties to conflicts, although the principles of neutrality and impartiality by which it is bound generally prevent that organisation from making public condemnations of violations.

(G) ACTION AGAINST INDIVIDUALS

There have been rare occasions when international tribunals have been established to hear cases against individuals charged with war crimes. The London Agreement of August 1945 for the Prosecution and Punishment of the Major War Criminals of the European Axis provided the basis for the prosecution of a number of major war criminals shortly after the Second World War. The Charter of the International Military Tribunal, annexed to the London Agreement, defined three categories of crime coming within the jurisdiction of the Tribunal – crimes against peace, war crimes and crimes against humanity.

Accounts of three other *ad hoc* tribunals established in the wake of conflicts, the International Criminal Tribunal for the former Yugoslavia, the International

---

[70] 1977 Additional Protocol I, article 88.

86

Criminal Tribunal for Rwanda, and the Special Court for Sierra Leone are given in Chapter 1 of Part I. The permanent International Criminal Court, which has jurisdiction over the crime of genocide, crimes against humanity, war crimes and the crime of aggression, is also described in the same chapter.

For the purposes of the Statute of the International Criminal Court genocide means any of a number of specified acts committed with intent to destroy, in whole or in part, a national, ethnical, racial or religious group. The specified acts include killing members of the group and causing serious bodily or mental harm to members of the group (article 6). Crime against humanity means any of a number of specified acts when committed as part of a widespread or systematic attack directed against any civilian population, with knowledge of the attack. The specified acts include murder, extermination, enslavement, deportation or forcible transfer of population, imprisonment or other severe deprivation of physical liberty in violation of fundamental rules of international law, torture, rape, sexual slavery, enforced prostitution, and enforced disappearance of persons (article 7). The jurisdiction of the Court extends to genocide and crimes against humanity committed in both international and non-international armed conflict. Indeed the crime of genocide can occur whether or not any form of armed conflict is taking place.

For the purposes of the same statute war crimes include grave breaches of the 1949 Geneva Conventions, and other serious violations of the laws and customs applicable in international armed conflict specified in the article. These are many and include intentionally directing attacks against the civilian population and intentionally directing attacks against civilian objects; that is, objects that are not military objects. In the case of an armed conflict not of an international character, war crimes include serious violations of article 3 common to the 1949 Geneva Conventions and other serious violations of the laws and customs applicable in armed conflicts not of an international character. These, also, are many and include pillage, rape, conscripting children under the age of fifteen years into armed forces or groups, killing or wounding treacherously a combatant adversary, and declaring that no quarter will be given (article 8).

(a) Individual Criminal Responsibility

The statutes of the International Criminal Tribunal for the former Yugoslavia, the International Criminal Tribunal for Rwanda, and Special Court for Sierra Leone each contain similar provisions on individual criminal responsibility. They establish the criminal liability of those directly or indirectly responsible for the commission of crimes; they deny immunity from prosecution to heads of State and government and government officials; they establish the criminal responsibility of superiors for the acts of their subordinates; and they deny the defence of superior orders to the authors of crimes.

Article 7 of the Statute of the Yugoslavia Tribunal may be taken as an example. The first paragraph of the article states that a person who planned, instigated, ordered, committed or otherwise aided and abetted in the planning, preparation or execution of a crime referred to in articles 2 to 5 of the Statute, shall be individually responsible for the crime. Paragraph 2 states that the official position of any accused person, whether as head of State or government or as a responsible government official, shall not relieve such person of criminal responsibility nor mitigate punishment. Paragraph 3 states that the fact that any of the acts referred to in articles 2 to 5 of the Statute was committed by a subordinate does not relieve his superior of criminal responsibility if he knew or had reason to know that the subordinate was about to commit such acts or had done so and the superior failed to take the necessary and reasonable measures to prevent such acts or to punish the perpetrators thereof. Paragraph 4 states that the fact that an accused person acted pursuant to an order of a government or of a superior shall not relieve him of criminal responsibility, but may be considered in mitigation of punishment if the International Tribunal determines that justice so requires. Articles 2 to 5 of the Statute refer to grave breaches of the 1949 Geneva Conventions, violations of the laws and customs of war, genocide and crimes against humanity respectively.

An account of a case in which the International Criminal Tribunal for the former Yugoslavia pronounced on the responsibility of superiors for the criminal acts of subordinates, termed command responsibility, is discussed below.

The Rome Statute of the International Criminal Court contains a number of provisions concerning individual criminal responsibility. Article 25 establishes the criminal liability of those directly or indirectly involved in committing crimes that fall within the jurisdiction of the Court. These include, *inter alia*, ordering, soliciting or inducing such crimes; aiding, abetting or assisting in their commission; and contributing in any other way to their commission or attempted commission by a group of persons acting with a common purpose.

Article 27 is headed 'Irrelevance of official capacity' and states that the Statute applies equally to all persons without any distinction based on official capacity. In particular heads of State or government, members of government or parliaments, and elected or government officials are not exempt from criminal responsibility under the Statute.

Article 28 defines the responsibility of commanders and other superiors where they fail to exercise proper control over forces under their command. Military commanders or those effectively acting as such are criminally responsible for crimes committed by forces under their effective command and control where they either knew or should have known that the forces were committing or about to commit such crimes, and failed to take all necessary and reasonable measures within their power to prevent or repress their commission or to submit the matter to the competent authorities for investigation and prosecution.

Concerning superior and subordinate relationships outside the above category, the same article provides that a superior is criminally responsible for crimes within the jurisdiction of the Court committed by subordinates under his or her effective authority and control, as a result of his or her failure to exercise control properly over such subordinates, where: the superior either knew, or consciously disregarded information which clearly indicated, that the subordinates were committing or about to commit such crimes; the crimes concerned activities that were within the effective responsibility and control of the superior; and the superior failed to take all necessary and reasonable measures within his or her power to prevent or repress their commission or to submit the matter to the competent authorities for investigation and prosecution.

Article 33 deals with the question of superior orders of governments or of superiors, whether military or civilian. The fact that a crime within the jurisdiction of the Court has been committed by a person pursuant to such an order shall not relieve that person of criminal responsibility unless the person was under a legal obligation to obey it; the person did not know that the order was unlawful; and the order was not manifestly unlawful. For the purposes of article 33, orders to commit genocide or crimes against humanity are manifestly unlawful.

(b) Command Responsibility – a case before the International Criminal Tribunal for the Former Yugoslavia

International Criminal Tribunals have addressed the issue of command responsibility and, most recently and authoritatively, the International Criminal Tribunal for the Former Yugoslavia has done so in the case *Prosecutor* v. *Zejnil Delalic, Zdravko Mucic, Hazim Delic and Esad Landzo*, also known as the *"Celebici"* case.[71] The pronouncement of the Tribunal on the concept of command responsibility was the first decision by an international judicial body on that doctrine since the cases decided in the wake of the Second World War.

---

[71] Case No. IT-96-21-T, judgment of 16 November 1998 (Trial Chamber); *see also* Case No. IT-96-21-A, judgment of 20 February 2001 (Appeals Chamber).

II:1

The trial related to events that took place in 1992 in a prison camp in the village of Celebici in Bosnia and Herzegovina. The four accused were charged with numerous counts of grave breaches of the Geneva Conventions of 12 August 1949 under article 2 of the Statute of the Tribunal and with violations of the laws or customs of war under article 3. The victims were Bosnian Serb detainees in the Celebici camp. The trial of the four accused commenced on 10 March 1997 and covered a period of some 19 months.

The Trial Chamber observed that, although no explicit reference was made to the concept of command responsibility in the Statute of the International Tribunal, its governing principles had been incorporated into article 7, paragraph 3. In this provision, it was stated that the fact that any of the acts referred to in articles 2 to 5 of the Statute (which set out the crimes over which the Tribunal has jurisdiction) was committed by a subordinate did not relieve his superior of criminal responsibility if he knew or had reason to know that the subordinate was about to commit such acts or had done so, and the superior failed to take the necessary and reasonable measures to prevent such acts or to punish the perpetrators of them.[72]

Before deliberating this provision, the Trial Chamber considered briefly the legal character of this species of criminal responsibility and its status under customary international law more generally. It observed that it was a well-established norm of customary and conventional international law that military commanders and other persons occupying positions of superior authority might be held criminally responsible for the unlawful conduct of their subordinates. Such criminal liability might arise out of the positive acts of the superior, sometimes referred to as direct command responsibility, or from his culpable omissions, indirect command responsibility or command responsibility *strictu sensu*. Thus, a superior might be held criminally responsible not only for ordering, instigating or planning criminal acts carried out by his subordinates, but also for failing to take measures to prevent or repress the unlawful conduct of his subordinates. The Trial Chamber noted the distinct legal character of the two types of superior responsibility.

While the criminal liability of a superior for positive acts followed from general principles of accomplice liability, the criminal responsibility of superiors for failing to take measures to prevent or repress the unlawful conduct of their subordinates was best understood when seen against the principle that criminal responsibility for omissions was incurred only where there existed a legal obligation to act.

---

[72] It is significant that a form of words very similar to this appears in principle 24 of the Basic Principles on Force and Firearms by Law Enforcement Officials, which are considered in Chapter 4 of this Part of the book.

The Trial Chamber pointed out that, in the case of military commanders, under article 87 of the Protocol Additional to the Geneva Conventions of 12 August 1949, and relating to the Protection of Victims of International Armed Conflicts (Additional Protocol I), international law imposed an affirmative duty on superiors to prevent persons under their control from committing violations of international humanitarian law. Ultimately, it was this duty that provided the basis for, and defined the contours of, the imputed criminal responsibility under article 7, paragraph 3, of the Statute of the Tribunal.

In the period following the Second World War until the present time, the Chamber observed, the doctrine of command responsibility had not been applied by any international judicial body. Nonetheless, there could be no doubt that the concept of the individual criminal responsibility of superiors for failure to act was today firmly placed within the corpus of international humanitarian law. Through the adoption of Additional Protocol I, the principle had now been codified and given a clear expression in international conventional law. Thus, article 87 of Additional Protocol I gave expression to the duty of commanders to control the acts of their subordinates and to prevent or, where necessary, to repress violations of the Geneva Conventions or Additional Protocol I. The concomitant principle under which a superior might be held criminally responsible for the crimes committed by his subordinates where the superior had failed to properly exercise this duty was formulated in article 86 of Additional Protocol I. The Trial Chamber concluded that the principle of individual criminal responsibility of superiors for failure to prevent or repress the crimes committed by subordinates formed part of customary international law.

The Trial Chamber then considered the elements of individual criminal responsibility under article 7, paragraph 3, of the Statute. It concluded that it was possible to identify the essential elements of command responsibility for failure to act: there existed a superior-subordinate relationship; the superior knew or had reason to know that the criminal act was about to be or had been committed; and the superior failed to take the necessary and reasonable measures to prevent the criminal act or punish the perpetrator of it. These elements were then considered in turn.

After deliberating on the first element, the Trial Chamber concluded that, in order for the principle of superior responsibility to be applicable, it was necessary that the superior had effective control over the persons committing the underlying violations of international humanitarian law, in the sense of having the material ability to prevent and punish the commission of these offences, with the caveat that such authority could have a *de facto* as well as a *de jure* character. The doctrine of superior responsibility extended to civilian superiors only to the extent that they exercised a degree of control over their subordinates which was similar to that of military commanders.

II:1

Concerning the mental element of command responsibility, (the superior knew or had reason to know), the Trial Chamber observed that the doctrine of superior responsibility did not establish a standard of strict liability for superiors for failing to prevent or punish the crimes committed by their subordinates. Instead, article 7, paragraph 3, of the Statute provided that a superior might be held responsible only where he knew or had reason to know that his subordinates were about to or had committed the acts referred to under articles 2 to 5. A construction of this provision in light of the content of the doctrine under customary law led the Trial Chamber to conclude that a superior might possess the *mens rea* required to incur criminal liability where he had actual knowledge, established through direct or circumstantial evidence, that his subordinates were committing or about to commit crimes referred to under articles 2 to 5 of the Statute; or where he had in his possession information of a nature, which at the least would put him on notice of the risk of such offences by indicating the need for additional investigation in order to ascertain whether such crimes were committed or were about to be committed by his subordinates.

Concerning the third element, that of taking necessary and reasonable measures, the Trial Chamber observed that the legal duty resting upon all individuals in positions of superior authority required them to take all necessary and reasonable measures to prevent the commission of offences by their subordinates or, if such crimes had been committed, to punish the perpetrators of them. It was the view of the Trial Chamber that any evaluation of the action taken by a superior to determine whether this duty had been met was so inextricably linked to the facts of each particular situation that any attempt to formulate a general standard *in abstracto* would not be meaningful. The Trial Chamber insisted it had to be recognised that international law could not oblige a superior to perform the impossible. Hence, a superior might only be held criminally responsible for failing to take such measures that were within his powers.

Ultimately, the Trial Chamber found three of the accused guilty, *inter alia*, of various charges of grave breaches of the Geneva Conventions and violations of the laws or customs of war, and they were sentenced to terms of imprisonment. In respect of superior responsibility the Trial Chamber concluded that one of these accused was the de facto commander of the camp exercising de facto authority. Accordingly, he was criminally responsible for the acts of personnel in the camp on the basis of the principle of superior responsibility.

(H) POLICE INVESTIGATION OF GENOCIDE, CRIMES AGAINST HUMANITY AND WAR CRIMES

Police officials have been involved in investigations of cases considered by the *ad hoc* tribunals, and, when the International Criminal Court becomes fully operative, it is certain that police officials will be required to investigate crimes that are subject to the jurisdiction of that Court.

On some occasions it may be possible for police officials, during the course of a conflict or in its immediate aftermath, to gather or preserve evidence of crimes. Evidence of this nature could be used to support prosecutions before domestic courts and international tribunals. Part 9 of the 1998 Rome Statute of the International Criminal Court contains a number of provisions on international co-operation and judicial assistance, and some of these have clear relevance to police. For example, some requests for cooperation may be transmitted through the International Criminal Police Organization (Interpol) or any appropriate regional organisation (article 87(1)(b)); the Court may transmit a request for the arrest and surrender of a person to any State on the territory of which that person may be found and request the cooperation of that State in the arrest and surrender of such a person (article 89(1)); other forms of cooperation include assisting in the identification and whereabouts of persons or the location of items, and the questioning of any person being investigated or prosecuted (article 93(1)(a) and (1)(c) respectively).

Crimes of this nature are among the most atrocious and heinous that can be committed. It is surely right that police officials should apply their skills, and experience in the most energetic and dedicated manner to bring such appalling criminals to justice.

Chapter 2. Types of Conflict and Rules of Behaviour

The provisions of international humanitarian law are many and detailed. For example, the four Geneva Conventions of 1949 contain a total of 429 articles. The two Additional Protocols of 1977 add another 130 articles between them. The Third Geneva Convention, which complements already existing rules for the protection of prisoners of war in the 1899 and 1907 Hague Regulations, contains 143 articles. This figure can be contrasted with the 95 articles of the most comprehensive human rights instrument setting out good principle and practice in the treatment of prisoners and the management of civil penal institutions, the Standard Minimum Rules for the Treatment of Prisoners.[73] Even if the 39 articles of another human rights instrument, the Body of Principles for the Protection of All Persons under Any Form of Detention or Imprisonment, are taken into account the provisions for the protection of captured combatants remain more numerous.

Clearly distinguishing between international humanitarian law instruments and human rights instruments on the treatment of prisoners purely on the basis of the number of articles is an unsatisfactory way of making a comparison. Furthermore the very specific human rights instruments designed to protect detainees from torture and mistreatment, and those for the protection of juvenile detainees, could also be taken into account. Nevertheless, it is a useful preliminary indication of the multiplicity of humanitarian law provisions to police officials who are probably more familiar with domestic and international human rights instruments for the protection of civil prisoners.

Given that the purposes of international humanitarian law are to regulate the conduct of hostilities and to protect victims of armed conflicts, and that the bulk of its provisions relate to international armed conflicts, this law is primarily the concern of the military. However, for the reasons indicated in the previous chapter, police officials should become familiar with humanitarian law, and comply with it and secure compliance with it. The point made there, that the lack of awareness of police officials about this subject should be remedied, will, it is hoped, be reinforced by the following account of some of its provisions, and especially the account of the status of police in times of armed conflict. In this respect, the distinction between combatant and civilian will first be made clear. The question of combatant and non-combatant status only arises in the circumstances of international armed conflict, and the conflicts to which this term applies are set out in the 1949 Geneva Conventions and 1977 Additional Protocol I to the Conventions.

---

[73] Standard Minimum Rules for the Treatment of Prisoners, *supra* note 61.

II:2

(A) INTERNATIONAL ARMED CONFLICT

The Geneva Conventions and the First Additional Protocol apply to all cases of declared war or of any other armed conflict arising between two or more parties to the Conventions and Additional Protocol I from the beginning of such a situation, even if a state of war is not recognised by one of them, and to all cases of partial or total occupation of the territory of a high contracting party, even if the occupation meets with no resistance. The treaties also cover armed conflicts in which people are fighting against colonial domination and alien occupation, and against racial regimes in the exercise of their right of self-determination.[74]

Members of the armed forces of a party to an international armed conflict (other than medical or religious personnel) are combatants, and any combatant captured by the adverse party is a prisoner of war.[75] Such armed forces must be organised, placed under a command responsible to that party for the conduct of its subordinates, and subject to an internal disciplinary system that enforces compliance with the rules of international law applicable in armed conflict.

Compliance with these rules implies, in particular, that combatants are obliged to distinguish themselves from the civilian population by a uniform or by some other distinctive sign, at least while they are engaged in an attack or in a military operation preparatory to an attack. In exceptional circumstances, owing to the nature of hostilities, they may distinguish themselves as combatants by carrying arms openly.

A civilian is any person who is not a member of armed forces, and where there is doubt as to whether or not a person is a civilian, a person is to be considered a civilian. The civilian population comprises all persons who are civilians, and the presence within the civilian population of individuals who do not come within the definition of civilians does not deprive the population of its civilian character.[76]

(a) Status of Police

Civil police forces are not armed forces in the sense in which that term is used in these definitions. It is clear that civil police forces have civilian status and that members of those forces have civilian and not combatant status.

This point is reinforced by article 43(3) of 1977 Additional Protocol I, which states that whenever a Party to a conflict incorporates a paramilitary or armed law

---

[74] Article 2 common to the 1949 Geneva Conventions, and article 1(4) of the 1977 Additional Protocol I.
[75] 1949 Geneva Convention III, article 4, and 1977 Additional Protocol I, articles 43 and 44.
[76] 1977 Additional Protocol I, article 50.

enforcement agency into its armed forces it shall so notify other parties to the conflict. This means that in order for a police official to be accorded combatant status, he or she must be a member of an (armed) law enforcement agency that is formally assimilated into the armed forces of a party to a conflict. Such an act of incorporation, coupled with notification to other parties, not only radically alters the status of members of such a law enforcement agency; it also confirms the civilian status of members of agencies to which the provision has not been applied.

A number of other provisions in Hague and Geneva Conventions underscore the non-combatant status of police. For example the 1954 Hague Convention for the Protection of Cultural Property in the Event of Armed Conflict grants special protection to cultural property in refuges established for that purpose, provided they are situated at an adequate distance from potential military targets and are not used for military purposes. Article 8(4) of the Convention states that the presence, in the vicinity of such cultural property, of police forces normally responsible for the maintenance of public order shall not be deemed use for a military purpose.

The same approach is taken in respect of the establishment of non-defended localities (which may not be attacked), and demilitarised zones (which may neither be attacked nor occupied) under articles 59 and 60 of 1977 Additional Protocol I. Both articles carry provisions which stipulate that the presence in such places of police forces retained for the sole purpose of maintaining law and order does not contravene the conditions under which such a locality or zone may be established.

The provisions of 1949 Geneva Convention IV on occupied territories contain an important provision on the status of public officials. Article 54 prohibits an occupying power from altering the status of public officials or judges in the occupied territories, or in any way applying sanctions to or taking any measures of coercion or discrimination against them, should they abstain from fulfilling their functions for reasons of conscience.

Under article 16 of the 1907 Hague Convention V on Neutrality in Land War, nationals of a State not taking part in the war are considered neutrals. However, a neutral can not avail himself of his neutrality if he commits acts in favour of a belligerent (Article 17(b)). Article 18(b) provides an exception to this rule, stating that services rendered in matters of police or civil administration shall not be considered as committed in favour of a belligerent. Thus, in making this distinction between neutrality and belligerency, an important distinction for those individuals concerned, the Convention is affirming the civilian character of the police function.

(b) **Some Rules Concerning Behaviour**

(i) Rules on Methods and Means of Warfare

Those police officials who, exceptionally, are accorded combatant status need to be aware that combatants can participate directly in hostilities and commit acts of violence which would be unlawful in time of peace. Furthermore they may be attacked; they may receive some protection during hostilities through measures designed to regulate methods and means of warfare; they are entitled to be treated as prisoners of war in the event of their capture by enemy forces; and they must comply with the rules of international law applicable in armed conflict.

As indicated in the preceding chapter, 'Hague Law' governs the conduct of hostilities, the permissible means and methods of warfare. However, many of the 'Hague Regulations' have been developed or superseded by the Geneva Conventions and their Additional Protocols. Examples here are taken from the 1977 Additional Protocol I. Basic rules on means and methods of warfare are set out in the three paragraphs of article 35 of that instrument. In paragraph 1 it is stipulated that in any armed conflict, the right of parties to the conflict to choose methods and means of warfare is not unlimited. Paragraph two prohibits the employment of weapons, projectiles and material and methods of warfare of a nature to cause superfluous injury or unnecessary suffering. Paragraph three prohibits the employment of methods or means of warfare which are intended, or may be expected, to cause widespread, long-term and severe damage to the natural environment.

Ensuing paragraphs then set out other, more specific, rules on means and methods of warfare. Examples of such rules are the prohibition on killing, injuring or capturing an adversary through perfidy; the prohibition on misuse of emblems (red cross, red crescent, white flag); the prohibition on refusing quarter; the requirement that a person who is recognised or who, in the circumstances, should be recognised to be *hors de combat* shall not be made the object of attack; and the requirement on captors to release persons entitled to protection as prisoners of war if they are unable to evacuate them from the combat zone. In such cases all feasible precautions shall be taken to ensure their safety.[77]

(ii) Protection of Wounded, Sick and Shipwrecked

The terms 'wounded' and 'sick' mean military or civilian persons in need of medical care and who refrain from any act of hostility. The term 'shipwrecked' means

---

[77] *Ibid.*, articles 37, 38, 40 and 41 respectively.

military or civilian persons in a perilous situation at sea or on any other waters following a misfortune which has befallen them and who refrain from any act of hostility.[78]

All police officials need to be aware of the general rule that wounded, sick and shipwrecked, to whichever Party they belong, shall be respected and protected.[79] They also need to be aware of the requirements to search for and collect wounded, sick and shipwrecked;[80] and protect and respect the wounded and sick, in particular protecting them against pillage and ill-treatment.[81]

Police officials, especially those with civilian status, must be aware of the provisions requiring the civilian population to respect the wounded, sick and shipwrecked, even if they belong to the adverse party, and to commit no act of violence against them; permitting the civilian population and aid societies (such as the Red Cross or Red Crescent), even on their own initiative, to collect and care for the wounded, sick and shipwrecked; forbidding harm against or prosecution, conviction or punishment of persons for such humanitarian acts; and permitting Parties to a conflict to appeal to the civilian population and aid societies to undertake humanitarian actions (e.g. collect and care for the wounded, sick and shipwrecked), and to grant protection and facilities to those who respond to such appeals.[82]

In 1994 the Working Group on Arbitrary Detention considered a case against Kuwait in which it was alleged that a Palestinian citizen, who served as a nurse at a hospital in Kuwait during the first Gulf war, was sentenced to 15 years' imprisonment for having collaborated with the enemy during that war.[83] It was claimed that the charge against him was unjust since, in the course of his duties as a nurse, he simply acted in a humanitarian spirit, without making distinctions between the sick and wounded for whom he was caring on the ground that they belonged to one side or the other. In coming to its decision in which it found, *inter alia*, the detention to be arbitrary, the Working Group recognised that in a war situation it was not lawful for medical personnel to extend the required humanitarian care only to the wounded of one side. Such action was contrary to the Geneva Conventions relating to the treatment of wounded prisoners and to civilians affected by the conflict.

---

[78] *Ibid.*, article 8.

[79] *Ibid.*, article 10.

[80] Articles 15 and 18 of the 1949 Geneva Conventions I and II respectively.

[81] 1949 Geneva Convention IV, article 16.

[82] 1949 Geneva Convention I, article 18, and 1977 Additional Protocol I, article 17.

[83] Decision No. 59/1993 (*Kuwait*), United Nations document E/CN.4/1995/31/Add.1, p. 22, decision adopted on 9 December 1994.

II:2

(iii) Prisoners of War

Article 12 of the Third Geneva Convention states that prisoners of war are in the hands of the enemy power but not of the individuals or military units who have captured them. Irrespective of the individual responsibilities that may exist, the detaining power is responsible for the treatment given. A prisoner of war camp must, however, be under the immediate authority of the regular armed forces of the detaining power.[84]

Article 13 of the same Convention requires all prisoners of war to be humanely treated at all times. Any unlawful act or omission by the detaining power causing death or seriously endangering the health of a prisoner of war in its custody is prohibited, and will be regarded as a serious breach of the Convention. Furthermore prisoners of war must at all times be protected, particularly against acts of violence or intimidation and against insults and public curiosity.

In view of the responsibilities of the detaining power towards prisoners of war, and the fact that the Convention includes provisions on their escape, capture, criminal offences committed by and against them, and on judicial proceedings, it is inevitable that a detaining power will meet some of its responsibilities in respect of prisoners of war through its civil police forces. This means that police officials need to be aware of some of the provisions of 1949 Geneva Convention III. For example prisoners of war shall be subject to the laws, regulations and orders in force in the armed forces of the detaining power;[85] in deciding whether an offence committed by a prisoner of war should be subject to disciplinary or judicial punishment, the detaining power shall ensure that the competent authorities exercise the greatest leniency and adopt, wherever possible, disciplinary rather than judicial measures;[86] as far as judicial sanctions are concerned a prisoner of war may be tried only by a military court, unless the existing laws of the detaining power expressly permit the civil courts to try a member of its own armed forces in respect of the particular offence alleged to have been committed by the prisoner of war;[87] prisoners of war who escape and are recaptured are liable to disciplinary punishment only, and on recapture they are to be handed over without delay to the military authority;[88] offences committed by prisoners of war with the sole intention of facilitating their escape and which do not entail any violence against life or limb, such as offences against public property, theft without intention of self-enrichment, the drawing up or

---

[84] 1949 Geneva Convention III, article 39.

[85] *Ibid.*, article 82.

[86] *Ibid.*, article 83.

[87] *Ibid.*, article 84.

[88] *Ibid.*, article 92.

use of false papers, or the wearing of civilian clothes, shall occasion disciplinary punishment only.[89]

Finally, and most importantly, article 121 of the Third Geneva Convention requires every death or serious injury of a prisoner of war caused or suspected to have been caused by a sentry, another prisoner of war, or any other person, as well as any other death the cause of which is unknown, to be immediately followed by an official enquiry by a detaining power. Investigating deaths or injuries that may have been caused by criminal acts is a police function, and it is highly likely that some of these enquiries would be carried out by civil police officers.

(iv) Civilians

Those police officials with combatant status need, in particular, to be aware of the basic rule which requires parties to a conflict to distinguish between the civilian population and combatants and between civilian objects and military objectives, and to direct operations only against military objectives.[90] They also need to be aware of the more detailed rules which follow that basic rule, and which are designed to secure compliance with it. For example the civilian population as such, as well as individual civilians, shall not be the object of attack, and acts or threats of violence the primary purpose of which is to spread terror among the civilian population are prohibited.[91]

Police officials with civilian status, as beneficiaries of the rules designed to protect civilians and as functionaries who may be able to secure or promote respect for them, need to have a good understanding of those rules. For example it is important for them to know that civilians may enjoy the protection afforded by those provisions which provide general protection to civilians against the effect of hostilities unless and for such time as they take a direct part in hostilities.[92] This means that they may not use force against enemy combatants except for purposes of individual self-defence or for the defence of other civilians against unlawful attacks; they may not defend their country, friendly combatants, or hinder enemy forces in military operations; and they may not use force to defend civilians (including themselves) against arrest. They should also know that attacks are to be strictly limited to military objectives (attacks against civilian objects being prohibited), and that military objectives are limited to those objects which by their nature, location, purpose or use make an effective contribution to military action.[93]

---

[89] 1949 Geneva Convention III, article 93.
[90] 1977 Additional Protocol I, article 48.
[91] *Ibid.*, article 51(2).
[92] *Ibid.*, article 51(3).
[93] *Ibid.*, article 52.

II:2

Such awareness may enable civil police officials to avoid actions that are likely to deprive them of the protection afforded by their civilian status, and to prevent police buildings from being used in such a way that they could be considered to be military objectives. By taking these measures they enhance their own ability to continue their civilian policing functions, and increase the possibility that they can continue to use the resources of their buildings and contents.

Implementation of some of the rules under Part II of 1949 Geneva Convention IV, designed to protect the whole of the populations of the countries in conflict against certain consequences of war, could be assisted by police action and, hence, by police awareness of them. For example the requirement for convoys of vehicles or hospital trains conveying wounded and sick civilians to be respected and protected, as set out in article 21 of the Convention, could be met in some circumstances by police action. Equally police may to be able to take the initial action necessary for parties to ensure that children orphaned or separated from their families as a result of war are not left to their own resources, as required by article 24.

The greater part of the provisions of the Fourth Geneva Convention are designed to protect those who find themselves, in case of conflict or occupation, in the hands of a party to the conflict or occupying power of which they are not nationals,[94] and some of these have great significance in policing terms. For example, article 27 requires protected persons to be protected against acts of violence or threats thereof, and women to be protected against any attack on their honour, and in particular against rape. These are police functions.

Other examples of provisions relevant to police are those prohibiting physical or moral coercion to obtain information from protected persons;[95] the punishment of a protected person for an offence he or she has not personally committed, collective penalties and also measures of intimidation or of terrorism, and pillage;[96] and hostage taking.[97]

(v) Occupied Territories

The provisions of article 54 of the Fourth Geneva Convention, protecting the status of public officials and judges in occupied territories should they abstain from fulfilling their functions for reasons of conscience, are referred to above.

---

[94] 1949 Geneva Convention IV, article 4.
[95] *Ibid.*, article 31.
[96] *Ibid.*, article 33.
[97] *Ibid.*, article 34.

Other important provisions on occupation include those on public order and law enforcement set out in regulations 42 and 43 of the Regulations annexed to the 1907 Hague Convention IV. Here it is stipulated that a territory is considered occupied when it is actually placed under the authority of the hostile army, and that, as legitimate power has passed to the hands of the occupant, he shall take all possible measures in his power to restore, and ensure, as far as possible, public order and safety, while respecting, unless absolutely prevented, the laws in force in the country.

These principles are reaffirmed and extended by article 64 of the Fourth Geneva Convention, which requires that the penal laws of the occupied territory shall remain in force, with the exception that they may be repealed or suspended by the occupying power in cases where they constitute a threat to its security or an obstacle to the application of the Convention.

Similar considerations apply to existing tribunals. However, article 64 also acknowledges that the occupying power may enact its own regulations if they are essential to enable the occupying power to fulfil its obligations under the Convention, to maintain orderly government of the territory, and to ensure the security of the occupying power, of the members and property of the occupying forces or administration, and likewise of the establishments and lines of communication used by them.

The principle is, therefore, that the institutions and the public and police officials in the occupied territory continue to function as before, in so far as they are able.

A number of other provisions relating to occupied territories are relevant to policing. For example, those of article 49 of the Fourth Convention, which prohibit individual or mass forcible transfers as well as deportations of protected persons from occupied territory; and those of article 70, which prohibit the arrest, prosecution or conviction of protected persons by the occupying power for acts committed or opinions expressed before the occupation. Provisions of this type are relevant because police could become the agents by which they are violated.

Another category of civilian to be considered under this heading is internees. Both in the case of enemy civilians on the territory of a Party to the conflict, and that of protected persons in occupied territory, there is a principle expressed in the Fourth Convention[98] that if the detaining power considers it necessary, for imperative reasons of security, to take safety measures concerning protected persons it may, at the most, subject them to assigned residence or internment.

---

[98] *Ibid.*, articles 41 and 78.

II:2

Police may well become involved in some stages of an internment process and they ought to be aware of some of the provisions relating to that process. Particularly relevant are those concerning the recapture of internees after escape (Articles 120 - 122),[99] and those designed to secure a fair hearing of disciplinary charges against internees (Article 123).

(vi) Additional Rules

A final category of person to be considered under the heading of 'Civilians' is that category specified in Section III of Part IV of the First Additional Protocol, persons in the power of a party to the conflict. Unlike the category specified in article 4 of the Fourth Geneva Convention the term 'of which they are not nationals' is omitted. The opening article of Section III, article 72, states that the provisions of the Section are additional to the rules concerning humanitarian protection of civilians and civilian objects in the power of a party to the conflict contained in the Fourth Geneva Convention, as well as to other applicable rules of international law relating to the protection of fundamental human rights during international armed conflict.

It is important for police to be aware of article 75 in that Section of Additional Protocol I, as that article sets out detailed provisions to protect persons who are in the power of a party to the conflict and who do not benefit from the more favourable treatment under the Conventions or Additional Protocol I. Its provisions are expressed in much the same way as provisions of human rights treaties. A person within this category could include a guerrilla fighter who has forfeited the right to be a prisoner of war because, when finding himself in an unusual combat situation as defined in article 44 of Additional Protocol I, he has failed to meet the minimum requirement of carrying arms openly. Another example would be a mercenary who, according to article 47 of Additional Protocol I, shall not have the right to be a combatant or a prisoner of war.

Article 75 prohibits such acts as murder, torture, mutilation, outrages upon personal dignity such as enforced prostitution and indecent assault, hostage taking and collective punishments. It then sets out minimum requirements to secure a fair trial in the event of protected persons being prosecuted for actions related to the armed conflict; requirements for the proper treatment of women detainees; and provisions on the prosecution of persons for war crimes and crimes against humanity. The

---

[99] These include provisions that internees who are captured after having escaped, or when attempting to escape, shall be liable only to disciplinary punishment in respect of that act, and escape, or attempted escape, shall not be deemed an aggravating circumstance in cases where an internee is prosecuted for offences committed during his escape.

provisions of this article are relevant to police with combatant status and civilian police.

(vii) Civil Defence

Part IV of the First Additional Protocol also contains a chapter on civil defence, and the provisions of articles within this chapter could be relevant to police. For example, civil defence is defined as the performance of a number of humanitarian tasks intended to protect the civilian population against the dangers, and to help it to recover from the immediate effects of hostilities and disasters and also to provide the conditions necessary for its survival.[100]

The provision of emergency aid and assistance is a basic policing function, and some of the tasks listed could be carried out by police, such as warning, evacuation, detection and marking of danger areas, emergency assistance in the restoration and maintenance of order in distressed areas. However, civil defence organisations are defined as those establishments and other units which are organised or authorised by the competent authorities of a party to the conflict to perform any of the specified tasks, and which are assigned and devoted exclusively to such tasks. Personnel of civil defence organisations are defined as those persons assigned by a party to a conflict exclusively to the performance of the specified tasks.

Civil defence personnel may carry light individual weapons for the purpose of maintaining order or for self-defence.[101]

(B) NON-INTERNATIONAL ARMED CONFLICT

A non-international armed conflict, or civil war, is generally understood as a conflict in which insurgents within a state seek to displace the government by force of arms. The question of combatant status does not arise in such conflicts, insurgents do not have prisoner of war status when captured, and they are liable under the criminal law of the state concerned for their act of insurgency and any other crimes arising out if it.

(a) Article 3 Common to the Geneva Conventions of 1949

The central concern of the four Geneva Conventions of 1949 is the protection of victims of international armed conflicts. Of the 429 detailed articles in the Conventions only one, article 3 common to them all, is designed for the protection of victims of non-international armed conflicts.

---

[100] 1977 Additional Protocol I, article 61.

[101] *Ibid.*, article 65(3).

II:2

The article extends basic humanitarian protection to the categories of people it protects by applying principles on which the Geneva Conventions are based to armed conflicts not of an international character occurring in the territory of one of the High Contracting Parties. In such cases each party to the conflict is bound to apply its provisions as a minimum. It is sometimes described as a convention within the Conventions, or a mini-convention. It provides no definition of the type of conflict it seeks to regulate.

The fundamental principle of humane treatment is embodied in paragraph 1 which also defines those protected under the article:

> "Persons taking no active part in hostilities, including members of armed forces who have laid down their arms and those placed hors de combat by sickness, wounds, detention, or any other cause, shall in all circumstances be treated humanely, without any adverse distinction founded on race, colour, religion or faith, sex, birth or wealth, or any other similar criteria."

The remainder of the paragraph sets out a number of acts that are prohibited at any time and in any place whatsoever in respect of the people it protects. Prohibited acts include murder, torture, hostage taking, outrages upon personal dignity and (in sub-paragraph (d)):

> "the passing of sentences and the carrying out of executions without previous judgement pronounced by a regularly constituted court, affording all the judicial guarantees which are recognised as indispensable by civilised peoples."

Paragraph 2 of common article 3 requires wounded and sick to be collected and cared for, and the final provisions include one that allows an impartial body (such as the International Committee of the Red Cross) to offer its services to parties to the conflict.

Whilst common article 3 has a number of strengths, including the fact that it does concisely embody the general principles of the Conventions, and the fact that it is binding on all parties to a conflict, it also has a number of shortcomings.

In the first instance its provisions are expressed in language that is somewhat imprecise and generalised, and the exact meaning of some of the terms it employs is arguable. For example in times of internal armed conflict governments tend to adopt emergency measures which reduce some of the judicial guarantees necessary to secure a fair trial. Those stipulations on judicial guarantees set out in sub-paragraph

(d) (see above) are insufficiently precise on the question of which of the judicial guarantees are actually indispensable. Secondly, the extent of the protection it offers is limited in scope.

Recognition of these, and other, shortcomings, and an increase in the number of non-international armed conflicts resulted in efforts, largely by or under the auspices of the International Committee of the Red Cross, to improve on the law protecting victims of such conflicts. These efforts resulted in the adoption of Geneva Protocol II Additional to the Geneva Conventions on 8 June 1977.

(b) 1977 Protocol II Additional to the Geneva Conventions of 12 August 1949, and Relating to the Protection of Victims of Non-International Armed Conflicts

This treaty develops and supplements common article 3 of the Geneva Conventions without modifying its existing conditions of application, and the Common Article continues as an essential part of humanitarian law - especially in relation to its scope and application.

The preamble to Additional Protocol II acknowledges that the humanitarian principles enshrined in Common Article 3 constitute the foundation of respect for the human person in cases of armed conflict not of an international character and that international instruments relating to human rights offer a basic protection to the human person. It then sets out the reason for the adoption of the Protocol - to ensure a better protection for the victims of non-international armed conflicts, and recalls that in cases not covered by the law in force, the human person remains under the protection of the principles of humanity and the dictates of public conscience. This last part of the preamble is a shortened version of the Martens Clause (named after the Russian delegate to the first Hague Conferences who expounded a fuller Declaration on the principles of limitation and constraint in warfare). The Martens Clause is embodied, in various forms, in treaties expressing both 'Hague' and 'Geneva' law.

The material field of application of Additional Protocol II is set out in article 1. That part of the article that establishes the relationship of the Protocol to common article 3 is referred to above. Article 1 then stipulates that the Protocol applies to all armed conflicts that are not covered by article 1 of the First Additional Protocol to the Geneva Conventions – where the types of conflict categorised as international are identified. The article then stipulates that conflicts to which it does apply must take place:

> "in the territory of a High Contracting Party between its armed forces and dissident armed forces or other organised armed groups which, under

responsible command, exercise such control over a part of its territory as to enable them to carry out sustained and concerted military operations and to implement the Protocol."

The second paragraph of article 1 states that Additional Protocol II does not apply to:

"situations of internal disturbances and tensions, such as riots, isolated and sporadic acts of violence and other acts of a similar nature, as not being armed conflicts."

In these ways the upper and lower limits of the field of application of Additional Protocol II are established.

The personal field of application of Protocol II extends, under article 2, to all persons affected by an armed conflict as defined in article 1. Anyone who takes a direct part in hostilities is not considered to be a person 'affected by an armed conflict', and this is an indication of an important distinction between the law on international armed conflicts and that on non-international conflicts.

Whilst the former recognises certain categories of people as combatants and makes provision for their protection against certain means and methods of warfare, the notion of combatant does not exist in the latter and neither does that of prisoner of war. This distinction is a reflection of the fact that those who take up arms against a state are generally characterised, by the state concerned, not merely as criminals, but also as traitors and terrorists, whatever the justice or otherwise of their cause.

Article 2 also includes a stipulation that Additional Protocol II is to be applied without any adverse distinction on such grounds as race, colour, sex, language, religion or belief.

Under the heading 'Humane Treatment', Part II of Additional Protocol II sets out fundamental guarantees for all persons who do not take a direct part or who have ceased to take a direct part in hostilities, whether or not their liberty has been restricted. All such people are entitled to respect for their person, honour and convictions and religious practices. Furthermore they shall in all circumstances be treated humanely without any adverse distinction. These provisions are set out in article 4, which concludes with the only protection provided in Protocol II for people taking part in hostilities, that "it is prohibited to order that there shall be no survivors".

Paragraph 2 of article 4 elaborates a number of acts against protected persons (in other words those not taking a direct part in hostilities) that are prohibited at any time and in any place whatsoever. These include violence to life, torture, hostage taking, acts of terrorism and outrages upon personal dignity. The article also addresses the specific problem of protection of children, with provisions on such matters as education, reunion with families, and a prohibition on children under 15 years of age being recruited into armed forces or taking part in hostilities.

Article 5 sets out safeguards for persons whose liberty has been restricted, making no distinction according to reason for restriction of liberty and creating no prisoner of war status. It provides rules on persons interned or detained, and rules for those responsible for detention, all designed to secure humane treatment for, and safety of, detainees. It is important to emphasise here that these provisions do apply to detained people who have taken part in hostilities. Whilst members of dissident armed forces involved in non-international armed conflicts do not have combatant or prisoner of war status, they do have rights as detainees. It is important also to note the extent to which provisions such as these overlap with human rights law, much of which is derogable, designed to protect people from arbitrary detention and to secure basic rights for people who have been detained (for example article 9 of the International Covenant on Civil and Political Rights and equivalent provisions in the regional treaties).

Article 6 applies to the prosecution and punishment of criminal offences related to the armed conflict, and sets out detailed rules to ensure those judicial guarantees necessary to secure a fair trial.

Part III of Protocol II contains six articles on those affected by an armed conflict by virtue of being wounded, sick or shipwrecked. It reaffirms the principle of humane treatment and sets out provisions to secure protection and care of such victims, and protection of medical personnel and medical duties, units and transports.

The six articles under Part IV of Additional Protocol II deal with protection of the civilian population, re-asserting the general principle that the civilian population and individual civilians shall enjoy general protection against the dangers arising from military operations. A proviso is added to the effect that civilians shall enjoy the protection afforded by Part IV unless and for such time as they take a direct part in hostilities.

There then follows a series of measures designed to secure compliance with the principle. These include prohibitions on making civilians the object of attack, and on acts or threats of violence the primary purpose of which is to spread terror among the civilian population. Measures are also included for the protection of objects indispensable to the survival of the civilian population; works and installations containing dangerous forces (such as dams and nuclear power stations); and cultural objects and places of worship. The displacement of the civilian population for reasons related to the conflict is prohibited unless the security of the civilians involved or imperative military reasons so demand.

Finally, under Part IV of Additional Protocol II, article 18 states that relief societies located in the territory of the high contracting party may offer their services to aid victims of the armed conflict. As indicated above, the comparable provision of Common Article 3 makes no stipulation concerning the location of relief societies.

(c) Common Article 3 and Additional Protocol II Compared and Contrasted

Whilst Additional Protocol II generally reaffirms and develops common article 3, the greater restriction on relief societies is only one way in which the Protocol is more limited than the common article. The stipulation in article 1 of Protocol II limiting its application to armed conflicts between armed forces of a party to the Protocol and dissident armed forces on its territory means that conflicts involving two or more non-governmental forces, but not involving State forces, are not covered by the Protocol. Furthermore the requirement that dissident armed forces should exercise control over territory excludes from the ambit of Protocol II many forms of armed conflicts involving highly mobile forms of guerrilla warfare. Common article 3 imposes neither of these conditions hence its continuing importance as it is applicable over a wider range of conflicts.

Where Additional Protocol II does meet the need identified in its Preamble, to ensure a better protection for victims of armed conflicts, is in terms of the substantive rights it embodies for such victims. In that sense it represents a considerable advance on common article 3, both in the extent of protection offered and in the precision with which it is expressed. This is exemplified by Part II of Protocol II, which concerns humane treatment. The three long and detailed articles (4, 5 and 6) substantially clarify and elaborate the fundamental principle and list of prohibited acts set out in paragraph 1 of common article 3.

These differences between the Common Article and the Protocol, the wider field of application of Common Article 3 and the more complete protection for victims provided by the Protocol, are significant, but so are the common characteristics of each. Both apply automatically as soon as the specific conditions are fulfilled; both seek to avoid conferring legal status on insurgents; neither recognises the quality of combatant nor confers prisoner of war status on captured fighters.

(d) Cases Arising out of Non-International Armed Conflicts

It is important and encouraging to note that international human rights courts do hold states to account for human rights violations committed during non-international armed conflicts

The case *Bámaca Velásquez* v. *Guatemala*,[102] is interesting for a number of reasons, including the observations of the Inter-American Court of Human Rights on the behaviour required of State forces engaged in a non-international armed conflict. The case concerned the human rights of the commander of a guerrilla force captured in such a conflict. During the course of its deliberations, the Court found that it was the practice of the army to capture guerrillas and keep them in clandestine confinement in order to obtain information that was useful for the army, through physical and mental torture. These guerrillas were frequently transferred from one military detachment to another. After several months, they were used as guides to determine where the guerrilla forces were active and to identify individuals who were fighting with the guerrillas. Many of those detained were then executed.

In its application, the Inter-American Commission on Human Rights asked the Court to decide whether the State had violated a number of rights of Efraín Bámaca Velásquez, including those embodied in article 3 common to the Geneva Conventions. In responding to the Commission's request on this matter, the Court noted that it had been proved that there was an internal armed conflict in Guatemala at the time of the facts of the case. Instead of releasing the State from its obligations to respect and guarantee human rights, the Court observed, this required the State to act in accordance with such obligations. The Court further stated that although it lacked the competence to declare that a State was internationally accountable for the violation of international treaties that did not grant it such competence, it could observe that certain acts or omissions violating human rights, protected by treaties it was competent to apply and interpret, also violated other international instruments for the protection of the individual, such as the Geneva Conventions and, in particular, their Common Article 3.

The Court pointed out the similarity between the content of Common Article 3 and the provisions of the American Convention on Human Rights and other international instruments regarding non-derogable human rights, such as the right to life and the right not to be submitted to torture or cruel, inhuman or degrading treatment. The Court also recalled what it had indicated on previous occasions, that although the State had the right and obligation to guarantee its security and maintain public order,

---

[102] Inter-American Court of Human Rights, Series C: *Decisions and Judgments*, No. 70 (2001), petition No. 11129, judgment of 25 November 2000.

II:2

its powers were not unlimited. It had the obligation, at all times, to apply procedures that were in accordance with the law and to respect the fundamental rights of each individual in its jurisdiction.

Ultimately, the Court found violations of a number of rights protected under the American Convention, including the right to life and to physical, mental and moral integrity protected by articles 4 and 5 respectively. Guatemala had the obligation to respect these rights and to guarantee them. It also found violations of the Inter-American Convention to Prevent and Punish Torture.

There have been a number of cases against Russia before the European Court of Human Rights arising out of the conflict in Chechnya. For example, in the case *Khashiyev and Akayeva* v. *Russia*,[103] the applicants alleged that their relatives were tortured and killed by members of the Russian federal military in Chechnya in February 2000. They also submitted that the investigation into their deaths was inefficient. The applicants relied on articles 2, 3 and 13 of the European Convention on Human Rights, which, respectively, protect the right to life, prohibit torture and ill-treatment and require an effective remedy.

In December 1999 the Russian federal army started an operation to take control of Grozny. Heavy fighting lasted until the end of January 2000, when the central parts of the city were finally taken. The applicants, residents of Grozny, left their homes prior to the hostilities but their relatives, the victims, remained to look after their property and houses. At the end of January 2000, the applicants learned that their relatives had been killed in Grozny. Having subsequently viewed the bodies, the applicants submitted, variously, that they bore marks of numerous stab and gunshot wounds and bruises, and that some bones were broken. There were also traces of beatings and torture on the bodies.

On the basis of the material in its possession the Court found it established that servicemen killed the applicants' relatives and that their deaths could be attributed to the State. It observed that no explanation had been forthcoming from the Russian Government as to the circumstances of the deaths, nor had they relied on any ground of justification in respect of any use of lethal force by their agents. Liability for the applicants' relatives' deaths was therefore attributable to the respondent State.

Ultimately, the Court held that there had been a violation of article 2 of the Convention in respect of the deaths; a violation of article 2 in that the authorities failed to carry out an adequate and effective investigation into the circumstances of the deaths; no violation of article 3 in respect of the failure to protect the applicants'

---

[103] Applications 57924/00 and 57945/00, judgment in Strasbourg on 24 February 2005.

112

relatives from torture; a violation of article 3 in respect of the failure to carry out an adequate and effective investigation into the allegations of torture; and a violation of article 13.

(C) INTERNAL DISTURBANCES AND TENSIONS

Three categories of internal conflict are apparent under the terms and conditions of common article 3 and Additional Protocol II. The first category, identified in article 1 of Protocol II, embraces those high-intensity internal armed conflicts in which rebel forces have control of territory. Protocol II regulates this type of conflict in some detail, supplementing considerably the provisions of common article 3, which, nevertheless, also apply. At a lower intensity are those conflicts that fall below the threshold of Protocol II and to which only the provisions of common article 3 apply. Finally, below that level is the category specifically excluded by article 1(2) of the Protocol, situations of internal disturbances and tensions.

Internal disturbances and tensions are exemplified in article 1(2) as riots, isolated and sporadic acts of violence and other acts of a similar nature, as not being armed conflicts. However, there remains some difficulty in distinguishing between armed conflicts and internal disturbances, particularly where the scale of violence fluctuates around that manifested in those internal disturbances and tensions specifically excluded by article 1(2) of the Protocol. Furthermore, whilst this threshold is not included in the provisions of Common Article 3, the article clearly deals with armed conflicts involving hostilities between armed forces. In any event when civil conflict does occur, the demarcation between civil war and disturbances and tensions is not always clear, and the need to alleviate the suffering of victims remains, however the conflict may be categorised, as does the legal and moral obligation to comply with human rights and humanitarian standards.

In order to assist in identifying those situations in which it may offer its services to governments for humanitarian purposes, beyond the field of application of the Geneva Conventions and the Additional Protocols (which it is authorised to do under its Statute), the International Committee of the Red Cross proposed descriptive definitions of internal disturbances and tensions. These were published in the *International Review of the Red Cross*.[104] It also set out ten characteristics, some or all of which may be present in situations of disturbance or tension. These definitions, and the list, assist in distinguishing between armed conflict and internal disturbances and also in characterising the nature of such disturbances which are described as:

---

[104] No. 262 (Jan – Feb 1988).

II:2

> "situations in which there is no non-international armed conflict as such, but there exists a confrontation within the country, which is characterised by a certain seriousness or duration and which involves acts of violence. These latter can assume various forms, all the way from the spontaneous generation of acts of revolt to the struggle between more or less organised groups and the authorities in power. In these situations, which do not necessarily degenerate into open struggle, the authorities in power call upon extensive police forces, or even armed forces, to restore internal order. The high number of victims has made necessary the application of a minimum of humanitarian rules."

The term 'internal tensions' is used to refer to situations of serious tension (political, religious, racial, social, economic, etc.) or to sequels of an armed conflict or internal disturbance. The ten characteristics include the introduction of various forms of detention, large scale and long term; torture and ill-treatment of detainees; suppression of fundamental judicial guarantees; forced disappearances and other acts of violence such as hostage taking; repressive measures against families and associates of detainees; and generally spreading terror among the population.

It is clear that the behaviour of police and other state agencies and officials in times of disturbance and tension is regulated by human rights law, and that international humanitarian law is not legally applicable in such situations. However, one of the advantages that international humanitarian law has over international human rights law in protecting people in times of armed conflict is that the provisions of international humanitarian law are binding on each party to a conflict whereas international human rights law is binding on governments of states, and not on entities which do not exercise state power. A second advantage is that its fundamental principles and its specific provisions are directly relevant to the situation of victims of armed conflict. Furthermore human rights law can be limited through measures of derogation.

It is argued in the preceding chapter that the application of international humanitarian law, even in those situations where it may not be legally applicable, is a matter of good police practice, and that some of its principles should form an important element in the strategy and tactics of policing civil disturbances, especially when those disturbances are serious in terms of scale or intensity of violence. Examples of principles that are especially relevant in such circumstances are prohibitions of hostage taking, pillage, collective punishments and acts of terrorism; special measures to protect children, and to safeguard them from being recruited into armed groups or from taking part in violence; and requirements to respect and protect medical and religious personnel, and to assist them in the performance of their duties.

114

The protection of victims and the process of post-conflict reconciliation would both be enhanced if these and other provisions of international humanitarian law were to be applied by police when responding to internal disturbances and tensions.

Considerations of this nature have led to a number of individual initiatives to produce fundamental rules of humanity applicable in all circumstances, and particularly in times of internal disturbance and tension. An example of one such text is the Turku (Abo) Declaration of Minimum Humanitarian Standards[105] embodying rules based on non-derogable rights and prohibitions set out in human rights treaties, the Geneva Conventions of 1949 (particularly common article 3) and Additional Protocol II. It was proposed that its provisions would apply in all situations of internal disturbance or tension, and that they should be respected by, and applied to, all persons and groups in such situations without discrimination. The text contained a statement embodying a general principle of humane treatment and respect for human dignity, and prohibiting various acts common in situations of internal disorder and tension. These include such atrocities as murder, torture, mutilations, rape, hostage taking, involuntary disappearances, pillage, and acts of terrorism. In particular the Declaration of Minimum Humanitarian Standards required detainees to be kept in recognised places of detention; accurate information on their detention and whereabouts to be made available to family and lawyers; the right to effective remedies, including *habeas corpus*, as a means to determine whereabouts or state of health of detainees; and entitlement to take proceedings to test lawfulness of detention. These are precisely the types of safeguard that may be lost when a state derogates from its obligations under human rights treaties unless there is proper supervision of measures of derogation by treaty bodies in cases where this is possible.

The Draft Declaration was submitted in one of the reports of the Secretary General to the Commission on Human Rights. [106]

The principal rationale for seeking to apply elements of international humanitarian law to situations not amounting to armed conflict is to encourage a measure of humanity in circumstances where it is required but may be lacking. Those are the

---

[105] First published in the *International Review of the Red Cross*, No. 282 (May–June 1991).

[106] *See* UN Doc. E/CN.4/1995/116. *See also* Commission on Human Rights resolution 1998/29 on minimum humanitarian standards, which recalled its resolution 1997/21 and welcomed the Secretary General's analytical report E/CN.4/1998/87/Add.1 on the issues of fundamental standards of humanity. More recent reports of the Secretary General on this matter are E/CN.4/1999/92, E/CN.4/2000/94 and E/CN.4/2001/91. For the most recent report by the Secretary General on fundamental standards of humanity, *see* E/CN.4/2006/87, this report was submitted pursuant to Commission on Human Rights decision 2004/118.

II:2

very circumstances in which police may feel that it is justifiable and even necessary to violate human rights and to breach basic humanitarian standards. They feel this justification and this necessity even though such actions are a form of disorder in themselves, a very serious form of disorder by people who have a fundamental duty to maintain or restore order, and a form of disorder that provokes further disorder on the part of others. Police officials need to understand and apply principles and provisions of humanitarian law and human rights law in times of conflict as a matter of good professional practice, for lawless and inhumane policing exacerbates conflict, prolongs conflict, and creates more victims of conflict, including victims among police ranks. That is the measure of the importance and significance of the law of rights and the law of conflict to police officials.

(D) TERRORISM

Terrorism is a form of conflict, a strategy or tactic adopted to achieve various ends. These include spreading fear among civilian populations, de-stabilising political institutions, securing publicity for a cause, and provoking state authorities to react in ways that serve the ends of the terrorists. There is no internationally agreed definition of the term 'terrorism', but it is generally accepted that terrorist acts are acts of violence and intimidation intended to coerce a government or community. Other characteristics of terrorism include randomness, unpredictability, inhumanity, and targeting of civilians or non-combatants.

Terrorism takes different forms and, regardless of the types of groups that practice it, the methods adopted and the rationale offered, it is an entirely criminal activity, whether committed by non-state or state entities or actors. Its various causes, historical, cultural, religious, economic and political need to be understood and addressed internationally and nationally. To understand terrorism and its causes is not to condone it. Understanding is a starting point for effective action. As terrorists are criminals, primary responses to them must come from criminal justice and policing systems of states. It is unwise, unhelpful and incorrect to refer to action against terrorism as a 'war'. To do so is to meet the wishes of terrorists. It enhances their status and their causes for a state, with all of its political, constitutional and legal legitimacy and authority, to declare that it is waging a war against them. To declare a 'war on terror' is to misstate the nature of the action that is to be taken against it, and it is, in legal terms, technically incorrect.

It may be necessary, on occasions, to engage a terrorist group with military forces. Military operations are then, as always, subject to the provisions of international humanitarian law, international human rights law and domestic law. Furthermore, in some circumstances, military forces may support the actions of police. However, the primary counter-terrorist role lies with police and intelligence agencies. It is their responsibility to prevent terrorist crimes and, when they occur, to investigate them and bring the perpetrators to justice, with 'justice' being the operative word. The causes of terrorists are promoted when police and other security officials operate outside the law. It is one of the designs of terrorists to provoke this, and to change the very nature of the societies they threaten. For example, in response to acts of terrorism democratic states governed by the rule of law enact repressive laws thus redefining the nature of those states in ways that terrorists wish. Furthermore states, democratic and otherwise, exploit the need to respond to terrorism as a cloak for action against legitimate opposition and the legitimate exercise of democratic rights. Police and other security forces exceed their powers, act unlawfully and inhumanely, create 'martyrs', and alienate communities or sections of communities that might otherwise help them respond effectively to terrorists. Great institutions of state, communications media, and large sections of states' populations think, emote and behave in accordance with the wishes and intentions of small groups of criminal fanatics.

Acts of terror are prohibited in both international and non-international armed conflicts. Article 51(2) of 1977 Additional Protocol I prohibits acts or threats of violence the primary purpose of which is to spread terror among the civilian population. Article 4(2)(d) of 1977 Additional Protocol II prohibits, at any time and in any place whatsoever, acts of terrorism against those protected by article 4(1)[107] Regardless of whether or not they are committed during the course of armed conflict, some large-scale acts of terrorism, such as those perpetrated against the USA in September 2001, could be classified as crimes against humanity under the Rome Statue of the International Criminal Court. Article 7, paragraph 1 states that, for the purpose of the Statute, 'crime against humanity' means any of a number of listed acts when committed as part of a widespread or systematic attack directed against any civilian population, with knowledge of the attack. The listed acts include the crime of murder. Paragraph 2 states that for the purpose of paragraph 1: "attack directed against any civilian population" means a course of conduct involving the multiple commission of acts referred to in paragraph 1 against any civilian population, pursuant to or in furtherance of a state or organisational policy to commit such attack. Other terms, although not that of 'terrorism' are defined in paragraph 2.

Due to the international dimensions of terrorism, the responses of states to it need to be coordinated, assisted and reinforced, and global and regional organisations have taken steps to those ends. Twelve global and seven regional Conventions have been

---

[107] More specifically, all persons who do not take a direct part or who have ceased to take part in hostilities.

II:2

adopted to deal with various forms of terrorism,[108] and efforts are currently being made within the United Nations system to adopt a comprehensive convention on terrorism. The Security Council, the General Assembly, the Economic and Social Council and the Human Rights Commission of the United Nations have each adopted resolutions and taken other action to counter terrorism[109]

A Security Council resolution unanimously adopted in July 2005 called on the Secretary-General to work with Interpol to provide better tools to assist the Council's 1267 Committee, which is responsible for monitoring various actions directed against groups and individuals associated with Al-Qaida and the Taliban.[110] In response to this resolution, Interpol-United Nations Security Council Special Notices, distributed to all of Interpol's 184 member countries using the organisation's global police communications system, have been issued for targeted individuals. If the whereabouts of suspects named in these notices become known to police, the Interpol National Central Bureau in the country concerned is to be notified immediately so that competent authorities can take the necessary action to implement the UN sanctions against them.

In order to operate effectively, lawfully and humanely in response to terrorism and, indeed, every other challenge, police must be properly resourced, trained, equipped, commanded, controlled and led. Fully professional police agencies cooperating across national boundaries are an essential element in humanity's resistance to the barbarities of terrorism.

---

[108] *See e.g.*, International Convention for the Suppression of the Financing of Terrorism, adopted by the General Assembly of the United Nations on 9 December 1999; International Convention for the Suppression of Acts of Nuclear Terrorism, adopted by the General Assembly of the United Nations, at New York, on 13 April 2005; European Convention on the Suppression of Terrorism, at Strasbourg, on 27 January 1977; Arab Convention on the Suppression of Terrorism, signed at a meeting held at the General Secretariat of the League of Arab States, at Cairo, on 22 April 1998.

[109] For example, on 28 September 2001, acting under Chapter VII of the United Nations Charter (concerning threats to international peace and security), the Security Council adopted resolution 1373 (2001), reaffirming its unequivocal condemnation of the terrorist attacks which took place in New York, Washington, D.C. and Pennsylvania on 11 September 2001, and expressing its determination to prevent all such acts. The resolution also established the Counter-Terrorism Committee (CTC), made up of all 15 members of the Security Council. The CTC monitors the implementation of resolution 1373 by all States and tries to increase the capability of States to fight terrorism.

[110] United Nations Security Council resolution 1617 of 29 July 2005.

118

Chapter 3. The Right to Life

The present chapter deals with the right to life in so far as it concerns the use of force by police although, clearly, other issues such as abortion and voluntary euthanasia also arise in connection with this right. Indeed the Human Rights Committee, as can be seen below, favours a broader interpretation of the right. The next chapter deals with the wider aspects of the use of force by police, and the essential message of both chapters is that the legal protection of the right to life is enhanced by the lawful and expert use of force by police, and it is undermined by unlawful and arbitrary police action.

The right to life is a fundamental human right, if not the fundamental right. It is enshrined in the Universal Declaration of Human Rights, and in global and regional human rights treaties. The right to life is elaborated, developed and delineated in the jurisprudence of human rights institutions. It is also considered to be a rule of general international law binding on all states. Under international humanitarian law, murder and other forms of unlawful killing are prohibited in times of international and non-international armed conflict.

The Universal Declaration of Human Rights proclaims the right to life under article 3, and links it with other essential rights in the following terms: "Everyone has the right to life, liberty and security of person."

Although it is arguably the most fundamental of human rights, and is expressed unconditionally in the Universal Declaration, the right to life is not given absolute protection under treaty law whereas, for example, the prohibitions of torture and of slavery are protected absolutely. However, it is among that small number of human rights from which the treaties allow no derogation by states parties in time of public emergency, apart from one particular exception under the European Convention on Human Rights (see below).

Exceptions to the general rule that the right to life shall be protected are expressed in treaties to indicate those limited circumstances under which life may be taken by the state. Indeed, given that the Universal Declaration of Human Rights and the principal human rights treaties followed in the wake of atrocities visited upon people by murderous regimes just prior to and during the Second World War, the overriding purpose of those provisions expressing the right to life is to protect people from being unlawfully killed by the state.

It is pertinent to recall here the observations made in Chapter 2 of Part 1 on the entitlement of police officials to human rights, and particularly the right to life. Given the numbers of police officials killed in the course of their duties it is surprising that, apparently, none of these deaths have resulted in applications to treaty bodies claiming violations of the right to life of the officials. It is almost inevitable that defects in training, equipment, planning and command and control of police operations have led to loss of police lives. Deficiencies in these areas provide

II.3

at least *prima facie* grounds for seeking remedy or redress through a human rights treaty body.

(A) TREATY PROVISIONS

(a) International Covenant on Civil and Political Rights

The International Covenant on Civil and Political Rights expresses the right to life in article 6(1): "Every human being has the inherent right to life. This right shall be protected by law. No one shall be arbitrarily deprived of life."

The remainder of the article (paragraphs 2 to 6) contains provisions on the death penalty and on the crime of genocide. The Covenant does not prohibit capital punishment, and thus does not provide absolute protection for the right to life, but it does seek to ensure that it is imposed only for the most serious crimes and carried out pursuant to a final judgement rendered by a competent court. Furthermore it stipulates that there should be a right to seek pardon or commutation of the sentence, and that it should not be carried out on persons below eighteen years of age or on pregnant women.

The first paragraph of the article, in addition to proclaiming the inherent right to life, places obligations on states to enact laws guaranteeing the right, and to ensure that such laws are not applied so as to arbitrarily deprive an individual of life. The term 'arbitrary' has a wider meaning than 'unlawful' in that a killing may breach article 6 even though it is within the domestic law of a state. In its General Comment No. 6 (16) concerning article 6 of the Covenant,[111] the United Nations Human Rights Committee characterised the right to life as the supreme right from which no derogation is permitted under article 4 of the Covenant, even in a time of public emergency threatening the life of the nation, and described the protection against arbitrary deprivation of life as one of paramount importance.

The Committee considers that States parties should take measures not only to prevent and punish deprivation of life by criminal acts, but also to prevent arbitrary killing by their own security forces. It adds, in its General Comment, that the deprivation of life by the authorities of the State is a matter of the utmost gravity and that, therefore, the law must strictly control and limit the circumstances in which a person may be deprived of his life by such authorities. Whilst it is useful for some purposes to distinguish, as the Committee does, deprivation of life by criminal acts and arbitrary killings by security forces, it is important to remember that arbitrary

---

[111] Adopted by the Human Rights Committee at its 378th meeting (sixteenth session), held on 27 July 1982.

killings by security forces are also criminal acts. Nevertheless the message of the Committee is clear; deprivation of life by the State is an extremely grave matter to be strictly regulated under the law.

In the same General Comment, the Committee insists that State parties should take specific and effective measures to prevent the disappearance of individuals as this, too often, leads to arbitrary deprivation of life. States should establish effective facilities and procedures to investigate thoroughly cases of missing and disappeared persons in circumstances that may involve a violation of the right to life.

Finally, on the General Comment, the Committee notes that the expression 'inherent right to life' cannot properly be understood in a restrictive manner, and the protection of the right requires that States adopt positive measures. In this connection the Committee considers that it would be desirable for States parties to take all possible measures to reduce infant mortality and to increase life expectancy, especially in adopting measures to eliminate malnutrition and epidemics. The requirement to adopt positive measures has significant implications for police officials and police operations. For example, governments and police leaders should institute positive measures, which would include such matters as training and equipment, to protect the right to life of police. They should ensure that positive measures to protect the right to life are included in planning, strategies, tactics, and briefing for, and command and control of, all police operations involving the use of force by police. This requirement features, explicitly and implicitly, in much of the jurisprudence of treaty bodies described below.

(b) Convention on the Rights of the Child

The Convention on the Rights of the Child contains a number of measures to protect the right to life of children.[112] For example, article 6 requires States Parties to recognise that every child has the inherent right to life, and to ensure to the maximum extent possible the survival and development of the child. Article 38 contains a number of provisions to protect children in times of armed conflict. These include requiring States Parties to undertake to respect and ensure respect for rules of international humanitarian law applicable to them in armed conflicts which are relevant to the child, and to take all feasible measures to ensure that persons who have not attained the age of fifteen years do not take a direct part in hostilities. Under this Convention a child means every human being below the age of eighteen years unless, under the law applicable to the child, majority is attained earlier.

---

[112] Adopted by the General Assembly of the United Nations on 20 November 1989.

II.3

(c) Convention on the Prevention and Punishment of the Crime of Genocide

The provisions of the Genocide Convention should also be noted.[113] Contracting Parties confirm that genocide, whether committed in time of peace or in time of war, is a crime under international law which they undertake to prevent and punish. Clearly, measures designed to prevent the crime of genocide are protective of the right to life.

Under the Convention, genocide means any of a number of specified acts committed with intent to destroy, in whole or in part, a national, ethnical, racial or religious group. The specified acts include killing members of the group, causing serious bodily or mental harm to members of the group, and deliberately inflicting on the group conditions of life calculated to bring about its physical destruction in whole or in part.

(d) African Charter on Human and Peoples' Rights

The African Charter[114] protects the right to life, and prohibits arbitrary deprivation of life in one succinct paragraph: "Human beings are inviolable. Every human being shall be entitled to respect for his life and the integrity of his person. No one may be arbitrarily deprived of this right."[115]

(e) American Convention on Human Rights

The scope of article 4 of the American Convention[116] is similar to that of article 6 of the International Covenant on Civil and Political Rights. The right to life and the prohibition on arbitrary deprivation of life are expressed in paragraph 1 in the following terms: "Every person has the right to have his life respected. This right shall be protected by law, and, in general, from the moment of conception. No one shall be arbitrarily deprived of his life."

The remainder of the article (paragraphs 2 to 6) contains provisions on the death penalty similar to those of the International Covenant on Civil and Political Rights, with the additional requirement that it shall not be inflicted for political offences.

---

[113] Approved by the General Assembly of the United Nations on 9 December 1948.
[114] Adopted by the Assembly of Heads of State and Government of the Organisation of African Unity on 27 June 1981.
[115] Article 4.
[116] Signed by States Members of the Organisation of American States on 22 November 1969.

(f) European Convention on Human Rights

Under the European Convention on Human Rights, the right to life is expressed in article 2(1) as follows: "Everyone's right to life shall be protected by law. No one shall be deprived of his life intentionally save in the execution of a sentence of a court following his conviction of a crime for which this penalty is provided by law." The second sentence of this paragraph is now redundant as there are two Protocols to the Convention concerning the abolition of that penalty, open to states parties to the Convention. Protocol No. 6 proclaims that the death penalty shall be abolished and that no one shall be condemned to such penalty or executed, but the death penalty may be applied in time of war. Protocol No. 13 extends the abolition of the death penalty to all circumstances.

In contrast to the International Covenant and the other two regional treaties, the European Convention makes no specific reference to arbitrary deprivation of life. However it does, in the second paragraph, set out those specific circumstances under which the taking of life will not contravene the Convention "when it results from the use of force which is no more than absolutely necessary". Those circumstances are:

"a. in defence of any person from unlawful violence;

b. in order to effect a lawful arrest or to prevent the escape of a person lawfully detained;

c. in action lawfully taken for the purpose of quelling a riot or insurrection."

In making these exceptions the article purports to define exhaustively permissible grounds for deprivation of life. No other grounds for deprivation of life by the state are permitted under the Convention save that allowed for under article 15. This article, which is referred to in Chapter 1 of this part, allows a High Contracting Party to take measures derogating from its obligations under the Convention in time of war or other public emergency threatening the life of the nation. In prohibiting derogation from, *inter alia*, article 2 of the Convention, article 15 only makes an exception for "deaths resulting from lawful acts of war".

It is important to note at this stage that whilst use of force may be justifiable in the circumstances set out in paragraph 2 of the article, its use must be both proportionate and necessary as required by the term "the use of force which is no more than absolutely necessary". The terminology of the article, as it is applied to specific cases, is considered under the next sub-heading.

II.3

(B) JURISPRUDENCE OF TREATY BODIES

The jurisprudence of the various treaty bodies includes a great number of cases on the right to life, and much of this has its origins in situations where police and other state officials used force. A few representative cases are considered here in order to expand upon what has already been said about the right, and to illustrate various aspects of the exercise, and also the abuse, of the power to use force.

(a) Arbitrary Deprivation of Life

Most of the cases selected for inclusion under subsequent sub-headings are also examples of arbitrary deprivations of life. However, an example of an egregious arbitrary deprivation of life can be found in the case *John Khemraadi Baboeram et al.* v. *Suriname*,[117] in which eight prominent people were arrested in their homes in Paramaribo, the capital of Suriname by Suriname military police and subjected to violence. Following an announcement by State authorities that a coup attempt had been foiled and that a number of detainees had been killed while trying to escape, their bodies were delivered to a mortuary. The bodies were seen by family members and other people who testified that they showed numerous wounds. Neither autopsies nor official investigations into the killings had taken place.

The Human Rights Committee observed that the right enshrined in article 6, paragraph 1, of the International Covenant on Civil and Political Rights was the supreme right of the human being and that the deprivation of life by the authorities of a State party was a matter of utmost gravity. This followed from the article as a whole. In particular, it was the reason for the provision in paragraph 2 of the article that the death penalty might be imposed only for the most serious crimes. The requirements that the right should be protected by law and that no one should be arbitrarily deprived of his life meant that the law had strictly to control and limit the circumstances in which a person might be deprived of his life by State authorities. It was evident from the fact that 15 prominent persons, including the victims in the present case, lost their lives as a result of the deliberate actions of the military police, that the deprivation of life was intended. The Committee concluded that the victims were arbitrarily deprived of their lives contrary to article 6, paragraph 1.

As the State party had failed to submit any evidence proving that these persons were shot whilst trying to escape, the Committee urged the State to take effective steps to investigate the killings; to bring to justice any persons found to be responsible for

---

[117] United Nations, *Official Records of the General Assembly, Fortieth Session, Supplement No. 40* (A/40/40), annex X, communications No. 146/ 1983, No.148/1983, No. 149/1983, No. 150/1983, No. 151/1983, No. 152/1983, No. 153/1983 and No. 154/1983, views adopted on 4 April 1985.

the death of the victims; to pay compensation to the surviving families; and to ensure that the right to life was duly protected in Suriname.

In the case *Villagrán Morales et al.* v. *Guatemala*, the *"Street Children"* case,[118] the five victims were killed, four of them after abduction and torture. In coming to its conclusions, the Inter-American Court of Human Rights observed that there was abundant concurring evidence that the abduction of four of the youths was perpetrated by State agents and, more specifically, by members of the State's national police force.

The Court observed that the right to life was a fundamental human right and that the exercise of this right was essential for the exercise of all other human rights. The right to life included not only the right of every human being not to be arbitrarily deprived of his life, but also the right not to be prevented from having access to the conditions guaranteeing a dignified existence. States had the obligation to guarantee the creation of conditions required for violations of this basic right not to occur and, in particular, the duty to prevent its agents from violating it.

In respect of the latter point the Court referred to general comment No. 6 (16) by the Human Rights Committee on article 6 of the International Covenant on Civil and Political Rights in which, it will be recalled, the Committee observed that States parties to the Covenant should take measures not only to prevent and punish deprivation of life by criminal acts, but also to prevent arbitrary killing by their own security forces. It went on to say that the deprivation of life by authorities of the State was a matter of utmost gravity and that the State had strictly to control and limit the circumstances in which a person might be deprived of his life by such authorities.

Finding a violation of the right to life of the five victims, the Court stated that it wished to indicate the particular gravity of the case. The victims were youths, three of them children. The conduct of the State not only violated the express provision of article 4 of the American Convention on Human Rights, but also numerous international instruments that devolved to the State the obligation to adopt special measures of protection and assistance for the children within its jurisdiction.

---

[118] *Supra* note 43.

II.3

(b) **Necessity and Proportionality**

The case *María Fanny Suárez de Guerrero* v. *Colombia*[119] is similar to the two cases cited above in the shocking and arbitrary way in which a number of lives were taken by the state. However, in this early case, the Human Rights Committee made some important observations on the principles of necessity and proportionality.

This case concerned a complaint submitted on behalf of Mr. De Guerrero in respect of the shooting of his wife and six other people by police who raided a house in Bogota. The police mounted an operation because it was suspected that a kidnap victim was being detained at the house, although the victim was not found by them when they arrived.

The police waited in the house for people suspected of being involved in the kidnapping. Eventually seven people arrived at different times. They were each shot dead by police. According to witnesses, the victims were not given the opportunity to surrender and neither were they armed. Furthermore, investigations failed to link the victims with the kidnapping crime.

The Committee eventually concluded that the police action had been disproportionate to the requirements of law enforcement and that Mrs. de Guerrero has been deprived of her life arbitrarily in contravention of article 6(1) of the International Covenant on Civil and Political Rights. On the question of necessity the Committee commented:

> "There is no evidence that the action of the police was necessary in their own defence or that of others, or that it was necessary to effect the arrest or prevent the escape of the persons concerned."

Another significant observation made by the Committee in this case was that the victims were no more than suspects of a crime. Their killing by the police deprived them of all the protections of due process of law laid down by the Covenant.

The concept of proportionality was one of the matters considered by the Inter-American Court of Human Rights in *Neira Allegría et al.* v. *Peru.*[120] The case arose out of the responses of the Peruvian republican guard, navy and police, to a serious riot in a prison located on an island. Whilst endorsing the right and duty of the State

---

[119] United Nations, *Official Records of the General Assembly, Thirty-seventh Session, Supplement No. 40* (A/37/40), annex XI, communication No. 45/1979, views adopted on 31 March 1982.

[120] Inter-American Court of Human Rights, Series C: *Decisions and Judgments*, No. 20 (1995), judgment of 19 January 1995.

to suppress the riot, the Court ultimately concluded that there had been arbitrary deprivation of life as a consequence of the disproportionate use of force by security forces in the operation. This included the demolition by explosives of a building occupied by prisoners.

Although those detained in the prison were highly dangerous and in fact armed, it was the opinion of the Court that these circumstances were not reasons sufficient to justify the amount of force used. It insisted that, whilst the State had the right and duty to guarantee its security, the power of the State was not unlimited. It could not resort to any means to attain its ends. The State was subject to law and morality, and disrespect for human dignity could not serve as the basis for any of its actions.

The term 'absolutely necessary' is used to qualify the circumstances in which the use of force resulting in death may not contravene article 2 of the European Convention on Human Rights. In the case *Stewart* v. *the United Kingdom*,[121] the European Commission on Human Rights clarified the meaning of this term and linked it to the principle of proportionality. In fact, the Commission's pronouncements on the interpretation of article 2 of the Convention in this case have been referred to by the European Court of Human Rights in subsequent judgements. Having reviewed the wording of article 2, and the jurisprudence of both the Commission and the Court, it was the Commission's opinion that the text of this article, read as a whole, indicated that paragraph 2 did not primarily define situations where it was permitted intentionally to kill an individual, but it defined the situations where it was permissible to use force which might result, as the unintended outcome of the use of force, in the deprivation of life.

The use of force, however, had to be no more than absolutely necessary for the achievement of one of the purposes set out in article 2, paragraph 2 (a), (b) or (c), of the Convention. In this respect, the Commission observed that the use of the term 'absolutely necessary' in that paragraph indicated that a stricter and more compelling test of necessity had to be employed from that normally applicable when determining whether State action was necessary in a democratic society under paragraph 2 of articles 8 to 11.[122] In particular, the force used had to be strictly proportionate to the achievement of the aims set out in article 2, paragraph 2 (a), (b) and (c). In assessing whether the use of force was strictly proportionate, regard had to be had to the nature of the aim pursued, the dangers to life and limb inherent in

---

[121] European Commission of Human Rights, *Decisions and Reports*, No. 39 (1984), p. 162, application No. 10044/82, decision of 10 July 1984.
[122] Articles 8–11 protect, respectively, the right to respect for private and family life; freedom of thought, conscience and religion; freedom of expression; and freedom of assembly and association.

II.3

the situation and the degree of the risk that the force employed might result in loss of life.

Disproportionate use of force was a significant factor in the findings of the European Court of Human Rights in the case *Güleç* v. *Turkey*.[123] This case concerned the killing of a 15 year old boy by security forces during an operation to quell a violent demonstration in a town in Eastern Turkey. In its judgement, the European Court of Human Rights commented on the security forces' tactics and on the lack of equipment that would have enabled them to adopt a graduated and proportionate response to the situation.

The European Commission of Human Rights concluded that the security forces had deployed an armoured vehicle equipped with a machine gun which had opened fire in the street where the demonstration was taking place, either in the air or at the ground, in order to disperse the demonstrators. The young victim had been hit by a fragment of a bullet, fired from the armoured vehicle, which had ricocheted off the ground or a wall. However, the Commission did not believe that the machine gun, a combat weapon with a very rapid rate of fire, had been used to kill demonstrators intentionally. It accepted that the form the demonstration had taken was such that it could be described as a riot within the meaning of article 2, paragraph 2 (c), of the Convention, but it expressed the view that the use of a combat weapon during a demonstration for the purpose of restoring order could not be regarded as proportionate.

The Court accepted the facts as set out by the Commission, and it accepted that the demonstration was far from peaceful, as was evidenced by the damage to property in the town and the injuries sustained by some members of the security forces. The Court observed that, confronted with serious acts of violence, the security forces, which were not present in sufficient strength, called for reinforcements, and at least two armoured vehicles were deployed. Whereas the driver of one such vehicle asserted that he had fired into the air, several witnesses said that shots had been fired at the crowd. Although this allegation was denied by the Government, the Court noted that it was corroborated by the fact that nearly all the wounded demonstrators were hit in the legs. This would have been perfectly consistent with ricochet wounds from bullets with a downward trajectory which could have been fired from the turret of an armoured vehicle.

The Court, like the Commission, accepted that the use of force might have been justified under article 2, paragraph 2 (c), of the Convention. However, it insisted, a

---

[123] European Court of Human Rights, *Reports of Judgments and Decisions*, 1998-IV, p. 1698, application No. 21593/93, judgment of 27 July 1998.

balance had to be struck between the aim pursued and the means employed to achieve it. The security forces had used a very powerful weapon, because they apparently did not have truncheons, riot shields, water cannon, rubber bullets or tear gas. The Court stated that the lack of such equipment was all the more incomprehensible and unacceptable, because this province of Turkey, as the Government had pointed out, was in a region where a state of emergency had been declared and where, at the material time, disorder could have been expected.

The Court concluded that in the circumstances of the case the force used to disperse the demonstrators which caused the death of the victim was not absolutely necessary within the meaning of article 2 of the Convention. It also concluded that there had been a breach of that article on account of the lack of a thorough investigation into the circumstances of his death.

(c) Disappearances

Two cases that had their origins in disappearances, dealt with respectively by the Human Rights Committee and the Inter-American Court of Human Rights, are selected for inclusion here as significant examples of this criminal and inhumane practice.

In the case *Herrera Rubio* v. *Colombia*[124] the author of the complaint claimed that, following his arrest by members of the Colombian armed forces on suspicion of being a 'guerrillero', he was tortured by the military authorities who also threatened to kill his parents unless he signed a confession. These people were, in fact, subsequently murdered.

In considering the application the Human Rights Committee referred to its General Comment No. 6 (16), providing, *inter alia*, that States parties should take specific and effective measures to prevent the disappearance of individuals. Furthermore, they should establish effective facilities and procedures to investigate thoroughly, cases of missing and disappeared persons in circumstances which might involve a violation of the right to life.

Responding to submissions by the State party on investigations carried out into the deaths, the Committee observed that the investigations appeared to have been inadequate in the light of the State party's obligations under article 2 of the International Covenant on Civil and Political Rights. According to this article, each

---

[124] United Nations, *Official Records of the General Assembly, Forty-third Session, Supplement No. 40* (A/43/40), annex VII, sect. B, communication No. 161/1983, views adopted on 2 November 1987.

II.3

State party undertakes, *inter alia*, to respect and ensure to all individuals within its territory and subject to its jurisdiction the rights recognised in the Covenant; to adopt laws or other measures to give effect to the rights recognised in the Covenant; and to provide an effective remedy to any person whose rights or freedoms have been violated.

An important element of the obligations under article 2 is that the protection of Covenant rights must be effective, and this requires a variety of measures. Effective protection of the right to life includes effective protection against abduction, torture and killing by forces of the State, and effective remedy requires an effective investigation. The Committee found a violation of article 6 of the Covenant, because the State party had failed to take appropriate measures to prevent the disappearance and subsequent killings of the parents of the complainant. It also found that he had been subjected to torture and ill-treatment during his detention, in violation of articles 7 and 10(1).

The case *Velásquez Rodríguez* v. *Honduras*[125] concerned the disappearance of a Honduran student in which the Inter-American Court of Human Rights found that the following facts had been proven in the proceedings: a practice of disappearances carried out or tolerated by Honduran officials existed between 1981 and 1984; the victim in this case had disappeared at the hands of or with the acquiescence of those officials within the framework of that practice; and the Government of Honduras had failed to guarantee the human rights affected by that practice.

As to the phenomenon of disappearances, the Court made a number of noteworthy observations. Disappearances were not new in the history of human rights violations. However, their systematic and repeated nature and their use not only for causing certain individuals to disappear, either briefly or permanently, but also as a means of creating a general state of anguish, insecurity and fear, was a recent phenomenon. Although this practice existed virtually worldwide, it had occurred with exceptional intensity in Latin America in the few years preceding this case.

The phenomenon of disappearances was a complex form of human rights violation that had to be understood and confronted in an integral fashion. In this context, the Court referred to the establishment of the Working Group on Enforced or Involuntary Disappearances, set up in 1980 by the United Nations Commission on Human Rights. The Court observed that this was a clear demonstration of general censure and repudiation of the practice of disappearances. This phenomenon had already received world attention within the United Nations. The practice of

---

[125] Inter-American Court of Human Rights, Series C: *Decisions and Judgments*, No. 4 (1988), petition No. 7920, judgment of 29 July 1988.

disappearances should be stopped, the victims reappear and those responsible be punished.

Without question, the Court observed, the State had the right and duty to guarantee its security. It was also indisputable that all societies suffered some deficiencies in their legal orders. However, regardless of the seriousness of certain actions and the culpability of the perpetrators of certain crimes, the State's power was not unlimited, nor could the State resort to any means to attain its ends. The State was subject to law and morality, and disrespect for human dignity could not serve as the basis for any State action.

The forced disappearance of human beings was a multiple and continuous violation of many rights under the Convention that the States parties were obliged to respect and guarantee. The kidnapping of a person was an arbitrary deprivation of liberty, an infringement of a detainee's right to be taken without delay before a judge and to invoke the appropriate procedures to review the legality of the arrest, all in violation of article 7 recognising the right to personal liberty.

Moreover, prolonged isolation and deprivation of communication were in themselves cruel and inhuman treatment, harmful to the psychological and moral integrity of the person and a violation of the right of any detainee to respect for his inherent dignity as a human being. Such treatment, therefore, violated article 5 of the Convention recognising the right to the integrity of the person. Investigations into the practice of disappearances, and the testimony of victims who had regained their liberty, showed that those disappeared often were subjected to merciless treatment, including all types of indignities, torture and other cruel, inhuman and degrading treatment, in violation of the right to physical integrity recognised in article 5.

The practice of disappearances often involved secret execution without trial, followed by concealment of the body to eliminate any material evidence of the crime and to ensure the impunity of those responsible. This was a flagrant violation of the right to life, recognised in article 4 of the Convention.

The Court concluded that the practice of disappearances, in addition to directly violating many provisions of the Convention, constituted a radical breach of the treaty in that it showed a crass abandonment of the values emanating from the concept of human dignity and of the most basic principles of the Inter-American system and the Convention. The existence of this practice, moreover, evinced a disregard of the duty to organise the State in such a manner as to guarantee the rights recognised in the Convention.

II.3

Ultimately, the Court declared that Honduras had violated its obligations to respect and to ensure the right to personal liberty set forth in article 7 of the American Convention on Human Rights, its obligations to respect and to ensure the right to humane treatment set forth in article 5 and its obligation to ensure the right to life set forth in article 4, all read in conjunction with article 1, paragraph 1, of the Convention.

(d) Command and Control of Operations Involving the Use of Force

Given the prohibition of arbitrary deprivation of life and the concomitant obligations on states to take positive steps to protect the right to life, it is unsurprising that treaty bodies have closely scrutinised the command and control of police operations involving the use of force that have resulted in loss of life.

A landmark case in this respect is *McCann et al.* v. *United Kingdom*,[126] which arose out of the killing of three terrorist suspects by four soldiers of the S.A.S. Regiment of the British Army on Sunday 6 March 1988 in Gibraltar.

Towards the end of 1987, British authorities received intelligence to the effect that an explosive device concealed in a car was to be detonated at a public place in Gibraltar where a changing of the guard ceremony was to take place on 8 March 1988. Although military personnel were deployed it was, in fact, a police operation to arrest and detain the suspects. Arrest procedures had been practised by the soldiers, and efforts had been made to find a suitable place in Gibraltar to detain the suspects after their arrest.

The case produced a long and detailed judgement from the European Court of Human Rights concerning the right to life and the use of force. In coming to its decision the Court scrutinised carefully not only whether the force used by the soldiers was strictly proportionate to the aim of protecting persons against unlawful violence, but also whether the anti-terrorist operation was planned and controlled by the authorities so as to minimise, to the greatest extent possible, recourse to lethal force. The reasoning behind the Court's decision in this case is noteworthy, and hugely important to those planning, and commanding and controlling operations involving the use of force. The Court placed the responsibility for violations of the right to life squarely on those in command of the operation.

Concerning the soldiers, the Court accepted that they honestly believed, in the light of the information they had been given, that it was necessary to shoot the suspects in

---

[126] Publications of the European Court of Human Rights, Series A: *Judgments and Decisions*, vol. 324 (1996), application No. 18984/91, judgement of 27 September 1995.

order to prevent them from detonating a bomb and causing serious loss of life. The actions which they took, in obedience to superior orders, were thus perceived by them as absolutely necessary in order to safeguard innocent lives.

The Court considered that the use of force by agents of the state, in pursuit of one of the aims delineated in article 2 paragraph 2, of the Convention, might be justified under this provision where it was based on an honest belief, perceived for good reasons to be valid at the time but subsequently turned out to be mistaken. To hold otherwise would be to impose an unrealistic burden on the state and its law enforcement personnel in the execution of their duty, perhaps to the detriment of their lives and those of others. It followed that, having regard to the dilemma confronting the authorities in the circumstances of the case, the actions of the soldiers did not, in themselves, give rise to a violation of article 2.

The question arose, however, whether the anti-terrorist operation as a whole was controlled and organised in a manner that respected the requirements of article 2 and whether the information and instructions given to the soldiers, in effect rendering inevitable the use of lethal force, took adequately into consideration the right to life of the three suspects. In considering this question, the Court examined the various strategic and tactical decisions taken by the authorities prior to and during the anti-terrorist operation.

Concerning the briefing attended by the soldiers, the Court noted that it was considered likely that the attack would be by way of a large car bomb, and a number of key assessments were made. In particular, it was thought that the bomb would be detonated by a radio-control device; that the detonation could be effected by the pressing of a button; that it was likely that the suspects would detonate the bomb if challenged; and that they would be armed and would be likely to use their arms if confronted. In the event, all of these crucial assumptions, apart from the terrorists' intentions to carry out an attack, turned out to be erroneous.

In fact, the Court observed, it appeared that insufficient allowances had been made for other assumptions. For example, since the bombing was not expected until 8 March when the changing of the guard ceremony was to take place, there was equally the possibility that the three terrorists were on a reconnaissance mission when they were killed on 6 March. While this was a factor which was briefly considered, it did not appear to have been regarded as a serious possibility.

In the absence of sufficient allowances being made for alternative possibilities and the definite reporting of the existence of a car bomb that, according to the assessments made, could be detonated at the press of a button, a series of working hypotheses were conveyed to the soldiers as certainties, thereby making the use of

II.3

lethal force almost unavoidable. Furthermore, the Court observed, the failure to make provision for a margin of error also had to be considered in combination with the training of the soldiers to continue shooting once they opened fire until the suspect was dead.

Against this background, the authorities were bound by their obligation to respect the right to life of the suspects to exercise the greatest of care in evaluating the information at their disposal before transmitting it to soldiers whose use of firearms automatically involved shooting to kill. Their reflex action in this vital respect lacked the degree of caution in the use of firearms to be expected from law enforcement personnel in a democratic society, even when dealing with dangerous terrorist suspects. It stood in marked contrast to the standard of care reflected in the instructions in the use of firearms by the police which emphasised the legal responsibilities of the individual officer in the light of conditions prevailing at the moment of engagement. This failure by the authorities also suggested a lack of appropriate care in the control and organisation of the arrest operation.

In sum the Court was not persuaded that the killing of the three suspects constituted the use of force not more than absolutely necessary in defence of persons from unlawful violence within the meaning of article 2, paragraph 2 (a), of the Convention. Accordingly, the Court held, by 10 votes to 9, that there had been a violation of article 2 of the Convention.

The *McCann* judgement has been cited subsequently in other cases where the planning, and command and control of operations involving the use of lethal force has been an issue in right to life cases.

(e) Investigations into Killings by State Officials

Another important feature of the *McCann* Case was the observation of the European Court of Human Rights that a general legal prohibition of arbitrary killings by the agents of the state would be ineffective if no procedure existed for reviewing the lawfulness of the use of lethal force by state authorities. The Court pointed out that the obligation to protect the right to life read in conjunction with the state's general duty under article 1 of the European Convention on Human Rights to secure to everyone within their jurisdiction the rights and freedoms defined in the Convention, requires by implication that there should be some form of effective official investigation when individuals have been killed as a result of the use of force by agents of the state. Having reviewed the adequacy of the Inquest proceedings in the *McCann* case, the Court concluded that there had been no violation of the right to life on this ground. However, in subsequent cases the Court has found violations of the right to life because of the minimal and defective nature of investigations into killings by state officials.

The *McCann* case was cited, on this and other matters, in *McKerr* v. *United Kingdom*[127] where the applicant alleged that his father had been shot and killed by police officers, and the Court held that there had been a violation of the right to life because of a failure of the State to conduct a proper investigation into the circumstances of the death. The judgment in this case was delivered on the same date as the judgments in three similar cases against the United Kingdom. The Court noted that, under article 2 of the Convention, investigations capable of leading to the identification and punishment of those responsible had to be undertaken into allegations of unlawful killings. It observed that proper procedures for ensuring accountability of State agents were indispensable in maintaining public confidence and meeting the legitimate concerns that might arise from the use of lethal force.

The case *Nachova and Others* v. *Bulgaria*,[128] is noteworthy for a number of reasons but primarily, in this context, because the European Court of Human Rights Court emphasised that the general obligation on states to conduct an effective investigation in cases of deprivation of life under article 2 of the European Convention on Human Rights had to be discharged without discrimination, as required by article 14. Following a judgment by the Court sitting as chamber, the final judgment was delivered by the Court sitting as a grand chamber.

The case concerned the killing of two men of Roma origin, conscripts in the Bulgarian army, by a military police officer in an arrest operation. The Court found that the State was responsible for the deprivation of life of the victims, in violation of article 2 of the Convention. Firearms were used to arrest people who were suspected of non-violent offences, were not armed and did not pose any threat to the arresting officers or others. The Court expressed grave concern that the relevant regulations on the use of firearms by the military police effectively permitted lethal force to be used when arresting a member of the armed forces for even the most minor offence. Furthermore, the violation was aggravated by the fact that excessive firepower was used, and the State was responsible for the failure to plan and control the arrest operation in a manner compatible with article 2. Under the same article, the Court also found a violation of the State's obligation to investigate deprivations of life effectively.

---

[127] Ibid., 2001-III, p. 475, application No. 28883/95, judgment of 4 May 2001.
[128] European Court of Human Rights, applications No. 43577/98 and No. 43579/98, judgment 6 July 2005.

II.3

This case is, however, particularly significant because of the Court's pronouncements on the prohibition of discrimination set forth in article 14 of the Convention. The applicants alleged that the events leading to the deaths of the victims constituted an act of racial violence. The Court held that there had been no violation of article 14 of the Convention, in conjunction with article 2, in that respect because it could not exclude the possibility that the police officer was simply adhering strictly to the regulations and would have acted as he did in any similar context, regardless of ethnicity. However, the Court held that there had been a violation in respect of these provisions in that the authorities failed to investigate possible racist motives behind the events.

The Court endorsed the analysis in the chamber's judgment of the procedural obligation of States parties to investigate possible racist motives for acts of violence. When investigating violent incidents and, in particular, deaths at the hands of State agents, State authorities had the additional duty to take all reasonable steps to unmask any racist motive and to establish whether or not ethnic hatred or prejudice might have played a role in the events. Failing to do so and treating racially induced violence and brutality on an equal footing with cases that had no racist overtones would be to turn a blind eye to the specific nature of acts that were particularly destructive of fundamental rights.

The Court also reiterated an observation of great significance to police officials and police agencies. In order to maintain public confidence in their law enforcement machinery, States parties had to ensure that in the investigation of incidents involving the use of force, a distinction was made both in their legal systems and in practice between cases of excessive use of force and of racist killing.

The Human Rights Committee has also insisted on investigations into killings by state officials, and the Inter-American Court of Human Rights has referred to the obligation on states to investigate any violation of the American Convention. For example it will be recalled that in *Baboeram et al* v. *Suriname* the Human Rights Committee urged the State to take effective steps to investigate the killings, to bring to justice any persons found to be responsible for the death of the victims, to pay compensation to the surviving families, and to ensure that the right to life was duly protected in Suriname. In the *Villigran Morales* case the Inter-American Court of Human Rights stated that it was clear from article 1(1) of the American Convention on Human Rights that the State is obliged to investigate and punish any violation of the rights embodied in the Convention in order to guarantee such rights.

Clearly this requirement for reviewing the lawfulness of the use of lethal force by state authorities has implications for police leaders in terms of ensuring the proper recording and documentation of intelligence and of the planning stages of operations; of briefing instructions; of accounts of the actual conduct of operations; and of the steps taken at the conclusion of operations to search for and safeguard forensic and other forms of evidence relating to the taking of life by state officials. The requirement also obliges police to ensure that an effective investigation into such killings is carried out when they have the responsibility for the investigation, and to cooperate fully with investigators when they do not.

(f) Protection of the Right to Life

Whilst the right to life is protected under article 6 of the International Covenant on Civil and Political Rights, the Human Rights Committee has found violations of article 9, paragraph 1 of the Covenant, which protects the right to liberty and security of person, where there have been threats to life. The victim in *Delgado Páez* v. *Colombia*,[129] having received death threats and been attacked personally, left his country, Colombia, and obtained political asylum in France. The Human Rights Committee reasoned that the concept of right to security did not apply only to situations of formal deprivation of liberty, even though it was expressed in an article addressing such situations. The Committee argued that States could not be allowed to ignore known threats to the life of persons within their jurisdiction just because he or she was not arrested or detained. States parties to the Covenant had a duty to take reasonable and appropriate measures to protect people whose lives had been threatened. The Committee found that the State party had not taken, or had been unable to take, appropriate measures to ensure Mr. Delgado's right to security of his person under article 9, paragraph 1, of the Covenant.

This reasoning was subsequently followed in other cases, including in *Chongwe* v. *Zambia*,[130] where the victim received a life threatening wound when shot by police whilst attending a political rally. The Committee observed that article 6, paragraph 1, of the Covenant entailed an obligation of a State party to protect the right to life of all persons within its territory and subject to its jurisdiction. In this case the author had claimed, and the State party failed to contest before the Committee, that the State party authorised the use of lethal force without lawful reasons, which could have led to the killing of the author. In the circumstances, the Committee found that the State party had not acted in accordance with its obligation to protect the author's right to life under article 6, paragraph 1.

---

[129] United Nations, *Official Records of the General Assembly, Forty-fifth Session, Supplement No. 40* (A/45/40), vol. II, annex IX, sect. D, communication No. 195/1985, views adopted on 12 July 1990.
[130] Ibid., *Fifty-sixth Session, Supplement No. 40* (A/56/40), vol. II, annex X, sect. K, Communication No. 821/1998, views adopted on 25 October 2000.

II.3

The Committee recalled its jurisprudence that article 9, paragraph 1, of the Covenant protected the right to security of person also outside the context of formal deprivation of liberty. The interpretation of article 9 did not allow a State party to ignore threats to the personal security of non-detained persons subject to its jurisdiction. In the present case, it appeared that persons acting in an official capacity within the Zambian police forces shot at the author, wounded him and almost killed him. The Committee concluded that the author's right to security of person under article 9, paragraph 1, had been violated.

The Human Rights Committee has considered a number of cases that concern the duty of the State to protect the right to life of detainees. For example, the victim in *Rickly Burrell* v. *Jamaica*[131] was awaiting execution at a prison when he was shot and killed by a warder during a prison disturbance in which some warders had been taken hostage by prisoners. The State party acknowledged that Mr. Burrell's death was the unfortunate result of confusion on the part of the warders. They panicked when seeing some of their colleagues being threatened by the inmates. The report submitted by the State party to the Committee acknowledged that the shooting continued after the warders were rescued. In the circumstances, the Committee concluded that the State party had failed in taking effective measures to protect Mr. Burrell's life, in violation of article 6, paragraph 1, of the Covenant.

In *Osman* v. *the United Kingdom*,[132] the European Court of Human Rights set out the very specific circumstances in which the authorities are required to take operational measures to protect the right to life. The case concerned the killing of a father and the wounding of his son by a schoolteacher who had formed an attachment to the boy.

The Court noted that the first sentence of article 2, paragraph 1, of the European Convention on Human Rights enjoined the State not only to refrain from the intentional and unlawful taking of life, but also to take appropriate steps to safeguard the lives of those within its jurisdiction. It pointed out that the State's obligation in this respect extended beyond its primary duty to secure the right to life by putting in place effective criminal law provisions to deter the commission of offences against the person, backed up by law enforcement machinery for the prevention, suppression and sanctioning of breaches of such provisions. Accordingly, article 2 might also imply, in certain well-defined circumstances, a positive obligation on the

---

[131] Ibid., *Fifty-first Session, Supplement No. 40* (A/51/40), vol. II, annex VIII, sect. R, communication No. 546/1993, views adopted on 18 July 1996.

[132] European Court of Human Rights, *Reports of Judgments and Decisions*, 1998-VIII, p. 3124, application No. 23452/94 judgment of 28 October 1998.

authorities to take preventive operational measures to protect an individual whose life was at risk from the criminal acts of another individual.

However, bearing in mind the difficulties involved in policing modern societies, the unpredictability of human conduct and the operational choices that had to be made in terms of priorities and resources, the Court pointed out that such an obligation had to be interpreted in a way not imposing an impossible or disproportionate burden on the authorities. Accordingly, not every claimed risk to life could entail for the authorities a requirement under the Convention to take operational measures to prevent that risk from materialising. Another relevant consideration for the Court was the need to ensure that the police exercised their powers in a manner which fully respected the due process and other guarantees which legitimately placed restraints on the scope of their action to investigate crime and bring offenders to justice, including the guarantees in articles 5 and 8 of the Convention.[133]

The Court stated that, where there was an allegation that the authorities had violated their positive obligation to protect the right to life in the context of their duty to prevent and suppress offences against the person, a number of points had to be established. The Court had to be satisfied that the authorities knew or ought to have known at the time of the existence of a real and immediate risk to the life of an identified individual or individuals from the criminal acts of a third party and that they failed to take measures within the scope of their powers which, judged reasonably, might have been expected to avoid that risk.

In the view of the Court, the applicants in this case had failed to point to any decisive stage when it could be said that the police knew or ought to have known that the lives of the Osman family were at real and immediate risk from the teacher. It concluded that there had been no violation of article 2 of the Convention in this case.

In *Mahmut Kaya* v. *Turkey*[134] the Court applied the principles set out in the *Osman* case to killing by individuals or groups who, it seemed, were acting with the knowledge or acquiescence of elements in the security forces in the context of a conflict in south-eastern Turkey. This phenomenon, referred to as 'unknown perpetrator killing', has been alleged in other conflicts, particularly where the State is responding to terrorism or other acts of insurgency. In this case it was alleged that the victim was kidnapped, tortured and killed by, or with the connivance of, State agents and that there was no effective investigation or remedy for his complaints.

---

[133] Article 5 of the European Convention on Human Rights protects the right to liberty and security of person and article 8 protects the right to respect for private and family life.
[134] Ibid., 2000-III, p. 149, application No. 22535/93, judgment of 28 March 2000.

II.3

The Court's observations on the State's duty to protect the right to life in such cases included the comment that the authorities were aware or ought to have been aware of the criminal collusion between killers and security forces. The Court noted that a wide range of preventive measures would have been available to the authorities regarding the activities of their own security forces and those groups allegedly acting under their auspices or with their knowledge. It concluded that the authorities had failed to take reasonable measures available to them to prevent a real and immediate risk to the life of victim, and that they had failed to carry out an adequate and effective investigation into the killing. On these grounds there had been violations of article 2 of the Convention.

(C) NON-TREATY INSTRUMENTS

A number of non-treaty instruments addressed to police set out standards on the use of force. Compliance with these reinforces protection of the right to life and enhances the professionalism and effectiveness of police. The provisions of the UN Code of Conduct for Law Enforcement Officials,[135] the Basic Principles on the Use of Force and Firearms by Law Enforcement Officials,[136] and the European Code of Police Ethics[137] in this respect are discussed in the next chapter.

In addition to embodying standards on the use of force, the European Code of Police Ethics, in article 35, deals explicitly with the right to life by requiring the police and all police operations to respect everyone's right to life. The Commentary to the Code states that article 35 is based on article 2 of the European Convention on Human Rights, and it implies that the police and their operations shall not engage in intentional killings. Furthermore, the Commentary continues, considering article 2 of the European Convention on Human Rights in the light of Protocol No. 6 to the same Convention, concerning the abolition of the death penalty, it should also be excluded that the police are being used for the execution of capital punishment.

The Commentary acknowledges that police actions may lead to the loss of life as a result of the use of force by the police, but that may not necessarily violate the respect for the right to life provided that certain conditions are fulfilled. It then cites article 2, paragraph 2 of the European Convention on Human Rights, and the observations of the European Court of Human Rights on the term 'absolutely necessary', both of which are set out above.

---

[135] Adopted by UN GA resolution 34.169 of 17 December 1979.
[136] Adopted by the Eighth United Nations Congress on the Prevention of Crime and the Treatment of Offenders, Havana, 27 August – 7 September 1990.
[137] Adopted by the Committee of Ministers of the Council of Europe on 19 Sept 2001.

The Commentary concludes by pointing out that the training of police personnel in this respect is of utmost importance.

Two other non-treaty instruments embody standards that protect the right to life. The Principles on the Effective Prevention and Investigation of Extra-legal, Arbitrary and Summary Executions[138] is an instrument consisting of twenty principles dealing with the prevention of extra-legal, arbitrary and summary executions; the investigation of such executions; and legal proceedings following investigations. Essentially extra-legal, arbitrary and summary executions are unlawful killings by state officials.

These principles include requirements that extra-legal, arbitrary and summary executions should be prohibited by law, and that strict command and control be exercised over officials responsible for arrest and detention, and over those authorised to use force and firearms. They call upon governments to initiate thorough, prompt and impartial investigations of all suspected cases of such executions, and they set out a series of other requirements designed to assist the investigative process. Governments are to ensure that those identified by investigations as having participated in extra-legal, arbitrary and summary executions are brought to justice. Families and dependent victims are entitled to fair and adequate compensation.

The Declaration on the Protection of All Persons from Enforced Disappearances[139] consists of 21 articles. Article 1 proclaims that any act of enforced disappearance is an offence to human dignity, and is a grave and flagrant violation of human rights and fundamental freedoms. Any such act places the person subject thereto outside the protection of the law, and it inflicts severe suffering on them and their families. Article 6 prohibits any order or instruction of any public authority, civilian, military or other, from being invoked to justify an enforced disappearance. Any person receiving such an order or instruction has the right and duty not to obey it. The same article requires States to ensure that orders or instructions directing, authorising or encouraging any enforced disappearance are prohibited. The final paragraph of article 6 requires these provisions to be emphasised in the training of law enforcement officials. Under article 7 no circumstances whatsoever, whether a threat

---

[138] Recommended by the Economic and Social Council of the United Nations on 24 May 1989.

[139] Proclaimed by the General Assembly of the United Nations on 18 December 1992.

II.3

of war, a state of war, internal political instability or any public emergency, may be invoked to justify enforced disappearances.

Given the circumstances of cases described above, in which violations of the right to life arose out of instances of disappearances, compliance with the provisions of this instrument can be an important factor in preventing such violations.

Chapter 4. The Use of Force by Police

In this chapter standards dealing with the use of force by police expressed in three international instruments are considered. The greater part of the chapter is devoted to the Basic Principles on the Use of Force and Firearms by Law Enforcement Officials. The other two instruments, the Code of Conduct for Law Enforcement Officials and the European Code of Police Ethics, deal with other important aspects of police behaviour and have only one article each devoted to the use of force. The chapter concludes with a review and summary of international standards on the use of force by police.

Whereas the global and regional treaties examined in the previous chapter are legally binding on states party to them, the instruments considered in this chapter are not. However, compliance with their provisions by governments, police agencies and police officials will reduce the likelihood of violations of the right to life, enhance the lawful and expert use of force by police, and may make it less likely that a state will be found in violation of its legal obligations.

(A) POWER, RESTRAINT AND EFFECTIVENESS

Police are given power under the law to use force. Without this and other powers, such as the power to deprive people of their liberty, it would not be possible for police to perform their functions. Indeed whilst policing can be expressed as a number of functions, for example to prevent and to investigate crime and to maintain and to restore order, it can also be expressed as one function, that of responding to every situation arising within a society in which force may have to be used to provide at least a temporary solution.[140]

At the same time, the principles that peaceful means should be attempted before force is applied, and that only minimum levels of force are to be applied in any event are fundamental to policing. Given these principles and the centrality of force, express or implied, to policing; given the nature of policing with its uncertainties and its dangers; and given the importance of policing in a society, it is clear that the power to use force should be vested only in those people qualified to exercise it properly. This requires extremely rigorous selection and training processes; effective command, control and supervision of police officials by police leaders; and strict accountability of police to the law when the power is abused.

The importance of ensuring that abuses of the power to use force are kept to a minimum cannot be over-emphasised. The application of unlawful force by police can result in serious human rights violations including, ultimately, violations of the right to life. Such violations will also, in many cases, amount to very serious crimes including murder. Furthermore it exacerbates the difficulties and dangers of policing, already sufficiently difficult and dangerous in itself, because of the immediate and longer term reactions it provokes. Unlawful police violence can

---

[140] *See* Bittner, *supra* note 19.

precipitate serious public disorder to which the police then have to respond, and it can thereby expose police unnecessarily to dangerous situations and make them vulnerable to retributive attacks. Unlawful police violence can lead to a loss of confidence in and support for the police on the part of the community, which is inimical to effective policing.

On the other hand the lawful and expert application of force is a demonstration of police respect for human rights, and of policing as a positive factor in the protection of human rights. It is also effective policing.

(B) CODE OF CONDUCT FOR LAW ENFORCEMENT OFFICIALS

United Nations General Assembly resolution 34/169 of 17 December 1979, under which this Code was adopted and transmitted to Governments, recommended that favourable consideration should be given to its use within the framework of national legislation or practice as a body of principles for observance by law enforcement officials.

The Code, which is described more fully in Chapter 4 of Part 1, consists of eight articles, each with an explanatory commentary. In paragraphs (a) and (b) of the commentary to article 1, the following definition is supplied:

> "a. The term 'law enforcement official' includes all officers of the law, whether appointed or elected, who exercise police powers, especially powers of arrest or detention.
>
> b. In countries where police powers are exercised by military authorities, whether uniformed or not, or by state security forces, the definition of law enforcement officials shall be regarded as including officers of such services."

Article 3 expresses standards on the use of force in the following terms: "Law enforcement officials may use force only when strictly necessary and to the extent required for the performance of their duty." Paragraph (a) of the Commentary states that the use of force by police should be exceptional, and that while police may use such force as is reasonably necessary for the prevention of crime or in effecting or assisting in the lawful arrest of offenders or suspected offenders, no force going beyond that may be used. Paragraph (b) points out that national law ordinarily restricts the use of force by police in accordance with the principle of proportionality, and asserts that it is to be understood that such national principles of proportionality are to be respected in the interpretation of this provision.

Paragraph (c) emphasises that the use of firearms is considered an extreme measure and that every effort should be made to exclude the use of firearms, especially against children. It states that in general firearms should not be used except when a suspected offender offers armed resistance or otherwise jeopardises the lives of others and less extreme measures are not sufficient to restrain or apprehend the suspect. It requires a report to be submitted promptly to the competent authorities in every instance in which a firearm is discharged by police.

The standards on the use of force by law enforcement officials embodied in the article and its commentary reiterate the important principles of proportionality (force to be used only to the extent required) and necessity (force to be used only when strictly necessary). The first paragraph of the commentary to the article sets out the purposes for which the use of force is considered necessary, to prevent crime and to exercise lawful powers of arrest. However the term 'reasonably necessary' used in this paragraph seems to dilute somewhat the term 'strictly necessary' used in the actual article (and indeed the term 'absolutely necessary' used in article 2(2) of the European Convention on Human Rights). This difference is probably attributable to a lack of care in the drafting process because, clearly, the standard required is one based upon the notion of strict or absolute necessity.

The third paragraph of the Commentary excludes the use of firearms for any purpose other than that of defence of the person. The significance of the requirement, expressed in this paragraph, for a report to be submitted when a firearm is discharged by police is part of the process for securing effective accountability of police for their actions. It is not a mere formality. It would be an important element in the obligatory investigation into the taking of life by police officials, and it may act as a deterrent against unlawful use of firearms by police.

(C) BASIC PRINCIPLES ON THE USE OF FORCE AND FIREARMS BY LAW ENFORCEMENT OFFICIALS

The primary concerns of these principles are to protect the right to life, including that of law enforcement officials; to ensure that law enforcement officials use force in accordance with the principles of necessity and proportionality; and to encourage the development and application of professional standards in relation to all aspects of the use of force and firearms.

The first and second preambular paragraphs of the Basic Principles refer to the need to improve the working conditions of law enforcement officials, and assert that a threat to the life and safety of law enforcement officials must be seen as a threat to the stability of society as a whole. The importance of the role of law enforcement officials in protecting the right to life, liberty and security of person is acknowledged in the third preambular paragraph. Article 3 of the Code of Conduct for Law Enforcement is Officials is cited in the fifth preambular paragraph, and in the penultimate preambular paragraph the personal safety of law enforcement officials is referred to, *inter alia*, in the context of their role in protecting the right to life.

In a footnote to the first preambular paragraph reference is made to article 1 of the Code of Conduct for Law Enforcement Officials, and the definition of 'law enforcement official' from that article is reproduced.

The instrument consists of 26 detailed principles addressed to governments and law enforcement agencies, or to law enforcement officials. It embodies not only rules that are essentially normative in character, but also rules embodying good practice on technical aspects of policing. This is illustrative of the interdependence of good behaviour and high standards of professional competence in policing. For the purposes of this book, the various principles may best be considered under ten sub-headings:

(a) Rules and Regulations

Basic principle 1 requires governments and law enforcement agencies to adopt and implement rules and regulations on the use of force and firearms by law enforcement officials. In doing so they are to keep the ethical issues associated with the use of force and firearms constantly under review.

Clearly any such rules and regulations must be based on national law, and on the state's obligation under international law to protect the right to life of people within its jurisdiction. The requirement to keep ethical issues constantly under review implies a systematic review of such issues in the light of different situations involving the use of force and firearms by law enforcement officials as they arise, and reviews of developments in techniques and equipment.

(b) Equipment

Basic principle 2 also places obligations on governments and law enforcement agencies. It requires them to develop a broad range of means, and to equip police officials with a variety of types of weapons and ammunition, to allow for a differentiated use of force and firearms. The development of non-lethal incapacitating weapons is encouraged. In order to decrease the use of weapons of any kind the principle requires law enforcement officials to be equipped with defensive equipment such as shields, helmets, bullet proof vests and bullet-proof means of transportation- measures also necessary for the personal safety of the officials.

Whilst compliance with these provisions may protect the right to life and secure compliance with the principle of proportionality in the use of force, care needs to be taken to avoid misuse of non-lethal incapacitating weapons. Some weapons of this nature deliver such high levels of force that they are appropriate for use only in those situations where firearms may otherwise be lawfully deployed. For example, taser guns can deliver electric shocks of a magnitude that causes very severe pain, and they are life threatening when used against some individuals.[141] The potential for abuse of non-lethal incapacitating weapons is very high, and the circumstances under which they may be used needs to be strictly regulated and supervised.

These dangers are recognised to some extent in basic principle 3 which requires the development and deployment of non-lethal incapacitating weapons to be carefully evaluated in order to minimise the risk of endangering uninvolved persons. Furthermore, the use of such weapons is to be carefully controlled. The concern expressed in this principle to avoid harm or injury to uninvolved persons is a reflection of the rule of international humanitarian law which requires protection for people taking no active part in hostilities, and the human rights law requirement for the use of force to be no more than strictly necessary.

(c) Selection and Training

Basic principle 18 requires governments and law enforcement agencies to ensure that all officials are selected by proper screening procedures, and have appropriate moral, psychological and physical qualities for the effective exercise of their functions. They are to receive continuous and thorough professional training, and their continued fitness to perform these functions is to be subject to periodic review.

Basic principle 19 requires governments and law enforcement agencies to ensure that all law enforcement officials are provided with training and are tested in accordance with appropriate proficiency standards in the use of force. Those law enforcement officials required to carry firearms should be authorised to do so only upon completion of special training in their use.

Basic principle 20 requires that, in the training of law enforcement officials, governments and law enforcement agencies shall give special attention to issues of

---

[141] Taser guns are dart-firing electro-shock stun weapons designed to cause instant incapacitation by delivering a powerful electric shock. They fire two barbed darts up to a distance of 21 feet (6.4 metres), which remain attached to the gun by wires. The darts are designed to penetrate up to two inches of the target's clothing or skin and deliver a high-voltage, low amperage electric shock along insulated copper wires. They can also be used without the darts, close-up, as stun guns.

police ethics and human rights, especially in the investigative process. They are also required to give special attention to alternatives to the use of force and firearms, including the peaceful settlement of conflicts, the understanding of crowd behaviour, and the methods of persuasion, negotiation and mediation, as well as to technical means, with a view to limiting the use of force and firearms. Law enforcement agencies are required to review their training programmes and operational procedures in light of particular incidents.

These principles between them require very sophisticated methods of selection, staff appraisal and training. 'Use of force' is to be a significant criterion for selection and assessment of law enforcement personnel, and emphasis in training is on the behavioural and normative aspects of law enforcement as well as on matters of technical competence.

Realistically, only well resourced law enforcement agencies have the capacity to meet all of the requirements of the Basic Principles on selection and training, and those on equipment. Given the importance of the power to use force in the processes of law enforcement, and the serious nature of human rights violations arising out of abuse of that power, the allocation of resources to those ends should be given high priority. However it needs to be recognised that even in under-resourced agencies determined efforts can be made by good police leaders to meet the standards, and that abuses of the power to use force continue to occur in well resourced agencies.

(d) Use of Force

(i) Use of Force and Firearms

The principles of proportionality and necessity, augmented by humanitarian principles concerning injured people, form the basis of the standards on use of force embodied in the Basic Principles.

Principle 5 stipulates that whenever the use of force and firearms is unavoidable law enforcement officials shall exercise restraint, and act in proportion to the seriousness of the offence and the legitimate objective to be achieved. They are required to minimise damage and injury, and respect and preserve human life; to ensure that assistance and medical aid are rendered to any injured or affected persons; and to ensure that relatives or close friends of injured or affected persons are notified. The latter two requirements are to be complied with at the earliest possible moment.

(ii) Use of Firearms

There are three principles expressing standards specifically on the use of firearms under a sub-heading 'Special provisions'. The core standard is expressed in basic principle 9 which reads:

> "Law enforcement officials shall not use firearms against persons except in self-defence or defence of others against the imminent threat of death or serious injury, to prevent the perpetration of a particularly serious crime involving grave threat to life, to arrest a person presenting such a danger and resisting their authority, or to prevent his or her escape, and only when less extreme means are insufficient to achieve these objectives. In any event, intentional lethal use of firearms may only be made when strictly unavoidable in order to protect life."

The standard expressed here is one based strictly on the notion of defence of the person. This notion is succinctly expressed in the first three lines of the principle concluding with the words death or serious injury. The remainder of the principle can be seen as superfluous in that the use of firearms to prevent crime, to arrest or prevent escape are all contingent upon the person concerned presenting grave threat to life. This elaboration suggests that those drafting the principle were concerned to make it clear that it applied in the various situations with which law enforcement officials are faced. A more general formulation confined simply to self-defence may have seemed too juridical, and perhaps insufficiently cognisant of actual circumstances confronting law enforcement officials.

Another important element of the standard on use of firearms is the requirement for the threat of death or serious injury to be imminent. This element informs the entire principle because, under the circumstances envisaged, a threat to life cannot be considered to be grave if lack of immediacy of the threat enables preventive or protective action to be taken, other than by the use of firearms.

Finally a lack of clarity of expression in this principle needs to be considered. It prohibits use of firearms against persons except in the circumstances it specifies, but it does not categorically state that use of firearms is limited to use against the person actually presenting the imminent threat of death or serious injury, or grave threat to life. This objection may seem somewhat pedantic, and it is almost certain that those drafting the principle meant to authorise use of firearms only against the person presenting the threat. It is possible to be reasonably confident about their intentions firstly because it would be difficult to argue that use of firearms against a person other than the one presenting the threat was proportionate or necessary, and secondly because of the wording of article 3 of the Code of Conduct for Law

II:4

Enforcement Officials. Paragraph (c) of the commentary to this article is specific in that it prohibits use of firearms except against a suspected offender who presents certain dangers.

Given the references to the Code of Conduct in the preamble to the Basic Principles, it is unlikely that it was intended that the Basic Principles should differ radically on such an important point from the Code of Conduct. However, this point needed to be considered at this stage because it takes on an additional importance when basic principle 14 (policing violent assemblies) is discussed.

Basic principle 10 states that in the circumstances provided for under principle 9, law enforcement officials must identify themselves as such and give a clear warning of their intent to use firearms, with sufficient time for the warning to be observed. Obedience to this rule is not expected if it would unduly place law enforcement officials at risk; would create a risk of death or serious harm to other persons; or would be clearly inappropriate or pointless in the circumstances.

Basic principle 11 stipulates a number of provisions which should be included in rules and guidelines on the use of firearms by law enforcement officials. These include provisions specifying the circumstances under which law enforcement officials are authorised to carry firearms and prescribing the types of firearms and ammunition permitted; prohibiting the use of those firearms and ammunition that cause unwarranted injury or present an unwarranted risk; and regulating the control, storage and issue of firearms, including procedures for ensuring that law enforcement officials are accountable for the firearms and ammunition issued to them.

(e) Use of Force and Firearms in Dealing with Unlawful or Violent Assemblies

The right to participate in lawful and peaceful assemblies, enshrined in human rights treaties, is recalled in principle 12. In principle 13, law enforcement officials are told that in the dispersal of unlawful but non-violent assemblies they are to avoid the use of force or, where this is not practicable, they are to restrict the use of force to the minimum.

Principle 14 deals with the dispersal of violent assemblies and reads as follows:

> "In the dispersal of violent assemblies, law enforcement officials may use firearms only when less dangerous means are not practicable and only to the minimum extent necessary. Law enforcement officials shall not use firearms in such cases, except under the conditions stipulated in principle 9."

150

At this point it is necessary to consider the wording of this principle more closely, and to revisit the discussion about the meaning of basic principle 9. According to principle 14 it is permissible to use firearms against persons in order to disperse violent assemblies, but use of firearms under such circumstances must be in accordance with principle 9. If it is accepted that principle 9 permits firearms to be used only against a person posing imminent threat of death or serious injury or grave threat to life, then firearms could not be used solely to disperse a violent assembly as indicated by the first sentence of principle 14, but they could be used against a particular person or persons in the assembly posing the specific threats set out in principle 9.

However it must be recognised that violent assemblies differ in the numbers of people involved, in the degree of violence manifested and in the imminence or gravity of the threat to life posed by the actions of participants. In an extreme case where there is a tumultuous and chaotic disturbance created by an assembly of people exhibiting a ferocious degree of violence; where it is genuinely believed that the actions of a large proportion of people forming the assembly pose an imminent or grave threat to life; and where it is not possible to distinguish between those who do pose that threat and those who do not, it could be argued that the only way to reduce the threat is to disperse the assembly, and that the only way to disperse the assembly is to use firearms.

On such an occasion it is probable that a number of individuals within the assembly, who are not themselves presenting an imminent or grave threat to life, and who, because of the circumstances cannot be distinguished from those who are posing the threat, would be killed or injured by firearms discharged to disperse the assembly. Furthermore, apart from the impossibility of distinguishing between people who themselves do or do not present the necessary threat to life at any specific instant, the fact of participation in an assembly of people which, collectively, presents the threat could be seen as justification under the basic principles, for use of firearms against them as individuals

In any event, the reference to basic principle 9 in principle 14 creates two difficulties. In allowing use of firearms to disperse an assembly, as it does in the first sentence, it seems to authorise use of firearms against people other than those presenting imminent or grave threat to life. In doing that it may be taking into account the extreme circumstances described above, but it also dilutes the notion, apparently implicit in basic principle 9, that firearms should only be used against the actual person presenting the threat. In insisting that firearms should not be used except under the conditions stipulated in principle 9, as it does in the second sentence, it seems to ignore extreme circumstances in which the only way to dispel

II:4

imminent or grave threat to life is to disperse the assembly, and the only way to disperse the assembly is to use firearms.

In order to sustain the general principle that firearms should be specifically targeted against those posing the threats stipulated, and to recognise the need to take extraordinary action in extraordinary circumstances, it seems that it is necessary to acknowledge that basic principle 14 is not entirely adequate and to urge upon police the importance of applying the principles of necessity and proportionality to those extraordinary circumstances. It is vitally important to limit, to the greatest extent possible, indiscriminate use of firearms to disperse assemblies where such use is unnecessary and, hence, results in arbitrary deprivation of life.

(f) Use of Force or Firearms against People in Custody or Detention

Principle 15 prohibits law enforcement officials, in their relations with persons in custody or detention, from using force except when strictly necessary for the maintenance of security and order within the institution or when personal safety is threatened. There are no other circumstances whatsoever under which force may be used against a detained person. Furthermore, the use of restraints on detainees should be considered to be use of force, and their unnecessary use prohibited. The international standards on the treatment of detainees, including the absolute prohibition of torture and ill-treatment and the right to humane treatment, are considered in Part 3 of this book.

Principle 16 states that law enforcement officials, in their relations with persons in custody or detention, shall not use firearms, except in self-defence or in defence of others against the immediate threat of serious injury, or when strictly necessary to prevent the escape of a person in custody or detention presenting the danger referred to in principle 9. The danger referred to in that principle is 'a grave threat to life'. In fact, it can be seen that principle 16 is expressed in very much the same terms as those of principle 9.

(g) Stress Counselling

The requirement for stress counselling is set out in basic principle 21, which requires governments and law enforcement agencies to make this facility available to law enforcement officials who are involved in situations where force and firearms are used. This is an enlightened provision which is beneficial to the health and welfare of individual law enforcement officials, to law enforcement agencies, and to the protection of human rights.

Police agencies which provide a stress counselling service usually make it available on a wider basis than that required by principle 21, in recognition of the fact that their officials face a variety of stressful situations in addition to those involving force or firearms.

(h) Reporting and Review Procedures

Principle 22 requires governments and law enforcement agencies to establish effective reporting and review procedures for all incidents in which injury or death is caused by the use of force and firearms by law enforcement officials, or where law enforcement officials use firearms in the performance of their duty. There must be an effective review process, and independent administrative or prosecutorial authorities must be in a position to exercise jurisdiction in appropriate circumstances.

It will be recalled from the previous chapter that treaty bodies, in considering cases involving violations of the right to life, have required prompt and effective investigations into killings by state officials.

Under principle 23 persons affected by the use of force and firearms, or their legal representatives, must have access to an independent process, including a judicial process. Principle 6 reinforces and supplements principles 22 and 23 by requiring law enforcement officials who cause injury or death by the use of force and firearms to report the incident promptly to their superiors.

(i) Responsibility for Actions

Legal accountability and command responsibility of law enforcement officials are addressed in four of the principles.

Principle 7 requires governments to ensure that arbitrary or abusive use of force and firearms by law enforcement officials is punished as a criminal offence, and principle 24 requires governments and law enforcement agencies to ensure that senior officials are responsible for the unlawful use of force and firearms by law enforcement officials under their command. This responsibility of police leaders is dependent upon whether they knew, or should have known, of the circumstances, and whether they took sufficient preventive action or reported such unlawful use. The terminology of principle 24 is similar to that used in the articles of the statutes of international criminal tribunals and the International Criminal Court, considered in chapter 1 of this Part, that deal with the responsibilities of commanders and other superiors in rank.

II:4

It will be recalled from Chapter 4 of Part 1 that, whereas the European Code of Police Ethics states that police personnel have a duty to refrain from carrying out orders which are clearly illegal and to report such orders without fear of sanction, the UN Code of Conduct for Law Enforcement Officials makes no such categoric requirement. Basic principle 25 is almost equally deficient in that it uses a form of words similar to the Code of Conduct. It simply requires that no criminal or disciplinary sanction shall be imposed on law enforcement officials who, in compliance with the Code of Conduct for Law Enforcement Officials or the Basic Principles, refuse to carry out an order to use force and firearms. Bearing in mind the likely effect of an unlawful order to use force and firearms, it is regrettable that this principle does not impose a clear duty on police officials to disobey orders that are manifestly unlawful.

This is particularly the case when the provisions of principle 26 are taken into account. Here, obedience to superior orders is denied as a defence if law enforcement officials knew that an order to use force and firearms resulting in death or serious injury was manifestly unlawful, and they had a reasonable opportunity to refuse to follow it. If a defence of obedience to superior orders is to be denied in the event of an unlawful order, then a requirement to disobey such orders should be all the more explicit.

(j)   Exceptional Circumstances

Principle 8 stipulates that no exceptional circumstances such as internal political instability or any other public emergency may be invoked to justify any departure from the Basic Principles on Force and Firearms.

Unfortunately it is exactly under such circumstances that lawful restraints on the use of force and firearms are sometimes breached. When dealing with conflict or disorder, or when social tension is heightened, police may abuse the power to use force for a variety of reasons. They may be inadequately trained or equipped, or there may be shortcomings in command and control. Whatever the reasons the requirements of good professional policing are not met, human rights standards are disregarded, and the immediate task of restoring order may be made more difficult because of reactions by the community against police misconduct. Furthermore prospects for effective policing in the longer term are diminished because of loss of respect for the police by the community.

(D) EUROPEAN CODE OF POLICE ETHICS

Article 37 of the Code states that the police may use force only when strictly necessary and only to the extent required to obtain a legitimate objective. The

Commentary to the article states that the article recognises the case law of the European Court of Human Rights with regard to article 2 of the European Convention on Human Rights, but adds that it should be noted that the present rule is applicable to all kinds of situations where the police are entitled to use force.

As a starting point, the Commentary continues, there must always be a legal basis for police operations, including the use of force. Arbitrary use of force can never be accepted. Moreover, article 37 indicates that the use of force by the police must always be considered as an exceptional measure and, when there is need for it, no more force than is absolutely necessary may be used. This implies that the force used should be proportionate to the legitimate aim to be achieved through the measure of force. There must, accordingly, be a proper balance between the using of force and the situation in which the force is used. In practical terms, this means, for example, that no physical force should be used at all, unless strictly necessary, that weapons should not be used, unless strictly necessary, and, if lethal weapons are deemed necessary, they should not be used more than what is considered strictly necessary; shoot to warn before shoot to wound and do not wound more than is strictly necessary, etc.

Normally, the Commentary points out, national legislation and regulations should contain provisions on the use of force based on the principles of necessity and proportionality. However, the practical approach to the problem in a given situation is more difficult, as the use of force, according to the above principles, places a heavy burden on the police and emphasises the need for police personnel not only to be physically fit and equipped but also, to a large extent, to have well developed psychological skills. The Commentary concludes by emphasising the importance of recruiting suitable personnel to the police, and of training.

(E) REVIEW AND SUMMARY OF INTERNATIONAL STANDARDS ON THE USE OF FORCE BY POLICE

(a) Principles

The use of force by state authorities for law enforcement purposes is regulated under international law by the principles of necessity and proportionality. These principles are expressed in international instruments, and they have been enunciated by treaty bodies interpreting treaty provisions prohibiting arbitrary deprivation of life by the state.

II:4

For example, in *Suárez de Guerrero* v. *Colombia*[142] the Human Rights Committee concluded that Mrs. de Guerrero had been arbitrarily deprived of her life because police action had been disproportionate to the requirements of law enforcement. In the same case the Committee also looked for evidence that the police action had been necessary for certain specific purposes.

The two principles are embodied in article 2 of the European Convention of Human Rights which declares that deprivation of life will not be in violation of the article when it results from the use of force which is no more than absolutely necessary for a number of specified purposes. In *Stewart* v. *United Kingdom*[143] the European Commission on Human Rights declared that the test of necessity includes an assessment as to whether interference with the Convention right was proportionate to the legitimate aims pursued. It also set out its test of proportionality - one requiring the nature of the aim pursued, the dangers to life and limb inherent in the situation, and the degree of risk that the force employed might result in loss of life to be taken into account. This ruling has been followed by the European Court of Human Rights in subsequent cases.[144]

The same principles form the basis of the standards embodied in the three non-treaty instruments considered in this chapter. The Code of Conduct for Law Enforcement Officials authorises law enforcement officials to use force only when strictly necessary and to the extent required. The Basic Principles on the Use of Force and Firearms by Law Enforcement Officials require non-violent means to be attempted first, and permit the use of force and firearms only if other means are ineffective. They require law enforcement officials to exercise restraint and to act in proportion to the seriousness of the offence and the legitimate objectives to be achieved. The European Code of Police Ethics stipulates that the police may use force only when strictly necessary and only to the extent required to obtain a legitimate objective; no more force than is absolutely necessary may be used; this implies that the force used should be proportionate to the legitimate aim to be achieved through the measure of force.

(b) **Purposes**

In *Suárez de Guerrero* v. *Colombia* the Human Rights Committee concluded, *inter alia*, that the police action had been disproportionate to the requirements of law enforcement and that there was no evidence that the action of the police was necessary in their own defence or that of others, or that it was necessary to effect the

---

[142] *Supra* note 119.

[143] European Commission on Human Rights, *Decisions and Reports*, No. 39 (1984), p. 162, application No. 10044/82, decision of 10 July 1984.

[144] *See e.g., McCann et al.* v. *United Kingdom supra* note 126.

arrest or prevent the escape of the persons concerned.[145] These purposes, and lawful action taken to quell riot or insurrection, are the exhaustive grounds on which use of force resulting in deprivation of life will not be regarded as being in violation of the article 2(2) of the European Convention on Human Rights.

The three non-treaty instruments allow use of force for any legitimate policing purpose, reinforcing the point made at the beginning of this chapter that use of force is integral to policing, and that the function of policing may be seen as one of seeking to resolve any situation in society in which force may be used. For example, the Code of Conduct for Law Enforcement Officials allows such officials to use force generally for the performance of their duty, and specifically to prevent crime or to arrest offenders or suspected offenders. In requiring law enforcement officials to apply non-violent means in carrying out their duty before resorting to force, the Basic Principles on Force and Firearms allow for an equally generalised use of force. The specific situations in which use of force is regulated by the Basic Principles are in the dispersal of assemblies, and against people in custody or detention. The European Code of Police Ethics states that the police may use force to obtain a legitimate objective.

As far as firearms are concerned, their use against persons is justifiable only on grounds of personal defence. That is the standard expressed in article 3 of the Code of Conduct for Law Enforcement Officials ("when a suspected offender offers armed resistance or otherwise jeopardises the lives of others"), and in the Basic Principles on Force and Firearms. The lack of clarity in basic principle 14 discussed above detracts only marginally from this personal defence principle.

The human rights treaties make no specific reference to firearms as such. However, it is clear from the pronouncements of treaty bodies in right to life cases that their use would have to constitute necessary and proportionate use of force under the circumstances, and on those grounds it would be difficult to offer any justification other than personal defence. Furthermore, it is interesting and relevant to note that the European Court of Human Rights referred to the UN Basic Principles on force and firearms in its judgement on the *McCann* case. In particular the Court noted that provision of basic principle 9 which states that intentional use of firearms may only be made when strictly unavoidable in order to protect life.

---

[145] *Supra* note 119.

PART III

THE TREATMENT OF SUSPECTS – DECENCY AND DETENTION

Chapter 1. The Phenomenon of Torture

(A) THE EXTENT AND PERSISTENCE OF TORTURE

Torture has been prevalent, customary, and legally sanctioned in many civilisations throughout recorded history. It remains prevalent and customary in some societies, despite now being comprehensively outlawed. The infliction of physical pain has formed part of the judicial process as a means of indicating innocence or guilt in 'trial by ordeal', and torture has been practiced as a means of securing confessions of guilt, 'the queen of proofs'. That form of proof now has a much less regal countenance, it having been tarnished by methods adopted to secure confessions, the extraction of false confession, and serious miscarriages of justice.

Torture has also been practiced to terrorise the victim of torture and a wider population, and to punish. In some cases it is clear that the end of torture has been the destruction of the individual as a person either through that person's death, or through the severity of the damage to the person's physical and mental integrity. It is degrading, disgracing those who practice it and those in whose name it is practiced.

There appear to be no geographical or ideological frontiers to torture. The United Nations Special Rapporteur on Torture, in his report to the UN Human Rights Commission in 1987,[146] indicated that it is a widespread phenomenon and that no society, whatever its political system, is totally immune. In his first report to the Human Rights Commission, in 1986,[147] the Special Rapporteur concluded that, in general, as long as there are situations in which human beings find themselves in the absolute power of other human beings, such situations will be conducive to the practice of torture. In the same report he indicated that when states of emergency are declared in response to civil strife or civil war, it is highly likely that torture will be practiced on opponents of the regime, especially when such people are held in incommunicado detention.

In subsequent reports the absence of democracy and the absence of the rule of law are identified as common elements in situations in which torture is practiced systematically. The lack of or disregard for legal and institutional safeguards to protect detainees (human rights violations in themselves) are also identified as being conducive to the practice of torture generally. However, in his report to the Commission in 1988[148] the Special Rapporteur pointed out that torture can occur in countries in which the rule of law prevails, reiterating his earlier observations that no State is wholly immune from the practice and that torture may occur in any situation where a person has complete power over others. Furthermore, the vulnerability of all types of detainee kept in incommunicado detention is re-emphasised in a number of the Special Rapporteur's reports.

---

[146] 43rd Session, UN Doc. E/CN.4/1987/13. An account of the functions and methods of the Special Rapporteur is given in the next Chapter.
[147] 42nd Session, UN Doc. E/CN.4/1986/15.
[148] 44th Session, UN Doc. E/CN.4/1988/17.

III:1

In his report to the General Assembly in 1999,[149] the Special Rapporteur on Torture stated that, based upon all the information available to him, he could only conclude that the phenomenon of torture continued to plague all regions of the world. In the introduction to the addendum of his report to the UN Commission on Human Rights in 2004,[150] the Special Rapporteur said that it contained, on a country-by country basis, summaries of reliable and credible allegations of torture and other cruel, inhuman or degrading treatment or punishment that were brought to his attention and then transmitted to the Governments concerned. It also contained replies from Governments. During the period under review, 16 December 2003 to 30 November 2004, the Special Rapporteur sent 223 letters to 77 governments. He also sent 330 urgent appeals to 72 governments on behalf of individuals for whom fears had been expressed that they might be at risk of torture and other forms of ill-treatment. Whilst the Special Rapporteur pointed out that the addendum did not illustrate the state of torture and other cruel, inhuman or degrading treatment or punishment throughout the world, but rather reflected the state of information brought to his attention, the countries listed continue to represent all regions of the world. They include, unsurprisingly, those countries with appalling human rights records and repressive political systems, as well as democratic countries where torture, if it occurs, does so as an aberration.

In his statement to the 61st Session of the UN Commission on Human Rights on 4 April 2005 the Special Rapporteur on Torture recalled that torture is one of the most serious violations of human rights, as it constitutes a direct attack on the core of the human personality and its dignity. As a consequence, the prohibition of torture and other cruel, inhuman or degrading treatment or punishment constitutes one of the few human rights that are absolute under international law and, therefore, permits no exception. The Special Rapporteur expressed his deep concern about attempts to circumvent the absolute nature of the prohibition of torture and other forms of ill-treatment in the name of countering terrorism. He reported that these attempts included, *inter alia*, narrow interpretations of the terms torture, cruel, inhuman or degrading treatment or punishment contrary to established case law of competent international and regional human rights bodies; attempts at evading the application of domestic or international human rights law by detaining and interrogating suspected terrorists abroad, by outsourcing interrogations with torture methods to private contractors or by returning suspected terrorists to countries which are well-known for their systematic torture practices (a process termed 'renditions'); and attempts to admit confessions made under torture abroad as evidence in domestic judicial proceedings.

---

[149] 54th Session, UN Doc. A/54/42.
[150] 61st Session, UN Doc. E/CN.4/2005/62/Add.1.

Observing that, from a legal point of view, the answer to these attempts is clear, the Special Rapporteur made the following points. Not only freedom from torture, but also the prohibition of other forms of cruel, inhuman or degrading treatment or punishment are absolute and non-derogable rights. Similarly, the principle of *non-refoulement* applies equally to torture and other forms of ill-treatment. Diplomatic assurances are not adequate means to satisfy the principle of *non-refoulement* in relation to countries where torture is systematically practiced. Governments are fully responsible for any practice of torture and ill-treatment committed by their agents (public officials as well as private contractors) at home or abroad. Any statement that is established to have been made as a result of torture, irrespective of the place where torture has been applied, shall not be invoked as evidence in any proceedings.

The question of torture and abuse of terrorist suspects is discussed further below.

(B) DEFINITION AND FORMS OF TORTURE

Human rights instruments prohibiting torture offer definitions of torture, and these, together with interpretations by courts and treaty bodies of the term, are considered in the next chapter. Torture is defined in the Oxford English Dictionary as "inflicting excruciating pain as practiced by cruel tyrants, savages, brigands, etc from a delight in watching the agony of the victim, in hatred or revenge, or as a means of extortion". The definition also refers to 'judicial torture' that is "inflicted by a judicial or quasi judicial authority for the purpose of forcing an accused or suspected person to confess, or an unwilling witness to give evidence or information". The deliberate infliction of intense suffering, official sanctioning of this, and malice and coercion would seem to comprise the essential elements of torture according to this type of general definition of the practice.

Torture takes many forms because people have applied their ingenuity assiduously and creatively to that end. Simple beating with fists or boots is the most favoured form of torture. Sometimes various implements such as bags or plastic tubes filled with sand, and coshes and whips are used. A particularly cruel form of beating is *falaka* or *bastinado* in which the soles of the feet are beaten with sticks or whips. Victims are deprived of sleep, food and drink; subjected to electric shocks on sensitive parts of their bodies; burned with lighted cigarettes; immersed in water to the point of drowning; and restrained, and sometimes suspended at the same time, by ropes and chains. Fingernails and teeth are extracted using pliers, and both men and women are raped. Indeed with the additional possibilities made available through modern technology, forms of torture are almost unlimited.

III:1

In addition to such instances involving serious physical assault, treaty bodies have held that other forms of serious distress caused to people have amounted to torture. These findings are described in the next chapter.

(a) The Effects of Torture on Victims

"Whoever has succumbed to torture can no longer feel at home in the world." These are the words of Jean Amery (1912 - 1978), a Jewish victim of the Nazis.[151] During interrogation by the SS, his hands were tied behind his back and he was suspended by his wrists from a hook in the ceiling (a common torture method known as 'Palestinian hanging'). His arms became dislocated from his shoulders and he was beaten with a horsewhip.

The devastating and enduring effects of torture, expressed so poignantly by Amery, were also identified by the Special Rapporteur on Torture in that part of his report to the UN General Assembly in 2004 where he dealt with the impact of torture on victims.[152] Echoing Amery, he observed that whilst some of the physical consequences of torture may be medically treated and may eventually disappear with time, others will remain a visible stigma, sometimes still painful, that victims will have to bear for the rest of their lives. It will constantly remind them of the torture experience, which has considerable psychological effects.

Emphasising that the death of the victim, intentional or otherwise, may be one of the consequences of torture in quite a number of instances, the Special Rapporteur identified the most common consequences. These are loss of hearing or sight, skin lesions, fractures, sexual dysfunction, cardiopulmonary, gastrointestinal, musculoskeletal and neurological problems, and infectious diseases. He pointed out, furthermore, that victims are often subjected to multiple forms of torture and ill-treatment, which may result in overlapping injuries. The most common diagnosis of psychiatric symptoms among torture survivors has been that of post-traumatic stress disorder. Torture victims may suffer from after-effects such as sleep disturbance, irritability, anxiety, impaired memory, concentration deficiencies and depression.

Beyond the effects on the victim, there are the effects on his or her family and even the wider community. The report indicated that physical and psychological impediments caused by torture might create difficulties in resuming satisfactory relationships with the family, in particular with spouses and children. The impact of torture on the local community and on a whole society may be intended by the

---

[151] J. Amery, *At the Mind's Limits: Contemplations by a Survivor of Auschwitz and Its Realities* (S. and S. P. Rosenfeld (trans.)) (Indiana University Press, Bloomington, 1980) p. x.
[152] 59th Session, UN Doc. A/59/324.

perpetrators. The Special Rapporteur observed that in some instances, the purpose of torture is to generate terror among the population.

(C) TORTURERS

Initial reflection on the types of torture described above seems to endorse the notion expressed in the dictionary definition that torture is practiced by "cruel tyrants, brigands, savages, etc". However, this is misleading to some extent because it disguises the very ordinariness of many torturers. Researchers have concluded that, apart from traits of authoritarianism and obedience, torturers are not noticeably different from their peers until they are recruited and trained.

Under experimental conditions it has been shown that high levels of obedience to authority figures are associated with high levels of violence to victims, and that in situations where abuse is made legitimate a certain proportion of people can become violent and destructive towards others. The development of these characteristics and tendencies has been associated with widespread child rearing practices and forms of socialisation that are common to different types of society.

What this means is that, globally, there is a significant number of people who have experienced a type of upbringing that has reduced their capacity to empathise with others, a type of upbringing that has created the potential for them to become torturers given the right conditions. These conditions include training, introduction to the practice of torture through a series of easy gradations, economic advantage, and status. Training programmes, and subsequent socialisation practices, provide those recruited to torture with the necessary psychological mechanisms to enable them to justify and rationalise their conduct.

The fact that reference is made to the recruiting and training of torturers is an indication of their official status, and of the institutional nature of the practice in some regimes. Torturers are to be found amongst the ranks of the military, police and other security agencies, and prison officials. Complicity in torture extends to senior members of those organisations, medical staff, members of the judiciary and political leaders who either actively encourage and assist those who practice torture, or fail to intervene to prevent the practice. The various ways in which a person can become legally implicated in the crime of torture are defined in the next chapter, and accounts of psychological research into why and how people may become torturers are given in Chapter 1 of Part IV herein.

Torture and other forms of serious mistreatment of detainees do occur in countries where torturers are not formally recruited and trained, where torture is not institutionalised. As the Special Rapporteur has indicated, no State is wholly

III:1

immune from the practice. Episodes of these serious malpractices in a State where the rule of law prevails are an indication of serious shortcomings in methods of recruitment, training, and supervision, and in the processes for securing accountability of public officials.

The bottom line is, of course, that torturers are criminals. They criminally abuse and violate people who, whatever they have done or are suspected of having done, are completely defenceless and at the mercy of their tormentors. In these early years of the twenty-first century it is crucially important to emphasise this fact, for humanity is in danger of losing the progress it made when it responded to the barbarities of the last century by establishing the international system for the protection of human rights. The ill-educated and desensitised guard; the skilled but emotionally retarded interrogator who believes that he or she has some higher mission to fulfil; the senior official who condones or fails to stop torture in complete dereliction of his or her duty; the political leader who knowingly presides over a system where such people operate with impunity, or who undermines or fails to reinforce norms that protect the physical and mental integrity of the human person, every human person – all are implicated in the barbarities of this century. Political leaders bear a particularly heavy responsibility for they have it in their power to establish the conditions under which human dignity is respected or under which torture is practiced. By what they say, or fail to say, they can reinforce or undermine norms that protect detainees from abuse. They can reinforce or undermine civilised values, the values of every great religious or secular belief system.

(D) WHY TORTURE SHOULD NOT BE PRACTICED

Torture and ill-treatment of detainees is inflicted on people involved in, or suspected of being involved in, ordinary criminality. In fact some officials see it as an integral part of a criminal investigation, necessary to secure a 'confession' to a crime. Apart from those who engage in this inept, unprofessional and criminal practice it is rare to find anyone prepared to argue that it is acceptable. However some are prepared to argue that torturing or abusing people suspected of being involved in terrorism should be legally sanctioned, and this proposition is addressed here.

(a) Torture and Abuse of Terrorist Suspects

The arguments, legal, moral and utilitarian, for and against torture and abuse are well rehearsed, especially in the context of terrorism. They have been conducted with some vehemence since the terrorist attacks on the United States of America in September 2001, and in relation to the subsequent misnamed 'war on terror'. The term 'terrorism' and the reasons why the use of the term 'war on terror' is unwise, unhelpful and incorrect are discussed in Chapter 2 of Part II.

One difficulty that people face in attempting to weigh up the arguments and come to a definitive conclusion is that the arguments cannot be weighed up, and it is not possible to come to a definitive conclusion based on an evaluation of concrete, quantifiable evidence. This is because much of what might be termed the evidence on each side of the argument is anecdotal and/or speculative. Furthermore the probability that an objective, scientific enquiry could resolve the argument in a manner convincing to both sides would seem to be remote.

This point can be illustrated with one such argument from each side of the debate.

Those arguing against torture in the context of a 'war on terror', or indeed other forms of conflict, assert that torture creates more terrorists or insurgents who plant more bombs that kill more people. Many people working in the field of human rights, including the author, have personal, anecdotal evidence of this. Those arguing for torture say that torture has prevented terrorist attacks. Again, the evidence is anecdotal and it is unlikely that enquiry into its veracity would be permitted. However, it is almost certain to have been true on some occasions.

What we will never know is, for example, how many terrorists have been created through torture in the current 'war on terror' or, indeed, any counter-terrorist action, and what casualties and damage they caused. Neither will we ever know how many terrorist attacks were prevented through torture. And even if we were able to compile a casualty list derived from each situation, the argument would still not be resolvable unless the figures were hugely disproportionate to each other. Ultimately it comes down to a matter of choice, which is well expressed by Tzvetan Todorov in his book 'Hope and Memory'.[153]

Todorov points out that "Israeli Supreme Court Judge Landau decided that in view of the Jews' long history of suffering, it was legitimate to use torture on Palestinian prisoners to protect Israeli civilians and combat terrorism; but in the same country, Professor Leibovitz, referring to the same past history, reached the opposite conclusion, namely that torture should be opposed by all possible means."[154] Todorov also writes that "[i]n 1957, a French official, Paul Teitgen, who happened to be a camp survivor, resigned his post as a senior administrator in the city of Algiers. Why? Because the marks he saw on the bodies of the tortured Algerian

---

[153] T. Todorov, *Hope and Memory – Reflections on the Twentieth Century* (Atlantic Books, London, 2003).
[154] *Ibid.*, p. 167.

III:1

prisoners looked just like those he had seen on his own skin after the Gestapo had dealt with him in the cellars of Nancy."[155]

We need to accept that even if the most draconian punishments were in place and security and police agencies had, literally, unlimited powers to arrest and torture, terrorist atrocities and serious criminality would continue to occur. Supposedly democratic states governed by the rule of law are already severely limiting human rights in the face of the terrorist threat. If torture were to be legitimised in response to that same threat what would the next proposal be – death squads? Where does it stop?

(b) Ticking Bombs and Kidnapped Children

The dilemma of the official faced with an impossible choice - one where, whichever decision he or she makes, there could be tragic or unwanted consequences, is referred to in Chapter 4 of Part I in the discussion on the ethics of policing. 'Ticking bomb' and 'kidnapped child' scenarios are examples of such situations, and it is appropriate to consider these in the context of the absolute prohibition of torture.

In a 'ticking bomb' scenario, it is posited that a bomb primed to explode within a short time has been hidden in a city centre and that, unless its whereabouts are discovered, there will be a massive loss of life when it explodes. The person responsible for planting the bomb has been arrested but he or she refuses to disclose its whereabouts. Under these circumstances it is argued that not only is it justifiable to torture that person to force him or her to give the necessary information, but failure to do so renders the authorities co-responsible for any deaths arising out of the explosion.

If this argument is accepted, how are the proposals it embodies to be actualised? Are the officials responsible for discovering the location of the bomb expected to commit crime by torturing the person who has planted the bomb? If so, how are they to be dealt with subsequently by the criminal justice system? Alternatively, is torture to be legalised?

The argument for justifying torture in the situation described above sometimes includes a proposal that legislation be adopted to legalise the use of torture when strictly defined circumstances arise and under strictly controlled conditions. Yet what of the situation described above? It refers to a person who has planted a bomb. How certain is the knowledge that the person has planted a bomb? A court has not pronounced guilt, a necessary condition if the rule of law is to prevail, therefore the

---

[155] *Ibid.*, p. 174.

proposal depends upon the suspicions of investigators. How strong are the suspicions to be in order that torture may be legally practiced? Is it possible to frame legislation so that the degree of suspicion agreed upon can be satisfactorily expressed? What about accomplices, friends, family of the suspect - they may know something, could they be tortured? It would be very difficult, if not impossible, to incorporate such strictly defined circumstances satisfactorily into the law of a democratic state governed by the rule of law.

What then of the strictly controlled conditions under which torture may be practiced? Are the permissible methods of torture to be described in the legislation? Is torture to be carried out under medical supervision? Are investigators to be trained in the permitted methods of torture? Is equipment to be used? If so, where is it to be stored and how is it to be issued? What if the suspect dies under torture, or the torturer exceeds the permitted limits - is he or she to be prosecuted? If so the charge would make interesting reading – 'Adam State whilst carrying out lawful torture, did unlawfully kill Eve Citizen'. In sum, is a legal and administrative edifice, based on torture, to be built in a state where the rule of law prevails?

If the answer to that question is 'yes', then how often is the system it houses to be used? How many times, anywhere in the world, has a person suspected of planting a bomb about to explode within a short time been arrested? If such an event ever has occurred, or ever does occur, how many such instances are required to justify construction of the edifice? Once the edifice has been constructed how can its misuse be prevented?

This last question is important because misuse is inevitable. Almost every aspect of a criminal justice system has been abused at some time, and this one would be no different. Once justification of torture is admitted under law, justification of its use will be extended in practice. The existence of law permitting torture and prescribing its uses and methods; the existence of administrative guidelines to practitioners of torture, their hierarchical supervisors and their medical supervisors; the existence of training programmes and equipment; the identification of places where torture is to take place - all of these would corrupt policing, the criminal justice system and the wider community they both serve.

When the edifice for the practice of torture is constructed clandestinely in a state, and its existence denied, corruption also arises because of efforts, inevitably unsuccessful, to conceal it. Torture, whether lawfully sanctioned, outlawed but encouraged or tolerated, or outlawed and occurring as an aberration is a cancer within a state. The severity of the disease and its symptoms may vary according to which of these three alternatives prevail, but it remains, nevertheless, a destructive disease.

III:1

States derive much of their authority, and governments their legitimacy, from their moral and legal standing. These are undermined, sometimes fatally, when torture is practiced in the name of the state or government. When the state is challenged because of dissent or disaffection on the part of some of its citizens, or through the activities of armed opposition groups, terrorists or more generalised public disorder, the likelihood of torture being practiced in defence of the state is very high indeed. This point is made on more than one occasion in the reports of the UN Special Rapporteur on Torture.

When torture is practiced on opponents of a regime under these circumstances, one of the principal distinctions between state organisations and those of their unconstitutional opponents is removed. That distinction is the constitutional, legal and moral authority and legitimacy vested in state organisations. Furthermore, the alienation felt by sections of the larger community because of abuse of power by the state, and by individuals subjected to torture or mistreatment, contributes to the creation of a climate that is favourable to unconstitutional or terrorist opposition groups, and to the recruitment of individuals to their numbers and cause.

Finally, the practice of torture is inimical to the development of the entire range of legitimate policing skills, including that of interviewing suspects of crime, for these skills are neglected when the focus of investigations is on securing confessions - especially by illegitimate means.

Much of the above reasoning can be applied to a 'kidnapped child' scenario, where a person suspected of kidnapping a child refuses to reveal his or her whereabouts. A genuine case of this nature occurred in 2002 in Germany where a suspect, under threat of serious bodily harm, disclosed the location of the victim who was, in fact, dead. One official, a Deputy Police Commissioner, ordered a subordinate official to use direct force on the suspect. That official then threatened the detainee with force during questioning and elicited information about the location of the dead child. Both of the officials were prosecuted, convicted and made the subject of probation orders. The kidnapper was sentenced to life imprisonment for murder. In passing sentence on the police officials, the judge is reported to have said she had handed down the lightest possible sentence because the officers had the "honourable motive of saving a life". She added: "But it must also be made clear that the laws have to be followed, including when one is in difficult situations". In this way the absolute prohibition of torture was maintained whilst, at the same time, the dilemma facing the officials was recognised.

Genuine 'ticking bomb' and 'kidnapped child' situations do arise, but they are rare, so rare that they could not, realistically, form the basis of legislation and should

170

make no difference to the absolute prohibition of torture. Police and other state officials need to be aware of the prohibition of torture and why it is an absolute prohibition. They also need to be equipped to deal with the moral dilemmas arising in those extremely rare cases so that they can make informed decisions about when there might be some moral justification for breaking the law. If they decide to do so after such deliberation, they would be better able to present arguments in mitigation of their actions in any prosecution to which they may be subjected.

Deliberations of this nature would address, for example, the argument that, as international human rights standards already allow the application of force, up to and including lethal force, to prevent harm in some circumstances, it should be permissible to cause severe physical harm to suspects in 'ticking bomb' and 'kidnapped child' situations in order to extract information that would prevent death or injury. They would address the distinction that must be made between two types of situation. One where a person, in almost all cases not a detainee, is about to, or is in the course of, perpetrating some act that creates an imminent threat of death or serious injury to a person, and who can manifestly be prevented from doing so by the application of force. The other where a detainee, completely at the mercy of his or her captors, who may or may not be responsible for an atrocious crime, and who may or may not have information that can prevent harm from that crime, is tortured in cold blood in the hope that he or she will provide information to prevent it or mitigate its effects. The immediacy of the harm and the near certainty that the application of force can prevent it are present in the former type of situation and absent in the latter.

Torture is a very serious crime. For a state, through its officials, to commit such a crime in response to the crimes of terrorists is indefensible, unlawful, immoral and utterly senseless. A state that permits its officials to torture in the face of the threat from terrorism has taken the soft option; it has surrendered to terrorists, handing them victory.

Chapter 2. The Prohibition of Torture and Ill-Treatment under International Law

(A) THE EXTENT OF THE PROHIBITION OF TORTURE AND ILL-TREATMENT

The second preambular paragraph of the Universal Declaration of Human Rights proclaims that "disregard and contempt for human rights have resulted in barbarous acts which have outraged the conscience of mankind". The acts of barbarism referred to include torture and other atrocities committed by Nazis and fascists during and immediately preceding the Second World War. The adoption of the Universal Declaration of Human Rights by the General Assembly of the United Nations in 1948 was one of the ways in which humankind was seeking to assuage its outraged conscience, and to eliminate torture and other abominations from the human experience.

The prohibition against torture is simply and unambiguously expressed in article 5 of the Declaration: "No one shall be subjected to torture or to cruel, inhuman or degrading treatment or punishment".

(a) The Prohibition under Human Rights Treaties

The International Covenant on Civil and Political Rights, the text intended to give legal force to the civil and political rights expressed in the Universal Declaration of Human Rights, in article 7 expresses the prohibition in identical terms to those of the Declaration. A second sentence is added to the article that prohibits subjecting people to medical or scientific experimentation without their free consent.

The unqualified nature of the prohibition becomes apparent when the terms of the article are compared with the terms of articles protecting some other rights. For example article 21 expresses the right of peaceful assembly, and it allows no limitations on this right "other than those imposed in conformity with the law and which are necessary in a democratic society in the interests of national security or public safety, public order (*ordre public*), the protection of public health or morals or the protection of the rights and freedoms of others". No limitations whatsoever are placed on the prohibition expressed in article 7.

More importantly, however, the article expressing the prohibition of torture is one of the seven articles of the Covenant cited in article 4 from which no derogation is permitted in time of public emergency that threatens the life of the nation.

III:2

In paragraph 2 of its General Comment No. 20 (44)[156] on article 7 of the Covenant, the Committee stated that the aim of the provisions of article 7 of the Covenant is to protect both the dignity and the physical and mental integrity of the individual. The Committee also insisted that it is the duty of the State party to afford everyone protection through legislative and other measures as may be necessary against the acts prohibited by article 7, whether inflicted by people acting in their official capacity, outside their official capacity or in a private capacity. In paragraph 3 of the same general comment, referring to the non-derogation provisions of article 4 of the Covenant, the Committee observed that no justification or extenuating circumstances may be invoked to excuse a violation of article 7 for any reasons, including those based on an order from a superior officer or public authority.

The regional human rights treaties (the African Charter on Human and Peoples' Rights, in article 5; the American Convention on Human Rights, in article 5; and the European Convention on Human Rights, in article 3) each express the prohibition of torture and ill-treatment in terms that are essentially similar to those of the International Covenant. Furthermore, the American and European Conventions each forbid derogations from the prohibition, even in times of public emergency. The African Charter has no provision on derogation of rights.

Article 37(a) of the Convention on the Rights of the Child requires States Parties to ensure that no child shall be subjected to torture or other cruel, inhuman or degrading treatment or punishment. Furthermore, neither capital punishment nor life imprisonment without possibility of release shall be imposed for offences committed by persons below eighteen years of age.

Other international human rights instruments (a UN Declaration on the Protection of All Persons from Being Subjected to Torture and Other Cruel, Inhuman or Degrading Treatment or Punishment; a Convention against Torture and Other Cruel, Inhuman or Degrading Treatment or Punishment; a Council of Europe Convention for the Prevention of Torture and Inhuman or Degrading Treatment or Punishment; and an Inter-American Convention to Prevent and Punish Torture) have been promulgated to make the prohibition against torture more effective. The provisions of these instruments are discussed in more detail below.

(b) The Prohibition under International Humanitarian Law Treaties

Principles and provisions of international humanitarian law are described and discussed in Chapters 1 and 2 of Part II of this book. As indicated there,

---

[156] Adopted by the Human Rights Committee, at its 1138th meeting (44th session), on 3 April 1992.

international humanitarian law is designed to regulate the conduct of armed conflict and to protect its victims.

Non-international armed conflict or civil war is regulated by article 3 common to the four Geneva Conventions of 1949, and the Second Protocol of 1977 Additional to the Conventions, which develops and supplements the Common Article. The provisions of both of these texts are considered in Chapter 2 of Part II, but it is important to recall that Common Article 3 describes a number of acts against the persons it protects which "are and shall remain prohibited at any time and in any place whatsoever". Prohibited acts include "violence to life and person, in particular murder of all kinds, mutilation, cruel treatment and torture"; and "outrages upon personal dignity, in particular humiliating and degrading treatment".

It is also important to recall that article 4 of the Second Additional Protocol prohibits "violence to the life, health and physical or mental well-being of persons, in particular murder as well as cruel treatment such as torture, mutilation or any form of corporal punishment"; and "outrages upon personal dignity, in particular humiliating and degrading treatment, rape, enforced prostitution and any form of indecent assault".

The four Geneva Conventions of 1949, apart from Common Article 3, are concerned with the protection of victims of international armed conflicts. They protect wounded and sick members of armed forces on land, and wounded, sick and shipwrecked members of armed forces at sea (Conventions I and II respectively); prisoners of war (Convention III); and civilian persons (Convention IV).

Each of these Geneva Conventions embodies provisions prohibiting torture of the categories of person they protect. For example, article 12 of each of the first and second Geneva Conventions strictly prohibits torture of wounded and sick combatants on land, and wounded, sick and shipwrecked combatants at sea respectively. Article 17 of the third Geneva Convention states that every prisoner of war, when questioned on the subject, is bound to give only his surname, first names and rank, date of birth and army, regimental, personal or serial number, or failing this, equivalent information. No physical or mental torture, or any other form of coercion, may be inflicted on prisoners of war to secure from them information of any kind whatsoever. Prisoners of war who refuse to answer may not be threatened, insulted, or exposed to unpleasant or disadvantageous treatment of any kind. Under article 32 of the fourth Geneva Convention, High Contracting Parties specifically agree that each of them is prohibited from taking any measure of such a character as to cause the physical suffering or extermination of protected persons in their hands. This prohibition applies not only to murder, torture, corporal punishment, mutilation and medical or scientific experiments not necessitated by the medical treatment of a protected person, but also to any other measures of brutality whether applied by civilian or military agents. Furthermore each Geneva Convention designates a small number of acts, which include torture or inhuman treatment, as grave breaches.

The First Protocol Additional to the Geneva Conventions extends the scope of the Conventions by, for example, bringing wars of national liberation into the category of conflicts to which the Conventions apply, and by affording legal recognition to certain types of guerrilla activity. This means that the prohibitions of torture expressed in the Conventions are extended accordingly. Furthermore, Section III of Additional Protocol I sets out provisions on the treatment of persons in the power of a party to the conflict. Within that section, article 75 sets out fundamental guarantees in respect of persons who are in the power of a Party to the conflict and who do not benefit from more favourable treatment under the Conventions or under the Protocol. They are to be treated humanely in all circumstances and are to enjoy, as a minimum, the protection provided by the article without any adverse distinction on any of the usual grounds such as race, colour, sex, language and religion. A number of acts, including torture of all kinds, whether physical or mental, are prohibited at any time and in any place whatsoever, whether committed by civilian or military agents. As indicated in Chapter 2 of Part II, persons entitled to protection under article 75 would include those such as guerrilla fighters who have forfeited the right to be prisoners of war, and mercenaries who, according to article 47 of Additional Protocol I, do not have the right to combatant or prisoner of war status.

(c) The Prohibition under General International Law

Given the extent and nature of the prohibition of torture, the main elements of which are described above, it is argued by international lawyers that the prohibition is one of general international law and therefore applicable to all states regardless of whether or not they are bound by any treaty prohibiting torture. It is further argued that the prohibition is one of *jus cogens*, that is to say a peremptory norm of international law, which under no circumstances may be encroached upon.

In sum there are no circumstances under which torture can have any legal justification, and there is no place in which torture may be lawfully practiced. No category of detainee is outside the protection of the law on this matter.

(B) DEFINITIONS OF TORTURE AND ILL-TREATMENT

The phrase 'torture or cruel, inhuman or degrading treatment or punishment' is not defined in the Universal Declaration of Human Rights or in the treaties that enforce it, nor are the differences between separate components of that phrase explained in those texts. However treaty bodies, in examining cases brought under the articles prohibiting torture and other ill-treatment, have pronounced on what constitutes torture and ill-treatment, and they have sometimes distinguished between the various terms expressed in the articles. Furthermore torture is defined in the UN Torture Declaration and the Convention against Torture.

The Human Rights Committee, which supervises the implementation of the International Covenant on Civil and Political Rights, referred to the question of definition in its General Comment No. 20(44).[157] In pointing out that the Covenant does not contain any definition of the concepts covered by article 7, the Committee indicated that it did not consider it necessary to draw up a list of prohibited acts or to establish sharp distinctions between different kinds of punishment or treatment. The Committee observed that the distinctions depend on the nature, purpose and severity of the treatment applied.

In the *Greek* case,[158] an inter-State case brought by the Governments of Denmark, Norway, Sweden and the Netherlands against Greece, the European Commission of Human Rights distinguished between the various forms of treatment prohibited by article 3 of the European Convention on Human Rights, by pointing out that there might be treatment to which all these descriptions applied, for all torture had to be inhuman and degrading treatment, and inhuman treatment had also to be degrading.

The Commission went on to observe that inhuman treatment covered at least such treatment as deliberately caused severe suffering, mental or physical, in the particular situation being unjustifiable. The word 'torture' was often used to describe inhuman treatment for a purpose, such as the obtaining of information or confessions or the infliction of punishment, and it was generally an aggravated form of inhuman treatment. Furthermore, treatment or punishment of an individual might be said to be degrading if it grossly humiliated him before others or drove him to act against his will or conscience.

In another inter-State case, *Ireland* v. *the United Kingdom*,[159] the Commission referred back to the term 'unjustifiable' that it had used in the *Greek* case. Noting that the term, in the particular situation, had given rise to some misunderstanding, it found it necessary to state clearly that it did not have in mind the possibility that there could be justification for any treatment in breach of article 3 of the European

---

[157] *Ibid.*

[158] The *Greek* case, *Yearbook of the European Convention on Human Rights, 1969* [vol. 12 *bis*], applications Nos. 3321/67 to 3323/67 and 3344/67, European Commission of Human Rights report adopted on 5 November 1969, Committee of Ministers of the Council of Europe resolution DH (70) 1 adopted on 15 April 1970.

[159] *Publications of the European Court of Human Rights*, Series A: *Judgments and Decisions*, vol. 25 (1978), judgment of 18 January 1978.

Convention on Human Rights. It went on to state that, under the European Convention, war or other state of emergency did not authorise a State party to derogate from its obligations under article 3. The prohibition under article 3 was absolute. There could never be under the European Convention or under international law a justification for acts in breach of that provision.

(a) Definitions under the Convention against Torture and the Torture Declaration

The Convention against Torture and Other Cruel, Inhuman or Degrading Treatment or Punishment defines torture in article 1 as follows:

> "For the purposes of this Convention, the term 'torture' means any act by which severe pain and suffering, whether physical or mental, is intentionally inflicted on a person for such purposes as obtaining from him or a third person information or confession, punishing him for an act he or a third person has committed or is suspected of having committed, or intimidating or coercing him or a third person, or for any reason based on discrimination of any kind, when such pain or suffering is inflicted by or at the instigation of or with the consent or acquiescence of a public official or other person acting in an official capacity. It does not include pain or suffering arising only from, inherent in or incidental to lawful sanction'".

This definition is based on a definition set out in article 1 of the UN Torture Declaration, the second paragraph of which states that "[t]orture constitutes an aggravated and deliberate form of cruel, inhuman or degrading treatment or punishment". This important defining sentence is missing from the Torture Convention, but the definition in the Convention is more complete in other ways. For example the Convention definition embodies a wider element of purpose of torture, that inflicted as a means of punishment for a third person's act, or for coercing the victim or a third person, or for a reason based on discrimination. The Convention also extends State responsibility from that expressed in the Declaration to cover 'consent or acquiescence' on the part of public officials.

From the foregoing it can be seen that there are essentially two elements that distinguish torture from other forms of ill-treatment – severity of pain and suffering and intention or purpose. These two elements need to be considered further, as does another element of the definition under the Convention against Torture, the perpetrator. It is necessary to consider his or her status and ways in which individuals with that status may be held responsible for the crime of torture.

(b) **Severity of Pain or Suffering**

The only international instrument to embody a definition of torture, apart from the Torture Declaration and the Convention against Torture, is the Inter-American Convention to Prevent and Punish Torture. The definition in that instrument refers simply to 'physical or mental pain or suffering' without stipulating any particular degree of pain or suffering.

The attitude of the Human Rights Committee on distinguishing between different types of punishment or treatment when considering violations of article 7 of the International Covenant on Civil and Political Rights has been described above. Although it observed that the distinctions do depend on the nature, purpose and severity of the treatment applied, the Committee did not consider it necessary to establish sharp distinctions between different kinds of punishment or treatment.

This approach is reflected in the pronouncements of the Human Rights Committee on a number of cases it considered in which, typically, victims were subjected to a variety of cruelties and barbarities – beatings (in various forms including *falaka*), electric shocks, submerging the victim's head in filthy water, suspension by the hands tied behind the back, and being made to adopt extremely uncomfortable postures for long periods of time. In such cases the Committee has concluded that victims were tortured without indicating whether it was a combination of the acts that constituted torture, or whether specific acts amounted to torture and others to ill-treatment. On other occasions they have concluded that the acts constituted torture and ill-treatment, or simply that a violation of article 7 of the Covenant had occurred.

For example, in *López Burgos* v. *Uruguay*[160] the author of the complaint, the victim's wife, asserted that her husband was subjected to torture and ill-treatment as a consequence of which he suffered a broken jawbone and perforation of the eardrums. In substantiation of her allegations the author furnished detailed testimony submitted by six ex-detainees who were held, together with Mr. Lopez Burgos, in secret detention places in Argentina and Uruguay. Some of these witnesses describe the arrest of Mr. Lopez Burgos and other Uruguayan refugees in Buenos Aires. On this occasion his lower jaw was allegedly broken by a blow with the butt of a revolver, and he and the others were then taken to a house where he was interrogated, physically beaten and tortured. The witnesses asserted that Mr. Lopez Burgos was kept hanging for hours with his arms behind him, that he was given

---

[160] United Nations, *Official Records of the General Assembly, Thirty-sixth Session, Supplement No. 40* (A/36/40), annex XIX, communication No. 52/1979, views adopted on 29 July 1981.

179

electric shocks, thrown on the floor, covered with chains that were connected with electric current, and kept naked and wet. These tortures allegedly continued for ten days until Lopez Burgos and several others were blindfolded and taken to a military base adjacent to the Buenos Aires airport. A Uruguayan plane then flew them to a military base in Uruguay where interrogation continued, accompanied by beatings and electric shocks. One witness alleged that in the course of one of these interrogations the fractured jaw of Mr. Lopez Burgos was injured further. Four of the witnesses further asserted that Lopez Burgos and several others were forced under threats to sign false statements, which were subsequently used in the legal proceedings against them. Without distinguishing between the various cruel acts inflicted on the victim, the Human rights Committee found a violation of article 7, because of the treatment (including torture) suffered by Lopez Burgos at the hands of Uruguayan military officers both in Argentina and Uruguay.

In other cases the Committee has been more precise. For example in *Celis Laureano* v. *Peru*,[161] it concluded that the abduction and disappearance of the victim and the prevention of contact with her family and with the outside world constituted cruel and inhuman treatment, in violation of article 7, *juncto* article 2, paragraph 1, of the Covenant. In the case *Quinteros and Almeida de Quinteros* v. *Uruguay*,[162] also involving abduction and disappearance, the Committee held that the victim had been tortured and that mother of the victim too was a victim of the violations of the Covenant suffered by her daughter, in particular of article 7. The Committee understood the anguish and stress caused to the mother by the disappearance of her daughter and by the continuing uncertainty concerning her fate and whereabouts. This case, in so far as the victim's mother is concerned, is an example of a violation of article 7 of the Covenant somewhat different to the more typical violation where the physical or mental integrity of a detainee is abused.

Another such case was *Rafael Rojas García et al.* v. *Colombia*,[163] in which the author alleged, on his own behalf and on behalf of his family, that a group of armed men from the Public Prosecutor's Office, wearing civilian clothes, forcibly entered the author's house through the roof. The group carried out a room-by-room search of the premises, terrifying and verbally abusing the members of the author's family,

---

[161] United Nations, *Official Records of the General Assembly, Fifty-first Session, Supplement No. 40* (A/51/40), vol. II, annex VIII, sect. P, communication No. 540/1993, views adopted on 25 March 1996.
[162] United Nations, *Official Records of the General Assembly, Thirty-eighth Session, Supplement No. 40* (A/38/40), annex XXII, communication No. 107/1981, views adopted on 21 July 1983.
[163] United Nations, *Official Records of the General Assembly Fifty-sixth Session, Supplement No. 40* (A/56/40), vol. II, annex X, sect. D, communication No. 687/1996, views adopted on 3 April 2001.

including small children. In the course of the search, one of the officials fired a gunshot. After noting this treatment received by the Rojas García family at the hands of the police, the Committee found a violation of article 7.

As indicated in the reference to the case against Greece above, the European Commission of Human Rights has been prepared to distinguish between the various acts prohibited under article 3 of the European Convention on Human Rights, and indeed to attempt to define the terms used. This approach is again apparent in *Ireland* v. *the United Kingdom,* also referred to above, which involved both the Commission and the Court of Human Rights. The case is particularly appropriate in this context because it refers to techniques adopted in the process of interrogating detainees in order to secure information or intelligence. The Commission concluded that the combined use of five interrogations techniques, referred to variously as interrogation in depth, disorientation or sensory deprivation techniques, amounted to torture. These techniques were described as, respectively, wall standing- forcing a detainee to remain for long periods in a stress position; hooding – putting a dark coloured hood over the detainees' heads; subjection to continuous, loud noise; deprivation of sleep; and deprivation of food and drink. The two determining factors in this decision were the use of techniques sufficient to break the will and their purpose, to obtain information.

The European Court of Human Rights disagreed with the Commission and concluded, on a majority basis, that the five techniques constituted inhuman and degrading treatment as they did not occasion suffering of the degree of intensity and cruelty implied by the word torture. The Court held that it had to have regard to the distinction embodied in article 3 between the notion of torture and that of inhuman or degrading treatment. This distinction derived principally from a difference in the intensity of the suffering inflicted. It was the intention that the European Convention, by the term 'torture', should attach a special stigma to deliberate inhuman treatment causing very serious and cruel suffering. In explaining their decision the Court referred to paragraph 2 of article 1 of the Torture Declaration, quoted above, in which torture is defined as an aggravated and deliberate form of cruel, inhuman or degrading treatment or punishment.

The observations and conclusions of the Court in this case should, however, be contrasted with those in a later case, *Selmouni* v. *France,*[164] in which the Court recalled that it had previously examined cases and concluded that there had been treatment that could only be described as torture. However, having regard to the fact that the European Convention was a living instrument to be interpreted in the light of present-day conditions, the Court considered that certain acts classified in the past

---

[164] *Selmouni* v. *France, supra* note 45.

III:2

as inhuman and degrading treatment as opposed to torture could be classified differently in future. It took the view that the increasingly high standard being required in the area of the protection of human rights and fundamental liberties correspondingly and inevitably required greater firmness in assessing breaches of the fundamental values of democratic societies.

The Court was satisfied that a large number of blows were inflicted on Mr. Selmouni, and that it could be presumed that such intensity of blows would cause substantial pain. Moreover, a blow did not automatically leave a visible mark on the body. However, it could be seen from the report of the forensic medicine expert that the marks of the violence Mr. Selmouni had endured covered almost all of his body. The Court also noted that the victim was dragged along by his hair; that he was made to run along a corridor with police officers positioned on either side to trip him up; that he was made to kneel down in front of a young woman to whom someone said, 'look, you're going to hear somebody sing'; that one police officer then showed him his penis, saying, 'here, suck this', before urinating over him; and that he was threatened with a blowlamp and then a syringe. Besides the violent nature of these acts, the Court observed that they would be heinous and humiliating for anyone, irrespective of their condition.

The Court noted, lastly, that the abuse was not confined to any one period of police custody during which, without this in any way justifying them, heightened tension and emotions might have led to such excesses. It had been clearly established that Mr. Selmouni endured repeated and sustained assaults over a number of days of questioning. Under these circumstances, the Court was satisfied that the physical and mental violence, considered as a whole, committed against the applicant's person caused severe pain and suffering and was particularly serious and cruel. Such conduct must be regarded as acts of torture for the purposes of article 3 of the Convention. It concluded, therefore, that there had been a violation of this provision.

(c) Intention or Purpose

In addition to the nature of the abuse, the other reason given by the Commission for considering that the five techniques amounted to torture was the purpose for which they were applied – the purpose of inducing a person to give information. As indicated above, the Commission also referred to 'purpose' in the case against Greece – purposes such as the obtaining of information or confessions, or the infliction of punishment.

Furthermore the definitions of torture in the Torture Declaration and the Convention against Torture both include 'purpose' as a necessary element of the crime of torture, with the Convention identifying a wider range of purposes – obtaining information or confession, punishment, intimidation or coercion, or any reason based on discrimination of any kind. The purposes specified in the Inter-American Convention are wider still – criminal investigation, intimidation, punishment, preventive measure, penalty, or any other purpose. Under that Convention, torture can also mean using methods 'intended to obliterate the personality of the victim or to diminish his physical or mental capacities, even if they do not cause physical pain or mental anguish'.

The inclusion of this final category of purposes is important and interesting because some researchers have concluded that torture is sometimes applied quite simply to destroy the individual as a person. Indeed the UN Special Rapporteur on Torture, in his report to the 43rd Session of the UN Commission on Human Rights,[165] argued that in many instances torture is even directed at wiping out the individual personality. This may be an indication of a shortcoming in the definition of the Convention against Torture, and purposes of this nature may be an aspect of torture that a treaty body will be confronted with in the future.

Bearing in mind all of the deliberations that have taken place on the degree of pain or suffering necessary to constitute torture, the final category of purposes set out in the definition of the Inter-American Convention is also interesting because it precludes the necessity of any degree of physical pain or mental anguish.

(d) The Perpetrator

It is clear from what has been said in preceding chapters about the nature of human rights abuses, that they are a category of harm that can only be committed by a person dignified by the authority of the state to exercise power on behalf of the state. Whilst the acts of cruelty described above would generally be of sufficient gravity to constitute criminal offences under the ordinary criminal law of the state in which they occur, they take on the additional designation of human rights abuses when they are committed by state officials.

The status of the perpetrator of torture and ill-treatment is, then, quite clear – he or she is a state official. However, situations arise in which individuals who are not state officials, and groups that are not state bodies, torture, abuse, and even kill people on behalf of the state. In order to be able to require states to meet their international legal obligations to protect and secure respect for human rights under such circumstances, the notion of state responsibility has been extended in some international instruments.

---

[165] *Supra* note 146.

III:2

This extension of responsibility can be seen in the definition of torture as set out in the Convention against Torture, described above. The definition in the Convention against Torture refers to pain or suffering "inflicted by or at the instigation of or with the consent or acquiescence of a public official or other person acting in an official capacity". This terminology means that responsibility for torture extends beyond the actual perpetrator, to State officials at all levels who encourage torture, order it to be carried out, agree to it being practiced, or who do not act to stop torture where it occurs or is about to occur. It extends responsibility to State officials who fail to act to prevent torture committed by other State officials acting outside their official capacity, or by individuals or groups having no such official capacity.

The Inter-American Convention to Prevent and Punish Torture is even more explicit on this point, and it extends responsibility for torture to people who, whilst acting at the instigation of public officials, have no such status themselves. Article 3 of that Convention reads:

> "The following shall be held guilty of the crime of torture:
>
> a. A public servant or employee who, acting in that capacity, orders, instigates or induces the use of torture, or who directly commits it or who, being able to prevent it, fails to do so.
>
> b. A person who at the instigation of a public servant or employee mentioned in subparagraph (a) orders, instigates or induces the use of torture, directly commits it or is an accomplice thereto."

In the case *Prosecutor* v. *Anto Furundzija*[166] before the International Tribunal for the Former Yugoslavia, the Trial Chamber analyzed ways in which individuals may be involved in, or responsible for, torture. This was a case in which the accused interrogated a female detainee whilst she was subjected to torture, including rape, by another person. Addressing the issue of who might be held responsible for torture as a perpetrator and who as an aider and abettor, the Chamber observed that it was crucial to ascertain whether the individual who took part in the torture process was also partaking in the purpose behind torture. If he was not, but gave some sort of assistance and support with the knowledge however that torture was being practiced, then the individual might be found guilty of aiding and abetting torture. If the person attending the torture process neither shared in the purpose behind torture, nor in any way assisted in its perpetration, then he should not be regarded as criminally liable. Here, the Trial Chamber gave the example of the soldier whom a superior had

---

[166] Case No. IT-95-17/1-T, judgment of 10 December 1998 (Trial Chamber), and Case No. IT-95-17/1-A, judgment of 21 July 2000 (Appeals Chamber).

ordered to attend a torture session in order to determine whether that soldier could stomach the sight of torture and thus be trained as a torturer.

The Trial Chamber then observed that account had to be taken of some modern trends in many States practicing torture. They tended to compartmentalise and dilute the moral and psychological burden of perpetrating torture by assigning to different individuals a partial and sometimes relatively minor, role in the torture process. Thus, one person could order torture to be carried out; another could organise the whole process at the administrative level; yet another could ask questions while the detainee was being tortured; a fourth one could provide or prepare the tools for executing torture although another physically inflicted torture or caused mental suffering; someone else could furnish medical assistance so as to prevent the detainee from dying as a consequence of torture or from subsequently showing physical traces of the sufferings he had undergone; another person could process the results of interrogation known to be obtained under torture; and finally, yet another could procure the information gained as a result of the torture in exchange for granting the torturer immunity from prosecution. The Trial Chamber concluded that international law rendered all these people equally accountable.

The Chamber stressed that this was to a large extent consistent with the provisions contained in the Convention against Torture, from which it could be inferred that they prohibited not only the physical infliction of torture, but also any deliberate participation in the practice. It followed that if an official interrogated a detainee while another person was inflicting severe pain or suffering, the interrogator was as guilty of torture as the person causing the severe pain or suffering, even if he did not in any way physically participate in such infliction.

Furthermore, the Trial Chamber observed, it followed that where several people were acting as co-perpetrators of the crime, accomplice liability might only occur within very narrow confines. Aiding and abetting in the commission of torture might only exist in such very limited instances as for example driving the torturers to the place of torture in full knowledge of the acts they were going to perform there; or bringing food and drink to the perpetrators at the place of torture, again in full knowledge of the activity they were carrying out there.

The responsibility of all State officials, prosecutors and the judiciary, and indeed political leaders, under the global and the regional Convention is clear; they are to ensure compliance with the absolute prohibition of torture.

(C) ACTION AGAINST TORTURE AND ILL-TREATMENT

(a) Procedures within the United Nations System

Action against torture is taken as part of the more generalised procedures adopted within the United Nations system for the protection of human rights. For example the work of the Commission on Human Rights concerning the investigation of allegations of human rights violations, and the handling of communications relating to those violations is referred to in Chapter 1 of Part I herein. As indicated there, this work is carried out according to two procedures. One is designed to respond to situations that reveal consistent patterns of gross violations of human rights (a public procedure initiated by governments). The other is designed to respond to communications from individuals or non-governmental organisations that appear to reveal a consistent pattern of reliably attested violations of human rights and fundamental freedoms (a confidential procedure).

Thematic procedures established within the UN system to deal with specific human rights issues are also referred to in the same chapter, and reports and comments of the Special Rapporteur appointed to deal specifically with torture have been quoted subsequently. At its forty-first session, the Commission on Human Rights adopted resolution 1985/33 of 13 March 1985,[167] in which it decided to appoint a special rapporteur to examine questions relevant to torture, requesting the Special Rapporteur to seek and receive credible and reliable information on such questions and to respond to that information without delay. The mandate has been renewed by the Commission in subsequent resolutions.

The Special Rapporteur submits annual reports on his activities and mandate, as well as his conclusions and recommendations, to the Commission on Human Rights and the General Assembly. To this end, he establishes contact with governments and asks them for information on the legislative and administrative measures taken to prevent torture and to remedy its consequences whenever it occurs.

The requirement to respond effectively to credible and reliable information has led to the urgent appeals procedure in which governments are requested to clarify the situation of individuals whose circumstances give grounds to fear that treatment falling within the Special Rapporteur's mandate might occur or be occurring. This procedure is not *per se* accusatory, but rather essentially preventive in nature and purpose. The government concerned is requested to look into the matter and to take steps aimed at protecting the right to physical and mental integrity of the person concerned, in accordance with the international human rights standards. As urgent

---

[167] UN Doc. E/CN.4/1985/SR.55.

appeals serve immediate humanitarian purposes, the Special Rapporteur may exceptionally decide to send such appeals to entities other than official *de jure* authorities in cases where the entities in question, as well as a channel of communication for reaching them, have been clearly identified. In the past, situations of armed conflicts have provoked such action.

The Special Rapporteur's mandate also permits him to undertaking fact-finding visits to States where information suggests that torture may involve more than isolated and sporadic incidents, with a view to gaining more direct knowledge of the situation and practice relating to matters falling within his mandate and identifying measures to prevent the recurrence of such cases and to improve the situation.

(b) **Treaty Based Procedures**

The bodies and procedures established under the International Covenant on Civil and Political Rights and the three regional human rights treaties are designed to secure protection of all of the rights, including the prohibition of torture, which they embody. Examples of the functioning, decisions and pronouncements of some of these bodies are set out in foregoing parts of this book and, indeed, of this chapter and these will not be expanded upon here. The intention is, rather, to focus on the instruments dealing exclusively with torture and ill-treatment.

(i) *The Committee against Torture*

The Committee against Torture was established under article 17 of the Convention against Torture and Other Cruel, Inhuman or Degrading Treatment or Punishment. It consists of ten experts of high moral standing and recognised competence in the field of human rights and, although they are appointed by States parties as is the case with members of the Human Rights Committee, they serve in their personal capacity. The Committee is empowered to examine periodic reports from States parties, and to make enquiries into apparent systematic practices of torture. Where a State has agreed, the Committee may receive complaints from other States parties of non-compliance with the provisions of the Convention; it may also receive complaints from, or on behalf of, individuals who claim to be victims of a violation of the provisions of the Convention. In the event of the Committee receiving reliable information from any person or body that indicates systematic torture, it has power to initiate its own investigations rather than await complaints.

The decisions of the Committee are not legally binding but it communicates its views on cases to the parties concerned, and requests information on action taken. Whilst there are no formal sanctions, the Committee may publicise lack of action or response. It reports annually on its work, both to States parties and to the UN General Assembly.

(ii) Other Action under the Convention against Torture

In addition to providing a definition of torture and establishing the Committee against Torture, the Convention against Torture and Other Cruel, Inhuman or Degrading Treatment or Punishment embodies a number of other provisions that require action against torture. It requires each State party to take effective legislative, administrative, judicial or other measures to prevent acts of torture in any territory under its jurisdiction, and it stipulates that no exceptional circumstances whatsoever, whether a state of war or a threat of war, internal political instability or any other public emergency, may be invoked as a justification of torture. Furthermore it prohibits an order from a superior officer or a public authority from being invoked as a justification of torture.

Each State party is to ensure that all acts of torture are offences under its criminal law; that an investigation is carried out wherever there is a reasonable ground for believing that torture has been committed on its territory; that there is an individual right of complaint for individuals who allege torture, and an investigation of that complaint; and that victims of torture have a right to obtain redress and fair and adequate compensation. Similarly worded articles embodying these provisions are contained in the Torture Declaration.

The Convention against Torture provides for universal jurisdiction over people alleged to have committed torture, and it includes procedures for extradition of such people. (The provision on universal jurisdiction means that a person accused of torture may be tried by any party to the Convention, regardless of where the crime was committed, the nationality of the accused or the nationality of the alleged victim). The Convention also forbids the return of people to countries where there are substantial grounds for believing that they would be subjected to torture.

Some other provisions of the Convention against Torture and the Torture Declaration, which require action against torture, are standards relevant to interviewing people suspected of crime. These are discussed in Chapter 4 of this Part.

On 18 December 2002, the UN General Assembly adopted the Optional Protocol to the Convention against Torture and Other Cruel, Inhuman or Degrading Treatment or Punishment. Any State that has ratified or acceded to the Convention may become a party to the Optional Protocol. It will enter into force when twenty States have ratified or acceded to it.

The purpose of the Optional Protocol is to establish a system of regular visits undertaken by independent international and national bodies to places where people are deprived of their liberty, in order to prevent torture and other cruel, inhuman or degrading treatment or punishment. For that purpose, the States parties will elect a Subcommittee on Prevention of Torture and Other Cruel, Inhuman or Degrading Treatment or Punishment of the Committee against Torture. Each State party also undertakes to maintain, designate or establish one or several independent national preventive mechanisms for the prevention of torture at the domestic level.

(iii) The Inter-American Convention to Prevent and Punish Torture

The terms of the Inter-American Torture Convention[168] embodying action to be taken against torture are analogous to those of the UN Convention against torture except that no enforcement body is established under the Inter-American Convention. For example, it requires States to outlaw torture and to take measures to prevent it; to investigate allegations of torture, punish offenders, and compensate victims; and to deny exceptional circumstances or superior orders as justifications of torture. There are also measures that provide for universality of jurisdiction over cases in which people are accused of crimes of torture.

The only references to enforcement at the international level are those stipulating that, after exhaustion of domestic remedies, a case may be submitted to the international fora whose competence has been recognised by the State in question; and that State parties undertake to inform the Inter-American Commission on Human Rights of any legislative, judicial, administrative or other measures they adopt in application of the Convention.

(iv) The European Convention for the Prevention of Torture and Inhuman or Degrading Treatment or Punishment

The European Committee for the Prevention of Torture and Inhuman or Degrading Treatment or Punishment was established under the Council of Europe Convention for the Prevention of Torture and Inhuman or Degrading Treatment or Punishment.[169] This Convention differs from the European Convention on Human Rights in that the latter instrument enables individuals to challenge a State action before judicial enforcement machinery, which then responds by requiring redress if a violation is found. The European Convention for the Prevention of Torture, on the

---

[168] Signed by Member States of the OAS on 9 December 1985, entered into force 28 February 1987.
[169] Signed by Member States of the Council of Europe on 26 November 1987, entered into force on 1 February 1989.

other hand, empowers the Committee to examine detention conditions and the treatment of detainees generally, seeking to prevent abuse rather than to secure redress once abuse has occurred.

Relations between the Committee and the parties to the Convention are governed by two principles, cooperation and confidentiality. Cooperation implies that the Committee may visit any place within its jurisdiction where people are deprived of their liberty by the State, unless there are exceptional circumstances that prevent them from doing so. The aim of the Convention is to assist States to strengthen the protection of detainees, not to condemn States. The principle of confidentiality is a corollary of the principle of cooperation, and the question of publicity arises only if a State fails to cooperate with the Committee, or refuses to make improvements following the Committee's recommendations.

There are two types of visits, periodic and *ad hoc*. Periodic visits are carried out to all parties to the Convention on a regular basis. *Ad hoc* visits are organised when they appear to the Committee to be required in the circumstances. The Committee is entitled to interview in private people deprived of their liberty, and to communicate freely with anyone whom it believes can supply relevant information. After each visit the Committee prepares a report on its findings, which includes, if necessary, recommendations and advice.

Unlike the UN mechanism, described above, which is a Subcommittee of the Committee against Torture, the European Committee for the Prevention of Torture and Inhuman or Degrading Treatment or Punishment is not directly linked to, nor derived from, other human rights institutions.

(c) Non-Treaty Instruments

(i) Code of Conduct for Law Enforcement Officials

The UN Code of Conduct for Law Enforcement Officials, described in Chapter 4 of Part I, was adopted by the UN General Assembly as part of the UN's standard setting work against torture. This work also led to the adoption of an ethical code for medical personnel by the General Assembly (Principles of Medical Ethics relevant to the Role of Health Personnel, particularly Physicians, in the Protection of Prisoners and Detainees against Torture and Other Cruel, Inhuman or Degrading Treatment or Punishment).

As indicated in Chapter 4 of Part I, the Code of Conduct for Law Enforcement Officials consists of eight articles each with an explanatory Commentary. Law enforcement officials are defined in the Commentary to article 1 as "all officers of the law, whether appointed or elected, who exercise police powers, especially the powers of arrest or detention".

Article 5 sets out the full extent of the prohibition against torture:

> "No law enforcement official may inflict, instigate or tolerate any act of torture or other cruel, inhuman or degrading treatment or punishment, nor may any law enforcement official invoke superior orders or exceptional circumstances such as a state of war or a threat of war, a threat to national security, internal political instability or any other public emergency as a justification of torture or other cruel, inhuman or degrading treatment or punishment."

The Commentary to the article refers to the UN Torture Declaration as the source of the prohibition it expresses, and it includes the definition of torture as set out in that instrument. Further guidance to law enforcement officials on terms used in the prohibition is provided in paragraph c to the Commentary. In pointing out that the term 'cruel, inhuman or degrading treatment or punishment' has not been defined by the General Assembly, the Commentary stipulates that it should be interpreted so as to extend the widest possible protection against abuses, whether physical or mental.

Article 8 of the Code of Conduct requires law enforcement officials to respect the law and the Code of Conduct and, to the best of their ability, prevent and rigorously oppose any violations of them. Law enforcement officials are further required to report any violations of the Code, which they have reason to believe have occurred or are about to occur, to superior authorities or other authorities with reviewing or remedial power.

Whilst Article 5 denies the defence of superior orders to law enforcement officials in respect of acts of torture or ill-treatment they commit, the provisions of article 8 do not provide sufficiently clear guidance to law enforcement officials in respect of unlawful orders from senior officers. This point is discussed in Chapter 4 of Part I, where it is pointed out that a law enforcement official who has received an unlawful order from a senior official would find difficulty in disobeying it if he or she were to rely on the terms of the Code for guidance or support. Furthermore his or her difficulties are likely to be greatly intensified if such orders are given in situations where police agencies are facing severe challenges, in responding to acts of terrorism for example. Those are the situations in which police officials may feel justified, however wrongly, in torturing, or ordering the torture of, suspects or those who may be able to provide intelligence.

III:2

(ii) Basic Principles on the Use of Force and Firearms by Law Enforcement Officials

This instrument is described in Chapter 4 of Part II where it can be seen that principles 15, 16 and 17 set out standards on the use of force in respect of persons in custody or detention. Principle 15, in particular, reinforces the prohibition of torture by prohibiting law enforcement officials from using force on detainees except when strictly necessary for the maintenance of security and order within the institution, or when personal safety is threatened.

Some protection for officials who disobey unlawful orders is provided by principle 25, which requires governments and law enforcement agencies to ensure that no criminal or disciplinary sanction is imposed on law enforcement officials who, in compliance with the Code of Conduct for Law Enforcement Officials and the Basic Principles, refuse to carry out an order to use force and firearms, or who report such use by other officials.

(iii) Body of Principles for the Protection of all Persons under any Form of Detention or Imprisonment

This instrument is dealt with in more detail in the next chapter. However, it should be noted here that principle 6 reinforces the prohibition of torture in the following way:

> "No person under any form of detention or imprisonment shall be subjected to torture or to cruel, inhuman or degrading treatment or punishment. No circumstances whatsoever may be invoked as a justification for torture or other cruel, inhuman or degrading treatment or punishment."

(iv) European Code of Police Ethics

The European Code of Police Ethics, discussed in Chapter 4 of Part I, was adopted by the Committee of Ministers of the Council of Europe in 2001. It applies to traditional public police forces or police services, or to other publicly authorised and/or controlled bodies with the primary objectives of maintaining law and order in civil society, and who are empowered by the State to use force and/or special powers for these purposes. Article 1 sets out the main purposes of the police in a democratic society governed by the rule of law, and these include the protection of and respect for the individual's fundamental rights and freedoms as enshrined, in particular, in the European Convention on Human Rights.

Article 36, in Part V, states that the police shall not inflict, instigate or tolerate any act of torture or inhuman or degrading treatment or punishment under any circumstances. The Commentary to the article reads as follows:

> "The prohibition of torture or inhuman or degrading treatment or punishment contained in this Article, derives from Article 3 of the European Convention on Human Rights. The European Court of Human Rights clearly and systematically affirms that Article 3 of the European Convention enshrines one of the fundamental values of democratic societies and that the prohibition is absolute. That means that under no circumstances can it be admissible for the police to inflict, instigate or tolerate any form of torture for any reason. The word "tolerate" implies that the police should even have an obligation to do their utmost to hinder such treatment, which also follows from the overall objectives of the police, see Articles 1 and 38.
>
> In addition to the fact that torture, inhuman or degrading treatment or punishment is a serious offence against human dignity and a violation of human rights, such measures, when used for the purpose of obtaining a confession or similar information, may, and are even likely to, lead to incorrect information from the person who is subject to torture or similar methods. Thus, there is no rational justification for using such methods in a state governed by the rule of law.
>
> It is clear that both physical and mental suffering are covered by the prohibition. For a more detailed analysis on what kind of behaviour that is covered by torture, inhuman or degrading treatment, reference is made to the case law of the European Court of Human Rights as well as to the principles developed by the European Committee for the Prevention of Torture and Inhuman or Degrading Treatment or Punishment (CPT). These bodies have provided a rich source of guidance for the police, which must govern police action and be used in the training of police personnel.
>
> It goes without saying that a police service that uses torture or inhuman or degrading treatment or punishment against the public, are unlikely to earn respect or confidence from the public."

Article 39 of the European Code states that, whilst police personnel shall carry out orders properly issued by their superiors, they shall have a duty to refrain from carrying out orders which are clearly illegal and to report such orders, without fear of sanction. In contrast to the terms of article 8 of the UN Code of Conduct, this article is unequivocal in obliging police officers to disobey and to report illegal orders. They have a duty to do so. Orders to torture or to become involved in torture in any way are clearly unlawful. The article is sufficiently explicit to give police

III:2

officers clear guidance and support in very difficult circumstances, and it is reinforced by article 38, which requires the police always to verify the lawfulness of their intended actions, and article 1, set out above.

General Comment No. 20(44) of the Human Rights Committee[170] is important and useful in this respect. Paragraph 13 of the Comment states: "Those who violate article 7, whether by encouraging, ordering, tolerating or perpetrating prohibited acts, must be held responsible. Consequently, those who have refused to obey orders must not be punished or subjected to any adverse treatment."

(d) Responsibility for Actions of Subordinates

As non-treaty instruments provide some guidance to subordinates on their responses to unlawful orders, it is reasonable to expect that they might also provide guidance to commanders and superiors on their responsibility for the actions of subordinates. The Code of Conduct for Law Enforcement Officials is silent on this important matter. However this deficiency is remedied to some extent by the terms of another UN instrument, the Basic Principles on the Use of Force and Firearms by Law Enforcement Officials. This reinforces the prohibition of torture in principle 15, and embodies a provision in principle 24 which states:

> "Governments and law enforcement agencies shall ensure that superior officers are held responsible if they know, or should have known, that law enforcement officials under their command are resorting, or have resorted, to the unlawful use of force and firearms, and they did not take all measures in their power to prevent, suppress or report such use."

This is a reasonable and satisfactory way of expressing the notion of command or supervisory responsibility in general, and it is certainly applicable to situations in which detainees are subjected to torture or ill-treatment, as those activities almost invariably entail unlawful use of force. In fact the terms of this provision are very similar to the articles in the statutes of international criminal tribunals and the International Criminal Court, considered in Chapter 1 of Part II, that deal with the responsibilities of commanders and other superiors in rank.

The European Code of Police Ethics also refers to the responsibility of senior officials for the acts or omissions of their subordinates. Article 16 states that police personnel at all levels shall be personally responsible and accountable for their own actions or omissions or for orders to subordinates. Article 17 requires that the police organisation shall provide for a clear chain of command within the police, and that it

---

[170] General Comment No. 20(44), *supra* note 156.

should always be possible to determine which superior is ultimately responsible for the acts or omissions of police personnel.

The term "which superior is responsible for the acts or omissions of police personnel" seems to indicate a wider responsibility than that set out in article 16 (i.e. for orders), however the Commentary to article 17 clarifies this point as follows:

> "This Article, which is complementary to Article 16, concerns the responsibility for orders within the police. The fact that all police personnel are responsible for their own actions, does not exclude that superiors may also be held responsible, for having given the order. The superior may be held responsible side by side with the "implementing" official, or alone in cases where the latter person followed orders in "good faith". (See also Article 38.) Through an established *chain of command*, ultimate responsibility for police action can be traced in an effective way."

In this sense the European Code is weaker than the UN Basic Principles on Force and Firearms, which states that superior officers are held responsible if they know, or should have known, of incidences of unlawful use of force and firearms by subordinates.

(e) Action against Individuals

The International Criminal Tribunals for the former Yugoslavia and for Rwanda, the Special Court for Sierra Leone, and the International Criminal Court are described in the first chapter of this book, and crimes of torture come within the jurisdiction of all of them. Torture falls under the headings of Grave Breaches of the Geneva Conventions and War Crimes in articles 2 and 6 respectively of the Statute of the Tribunal for the former Yugoslavia; Crimes against Humanity and Violations of Article 3 Common to the Geneva Conventions and of Additional Protocol II in articles 3 and 4 respectively of the Statute of the Rwanda Tribunal; the same headings in articles 2 and 3 respectively of the Statue of the Special Court for Sierra Leone; and crimes against humanity and war crimes under articles 7 and 8 respectively of the Statute of the International Criminal Court.

The fact that individuals can be, and are being, prosecuted for crimes of torture before international tribunals is a most welcome development in the field of human rights protection, and in securing justice for victims of torture. The case *Prosecutor* v. *Furundzija* before the International Tribunal for the Former Yugoslavia, referred to above, is one example of a successful prosecution for this crime.[171]

---

[171] *Prosecutor* v. *Anto Furundzija, supra* note 166.

III:2

(f) Legal Liability and Responsibilities of Officials Receiving Information Obtained through Torture

Information obtained through torture is shared across national boundaries between state officials. Given that torture is a very serious crime under international and national criminal law, the legal liability and responsibilities of state officials who receive and act upon such information needs to be addressed. This is particularly important in the case of officials in democratic states governed by the rule of law.

Article 1 of the Convention against Torture and Other Cruel, Inhuman or Degrading Treatment or Punishment states that torture is committed by or at the instigation of, or with the consent or acquiescence of, a public official or other person acting in an official capacity. In his book *The Treatment of Prisoners under International Law*,[172] Professor Sir Nigel Rodley (a former UN Special Rapporteur on torture), referring to the language of the Convention, states that "government officials at all levels may be held responsible if they fail to act to stop torture where it occurs. Failure to so act could well be interpreted at least as acquiescence". His use of the term 'government officials at all levels' and, indeed the terminology of the Convention at this point, suggests a hierarchy of officials acting within an entirely domestic context. Realistically it also implies that an official has the power to stop torture, or can report to an authority having that power.

However, what of the situation in which a state official in one country requests a state official in another country to commit torture in order to secure information? It is arguable that the requesting official is implicated in the crime as an instigator. A logical, but possibly unrealistic extension of this argument goes as follows. An official who, knowing that information passed to him or her is being obtained through torture in another country, and who fails to take action to prevent it, is acquiescing in the crime of torture. This argument appears more compelling where there is an ongoing situation in which a victim is subjected to a series of torture sessions during each of which information is obtained and passed, as it is obtained, to an official in another country.

Clearly an official in one country does not have power to stop torture by an official in another country, but the fact that these situations arise in an international context, as opposed to a domestic one, does not prevent an official from acting to prevent torture. He or she can do so through diplomatic channels, or by invoking international mechanisms for the protection of human rights and for the investigation and punishment of acts or omissions recognised as crimes under

---

[172] N. S. Rodley, *The Treatment of Prisoners under International Law* (Oxford University Press, Oxford, 1999).

international law. For example where torture is committed in the context of armed conflict the International Committee of the Red Cross could be alerted and, whatever the context, the Special Rapporteur on Torture could be informed with a view to his transmitting an urgent appeal to the government concerned. When torture is committed in situations where the jurisdiction of the International Criminal Court applies (or, indeed, that of an *ad hoc* international tribunal) details could be passed to the prosecutor of that body.

If state officials do have these legal liabilities and responsibilities, there are serious implications for cooperation between police and security agencies of different states, and that cooperation is vital in dealing with terrorism and other forms of organised crime. Clearly, if officials of police and security agencies in one state were to take the sort action I have described those agencies would very quickly become isolated internationally. On the other hand, the very powerful legal, moral and utilitarian arguments against torture remain. At the very least policy and practice of state agencies need to take into account the ways in which their officials could become implicated in the crime of torture. Furthermore officials need to be able to modulate and adapt their behaviour on a case-by-case and a state-by-state basis. For example some detainees may be in a position to provide information on a genuine 'ticking bomb' situation. Others may have been arbitrarily detained and subjected to speculative torture simply to establish whether or not they have any information to disclose. Whilst it may be possible to plead mitigation in respect of criminal acts done in response to a genuine 'ticking bomb' situation, complicity in torture in the latter case could not be mitigated. Concerning states, officials need to distinguish between those where torture is the norm and those where it is an aberration, and to adapt their behaviour accordingly.

Police and other state officials at the junior level who torture and abuse detainees under the belief, mistaken or otherwise, that their seniors or the political elite require them to torture or that they condone torture should bear the following in mind. When it is in the interests of the state to hold somebody to account for the crime of torture, it is more likely that junior officials will be made subject to criminal proceedings. Political leaders and senior officials tend to escape sanction before domestic tribunals. On the other hand, politicians and senior officials have been successfully prosecuted before international tribunals.

Chapter 3. The Rights of Detainees

(A) CATEGORIES OF DETAINEE AND FUNDAMENTAL PRINCIPLES

The rights of detainees considered in this chapter are largely positive rights that complement the prohibitions of torture and ill-treatment. The effects of securing respect for these rights are to prevent or remedy arbitrary detention, to ensure humane treatment of detainees, and to contribute to the protection of the right to a fair trial. The probability of torture and ill-treatment of detainees inducing false confessions of crime, and hence subverting the right to a fair trial, has already been alluded to. Violation of other rights of detainees carries with it the same danger. Indeed the right to a fair trial may be weakened in a number of ways when these rights are not respected.

The lawful exercise of power to deprive a person of his or her liberty is an essential police power and, whilst the right to liberty of person may in this way be curtailed, the person so deprived of liberty is not deprived of other fundamental rights. Furthermore the detainee is vested with additional rights to secure his or her protection whilst in detention.

Detainees in the hands of the police are, almost invariably, people suspected of crime whereas those convicted of crime are usually in the custody of prison officials. This distinction is made in the Standard Minimum Rules for the Treatment of Prisoners and the Body of Principles for the Protection of All Persons under Any Form of Detention or Imprisonment.[173] The former instrument refers to 'untried prisoners' and 'convicted prisoners', and to 'prisoners under sentence' and 'prisoners under arrest or awaiting trial'. The latter instrument, defines a 'detained person' as 'a person deprived of personal liberty except as a result of conviction for an offence', and an 'imprisoned person' as 'a person deprived of personal liberty as a result of conviction for an offence'.

These instruments express rights having legal force in human rights treaties and they embody detailed rules and guidelines designed to give effect to those rights. Each category of detainee is endowed with rights appropriate to the form of his or her detention, and the detailed rules and guidelines reinforce these. There is, however, one important principle on which all of these rights are based - that no detainee is to be subjected to privations or constraints other than those arising from lawful deprivation of liberty. Rights separately enjoyed by untried detainees are based on the principle of the presumption of innocence, which is expressed as a right in human rights treaties.

---

[173] Standard Minimum Rules for the Treatment of Prisoners, *supra* note 73, and Body of Principles for the Protection of All Persons under Any Form of Detention or Imprisonment, *supra* note 12.

III:3

It is essential that the conduct of police officials towards detainees in their care should be informed by these two principles, by the fundamental human rights to which detainees are entitled, and by the detailed rules and guidelines which derive from these principles and rights.

(B) RIGHTS, RULES AND GUIDELINES

(a) The Prohibition of Arbitrary Arrest and Detention

Unlawful deprivation of liberty is a matter for concern not only because it is a serious human rights violation in itself but also because it can be the first of a series of human rights abuses to which detainees are vulnerable. The Universal Declaration of Human Rights protects the rights to liberty and security of person in article 3, which also protects the right to life. Arbitrary arrest, detention or exile are prohibited under article 9 of the Universal Declaration.

The right to liberty and security of the person and the prohibition of arbitrary arrest or detention are incorporated in article 9(1) of the International Covenant on Civil and Political Rights, which also stipulates that no one shall be deprived of liberty except on such grounds and in accordance with such procedures as are established by law. Arbitrary arrest or detention is also prohibited under the African Charter on Human and Peoples' Rights (article 6); the American Convention on Human Rights (article 7(1)-(3)); and the European Convention on Human Rights (article 5(1)). In fact, the article in the European Convention on Human Rights sets out an exhaustive list of permissible grounds for deprivation of liberty which may be summarised as arrest or detention following conviction by a competent court; for non-compliance with a lawful order of a court or to secure an obligation prescribed by law; of a person for the purpose of bringing him or her before the competent legal authority on reasonable grounds of having committed an offence; of a minor by lawful order for the purposes of educational supervision or bringing him or her before a competent legal authority; of persons for the purposes of preventing the spread of infectious diseases, of persons of unsound mind, alcoholics or drug addicts, or vagrants; of a person to prevent unauthorised entry into, or residence in, the country.

Clearly, depending upon the specific functions of a police agency, all of the grounds set out in article 5(1) of the European Convention could be invoked in some jurisdictions to justify deprivation of liberty by police, but the third, fourth and fifth reasons have most general relevance to police functions.

(b) Rights of Detainees on Arrest

These are also set out in article 9 of the International Covenant on Civil and Political Rights. Under paragraph 2, anyone who is arrested is to be informed, at the time of arrest, of the reasons for arrest and to be promptly informed of any charges against him. Under paragraph 3, anyone arrested on a criminal charge is to be brought promptly before a judge or other officer authorised by law to exercise judicial power, and is entitled to trial within a reasonable time or to release. Paragraph 4 stipulates that anyone deprived of liberty by arrest or detention is to be entitled to take proceedings before a court, in order that the court may decide without delay on the lawfulness of his detention and order his release if his detention is not lawful. Paragraph 5 states that anyone who has been the victim of unlawful arrest or detention shall have an enforceable right to compensation. Similar provisions are repeated in the American Convention on Human Rights (article 7), and the European Convention on Human Rights (article 5). No such provisions are embodied in the African Charter on Human and Peoples' Rights.

Articles prohibiting arbitrary arrest or detention, and protecting the right to liberty and security of person and the rights of detainees on arrest have been the subject of a great number of applications to the bodies established under global and regional human rights treaties.

The notion of arbitrariness arose in the case *van Alphen* v. *the Netherlands*.[174] Here, the State argued that it had observed the rules governing pre-trial detention laid down in its Code of Criminal Procedure. However the Human Rights Committee observed that it remained to be determined whether other factors might render arbitrary an otherwise lawful detention. In considering this point, the Committee noted that arbitrariness was not to be equated with against the law, but it had to be interpreted more broadly to include elements of inappropriateness, injustice and lack of predictability. This meant that remand in custody pursuant to lawful arrest had to be not only lawful but reasonable and necessary in all the circumstances, for example to prevent flight, interference with evidence or recurrence of crime. As the State party had not shown that these factors were present in this case, the Committee found that continued detention was arbitrary and in violation of article 9, paragraph 1 of the International Covenant on Civil and Political Rights.

In other cases the Committee has ruled that kidnapping by agents of one State in the territory of another State constituted unlawful arrest. In *Burgos* v. *Uruguay*,[175] the kidnapping of a man in Argentina and his removal to Uruguay by members of the Uruguayan security forces was found to be a violation of article 9, paragraph 1, of the Covenant on the grounds that the arrest was unlawful. There was a similar

---

[174] United Nations, *Official Records of the General Assembly, Forty-fifth Session, Supplement No. 40* (A/45/40), vol. II, annex IX, sect. M, communication No. 305/1988, views adopted on 23 July 1990.
[175] *Burgos* v. *Uruguay, supra* note 160.

III:3

finding in another such case, *Domukovsky* v. *Georgia*,[176] in which the applicant claimed that the Government of Azerbaijan refused Georgia's request to extradite him, whereupon he was kidnapped from Azerbaijan and illegally arrested.

The victim in *Caldas* v. *Uruguay*[177] was arrested by officials who did not identify themselves or produce any judicial warrant. He was informed that he was being arrested under the prompt security measures, but was not given more specific reasons for his arrest. It was the opinion of the Committee that article 9, paragraph 2, of the Covenant required that anyone arrested should be informed sufficiently of the reasons for his arrest to enable him to take immediate steps to secure his release if he believed that the reasons given were invalid or unfounded. It was not sufficient simply to inform a person that he was being arrested under the prompt security measures, without any indication of the substance of the complaint against him and, consequently, there was a violation of article 9, paragraph 2.

The requirement that an arrested or detained person should be brought promptly before a judge or other officer authorised to exercise judicial powers was considered by the Human Rights Committee in the case *Borisenko* v. *Hungary*.[178] The author was detained for three days before being brought before a judicial officer. In the absence of an explanation from the State party on the necessity to detain him for this period, the Committee found a violation of article 9, paragraph 3, of the International Covenant on Civil and Political Rights. Whilst this may indicate that the Committee was setting the standard required for compliance with this provision at less than three days, there were two dissenting opinions in the case. In one of them, the member of the Committee stated that he was unable to agree that article 9, paragraph 3, envisaged a rigid, inexorable rule that a person detained must be produced before a judicial officer within 48 hours of his arrest. He added that the determination of compliance or non-compliance with the requirement of this paragraph had ultimately to depend on the facts of each case.

---

[176] *See* United Nations, *Official Records of the General Assembly, Fifty-third Session, Supplement No. 40* (A/53/40), vol. II, annex XI, sect. M, communication No. 623/1995, views adopted on 6 April 1998.

[177] United Nations, *Official Records of the General Assembly, Thirty-eighth Session, Supplement No 40* (A/38/40), annex XVIII, communication No. 43/1979, views adopted on 21 July 1983.

[178] United Nations, *Official Records of the General Assembly Fifty-eighth Session, Supplement No. 40* (A/58/40), vol. II, annex VI, sect. J, communication No. 852/1999, views adopted on 14 October 2002.

A case against the United Kingdom before the European Court of Human Rights, *Brogan et al.* v. *the United Kingdom*,[179] concerned four applicants who were arrested under emergency domestic legislation designed to counter acts of terrorism, and who were each detained for different periods of time. The Court acknowledged that the investigation of terrorist offences presented the authorities with special problems. It acknowledged safeguards of ministerial control, monitoring of the need for emergency legislation by parliament and reviews of the operation of legislation. Furthermore, the Court accepted that the context of terrorism had the effect of prolonging the permissible period of detention prior to appearance before a judge or judicial authority. Nevertheless, the Court decided that even the shortest of the four periods of detention (four days and six hours) fell outside the strict time constraints permitted by the notion of promptness required by article 5, paragraph 3 of the European Convention on Human Rights. It concluded that none of the applicants were brought promptly before a judicial authority, nor were they released promptly following arrest.

In a similar case, *Aksoy* v. *Turkey*,[180] the European Court of Human Rights accepted that, because of the extent and impact of terrorist activity in South East Turkey, a public emergency threatening the life of the nation existed. In considering whether the measures of derogation the State had introduced in response to this were strictly required by the exigencies of the situation, the Court could not accept that it was necessary to hold a suspect for fourteen days without judicial intervention. This period was exceptionally long, the Court observed, and left the applicant vulnerable not only to arbitrary interference with his right to liberty but also to torture. In fact, the Court found that the victim had been cruelly tortured. It referred to the various rights of arrested and detained people as 'safeguards' and considered that, in this case, insufficient safeguards were available to the applicant who was detained over a long period of time. In particular, the denial of access to a lawyer, doctor, relative or friend and the absence of any realistic possibility of being brought before a court to test the legality of the detention meant that he was left completely at the mercy of those holding him. The Court was not persuaded that that the exigencies of the situation, the serious problem of terrorism, necessitated the holding of the applicant on suspicion of involvement in terrorist offences for fourteen days or more in incommunicado detention without access to a judge or other judicial officer.

---

[179] *Publications of the European Court of Human Rights*, Series A: *Judgments and Decisions*, vol. 145-B (1989), judgment of 29 November 1988.
[180] European Court of Human Rights, *Reports of Judgments and Decisions*, 1996-VI, p. 2260, judgment of 18 December 1996.

III:3

The right to challenge lawfulness of arrest or detention arose in *Suarez Rosero* v. *Ecuador*,[181] considered by the Inter-American Court of Human Rights, in which the Court found breaches of, *inter alia*, article 7 paragraph 6 and article 25 of the American Convention on Human Rights. Article 25 sets out the right to prompt recourse for protection against acts that violate a person's fundamental rights. It is important to note what the Court said about the nature and purpose of this right. In the judgment the Court referred to one of its earlier Advisory Opinions in which it had held that in order for *habeas corpus* to achieve its purpose, to obtain a judicial determination of the lawfulness of a detention, it was necessary for the detained person to be brought before a competent judge or tribunal with jurisdiction over him. Here *habeas corpus* performed a vital role in ensuring that a person's life and physical integrity were respected, in preventing his disappearance or the keeping of his whereabouts secret and in protecting him against torture or other cruel, inhuman or degrading punishment or treatment.

The Court considered it proven that the writ of *habeas corpus* filed by the victim was disposed of by the Supreme Court of Justice of Ecuador more than 14 months after it was filed. The application was ruled inadmissible on the ground that he had omitted certain information, whereas, under the domestic law of the State, such information was not a prerequisite for admissibility.

As to article 25 of the American Convention, the Court, in a previous case, had ruled that this provision constituted one of the basic pillars not only of the American Convention on Human Rights, but of the very rule of law in a democratic society in the sense of the Convention. Article 25 was closely linked to the general obligation to respect the rights, contained in article 1, paragraph 1, of the Convention, in assigning protective functions to the domestic law of States parties. The purpose of *habeas corpus* was not only to ensure respect for the right to personal liberty and physical integrity, but also to prevent the person's disappearance or the keeping of his whereabouts secret and, ultimately, to ensure his right to life. On the basis of this, and especially since the victim had not had access to simple, prompt and effective recourse, the Court found that the State had violated articles 7, paragraph 6, and 25 of the Convention.

(c) The Right to Humane Treatment and Conditions of Detention

The right to humane treatment is expressed in article 10(1) of the International Covenant on Civil and Political Rights in the following way: "All persons deprived

---

[181] Inter-American Court of Human Rights, Series C: *Decisions and Judgments*, No. 35 (1999), judgment of 12 November 1999.

of their liberty shall be treated with humanity and with respect for the inherent dignity of the human person."

The second paragraph contains provisions that recognise the presumption of innocence and the special status of juvenile detainees. It requires accused persons to be segregated from convicted persons and to be subject to separate treatment appropriate to their status as unconvicted persons; and it requires accused juveniles to be separated from adults and brought as speedily as possible for adjudication. The paragraph includes a third part that stipulates that the aim of the penitentiary system shall be the reformation and social rehabilitation of prisoners. The American Convention on Human Rights embodies similar provisions (article 5), but the African Charter and the European Convention do not. However, the European Committee for the Prevention of Torture and Inhuman or Degrading Treatment or Punishment has set out what it considers to be elementary material requirements for detainees in police custody, and these are described below.

In General Comment No. 21(44)[182] the Human Rights Committee states that article 10, paragraph 1 of the International Covenant on Civil and Political Rights applies to anyone deprived of liberty under the laws and authority of the State who is held in prisons, hospitals – particularly psychiatric hospitals – detention camps or correctional institutions or elsewhere. In the third paragraph of the General Comment, the Committee asserts that paragraph 1 of article 10 imposes on States parties a positive obligation towards persons who are particularly vulnerable because of their status as persons deprived of their liberty, and complements for them the ban on torture or other cruel, inhuman or degrading treatment or punishment contained in article 7 of the Covenant. Thus not only may persons deprived of their liberty not be subjected to treatment that is contrary to article 7, but neither may they be subjected to any hardship or constraint other than that resulting from the lawful deprivation of liberty; respect for the dignity of such persons must be guaranteed under the same conditions as for that of free persons. The third paragraph of the General Comment concludes with the observation that persons deprived of their liberty enjoy all the rights set forth in the Covenant, subject to the restrictions that are unavoidable in a closed environment.

In the fourth paragraph the Committee insists that treating all persons deprived of their liberty with humanity and with respect for their dignity is a fundamental and universally applicable rule, and that the application of this rule, as a minimum, cannot be dependent on the material resources available to the State party. The rule is to be applied without distinction of any kind, such as race, colour, sex, language,

---

[182] Adopted by the Human Rights Committee, at its 44th session, on 6 April 1992.

religion, political or other opinion, national or social origin, property, birth or other status.

In *Mukong* v. *Cameroon*,[183] considered by the Human Rights Committee, the author of the complaint alleged that, for a period of 26 days, he was continuously held in a cell measuring approximately 25 square meters, together with 25 to 30 other detainees. The cell did not have sanitary facilities and, as the authorities initially refused to feed him, the author was without food for several days until his friends and family located him. He further alleged that for a period of 29 days he was detained in a cell at police headquarters, where he was not allowed to keep his clothes and forced to sleep on a concrete floor. Within two weeks of detention under these conditions, he fell ill with a chest infection. Thereafter, he was allowed to wear his clothes and to use old cartons as a sleeping mat.

In responding to this complaint the State argued that the situation and comfort in the country's prisons had to be linked to the state of economic and social development of Cameroon. The Human Rights Committee responded that certain minimum standards regarding the conditions of detention had to be observed regardless of a State party's level of development. These included, in accordance with rules 10, 12, 17, 19 and 20 of the Standard Minimum Rules for the Treatment of Prisoners, minimum floor space and cubic content of air for each prisoner, adequate sanitary facilities, clothing in no manner degrading or humiliating, provision of a separate bed and provision of food of nutritional value adequate for health and strength. Echoing its General Comment 21, the Committee insisted that these were minimum requirements always to be observed, even if economic or budgetary considerations might make compliance with these obligations difficult.

In view of these general conditions of detention, and other cruelties, which included threats of torture and death, the Committee found that the author had been subjected to cruel, inhuman and degrading treatment, in violation of article 7 of the International Covenant on Civil and Political Rights. Other treaty bodies have concluded that inhumane conditions of detention have violated treaty provisions prohibiting torture and ill-treatment.

In three cases against Malawi[184], the African Commission on Human and Peoples' Rights considered, *inter alia*, prison conditions endured by two victims, a man and his wife. Their ill-treatment and punishment for disciplinary reasons included

---

[183] United Nations, *Official Records of the General Assembly, Forty-ninth Session, Supplement No. 40* (A/49/40), vol. II, annex IX, sect. AA, communication No. 458/1991, views adopted on 21 July 1994.
[184] Case Nos. 64/92, 68/92 and 78/92.

reduction in diet, chaining for two days of the arms and legs with no access to sanitary facilities, detention in a dark cell without access to natural light, water or food, forced nudity, and beating with sticks and iron bars. The Commission held that these were examples of torture, and cruel and degrading punishment and treatment, and, jointly and separately, clearly constituted a violation of article 5 of the African Charter on Human and Peoples' Rights.

General prison conditions in Malawi, described in these cases, included shackling of hands in the cell so that the prisoner was unable to move, serving rotten food, solitary confinement, or overcrowding such that cells for 70 people were occupied by up to 200. The Commission held that such conditions offended the dignity of the person and violated article 5 of the Charter, which prohibits torture and other ill-treatment. In addition, the inability of prisoners to leave their cells for up to 14 hours at a time, lack of organised sports, lack of medical treatment, poor sanitary conditions, and lack of access to visitors, post and reading material were all held to be violations of article 5.

The European Committee for the Prevention of Torture and Inhuman or Degrading Treatment or Punishment, described in the preceding chapter, has set out standards for conditions of detention of those in police custody.[185] The standards are referred to as elementary material requirements, which the Committee insists should be met. For example, all police cells should be of a reasonable size for the number of persons they are used to accommodate, and have adequate lighting (i.e. sufficient to read by, sleeping periods excluded) and ventilation; preferably cells should enjoy natural lighting. Cells should be equipped with a means of rest (e.g. a fixed chair or bench), and persons obliged to stay overnight in custody should be provided with a clean mattress and blankets. There should be adequate toilet and washing facilities and persons in custody should be given food at appropriate times, including at least one full meal.

(d) Provisions of Non-Treaty Instruments

The two principal non-treaty instruments containing provisions on detainees are identified above. Of these, the Standard Minimum Rules for the Treatment of Prisoners set standards for the treatment of prisoners and the management of penal and correctional institutions. For this reason they are more relevant to the work of prison officials. However they may have some relevance to the work of those police officials who do have specific responsibilities for the care and custody of prisoners.

---

[185] The CPT Standards, CPT/inf/E (2002)1- Rev 2004, paragraphs 42 and 43.

III:3

For example rules 84 to 93 under Part II concern 'Prisoners under Arrest or Awaiting Trial'. Under these provisions the presumption of innocence in relation to unconvicted prisoners is reiterated, as is the requirement that untried prisoners shall be kept separate from convicted prisoners. There are also rules on such matters as sleeping accommodation; the purchase of food by untried prisoners from outside the prison as an alternative to prison food; the purchase of books, newspapers and writing material; contact with family or friends; and contact with legal advisers.

Part I of the rules, which comprises the bulk of the instrument, covers the general management of institutions, and is applicable to all categories of prisoners – criminal or civil, untried or convicted. It includes provisions on such matters as accommodation, personal hygiene, clothing and bedding, exercise and sport, medical services, discipline and punishment, instruments of restraint, institutional personnel, and inspection of institutions.

The provisions on 'separation of categories' set out in rule 8 are particularly important in the context of this chapter. This rule requires the different categories of prisoner to be kept in separate institutions or parts of institutions, taking account of their sex, age, criminal record, the legal reason for their detention and the necessities of their treatment. For example, whenever it is possible, men and women are to be detained in separate institutions, and in institutions that receive both men and women the whole of the premises allocated to women are to be entirely separate. Furthermore untried prisoners are to be kept separate from convicted prisoners, and young prisoners are to be kept separate from adults.

The Body of Principles for the Protection of All Persons under Any Form of Detention or Imprisonment is of more direct relevance to the treatment of detainees in police custody (as opposed to penal institutions) suspected, but not convicted, of any crime. This is a very detailed instrument of 39 Principles.

Principle 1 embodies the basic requirement to treat detainees humanely, and principle 6 repeats the prohibition of torture. The instrument also includes a number of provisions on such matters as judicial supervision of detainees; the right to consult legal counsel; the right to communicate with families; adequate medical supervision of detainees; and records to be kept of circumstances of arrest and custody. Under principle 7.2 officials who believe that a violation of the instrument has occurred or is about to occur are to report the matter to superior authorities. Provisions on interrogation of detainees are considered in the following chapter.

Principle 5 embodies important provisions on equality of treatment and on especially vulnerable categories of detainee. It requires that the Principles be applied to all persons without distinction of any kind such as race, colour, sex, language, religion or religious belief, political or other opinion, national, ethnic or social origin, property birth or other status. It also stipulates that measures applied under the law and designed solely to protect the rights and special status of women, especially pregnant women and nursing mothers, children and juveniles, aged, sick or handicapped persons shall not be deemed to be discriminatory.

Surprisingly no international instrument specifically requires that women detainees should be supervised by women officials, nor are there any stipulations to the effect that personal searches of detainees are to be carried by officials of the same sex as the detainee. However such basic good practice, followed in most states, would seem to be required by the principle of respect for the inherent dignity of the human person - a principle on which the protection of all human rights is based, and which is repeated in most human rights instruments including the Body of Principles referred to here.

Finally, on standards expressed in non-treaty instruments, the Basic Principles on the Use of Force and Firearms by Law Enforcement Officials are also relevant. It will be recalled from Chapter 4 of Part II that principle 15 permits law enforcement officials to use force against detainees only when strictly necessary for maintaining order within the institution or when personal safety is threatened. Principle 16 prohibits the use of firearms against detainees except in self-defence or defence of others against the immediate threat of death or serious injury, or when strictly necessary to prevent the escape of a person presenting a grave threat to life.

(e) The Treatment of Juvenile Detainees

Juveniles in detention enjoy the same basic rights as adults but there are also specific international standards on the protection of juvenile detainees. These are largely embodied in the UN Standard Minimum Rules for the Administration of Juvenile Justice (also know as the Beijing Rules); the UN Rules for the Protection of Juveniles Deprived of their Liberty; and the Convention on the Rights of the Child.[186]

Under the UN Standard Minimum Rules for the Administration of Juvenile Justice, a juvenile is defined as a child or young person who, under the respective legal systems of Member States, may be dealt with for an offence in a manner that is different from an adult. Rule 5.1 requires that juvenile justice systems should emphasise the well being of the juvenile, and ensure that any reaction to juvenile

---

[186] The Beijing Rules were adopted by General Assembly resolution 40/33 of 29 November 1985. The UN Rules for the Protection of Juveniles Deprived of their Liberty were adopted by General Assembly resolution 45/113 of 14 December 1990. The Convention on the Rights of the Child, *supra* note 9.

III:3

offenders is always in proportion to the circumstances of both the offenders and the offence.

Part Two of the instrument concerns 'Investigation and Prosecution' and has most relevance to treatment of juveniles by police. For example rule 10 states that on arrest of a juvenile, parents or guardians are to be notified immediately, and a judge or other competent body must consider the issue of release without delay. The rule also requires contacts between a police agency and a juvenile to be managed in such a way as to respect the legal status of juvenile, promote the well-being of the juvenile, and to avoid harm to him or her, with due regard to the circumstances of the case. Rule 12 requires specialist police officials and police units to deal with juveniles and juvenile crime.

The UN Rules for the Protection of Juveniles Deprived of their Liberty define a juvenile as a person under the age of 18 years. Part Three of this instrument is of most relevance to police as it concerns 'Juveniles under Arrest or Awaiting Trial'. The two rules in this part, rules 17 and 18, stress the presumption of innocence and the special treatment that derives from that status. They set out rights of untried juveniles, and requirements relating to untried juveniles who are detained. These include the right to legal counsel, and requirements for opportunities to undertake work for remuneration, opportunities for education and training, and provision of material for leisure and education.

The Convention on the Rights of the Child defines a child as every human being below the age of eighteen years unless, under the law applicable to the child, the majority is attained earlier. Article 37 of the Convention contains a number of provisions relevant to this book, namely reiterations of the prohibitions of torture and ill-treatment, and of unlawful or arbitrary deprivation of the liberty but re-emphasising these prohibitions in relation to children. The article also reiterates the rights of detainees to be treated with humanity and with respect for the inherent dignity of the human person - again in relation to child detainees.

Further provisions of article 37 require child detainees to be treated in a manner which takes into account the needs of persons of their age; to be kept separate from adults; to have the right to maintain contact with family; to have the right of prompt access to legal assistance; and to have the right to challenge legality of detention through a court or other competent authority.

(C) PUBLIC EMERGENCIES AND MEASURES OF DEROGATION

Provisions of the International Covenant on Civil and Political Rights and of regional treaties, enabling States parties to take measures derogating from their obligations under the treaties during an officially proclaimed emergency which threatens the life of the nation, are described in Chapter 1 of Part II of this book.

It is appropriate to recall within the context of this part of the book, that no derogation is allowed from obligations under a number of articles, including those that protect the right to life, and prohibit torture and ill-treatment. It is also important to recall that the existence of a public emergency and the extension of powers of arrest and detention have created conditions conducive to torture and ill-treatment of detainees because, for example, of derogations from articles protecting the right to liberty of person.

Under these circumstances it is clearly of vital importance that powers of arrest and detention should only be enhanced to the extent strictly required by the exigencies of the situation; that those enhanced powers should be exercised in a strictly lawful manner; that safeguards outlined in this chapter to secure humane treatment of detainees and to promote the right to a fair trial should be respected; and, especially, that the prohibition of torture and ill-treatment should continue to be respected absolutely.

It is also of vital importance that there should be proper scrutiny of the effects of emergency legislation by treaty bodies, thereby ensuring that such safeguards are retained to a sufficient extent.

(D) NECESSARY CONDITIONS TO SECURE THE RIGHTS OF DETAINEES

The positive obligations on States to secure the rights of detainees, expressed in international instruments and reinforced by the observations of the Human Rights Committee and other treaty bodies, take a number of forms. They require States to enact adequate laws and promulgate detailed guidelines to ensure that arrests and detentions are lawful and necessary, and that people deprived of liberty in these ways are treated humanely. They require States to adopt other measures to ensure that laws and guidelines are complied with. These measures must include enforcing the legal accountability of all police officials for their own acts or omissions, and the legal accountability of senior officials for the acts or omissions of their subordinates. They must include proper selection and screening of people recruited into police agencies, and adequate training of police. Training must embrace not only the legal and procedural requirements on these matters, but the necessary technical policing skills and interpersonal skills, as well as leadership skills for police commanders and managers.

III:3

All of these measures are conducive to creating and maintaining that ethos of good behaviour in police agencies, which is necessary to secure protection of and respect for human rights by police. However it must be acknowledged that all of the measures make some demands upon resources, and that some make quite heavy demands. To make this acknowledgement is not to undermine the Human Rights Committee's insistence that humane treatment of detainees cannot be dependent on the material resources available to a State. It is an acknowledgement that allocation of resources to that end is a very high priority indeed, and that those measures which do not make heavy demands on resources should be rigorously adopted and enforced.

For example enacting and enforcing laws for the protection of detainees; denying immunity for wrongdoing by police; requiring police leaders to ensure the proper behaviour of their subordinates; adopting schemes for the inspection of places of detention; and introducing a substantial human rights element to police training programmes need not be expensive measures to implement. Furthermore the mutual dependency of good behaviour by police and technical policing skills upon each other must be recognised. Police are less able to protect and respect human rights when they do not possess the necessary technical policing skills, and they are less able to develop those skills when they continue to rely upon unlawful methods to secure results. Recognition of this link provides an additional reason for enhancing the human rights element of police training, and for focusing on those policing skills the lack of which is detrimental to effective policing and to human rights.

Chapter 4. International Norms and Standards on Interviewing

(A) THE TERMS 'INTERVIEW' AND 'INTERROGATION'

The provisions of international instruments that concern the questioning of people suspected of crime by police use the term 'interrogation' to describe that process. However, whilst dictionary definitions of 'interrogation' indicate that the general meaning of the term is to ask questions of a person, especially closely, thoroughly or formally, it has taken on somewhat negative connotations in relation to the questioning of suspects by police. At the very least, it can be considered to mean the questioning of suspects by investigators for the purpose of securing confessions to crime. It is argued later that this purpose provides an unsound basis for effective, lawful and ethical questioning processes. More damagingly, 'interrogation' can also imply 'third degree' methods of questioning and other forms of brutality.

Considerations such as these have led theorists and practitioners concerned with developing best practice in this field to prefer the term 'interview'. This word is sometimes qualified in some way to emphasise the lawful or ethical nature of the process, or to indicate that it is seen as an aspect of the information gathering part of an investigation. Interestingly, dictionary definitions of 'interview' include the meaning 'a session of formal questioning by police', but the term, as yet, seems to carry with it no sinister implications. Furthermore, 'interview' is also used to describe the questioning of victims of crime and witnesses, as well as suspects.

(B) TORTURE AND OTHER FORMS OF DURESS

In his first report to the United Nations Commission on Human Rights, in February 1986,[187] the Special Rapporteur on torture commented on torture, duress and interrogation in the following terms:

> "Until the nineteenth century, physical torture was officially admitted as a method of interrogation in many national systems. It was only when the concept of fundamental human rights, among which the right to physical integrity figured prominently, developed within national systems that this method of interrogation was officially abolished. The recognition that information or confessions obtained under duress are in many cases far from reliable and, therefore, cannot be admitted as evidence in a judicial process may also have been important."

Even though torture is a very serious crime, and torture and other forms of ill-treatment have been comprehensively outlawed, the Special Rapporteur has had cause to revisit the question of torture, duress and interrogation in subsequent reports. Most recently, as can be seen below, to respond to attempts by States to

---

[187] *Supra* note 147.

III:4

narrow the scope of the definition of torture contained in article 1 of the Convention against Torture, and to remind States that forms of ill-treatment below the threshold of torture are also prohibited. Whilst the primary reason for complying with the prohibition is to respect and protect the physical and mental integrity of the human person, an extremely important secondary reason to ensure the reliability and admissibility of evidence obtained during the interview process. Indeed it is clear, from the standards on interviewing people suspected of crime discussed in this chapter, that forms of duress and methods of interrogation that fall below the threshold of both torture and ill-treatment are prohibited for these same reasons.

It is useful to recall, in this respect, the right of detainees to be treated with humanity and with respect for the inherent dignity of the human person, protected under article 10 of the International Covenant on Civil and Political Rights. This right imposes on States parties a positive obligation towards persons who are particularly vulnerable because of their status as persons deprived of their liberty, and complements for them the ban on torture or other cruel, inhuman or degrading treatment or punishment contained in article 7 of the Covenant. It prohibits them from being subjected to any hardship or constraint other than that resulting from the derivation of liberty.[188]

(C) LIMITATIONS ON THE USE OF FORCE

Standards on the use of force and firearms, including their use against detainees, are discussed in preceding chapters, and it is useful to re-examine them here. It will be recalled that article 3 of the UN Code of Conduct for Law Enforcement Officials states that law enforcement officials may use force only when strictly necessary and to the extent required for the performance of their duty. The Commentary to the article expands its provisions by pointing out that law enforcement officials may be authorised to use force as is reasonably necessary in the circumstances for the prevention of crime or in effecting or assisting in the lawful arrest of offenders or suspected offenders. It is clear that these provisions relate to circumstances under which a police officer would use force against a person about to commit a crime in order to prevent that crime, or against a person who has committed a crime or is suspected of having done so in order to effect the lawful arrest of that person. They do not authorise use of force on a detainee in order to secure information or confession in order to prevent crime or to secure the arrest of offenders.

Any doubts that this may be the case are removed by reference to principle 15 of the Basic Principles on the Use of Force and Firearms by Law Enforcement Officials which states that law enforcement officials, in their relations with persons in custody

---

[188] General Comment No. 21(44), *supra* note 182.

or detention, shall not use force, except when strictly necessary for the maintenance of security and order within the institution, or when personal safety is threatened. These two grounds are the only two lawful grounds for using force against a detainee.

Article 37 of the European Code of Police Ethics states that police may use force only when strictly necessary and only to the extent required to obtain a legitimate objective. Needless to say, the use of force to secure information or confession during an interview is not a legitimate objective. The commentary to the article includes the observation that arbitrary use of force can never be accepted.

(D) STANDARDS ON INTERVIEWING PEOPLE SUSPECTED OF CRIME

(a) Declaration on the Protection of All Persons from Being Subjected to Torture and Other Cruel, Inhuman or Degrading Treatment or Punishment, and Convention against Torture and Other Cruel, Inhuman or Degrading Treatment or Punishment

Article 6 of the Torture Declaration requires States to keep under systematic review interrogation methods and practices with a view to preventing torture or other ill-treatment prohibited under the Declaration. The same article also requires such systematic reviews of arrangements for the custody and treatment of persons deprived of their liberty. The Convention against Torture, in article 11, imposes similar obligations on each State party to the Convention, although it additionally requires systematic reviews of interrogation rules and instructions as well as of methods and practices.

Systematic reviews of this nature can result in a number of desirable consequences. Apart from evaluating the continuing relevance of a state's rules, instructions, methods and practices in light of its obligations to prevent torture and ill-treatment, they provide a check on the level of compliance with them. Furthermore, they could encourage the spread of best practice in the technical aspects of interviewing, especially when such reviews include studies of lawful, ethical and effective interrogation methods and practices developed in other states.

Other provisions in the Torture Declaration and the Torture Convention relevant to interviewing people suspected of crime are those stipulating that statements made as a result of torture or other ill-treatment may not be invoked as evidence (articles 12 and 15 respectively). The Declaration prohibits their use against the person concerned or against any other person in any proceedings, whereas the Convention permits their use against a person accused of torture as evidence that the statement was made.

(b) **Inter-American Convention to Prevent and Punish Torture**

This instrument also includes a provision (in article 10) rendering inadmissible as evidence in a legal proceeding statements obtained through torture. Such a statement would, however, be admissible in a legal action against a person accused of having elicited it through acts of torture, as evidence that it was obtained by such means.

(c) **Body of Principles for the Protection of All Persons under any Form of Detention or Imprisonment**

Principle 21 of the Body of Principles embodies significant provisions in its two paragraphs, which deserve to be quoted in full:

> "1. It shall be prohibited to take undue advantage of the situation of a detained or imprisoned person for the purpose of compelling him to confess, incriminate himself otherwise or to testify against any other person.
>
> 2. No detained person while being interrogated shall be subject to violence, threats or methods of interrogation which impair his capacity of decision or his judgement."

The provisions of paragraph 1 recognise, and prohibit, perhaps one of the most common features of interrogation of suspects by police, the exploitation of the situation of the detainee to cause him or her to confess or to respond in the other ways mentioned in the paragraph. The very fact of confinement, especially if there is little or no opportunity to consult legal advisers, family or friends, means that detainees are extremely vulnerable to this type of manipulation. It is a form of exploitation that is unethical and in some circumstances unlawful, and which can lead to false confessions of crime and false incrimination of others.

All of the 'techniques' referred to in paragraph 2, it should be noted, are forbidden regardless of whether or not they reach the threshold of torture or other ill-treatment prohibited by treaty articles. By impairing capacity of decision or judgement they could induce false confessions of crime, which, in turn, could lead to the conviction and punishment of innocent people, and the consequent escape from justice of those actually responsible for crime. They could also cause the interviewee to provide false information about the matter on which he or she is being questioned which could be, at least, time wasting and, at most, dangerous.

Principle 23 of the Body of Principles is the other provision of that instrument directly addressing interrogation of detainees. This requires the duration of any interrogation of a detainee to be recorded, as well as intervals between interrogations, the identity of officials conducting the interrogations and other persons present. A detainee or his counsel is to have access to these records. Clearly these requirements are designed to prevent abuse of detainees during the interrogation process; to secure compliance with the provisions in principle 21; and to assist a court in deciding whether evidence secured during interrogation has been obtained in a manner that would make that evidence inadmissible.

(d) **European Code of Police Ethics**

Article 50 of the European Code of Police Ethics requires guidelines for the proper conduct and integrity of police interviews to be established. It stipulates that guidelines should, in particular, provide for a fair interview during which those interviewed are made aware of the reasons for the interview as well as other relevant information. Systematic records of police interviews are to be kept. The Commentary to the article indicates that the rule originates in statements with regard to the interrogation process in custody made by the European Committee for the Prevention of Torture and Inhuman or Degrading Treatment or Punishment, as contained in its Second General Report (1992):

> "[T]he CPT considers that clear rules or guidelines should exist on the way in which police interviews are to be conducted. They should address inter alia the following matters: the informing of the detainee of the identity (name and/or number) of those present at the interview; the permissible length of an interview; rest periods between interviews and breaks during an interview; places in which interviews may take place; whether the detainee may be required to stand while being questioned; the interviewing of persons who are under the influence of drugs, alcohol, etc. It should also be required that a record be systematically kept of the time at which interviews start and end, of any request made by a detainee during an interview, and of the persons present during each interview.
>
> The CPT would add that the electronic recording of police interviews is another useful safeguard against the ill-treatment of detainees (as well as having significant advantages for the police)."

The commentary concludes by pointing out that article 50 is applicable to all police interviews, regardless of whether those subject to the interview are in custody or not.

(E) **THE UN SPECIAL RAPPORTEUR ON TORTURE – OBSERVATIONS AND RECOMMENDATIONS ON INTERROGATION**

In his reports to the General Assembly of the United Nations and to the Commission on Human Rights, the Special Rapporteur on torture has made observations and recommendations concerning interrogation of detainees on a number of occasions.

III:4

These amount to expressions of good practice to be followed, and of bad practice to be avoided and prohibited.

For example, in his 1986 report to the Commission,[189] the Special Rapporteur's recommendations included the following: that evidence extracted under torture should not be admissible in legal proceedings; that interrogation procedures be subject to internal scrutiny; that interrogation only be carried out at official interrogation centres; and that all security and law enforcement personnel be provided with the UN Code of Conduct for Law Enforcement Officials, and be instructed on its requirements and on the absolute prohibition of torture. In his report to the Commission in 1987,[190] he observed that information extracted by torture in many cases is completely unreliable, adding that he had seen many reports in which victims stated that in the end they had said whatever the interrogator wanted them so say.

The Special Rapporteur has repeated, reinforced and expanded upon these observations and recommendations in subsequent reports. For example in his report to the Commission on Human Rights in 2003[191] the Special Rapporteur observed that incidents of torture or other forms of ill-treatment frequently occur in the period immediately following deprivation of liberty and during interrogation. He recalled that, in compliance with article 15 of the Convention against Torture, confessions made as a result of torture shall not be used as evidence in any proceedings, except against a person accused of torture as evidence that the statement was made.

In the same report, the Special Rapporteur referred to some basic guarantees that should be applied to avoid torture during interrogation. In accordance with article 11 (combined with article 16) of the Convention against Torture, interrogation rules, instructions, methods and practices shall be kept under systematic review with a view to preventing cases of torture and other forms of cruel, inhuman or degrading treatment. According to principle 23 of the Body of Principles on Detention the duration of interrogations, the intervals between each interrogation and the identity of the officials conducting the interrogation shall be recorded. The information recorded shall be available to the interrogated person and, when provided by the law, to his or her counsel.

The Special Rapporteur then recalled one of his previous recommendations, namely:

---

[189] *Supra* note 147.
[190] *Supra* note 146.
[191] UN Doc. E/CN.4/2004/56.

"[E]ach interrogation should be initiated with the identification of all persons present. All interrogation sessions should be recorded, and preferably video-recorded, and the identity of all persons present should be included in the records. Evidence from non-recorded interrogations should be excluded from court proceedings. The practice of blindfolding and hooding often makes the prosecution of torture virtually impossible, as victims are rendered incapable of identifying their torturers. That practice should be forbidden. Those legally arrested should not be held in facilities under the control of their interrogators or investigators for more than the time required by law to obtain a judicial warrant of pre-trial detention which, in any case, should not exceed a period of 48 hours. They should accordingly be transferred to a pre-trial facility under a different authority at once, after which no further unsupervised contact with the interrogators or investigators should be permitted."

In relation to guarantees during interrogation, the Special Rapporteur is of the opinion that, as provided by article 10 of the Convention against Torture, interrogators should receive training in order to ensure that they have the necessary skills to conduct interrogations and interview victims and witnesses.

Focusing on incommunicado detention, in the same report, the Special Rapporteur observed that this is aggravated when individuals are held in secret places of detention. He reiterated that the maintenance of secret places of detention should be abolished under law. It should be a punishable offence for any official to hold a person in a secret and/or unofficial place of detention. Any evidence obtained from a detainee in an unofficial place of detention and not confirmed by the detainee during interrogation at official locations should not be admitted as evidence in court.

Concerning female detainees, he reiterated that female security personnel should be present during the interrogation of women, as the interrogation and detention of female detainees by exclusively male personnel constitute conditions that may be conducive to rape and sexual abuse of women prisoners.

The Special Rapporteur has made some trenchant and timely observations on the question of interrogating detainees suspected of crimes of terrorism. An example of these, expressed in his statement to the Human Rights Commission in April 2005, is given in Chapter 1 of this part. In his report to the General Assembly of the United Nations in 2004,[192] he noted with serious concern that attempts have been made to narrow the scope of the definition of torture contained in article 1 of the Convention against Torture and Other Cruel, Inhuman or Degrading Treatment or Punishment. For instance, torture has reportedly been defined by the United States as physical

---

[192] *Supra* note 152.

III:4

pain that is difficult to endure, and which should be equivalent to the pain accompanying serious physical injury, such as organ failure, impairment of bodily function, or even death. Furthermore, it has reportedly been argued that some harsh methods should not be considered as torture, but merely as cruel, inhuman or degrading treatment or punishment and therefore not absolutely prohibited and permissible in exceptional circumstances. In particular, it was reportedly asserted that permissible methods of interrogation could include the deprivation of essential human needs, suffocation with a wet cloth and death threats. In this respect, the Special Rapporteur stressed that the definition contained in the Convention cannot be altered by events or in accordance with the will or interest of States. He also recalled that the prohibition applies equally to torture and to cruel, inhuman or degrading treatment or punishment.

In the same report, the Special Rapporteur indicated that he had received information on certain methods that have been condoned and used to secure information from suspected terrorists. They notably included holding detainees in painful and/or stressful positions, depriving them of sleep and light for prolonged periods, exposing them to extremes of heat, cold, noise and light, hooding, depriving them of clothing, stripping detainees naked and threatening them with dogs. He pointed out that jurisprudence of both international and regional human rights mechanisms is unanimous in stating that such methods violate the prohibition of torture and ill-treatment.

(F) TREATY BODIES AND INTERROGATION

(a) General Comments of the Human Rights Committee

Paragraphs 11 and 12 of the Committee's General Comment No. 20(44)[193] on article 7 of the Covenant, repeat and reinforce the provisions of human rights instruments on interrogation, and the recommendations of the Special Rapporteur on torture.

In paragraph 11 the Committee states, *inter alia*, that it should be noted that keeping under systematic review interrogation rules, instructions, methods and practices is an effective means of preventing cases of torture and ill-treatment; and that the time and place of all interrogations should be recorded, together with the names of all those present, and this information should be available for purposes of judicial or administrative proceedings.

---

[193] General Comment No. 20(44), *supra* note 156.

In paragraph 12 the Committee underlines the importance of prohibiting the admissibility in judicial proceedings of statements or confessions obtained through torture or other prohibited treatment

(b) Observations and Findings of Courts

Some of the interrogation techniques condemned by the Special Rapporteur on torture were considered by the European Commission of Human Rights and the European Court of Human Rights in *Ireland* v. *the United Kingdom*,[194] The techniques applied in this case were wall standing; putting a dark coloured hood over the detainees' heads; subjection to continuous, loud noise; deprivation of sleep; and deprivation of food and drink. It will be recalled from the account of this case in Chapter 2 of this part that, ultimately, the European Court of Human Rights concluded that the techniques, referred to variously as interrogation in depth, disorientation or sensory deprivation techniques, constituted inhuman and degrading treatment as they did not occasion suffering of the degree of intensity and cruelty implied by the word torture. However in a later case, *Selmouni* v. *France*,[195] the Court observed that, having regard to the fact that the European Convention on Human Rights was a living instrument to be interpreted in the light of present-day conditions, certain acts classified in the past as inhuman and degrading treatment as opposed to torture could be classified differently in future. It took the view that the increasingly high standard being required in the area of the protection of human rights and fundamental liberties correspondingly and inevitably required greater firmness in assessing breaches of the fundamental values of democratic societies. It had been clearly established to the Court that Mr. Selmouni endured repeated and sustained assaults over a number of days of questioning. The report of the case shows that he was subjected to a variety of painful, humiliating and degrading indignities and cruelties, and the Court found that these amounted to torture.

Other cases that involved criminal, cruel and unprofessional interrogation techniques are described in chapter 2 of this Part. In *López Burgos* v. *Uruguay* the victim, after atrocious treatment, was forced under threats to sign false statements, which were subsequently used in the legal proceedings against him.[196] In the case *Prosecutor* v. *Anto Furundzija* before the International Tribunal for the Former Yugoslavia the accused, who interrogated a female detainee whilst she was subjected to torture, including rape, by another person was convicted of the crime of torture and imprisoned.[197]

---

[194] *Ireland* v. *the United Kingdom*, *supra* note 159.

[195] *Selmouni* v. France, *supra* note 45.

[196] *López Burgos* v. *Uruguay* , *supra* note 160.

[197] *Prosecutor* v. *Anto Furundzija, supra* note 166.

III:4

(c) **Observations and Recommendations of the European Committee for the Prevention of Torture and Inhuman or Degrading Treatment or Punishment**

The European Committee has expressed informed and constructive observations and recommendations on the questioning of detainees suspected of crime.[198] The Committee points out that the questioning of criminal suspects is a specialist task which calls for specific training if it is to be performed in a satisfactory manner. First and foremost, the Committee observes, the precise aim of such questioning must be made crystal clear: that aim should be to obtain accurate and reliable information in order to discover the truth about matters under investigation, not to obtain a confession from someone presumed, in the eyes of the interviewing officers, to be guilty. In addition to the provision of appropriate training, it is the Committee's view that ensuring adherence of law enforcement officials to the above mentioned aim will be greatly facilitated by the drawing up of a code of conduct for the questioning of criminal suspects.

The Committee reports that, over the years, its delegations have spoken to a considerable number of detained persons in various countries, who have made credible claims of having been physically ill-treated or otherwise intimidated or threatened, by police officers trying to obtain confessions in the course of interrogations. It is self-evident to the Committee that a criminal justice system that places a premium on confession evidence creates incentives for officials involved in the investigation of crime – and often under pressure to obtain results – to use physical or psychological coercion. In the context of the prevention of torture or other forms of ill-treatment, the Committee urges the development of methods of crime investigation capable of reducing reliance on confessions, and other evidence and information obtained via interrogations, for the purpose of securing convictions.

The Committee observes that the electronic (i.e. audio and/or video) recording of police interviews represents an important additional safeguard against the ill-treatment of detainees, and is pleased to note that the introduction of such systems is under consideration in an increasing number of countries. Such a facility can provide a complete and authentic record of the interview process, thereby greatly facilitating the investigation of any allegations of ill-treatment. The Committee points out that this is in the interests both of persons who have been ill-treated by police and of police officers confronted with unfounded allegations that they have engaged in physical ill-treatment or psychological pressure. Electronic recording of police interviews also reduces the opportunity for defendants later to falsely deny that they have made certain admissions.

---

[198] The CPT Standards, *supra* note 185, paragraphs 33 – 39.

The Committee states that it has, on more than one occasion and in more than one country, discovered interrogation rooms of a highly intimidating nature: for example, rooms entirely decorated in black and equipped with spotlights directed at the seat used by the person undergoing interrogation. Facilities of this kind, the Committee rightly insists, have no place in a police service. It could have added that they have no place on the premises of any agency of a democratic State governed by the rule of law.

The Committee recommends standards for rooms in which interviews of suspects are conducted. In addition to being adequately lit, heated and ventilated, interview rooms should allow for all participants in the interview process to be seated on chairs of a similar style and standard of comfort. The interviewing officer should not be placed in a dominating (e.g. elevated) or remote position vis-à-vis the suspect. Further, colour schemes should be neutral.

In certain countries, the Committee reports that it has encountered the practice of blindfolding persons in police custody, in particular during periods of questioning. Its delegations have received various – often contradictory – explanations from police officers as regards the purpose of this practice. From information gathered over the years, it is clear to the Committee that in many if not most cases, persons are blindfolded in order to prevent them from being able to identify law enforcement officials who inflict ill-treatment on them. Even in cases where no physical ill-treatment occurs, to blindfold a person in custody – and in particular someone undergoing questioning – is a form of oppressive conduct, the effect of which on the person concerned will frequently amount to psychological ill-treatment. The Committee recommends that the blindfolding of persons who are in police custody be expressly prohibited.

Finally, in its observations and recommendations on this matter, the Committee reports that it is not unusual for its delegations to find suspicious objects on police premises, such as wooden sticks, broom handles, baseball bats, metal rods, pieces of thick electric cable, imitation firearms or knives. The presence of such objects has, on more than one occasion, lent credence to allegations received by Committee delegations that the persons held in the establishments concerned have been threatened and/or struck with objects of this kind.

A common explanation received by the Committee from police officers concerning such objects is that they have been confiscated from suspects and will be used as evidence. The fact that the objects concerned are invariably unlabelled, and frequently are found scattered around the premises (on occasion placed behind curtains or cupboards), only invites the scepticism of the Committee as regards that explanation. In order to dispel speculation about improper conduct on the part of

III:4

police officers and to remove potential sources of danger to staff and detained persons alike, the Committee recommends that items seized for the purpose of being used as evidence should always be properly labelled, recorded and kept in a dedicated property store. All other objects of the kind mentioned above, the Committee insists, should be removed from police premises.

(G) INTERVIEWING WITNESSES TO CRIME

There are no international standards on interviewing witnesses to crime, however one instrument establishes standards on the treatment of victims of crime, who sometimes fall into the category of witnesses, and another deals specifically with the special needs of witnesses.

The Declaration of Basic Principles of Justice for Victims of Crime and Abuse of Power[199] requires, in article 4, victims to be treated with compassion and respect for their dignity, and, in article 6(d), measures to be taken to minimise inconvenience to victims, protect their privacy, ensure their safety, as well as that of their families and witnesses on their behalf, from intimidation and retaliation.

Article 16 of the Declaration requires police and other relevant personnel to be trained to sensitise them to the needs of victims, and guidelines to ensure proper and prompt aid. Article 17 states that in providing services and assistance to victims, attention should be given to those who have special needs because of the nature of the harm inflicted. This last provision is particularly relevant to victims of sexual crimes and special measures are necessary to secure their welfare not only for the benefit of the victim, but also to enable them to provide the best possible evidence and to testify to the maximum effect.

The European Code of Police Ethics, in article 51, stipulates that police shall be aware of the special needs of witnesses and shall be guided by rules for their protection and support during investigation, in particular, where intimidation of witnesses is at risk. The commentary to the article states that police personnel must be competent in handling the early stages of an investigation, in particular, contacts with those implicated by a crime. The commentary points out that the proper protection of witnesses is necessary for their safety, which is a crucial condition for them to give evidence and thus for the outcome of the investigation. When intimidated witnesses are afraid of the possible consequences of giving evidence, investigative techniques must be flexible, and take this into account. The problem of intimidated witnesses is particularly critical in situations, such as those related to

---

[199] Declaration of Basic Principles of Justice for Victims of Crime and Abuse of Power, *supra* note 33.

terrorism, to organised crime, to drug related crime and to violence within the family. Moreover, in cases where the witnesses are also victims of the crime, the handling of witnesses becomes even more complex.

The commentary concludes by underlining how important it is for the police to be aware of the special needs of witnesses in different situations, and their protection. This calls for special training of police personnel, and guidelines to determine the proper handling of witnesses by the police.

Clearly all witnesses to crime are entitled to respect for their dignity. It is important for police to be trained not only in the competent and humane treatment of witnesses and victims, but also in the specific policing skill of interviewing such people.

(H) GOOD BEHAVIOUR AND TECHNICAL SKILL

There are no legal grounds, no moral grounds and no practical grounds that can justify the conduct of interviews by unlawful, unethical or inhumane means. Interrogation by ordeal is intolerable, unnecessary and counter productive. In the investigation of crime or the search for intelligence there is only one option for police officials and other professional interviewers, the lawful option.

Good behaviour in the investigative process, and specifically in the conduct of interviews, is one element essential for the delivery of high quality, proficient service to the community. The other element is the application of a high degree of expertise and skill in the craft of policing. In the practice of this craft, no operation or activity can be judged independently of the means by which it is effected. As has been argued in other parts of this book, the normative and the technical aspects of policing are mutually dependent.

Having considered the normative aspects of the treatment of detainees and the conduct of interviews, it is now appropriate and necessary to consider the theory and practice of the technical policing skill of investigative interviewing. Part IV of this of the book is devoted to this important matter.

As a prelude to Part IV it is important to acknowledge the good work of police officials, and to note that most do not torture or mistreat people with whom they deal, and that most treat detainees humanely. Nevertheless many police officials see human rights as being in conflict with their work, and the international standards for the protection of human rights are not as widely known amongst police as they should be. This is inimical to effective policing and to the enjoyment of human rights.

III:4

These are the reasons for locating the following account of the theory and practice of a technical policing skill within the context of normative standards expressed by human rights law generally, and for identifying specific human rights standards relevant to this aspect of policing. In this way the link between the normative and the technical aspects of policing is reinforced, and effective policing and the enjoyment of human rights may be enhanced.

Perhaps the last words on interviewing in this chapter should be those of a US army intelligence corps interrogator. Although they refer to a specific situation they have universal application.

> "The abuses at Abu Ghraib are unforgivable not just because they were cruel, but because they set us back. The more a prisoner hates America, the harder he will be to break. The more a population hates America, the less likely its citizens will be to lead us to a suspect. One of our biggest successes in Afghanistan came when a valuable prisoner decided to cooperate not because he had been abused (he had not been), but precisely because he realised he would not be tortured."[200]

---

[200] C. Mackey and G. Miller, *The Interrogator's War* (John Murray (Publishers), London, 2004), p. xxiii.

PART IV

INVESTIGATIVE INTERVIEWING: PROFESSIONALISM AND BEST PRACTICE

Chapter 1: Why Ordinary People Get Involved with Terrorism, Civil Conflict and Torture

At this juncture in the book we move from the theory and international framework of human rights law to consider how these principles can be applied to policing and investigative practice. In any civilised world, torture should belong to the history books, yet it remains horrifyingly commonplace, even if terrorist atrocities and civil emergencies remain the exception rather than the rule. The extent and the absolute nature of the prohibition of torture are described in Chapter 2 of Part III herein. There are no circumstances under which torture may be lawfully practiced. Furthermore, it is a very serious crime. Despite this unambiguous legal position, it would appear that, in responding to acts of terror and to internal armed conflicts, disturbances and tensions, torture is being sanctioned by some governments, or condoned and carried out on their behalf by nations with fewer scruples and concerns for human rights. In some democratic countries classified and secret evidence against terrorist suspects that may have been extracted under torture is being used in secret trials.[201]

The temptation to use torture is sometimes justified because of a belief that policing based on human rights principles will result in ineffectual investigations or diminish the elicitation of information from suspects during questioning. The authors refute this and maintain that it is precisely when human rights are respected that the professional standard of effective policing that should be required in democratic societies is made possible. The following chapters demonstrate that there is much to commend in this approach as rights form a basis for a relationship of trust and reciprocity between states and their intelligence and law enforcement agencies, and the individual. Respect for citizens' rights provides a solid basis for reciprocity between state and citizen.[202]

Our experience is that where investigations and interviews are conducted in ways that protect human rights it not only strengthens reciprocity, accountability and democracy, but it is also more likely to yield accurate and reliable information that is the lifeblood of intelligence and law enforcement agencies. Police in democracies are under pressure to respond to the threat of terrorist attack by interviewing terrorist

---

[201] T. Williamson (ed.), *Investigative Interviewing: Rights, Research and Regulation* (Willan Press, Cullompton, Devon, England, 2006).
[202] A. Wright, *Policing: An Introduction to Concepts and Practice* (Willan Press, Cullompton, Devon, England, 2002).

suspects in inhumane ways, including torture. This departure from international norms is made on the assumption that such treatment would yield information that could be used to prevent further atrocities. It was the atrocities committed during the Second World War that led the newly formed United Nations to adopt the Universal Declaration of Human Rights on 10 December 1948 in San Francisco. It could be argued that if the following 50 years were spent winning international respect for the *principle* of human rights, it was hoped that the second 50 years would be spent in achieving the routine *practice* of respect for human rights by all Member States and their agents, including law enforcement and intelligence agencies.

Of course, western democracies are not the only countries facing the threat of terrorism; bombs have exploded in many other countries recently, including in Iraq, Indonesia and Russia. No doubt these attacks will continue to affect others into the foreseeable future as more countries experience the scourge of terrorism. Indeed, it has been argued that civil emergencies including ethnic cleansing and the use of terror are likely to increase in the 21st Century as more countries aspire to become nation states and that such aspirations inevitably result in conflicts over nationality, ethnicity and religion[203]. If this analysis is right there will be a temptation to respond to such civil emergencies with the use of torture. We need to be clear that it is not only illegal and immoral, but counter-productive. As Kofi Annan, Secretary General of the United Nations has said: "There is no trade-off between effective action against terrorism and the protection of human rights. On the contrary, I believe that in the long term we shall find that human rights, along with democracy and social justice, are one of the best prophylactics against terrorism."[204]

Respecting the principles of human rights and developing appropriate practice will be an essential ingredient of solving future conflicts. This has been shown in the steps towards peace in Northern Ireland following a period of civil emergency that lasted from the 1960s. The creation of a model of policing based on respect for human rights was an essential part of the peace process.[205] When democracies are faced with the threat of terrorism it is easy to dismiss the protection of human rights as naïve. We should recognise that the appalling abuses and erosion of civil liberties of detainees suspected of involvement in terror and civil emergencies is an aberration. The type and level of threat does not provide a reason to abandon the

---

[203] M. Mann, *The Dark Side of Democracy: Explaining Ethnic Cleansing* (Cambridge University Press, Cambridge, 2005).
[204] Secretary General's statement at the UN Security Council meeting on counterterrorism on 18 January 2002.
[205] Independent Commission on Policing for Northern Ireland, Report: *A New Beginning: Policing in Northern Ireland,*1999; A. Mulcahy, *Policing Northern Ireland: Conflict, Legitimacy and Reform* (Willan Press, Cullompton, Devon, England, 1999).

concept of universal rights. It is the authors' experience that widely publicised examples of egregious human rights violations committed by representatives of democratic states governed by the rule of law have had at least two contrasting effects on officials from states in transition to democracy. In some instances examples of torture and abuse of detainees have been so graphic that they have sickened and appalled such officials, and it has been unnecessary to make out the case for the prohibition of torture and ill-treatment. The reasons for complying with the prohibition have been apparent. In contrast, other officials from states in transition have taken the position that international human rights standards can be of little value if they are violated by states that, supposedly, embrace human rights, democracy, and the rule of law. It may be understandable that a country facing terrorism or a civil emergency would want to take draconian action, but experience has shown that undermining human rights only exacerbates the situation. The Commission that redefined policing and put in place a fundamental process of change from quasi-military policing to human rights based civil policing in Northern Ireland argued that:

> "It is a central proposition of this report that the fundamental purpose of policing should be the protection and vindication of the human rights of all, *policing means protecting human rights.*"[206]

If this is the gold standard for policing in civil society, why is the use of torture and other forms of inhuman and degrading treatment of people by police and security forces around the world so pervasive? To answer this question we need to understand the conditions that allow it to happen. Most interviews will not involve torture, but the growing post-war consensus around the principle of respect for human rights does face a serious challenge. A global survey on torture by Amnesty International found over 150 countries practicing torture or ill treatment by state agents and more than 70 countries where torture was widespread. They found that most victims of torture by state agents are criminal suspects from the poorest or most marginalized sectors of society. Most of the torturers are police officials.[207]

When society fails to challenge human rights abuses it offers support for such conduct, despite the fact that in the long-term it has little utilitarian benefit. Whatever short-term gains may have been obtained, no terrorist campaign has been defeated or civil emergency resolved through the use of torture. Given the seriousness of the threat that countries face from terrorism and the prevalence of the use of torture as a response to the threat, there has been a debate about whether, in contravention of international law and, indeed, the laws of states, torture should

---

[206] *Ibid.*
[207] Amnesty International, *Torture Survey*, 2000.

IV:1

become an accepted tool to aid investigation and information gathering. It has been argued that states should make arrangements to authorise and regulate it. Arguments against torture, and specifically torture of terrorist suspects, were set out in Chapter 1 of Part III. However, it is useful to develop these arguments here, specifically in the context of interviewing. Dershowitz, an American lawyer, has argued for the introduction of a 'torture warrant', which would provide judicial authorisation for torturing a suspect in particular circumstances. He makes this suggestion on the basis that "at least moderate forms of non-lethal torture are in fact being used by the United States" (the so-called 'torture lite' option),[208] and that the US already subcontracts torture by 'rendering' suspects to Egypt, Morocco and Jordan.[209] The rendition of suspects to places where they may be tortured is a serious breach of international law. For example, article 3 of the Convention against Torture states:

> "No State Party shall expel, return ('refouler') or extradite a person to another State where there are substantial grounds for believing that he would be in danger of being subjected to torture."

The grounds for consideration include the existence in the State concerned of a consistent pattern of gross, flagrant or mass violations of human rights. Dershowitz's 'authorise and regulate' strategy would not only be in breach of international law, it has been criticised as unlikely to succeed as it would inevitably result in torturers and their superiors straying beyond the parameters set.[210] What might these parameters be and who would write them? A relevant ethical principle is that the end does not justify the means, especially when the end is likely to be information that is unreliable and misleading.

Dershowitz's argument that torture be used to collect information faces another problem because this is not how torture is mainly used. There are two other principal uses of torture. The first is to punish dissidents who are considered to be enemies of the state, and the second is to use the fact of torture as a form of coercive power to intimidate dissident populations. Gathering accurate and reliable information through the use of torture is rarely, if ever, the objective, despite this being the justification that is most frequently advanced. If that were occasionally the objective, there are more effective ways of achieving it through humane methods of

---

[208] A. M. Dershowitz, 'The Torture Warrant: A Response to Professor Strauss', 48 *New York Law School Law Review* (2003) pp. 275-94.

[209] Committee on International Human Rights of the Association of the Bar of the City of New York and Center for Human Rights and Global Justice, *Torture by Proxy: International and Domestic Law Applicable to 'Extraordinary Renditions'*, New York, 2004.

[210] D. Dixon, 'Regulating Police Interrogation', in T. Williamson (ed.), *Investigative Interviewing: Rights, Research and Regulation* (Willan Press, Cullompton, Devon, England, 2006).

interviewing. Dershowitz's arguments are egregious and flawed but they merit consideration here because they masquerade as a utilitarian justification for breaking a strongly entrenched rule of international and domestic law. Utilitarian arguments in favour of torture are rehearsed in police and intelligence agencies. They have been the subject of government inquiries such as the Landau Commission in Israel,[211] although physical pressures to aid interrogation such as sleep deprivation, enforced stress positions, shaking, hooding and the playing of loud music have been deemed to be unlawful by the Israeli Supreme Court in its ruling a decade later on 6 September 1999 in the case of *Public Committee Against Torture in Israel* v. *State of Israel*.

Ironically, the best argument against torture is also a utilitarian one, namely that in the long term, it does not work and it undermines the legitimacy of the state itself. For example, the French used torture in the colonial struggle in Algeria, but over time they lost the respect of the Arab population and departed Algeria in ignominy. According to Mann[212] ethnic and nationalist violence that leads to civil emergencies may be a product of our time. In the 20th Century over 70 million people died in ethnic and nationalist conflicts, a number which dwarfs those of previous centuries. The media is dominated by reports of ethnic strife. The aspiration for democracy represented in the form of the modern nation state can result in clashes between different ethnic groups as the state defines itself in terms of a common culture and a sense of heritage distinct from other peoples. When one ethnic group forms a majority it can rule democratically but also tyrannically. Tougher treatment for ethnic enemies is demanded.[213] This is a perversion of democracy because ethnic unity then outweighs respect for diversity, which is central to democracy. Who then would perpetrate such a thing as ethnic cleansing? Having studied civil emergencies Mann concludes that "ordinary people are brought by normal social structures into committing murderous ethnic cleansing".[214]

He concurs with the conclusion reached by a psychologist, Charny, who observed that "the mass killers of humankind are largely everyday human beings – what we have called normal people according to currently accepted definitions by the mental health profession".[215]

---

[211] Landau Commission (named after Justice Mann Landau), *Report of the Commission of Inquiry into the Methods of Investigation of the General Security Service with Respect to Hostile Terrorist Activity*, Jerusalem, 1987.

[212] *Ibid.*

[213] *Ibid.*

[214] *Ibid.*

[215] I. Charny, 'Genocide and Mass Destruction: Doing Harm to Others as a Missing Dimension in Psychopathology', 49 *Psychiatry* (1986) pp.144-157.

IV:1

If nationalist and ethnic conflict demonstrates that ordinary people can become mass killers in times of civil emergency might ordinary people not also become torturers? In the next section we will briefly consider the social psychological research demonstrating who becomes a torturer and why, and that both ethnic cleansing and torture can be state sponsored.

(A) THE FUNDAMENTAL ATTRIBUTION ERROR: WHO BECOMES A TORTURER AND WHY?

To torture another human being is such an evil thing to do that it is easy to assume that torturers are mentally unbalanced psychopaths. Nothing could be further from the truth. The research evidence all points to the banality of torture and inhumane treatment. To assume that there is something in the character of torturers is to fail to appreciate the very powerful social factors that shape and develop their behaviour. This is a classic illustration of the fundamental attribution error that occurs when we *underestimate the power of external situational forces* and *overestimate the strength of individual character factors* guiding behaviour.[216] The likelihood of torture increases when governments, often military juntas, come to power by coup d'etat rather than democratic means. State sponsorship of torture involves very serious breaches of international law. Who the state agents are and how they are recruited and trained is widely misunderstood, they begin as ordinary people whose behaviour is then shaped by situational forces. Research into torturers in Greece and Brazil when under military government allows a picture to develop of how torturers are selected and trained.[217] In the case of Greece, after graduation from basic military training cadets were assigned to elite units to shape them into military policemen and torturers. Torture training took place in a special prison and inclusion in the torture unit enhanced the status of these soldiers. The initiation of these soldiers began when they were recruits where they were brutalised and humiliated for weeks. Recruits in Brazil went through a similar process where their violent treatment at the hands of their superiors desensitised them to pain and suffering and promoted total obedience to authority and acceptance of the need to destroy enemies of the state. Some torture techniques would be perpetrated on the recruits.

The first surprising finding from these studies is that there is no evidence that these torturers were recruited and selected because they were psychopathic or suffered from other personality disorders. Rather, the reverse was the case. The recruiters were looking for people with stable personalities that could be shaped by the regime

---

[216] L. Ross, 'The intuitive psychologist and his shortcomings: distortions in the attribution process', 10 *Advances in Experimental Social Psychology* (1977).
[217] M. Haritos-Fatouros, *The Psychological Origins of Institutionalized Torture* (Routledge, New York, London, 2002); M. K. Huggins *et al.*, *Violence Workers: Police Torturers and Murderers Reconstruct Brazilian Atrocities* (University of California Press, London, 2002).

to torture people who were considered to be a threat. They selected people who neither became angry nor took pity on their victims. Recruits who were considered to be fragile were weeded out. There is no evidence of premorbid personalities that would have disposed the recruits to become torturers, and they were initially no different from the normal population. The recruits were gradually introduced into torture routines. A recruit would be given training in torture strategies, tactics and technologies. The recruit would begin by watching a torture session, then join a small group of torturers where he would at first play a minor part before being presented with the challenge of himself torturing a detainee in order to obtain a confession. The initiation in Brazil was less formalised but followed a similar pattern. Torture was commonplace. The ordinariness of the people engaged in such evil behaviour and the banality of this process is what is so striking and pertinent.

This was also the finding to emerge from a famous study of Adolph Eichmann's personality. Eichmann had engaged in some of the most evil deeds the world has ever known, designing and organising the Nazi extermination camps during the Second World War. When he was put on trial in Israel he was examined by psychiatrists who found, contrary to expectations, that he was not a psychopath. On the contrary his personality and demeanour were socially 'desirable'. Social philosopher Hannah Arendt was an observer at the trial of Eichmann. She studied him carefully and found that he was a dull, ordinary bureaucrat who saw himself as no more than a little cog in the big Nazi machine. She too found him to be terrifyingly normal.[218] The enormity of the acts perpetrated by people who appear so normal that they could be anyone's neighbour was so disturbing that she tried to capture this finding by referring to it as 'the banality of evil'. This phrase offers a chilling reminder of how commonplace this kind of behaviour can be. Therefore, given this banality, the fundamental attribution error must be avoided. Instead of looking for personality factors suggesting that these were inherently evil people, we are forced to consider in greater depth the powerful social influences that made ordinary people engage in acts that were exceedingly evil.

The social context that allows torture to occur is a more powerful determinant than the personality of the torturers. Both Greece and Brazil were under military governments and these regimes painted a picture that they were facing a national emergency. This was supported by a national security ideology in which communists, socialists and intellectuals were seen as enemies of the state. This meant that the torturers were able to excuse their behaviour by accepting the rhetoric of national security. It is the state that allows organisations to emerge that shape the values, thoughts and perceptions of the people within its systems. In Brazil, prior to

---

[218] H. Arendt, *Eichmann in Jerusalem: A Report on the Banality of Evil* (Viking Press, New York, 1963).

IV:1

the military government there was a long history of violent mistreatment of the poor that continues to this day. However, under the military, torture was planned and budgeted for, with sites for carrying out torture, sophisticated equipment and direct participation of doctors and nurses who advised the torturers and revived the victims when they lost consciousness.[219] According to Huggins *et al.* the Brazilian military regime "did what most repressive governments do: it created enemies of the State who must be identified, searched out, collected in secure settings, interrogated if they might have information of value, tortured if they do not comply, and executed when they are of no further value to the State's mission".[220]

State violence was deemed both necessary and appropriate. The torturers had internalised an image of a hated or feared enemy; the state was perceived as under siege. When the political ideology, bureaucracy and resources for state sponsored torture are in place, citizens who were once good are then enabled to do evil deeds with impunity, free from the fear of sanction. People can then rationalise their behaviour as being necessary to protect the state from its enemies who seek its destruction.

It is the case that in some regimes torture is prevalent but not institutionalised and may be the method some individuals choose to use to gain a confession or information. In other regimes torture is institutionalised, practiced systematically as part of a violent assembly line of repression, with the work organised around search and destroy teams using lethal force to execute subversives, and capture and interrogation units where detainees are tortured.[221]

What are the processes by which such moral transformations occur? Huggins *et al.* argue that four factors are necessary for ordinary people to do evil such as torture:

- Previous moral considerations are overridden.
- Blind obedience is mandated – mindless obedience to authority becomes necessary.
- Victims are dehumanised.
- Personal and social accountability is neutralised.[222]

There are strong social and organisational influences that have been identified in psychological laboratory research that are relevant to the phenomenon of torture. Bandura has described a process of moral disengagement where previously held

---

[219] Archdiocese of Sao Paulo, *Torture in Brazil* (Vintage, New York, 1998).

[220] *Ibid.*

[221] Huggins *et al.*, *supra* note 217, p. 246.

[222] *Ibid.*

moral values can be put to one side, and people engage in reprehensible behaviour they would not previously have countenanced. The conditions necessary for this to happen are those where there is an absence of either self-regulation or external surveillance.[223] Authoritarian systems require total, unquestioning obedience. A hierarchy of authority obviates individual responsibility for action, with people justifying their behaviour as only following orders. Nor need the orders be explicitly stated; blind obedience means that they may be implicit and inferred.

Although it may be difficult to accept that people will be mindlessly obedient to authority figures, there is a considerable amount of psychological research on how ordinary people in a democracy will follow instructions with blind obedience. A classic experiment was conducted by Stanley Milgram, a psychologist at Yale University. He advertised in a newspaper and recruited ordinary men and women who were offered USD 4 per hour to take part in a one hour experiment in what they were told was a memory study. When they arrived at the laboratory they met another participant who was a confederate of the experimenter. The real participant was assigned to the role of teacher and the confederate to the role of learner. The participant was required to read a list of word pairs to the learner and then test his memory by reading the first word of each pair and to then ask him to select the correct second word from four alternatives. Each time the learner made an error (and the participant was always told he had made an error) the participant was to press a lever that delivered an electric shock to him, ostensibly to aid his learning. The participant saw the learner strapped into a chair and an electrode attached to his wrist. The participant was seated in front of a shock generator with voltage ratings from 15 to 450 volts and there were labels showing 'Slight Shock' through to 'Danger: Severe Shock' and at the extreme a label marked 'XXX'. The participant was given a sample shock of 45 volts from the generator. The learner did not in fact receive any shocks, but as the shock levels were escalated by the participants he could be heard protesting through an adjoining wall. As the shocks became stronger he began to shout and curse. At 300 volts he began to kick the wall and at the next shock level, 'Extreme Intensity shock' he no longer answered any questions or made any noise. When the participants objected to the experiment they were simply told, 'Please continue', 'The experiment requires that you continue', 'It is absolutely essential that you continue' and 'You have no other choice – you must go on'.

Obedience to authority was measured by the maximum amount of shock the participant would administer before refusing to continue. Prior to the experiment Milgram consulted 40 psychiatrists who predicted that most participants would refuse to go on after reaching 150 volts and that only 4 per cent would go on beyond

---

[223] A. Bandura, 'Moral Disengagement in the Perpetration of Inhumanities', 3:3 *Personality and Social Psychology Review* (1999) pp. 193–209.

IV:1

300 volts and less than 1 per cent would go all the way to 450 volts. In fact 65 per cent of the participants continued to obey throughout going all the way to the end of the shock series (450 volts, labelled 'XXX'). The results of this experiment clearly demonstrate the fundamental attribution error, mentioned previously, that we erroneously attribute behaviour to peoples' character and personality and *overlook the power that situations hold over us*. The participants may not have wanted to do any harm but this failed to govern their behaviour. The contextual features of the experimental situation created blind obedience from ordinary people.[224] In 19 subsequent studies Milgram replicated the experiment using over 1,000 U.S. participants from all walks of life. In each replication he would vary one aspect of the experiment to see if obedience levels would change. Maximum obedience could be pushed to 90 percent where the participant watched another peer carry out the behaviour.[225] Milgram's experiment involved a gradual escalation of harm which is similar to the way that the recruits in Greece and Brazil were inducted into torture.

Another classical psychological experiment has examined the process of dehumanising that accompanies custodial detention and facilitates torture and inhuman and degrading treatment. When people are considered to be less than human, restraints are lifted on what is permissible to do to them. Another factor is lack of accountability. If people think that no one knows who they are or cares what they do it can result in what Zimbardo has called 'deindividuation'.[226] Dehumanising victims and the neutralising of personal and social responsibility were found in the Stanford Prison Experiment.[227]

In another famous study Zimbardo and his colleagues created a simulated prison in the basement of the psychology department at Stanford University and placed an advertisement in a local newspaper for participants to take part in a psychological experiment for pay. They selected 24 "mature, emotionally stable, normal,

---

[224] S. Milgram, 'Behavioral Study of Obedience', 67 *Journal of Abnormal and Social Psychology* (1963) pp. 371-378; S. Milgram, *Obedience to Authority: An Experimental View* (Harper & Row, New York, 1974).

[225] T. Blass (ed.), *Obedience to Authority: Current Perspectives on the Milgram Paradigm* (Erlbaum, Mahwah, New Jersey, 2000).

[226] P. G. Zimbardo, 'The Human Choice: Individuation, Reason, and Order Versus Deindividuation, Impulse, and Chaos', 17 *Nebraska Symposium on Motivation* (1969) pp. 237-307.

[227] P. G. Zimbardo, 'Pathology of Imprisonment', 9 *Society* (1972) pp. 4-8; P. G. Zimbardo *et al.*, 'The Mind is a Formidable Jailer: A Pirandellian Prison', *New York Times Magazine,* 8 April 1973, p. *38 et seq.*; P. G. Zimbardo *et al.*, 'Reflections on the Stanford Prison Experiment: Genesis, Transformations, Consequences', in T. Blass (ed.), *Obedience to Authority: Current Perspectives on the Milgram Paradigm* (Erlbaum, Mahwah, New Jersey, 2000).

intelligent white male college students" from middle-class homes throughout the United States and Canada. They shared similar values and none had a prison record. Half were randomly assigned to the roles of guards and the other half assigned roles as prisoners. The guards were instructed about their responsibilities and made aware of the potential danger of the situation and of the need to protect themselves. The prisoners were unexpectedly arrested at their homes, handcuffed, blindfolded and taken to the improvised jail where they were searched, deloused, fingerprinted, given numbers and placed in cells with two other prisoners. The participants expected the experiment to run for two weeks but it had to be abandoned by the sixth day as, far faster and more thoroughly than the researchers thought possible, an experiment had turned a reality. According to Zimbardo:

> "It was no longer apparent to most of the participants (or to us) where reality ended and their roles began. The majority had indeed become prisoners or guards, no longer able to clearly differentiate between role playing and self. There were dramatic changes in virtually every aspect of their behaviour, thinking, and feeling. In less than a week the experience of imprisonment undid (temporarily) a life-time of learning; human values were suspended, self-concepts were challenged, and the ugliest most base, pathological side of human nature surfaced. We were horrified because we saw some boys (guards) treat others as if they were despicable animals, taking pleasure in cruelty, while other boys (prisoners) became servile, dehumanised robots who thought only of escape, of their own individual survival, and of their mounting hatred for the guards."[228]

Bear in mind that the participants were randomly assigned to the roles of prisoner and guard, and that nothing in their character or backgrounds could explain their behaviour. Yet within a matter of days the guards became authoritarian and, in some cases, even sadistic. The guards dehumanised prisoners through punishment and harassment. During long night shifts, guards relieved their boredom by tormenting prisoners whom they treated as playthings. Some took pleasure in their own inventive cruelty. As the process of deindividuation, dehumanisation and moral disengagement unfolded it no longer mattered that they were just in an experiment. These findings suggest that custody itself is such a powerful situation that it can distort and change the behaviour of normal individuals.

Discussions of the Stanford Prison Experiment tend to focus on the behaviour of the prisoners and their guards but Huggins, Haritos-Fatouros and Zimbardo have broadened the discussion in the light of their research into torture. Using the metaphor of a theatre they point out that the prisoners and guards were actors in a

---

[228] *Ibid.*

larger drama that included directors, producers and audiences without whom the drama would lose its intensity and significance. Added credibility was given to the experiment by having the local police take part in the experiment for the arrest of the prisoners and these arrests were recorded by a local TV station. A Catholic priest interviewed the prisoners in the presence of guards; parents and friends visited during planned visiting hours and did nothing to force the prisoners' release despite their haggard appearance. A mock 'parole board' heard their complaints and sided with the guards. Many psychologists came to view the experiment and did not challenge its premises. The sadistic behaviour of some guards was always supported by at least one other guard on the same shift. The good guards never openly challenged the bad guards and never complained to the authorities about their colleagues' violations of prison rules. They enjoyed the positive comparison between themselves and the bad guards.[229]

The similarity between the experiment and a play is used by Zimbardo *et al.* to argue that in real life perpetrators of atrocities are facilitated by international governments (inter-governmental organisations), their representatives and the international corporations that supply atrocity technologies; national governments that provide the ideology, the cast of actors and the system of rewards and sanctions as well as the legal and financial structure that supports and excuses atrocity; and bystander communities, both in the perpetrators' society and in the broader world, who watch the play unfold in silence. They conclude that the nearly universal lack of accountability for torture makes it the perfect crime in most societies.

The psychological research by Bandura, Milgram and Zimbardo, briefly reviewed in this chapter points to a psychology of evil in which ordinary people can harm and degrade totally innocent people. Zimbardo *et al.* come to the chilling conclusion that

> "anyone could become a torturer or an executioner under a set of quite well-known conditions. Therefore, we must collectively strive to first expose these socio-political conditions wherever they appear and then to join others in denouncing and challenging them." This is not to excuse the individual perpetrator but to recognise that, "the decision to engage in evil is essentially one that each human must make and either to become a perpetrator or to resist the powerful situational pressures and choose the path of goodness."[230]

Taking the above psychological research studies into account, the abuse of detainees in custody is entirely predictable as a by-product of the various forms of action that states take in response to acts of terrorism. Although the individuals concerned

---

[229] *Ibid.*
[230] *Ibid.*

involved in human rights abuses should be held accountable, and occasionally some have been, we should take note of the wider context to which Zimbardo and colleagues draw attention. The wider cast may be discerned from a recent example, namely the United States of America policy papers that are now in the public domain which were passing up and down the chain of command when insufficient intelligence was being obtained from detainees.[231] These are the reports which USA government lawyers and officials wrote to prepare the way for, and to document, coercive interrogation and torture. These documents describe the systematic attempt of the USA Government to prepare the way for torture techniques and coercive interrogation practices, forbidden under both international human rights law and international humanitarian law, with the express intent of evading legal punishment in the aftermath of any discovery of these policies. The paper trail of approved interrogation techniques shows that the following were sanctioned:

- Sleep deprivation
- Detainees being shackled in stressful positions
- Extreme temperatures and noise
- Sexual humiliation
- Use of dogs to terrify detainees

There was also a request to permit the use of 'submarining', where detainees are held under water and fear that they will drown, but this was refused.[232] Confirmation that some of the methods were used has come from military officers involved in the questioning of detainees.[233]

The four key processes mentioned above that appear to be both necessary and sufficient for ordinary men and women to engage in torture and other evil acts can be discerned. It requires:

- creating new moralities, such as defending national security against a hated enemy;
- instilling blind obedience;
- dehumanising the victims; and
- neutralising personal and social responsibility.

---

[231] J. L. Dratel and K. J. Greenberg (eds.), *The Torture Papers: The Road to Abu Ghraib* (Cambridge University Press, Cambridge, 2005).
[232] D. Rose, 'American Interrogation Methods in the War on Terror', in T. Williamson (ed.), *Investigative Interviewing: Rights, Research and Regulation* (Willan Press, Cullompton, Devin, England, 2006).
[233] C. MacKey and G. Miller, *supra* note 200.

IV:1

These are sufficient to create a climate of moral disengagement to allow torture, summary executions and ethnic cleansing to occur.

The use of these techniques is predicated on the mistaken assumption that they work. As has been argued elsewhere in this book, it is difficult to disprove this assertion, in the short-term, because by the nature of these unlawful and secret activities we are unlikely to know whether useful information has been obtained. We do know however that the interrogation of detainees is frequently conducted in a ham-fisted and incompetent way, and that seasoned intelligence experts argue strongly that the best way of obtaining valuable, accurate and reliable information from detainees is through humane questioning.[234] It is to more humane and prosaic methods of interviewing that we now turn our attention.

---

[234] M. G. Gelles *et al.*, 'Al-Qaeda-Related Subjects: A Law Enforcement Perspective', in T. Williamson (ed.), *Investigative Interviewing: Rights, Research and Regulation* (Willan Press, Cullompton, Devin, England, 2006); J. Pearse, 'The Interrogation of Terrorist Suspects: The Banality of Torture', in T. Williamson (ed.), *Investigative Interviewing: Rights, Research and Regulation* (Willan Press, Cullompton, Devon, England, 2006).

Chapter 2. Investigative Interviewing: A Professional Approach to Investigations

(A) INTERVIEWING IN THE CONTEXT OF INVESTIGATIONS

An investigation should be a search for the truth. Unfortunately, in most criminal justice systems there is still an over-reliance on confession evidence, and in some cases it may be the only evidence. According to Dr Silvia Casale, President of the European Committee for the Prevention of Torture and Inhuman or Degrading Treatment or Punishment:

> "In many jurisdictions across the world, a confession is accepted as what is needed to complete an investigation, without the requirement for supporting evidence. Not surprisingly in such systems it is implicitly, or even explicitly, recognised that some police officials, relying heavily on gaining confessions from suspects in order to solve crimes, will resort to excessive use of force and ill-treat persons held for questioning. Such systems carry the greatest risk of denial of human rights. Whatever the pressures and expectations of the legal systems in which they operate, police officials cannot absolve themselves of their responsibilities under international law."[235]

The international instruments considered in previous parts of this book are intended to provide basic protection from physical or psychological abuse. That still leaves open the question of 'what is good interviewing?' and secondly, 'how does it fit into the way that investigations are conducted?' The specific purpose of this chapter is to explain the basic principles of investigative interviewing, and to describe how they can contribute to better police investigations and higher standards of professionalism consistent with international obligations.

Firstly it is necessary to place the interviewing of victims, witnesses or suspects in the context of the investigation. In some cases the investigator may find that the victim is dead; there are no witnesses to the offence; the witnesses are too afraid to give evidence or information; or there may be no forensic evidence. In such cases the investigator may have to rely on obtaining a confession from a suspect, and this

---

[235] B. Denmark, *Ethical Investigation: Practical Guide for Police Officers*, Foreign and Commonwealth Office, London, 2005.

is acceptable in those jurisdictions where a person may be found guilty by a court on the basis of an uncorroborated confession.

Since most interviews take place in private where the suspect is alone with the interviewer(s) and there is no independent record of what happened, there is, as Casale observed, a temptation for law enforcement officials to resort to physical or psychological abuse of the detainee. Sometimes the reasons for this can be understood, but such action is never justifiable. The offences under investigation may be heinous and there may be pressure on officials to solve the crime quickly and, as these situations have arisen in many countries, it is vitally important for all law enforcement officials to have a clearer understanding of the principles of ethical investigation and ethical interviewing based on respect for human rights. The model of investigation described here is intended to promote effective investigation of crime and respect for human rights in that process, and to encourage and maintain the support of the public for the police.

In most investigations it is normally the case that there are victims and witnesses from whom information can be obtained. Rather than over-relying on confession evidence, steps should instead be taken to identify those witnesses who may be able to provide relevant information. Sometimes enquiries for this purpose have to be made a considerable time after the event, and a number of methods have been found to be successful in tracing witnesses. For example, 'house to house enquiries' – the methodical visiting of all premises in the vicinity of a crime in order to establish whether occupants are able to provide relevant information; appeals for witnesses through the news media; the distribution of leaflets giving details of a crime and appealing for information; dramatised reconstructions of a crime on television programs (in some countries there are T.V. programs which specialise in this).

Forensic science can contribute greatly to investigations. In some countries techniques may be basic but nevertheless sound – for example the physical (as opposed to computerised) comparison of fingerprints found at the scene of a crime with those in a collection of previously convicted criminals. Other forensic science techniques, such as 'DNA profiling', are sophisticated and expensive, and may only be available in well-resourced police agencies. DNA is a very powerful tool and there are now many cases of people who have been wrongly convicted of serious offences where subsequent DNA tests showed that they could not have been responsible for the crime. In 9 per cent of these cases false confessions had been coerced from the suspect.[236] Regardless of the degree of sophistication of techniques or facilities available, it is essential that police officials should be aware of them and

---

[236] J. Dwyer *et al.*, *Actual Innocence: Five Days to Execution and Other Dispatches From the Wrongly Convicted* (Doubleday, New York, 2000).

maximise their use in order that they may be able to avoid conducting an investigation which relies solely on persuading a suspect to confession.

A fundamental flaw is created in many investigations when the investigator secures a confession from a suspect at an early stage, and then attempts to establish a case against the suspect by selectively building up supporting evidence around the confession. The key word here is 'selectively' for it means that the investigator is prepared to ignore, and even conceal, evidence which does not support the case against the accused, which was a factor in a further 9 per cent of cases of people who had been convicted and then later proved innocent on the basis of DNA evidence.[237] This can be fatal to the proper conclusion of any investigation, but especially so if the suspect has falsely confessed to a crime which he or she has not committed. If a person is convicted of a crime on the basis of evidence produced by such an 'investigation', a double miscarriage of justice occurs – the wrongful conviction of an innocent person, and the real offender manages to escape justice. It is more professional and ethical to approach the case with an open mind, and gather information systematically. In order for an investigation to be conducted on this methodical basis it is essential that each step of the investigation should be documented.

In complex or serious cases, on which a team of investigators is deployed, the senior investigating officer should set out in a book what the main lines of enquiry are, and record his or her reasons for following those particular lines of enquiry. This should be updated and the main lines of enquiry reviewed as the investigation progresses. It is also important to keep a record of all exhibits seized, and of all actions taken by the enquiry team. This means that when information is being recorded 'manually' (as opposed to on a computer system), three books are required which record 'Main Lines of Enquiry and Decisions'; 'Exhibits' – including a description of each item, and an account of who found them and where they were found; and 'Actions' – a record of all enquiries made and the results of those enquiries.

Commercial computerised major incident management systems are available for all of these purposes but, in their absence, the systematic and painstaking collation of information by non-technical means is not only possible – it is absolutely essential. The methodical collection of evidence is very important for the questioning of suspects. It means that all relevant information can be available for use by the interviewer. By approaching an investigation in this way the interview with a suspect can be based on the evidence and intelligence collected rather than just relying on trying to obtain a confession.

---

[237] *Ibid.*

IV:2

Where it has been possible to conduct research into how the police interview suspects it has almost always demonstrated that with a few notable exceptions, the standard of interviewing skill was poor. In what has been described by researchers as the 'standard police interview', there are a number of common features of bad interviewing that have been found in various jurisdictions. The interviewer starts with the objective not of seeking the truth but of getting a confession and shaping a story that emerges through questioning with the intention that it is damaging to the interviewee and incriminates them. The interview is conducted with little empathy for the interviewee and there is no attempt to establish rapport. The interview frequently commences abruptly with little or no explanation about what is going to happen which reinforces the perceived lack of rapport. There is no attempt at getting the suspect to provide their account. Instead, the interview is conducted in a question and answer session, typically with the use of closed questions, e.g. 'were you in the yellow car?'. Closed questions reduce the amount of information that is likely to be elicited. The interviewer endeavours to retain control of the interview, but if this is not done skilfully control moves around during the interview. When the interviewee is trying to provide an account, this is disrupted by frequent interruptions by the interviewer. Analysis of the whole interview shows that there is rarely any logical sequence to it, with questioning skipping from topic to topic leaving many lines of enquiry unanswered. Overall, the interviewee is likely to consider that the interviewer has been domineering, judgmental and socially unskilled.[238] One of the reasons for this low level of interviewing competence is that the interviewers generally have not had any formal training in how to conduct an investigative interview properly.

Where training has been provided it can all too frequently fall into the category of reinforcing the over-reliance on confession evidence. A very popular model of this kind of interview training is that provided by the Reid Organization.[239] This technique has been criticised for creating the conditions in which false[240] confessions can be an outcome.[241] We shall therefore briefly consider the Reid

---

[238] J. Baldwin, *Video Taping Police Interviews with Suspects: An Evaluation*, *Police Research Series*, Paper 1, Home Office Police Department, London, 1992; T. Williamson, 'Investigative Interviewing and Human Rights in the War on Terrorism', in T. Williamson (ed.), *Investigative Interviewing: Rights, Research and Regulation* (Willan Press, Cullompton, Devon, England, 2006).

[239] J. P. Buckley, 'The Reid Technique of Interviewing and Interrogation', in T. Williamson (ed.), *Investigative Interviewing: Rights, Research and Regulation*, (Willan Press, Cullompton, Devon, England, 2006).

[240] *Ibid.*

[241] G. H. Gudjonsson, 'The Psychology of Interrogations and Confessions', in T. Williamson (ed.), *Investigative Interviewing: Rights, Research and Regulation*, (Willan Press, Cullompton, Devon, England, 2006); S. Kassin, 'A Critical Appraisal of the Reid

technique, which is a highly confrontational and accusatory process of interrogation aimed at breaking down resistance and consists of the following nine steps:

Step 1: involves the suspect being told with absolute certainty that he or she committed the alleged offence. Where the interrogator has no evidence against the suspect they should pretend that there is evidence. If the suspect persists in denying the allegation the interrogator proceeds to step 2.

Step 2: is where various themes are suggested to the suspect aimed at minimising the moral implications of the alleged crime.

Step 3: is where the interrogator is trained to stop persistent denials by persistently interrupting the suspect and telling them to listen to what they have to say.

Step 4: requires the interrogator to overcome objections that the suspect may give as explanations for his or her innocence. When the suspect begins to show signs of withdrawal from active participation in the interrogation they are believed to be at their most vulnerable and this leads to step 5.

Step 5: requires the interrogator to secure the suspect's attention. They are trained to reduce the physical distance between themselves and the suspect, leaning forward towards the suspect, touching the suspect gently, mentioning the suspect's first name and maintaining good eye contact with the suspect. Through these means the suspect should become more attentive to the suggestions made by the interrogator.

Step 6: when it looks as though the suspect's resistance is about to break down, the interrogator will display signs of understanding and sympathy. Silence is taken as an indication that the interrogator should proceed to step 7.

Step 7: here the interrogator presents the suspect with two possible alternatives but both are highly incriminating. They are worded in such a way that one alternative acts as a face-saving device whilst the other implies some repulsive or callous motivation. It provides an incentive to confess and may be one of the most important parts of the Reid model. According to Gudjonsson (2006:127)[242] it is a coercive procedure where suspects are pressured to choose between two incriminating alternatives and it is particularly dangerous with suspects who are of below-average intelligence. Once the suspect has accepted one of the alternatives the interrogator moves on to Step 8.

Technique', in T. Williamson (ed.), *Investigative Interviewing: Rights, Research and Regulation*, (Willan Press, Cullompton, Devon, England, 2006); G. H. Gudjonsson and S. Kassin, 'The Psychology of Confessions: A Review of the Literature and Issues', 5:2 *Psychological Science in the Public Interest* (November 2004).

[242] Gudjonsson 2006, *ibid.*, p. 127.

IV:2

Step 8: here the suspect is required to orally relate various details of the offence once he or she has accepted one of the alternatives given to him or her in Step 7 and to provide a self-incriminating admission.
Step 9: is where the interrogator translates the oral confession into a written confession.

The main psychological manipulation involves maximisation by exaggerating the strength of evidence against the suspect and the seriousness of the offence, and minimisation by tricking the suspect into a false sense of security by offering sympathy and face saving excuses. The technique has been criticised as unethical due to the use of trickery, deceit and dishonesty as a way of breaking down resistance. There is no way of knowing what number of confessions obtained using the Reid technique are in fact false confessions. The use of deceit in an interview is permitted in some jurisdictions, such as the USA and Canada, and strongly proscribed in others such as England and Wales, because of the risk that it leads to false confessions.

Various models have been developed to explain why some suspects confess during questioning. According to Gudjonsson:

"Taken as a whole, the models suggest that suspects confess when they perceive that the evidence against them is strong (irrespective of whether this is real or distorted), when they need to relieve feelings of guilt, when they have difficulties coping with the custodial pressure (i.e. interrogation and confinement) and when they focus primarily on the immediate consequences of their actions rather than the long-term ones."[243]

False confession cases have been a feature of most jurisdictions and in some this has resulted in government inquiries into the circumstances leading to the false confession. Frequently such inquiries have recommended that improved training in interviewing should be provided and this has led to a search for more ethical interviewing methods that reduce the risk of false confessions but are still effective. There is considerable common ground regarding what constitutes best practice in investigative interviewing, although the particular training models have in some cases been developed independently. Not surprisingly, the best practice turns out to be the opposite of the features of the standard police interview observed in various studies, and of many of the features of the Reid technique.

In a good investigative interview the object is:

---

[243] For a detailed description of an interactional model of the interrogative process involving police factors, vulnerabilities and support factors, *see ibid.*, pp. 138-142.

- To keep an open mind, to search for the truth and to obtain information that is accurate and reliable.
- A thorough pre-interview investigation and collection of as much information as possible before conducting the interview. Recognition that the outcome of an interview will be associated with the amount of evidence. In interviews with suspects, strong evidence will be associated with a confession but where the evidence is weak it will encourage denials.
- Thorough preparation and planning prior to the interview.
- To begin with establishing rapport, where the interviewee is treated with respect and not demeaned, irrespective of the offence they are suspected of. Good interviewers display cultural sensitivity.
- To invite the interviewee to provide an account without interruption, which is sometimes known as 'free recall'.
- To initially ask open questions, before going to the use of closed questions for the purposes of clarifying or checking a particular point, initially avoiding leading questions, e.g. 'Did she have red hair?'
- To try to achieve a positive closure that will facilitate any future meetings. Remember that an interview is only one episode during an investigation and where an interview finishes positively it could be the basis for a useful long-term relationship, and this may be jeopardised if the interview finishes with the interviewee feeling negatively towards the interviewer.

Why is establishing rapport such an important factor in successful interviews? Many research studies have shown that the police tend to use a domineering approach in interviews and that this reduces the likelihood of rapport being established and is counter-productive. In a study in Sweden of men convicted of murder or sexual offences it was found that interviews characterised as dominant resulted in more denials. Interviews characterised as humane were associated with admissions. Similarly in a study of victims of rape or aggravated assault those interviews characterised as dominant by the witness were associated with victims who omitted to supply important information. Interviews that the witness characterised as being humane were associated with victims who provided all relevant information.[244]

Humane and ethical interviewing is therefore better than the other methods discussed herein because it is more effective, resulting in more information being obtained, and reduces the risk of confessions being obtained that are false. The next chapter describes one model of investigative interviewing and the arrangements that

---

[244] U. Holmberg, *Police Interviews with Victims and Suspects of Violent and Sexual Crimes: Interviewees' Experiences and Interview Outcomes'*, Stockholm University, Department of Psychology, Stockholm, Sweden, 2004, <www.diva-portal.org/su/abstract.xsql?dbid=64>, last visited September 2006.

have been made to regulate custodial questioning. Similar models have been developed in other jurisdictions that share the common features of humane interviewing.[245]

---

[245] M. St-Yves, 'The Psychology of Rapport: Five Basic Rules', in T. Williamson (ed.), *Investigative Interviewing: Rights, Research and Regulation* (Willan Press, Cullompton, Devon, England, 2006); P. Ekman *et al.*, 'Investigative Interviewing and the Detection of Deception', in T. Williamson (ed.), *Investigative Interviewing: Rights, Research and Regulation* (Willan Press, Cullompton, Devon, England, 2006); R. P. Fisher and R. E. Geiselman, *Memory Enhancing Techniques for Investigative Interviewing: The Cognitive Interview* (Thomas, Springfield, Illinois, 1992).

Chapter 3. Investigative Interviewing: Best Practice in Questioning Witnesses and Suspects

The function of an investigator is to collect information. Victims and witnesses are a major source of information. Whenever possible, a full investigation, including the interviewing of victims and witnesses, should be carried out before any suspects are interviewed. The subsequent questioning of suspects in detention in accordance with the principles of investigative interviewing helps to ensure that what is said during questioning by a suspect is said freely and can be relied upon by the judicial authorities. In this chapter the skills necessary to conduct an effective investigative interview are considered; the structure of an investigative interview is explained; and a model of interviewing that has been given the acronym 'PEACE' is introduced. This shows the different tasks that need to be performed, and suggests that they can be organised around five sequential stages.

(A) CREATING AN INVESTIGATIVE INTERVIEW – THE PEACE MODEL

It is highly likely that accurate and reliable information will be obtained from a well-planned and carefully conducted investigative interview. The PEACE model provides a structure for such an interview.[246] The acronym PEACE is derived from the first letters of the following terms:

- **P**reparation and Planning

- **E**ngage and Explain

- **A**ccount, Clarification, and Challenge

- **C**losure

- **E**valuation

---

[246] For a description of some similar models, *see* Williamson, *supra* note 201.

IV:3

(a) **Preparation for Interviews**

There are a number of points to be considered in the preparation and planning phase of all interviews. These points can form the basis of a written plan:

- How might this interview contribute to the investigation?

- What is known about the interviewee?

- What are the legal requirements?

- What points must be established to prove an offence has been committed?

- Practical arrangements for the interview.

Preparing for an interview gives an opportunity to review the investigation, establish what evidence is available and decide what is to be achieved from the interview. This phase of the preparation and planning stage covers such questions as:

- Which persons need to be interviewed and in what order?

- Why is the evidence from this particular person important?

- Is there information that needs to be obtained urgently?

- Should the interview with the suspect take place now, or be left until more information about the circumstances of the offence has been obtained?

To interview effectively the interviewer needs to take account of the interviewee as an individual. Every interview must be approached with an open mind, and interviewers are required to act fairly in the circumstances of each case. In these respects the following factors are worth considering:

- *Age, gender and domestic circumstances of the interviewee.* This helps in establishing a relationship with the interviewee. In certain types of crime, for example rape, it is important to consider the gender of the interviewer.

- *Cultural background of the interviewee.* This affects such matters as the way in which the person prefers to be addressed, and provides an indication of how formal the approach needs to be. The interviewer must also consider whether or not the person understands the language in which the interview is to be conducted. If not an interpreter is required.

- *Intellectual level of interviewee.* Knowing the educational background of a person can provide an indication of vulnerability, and therefore of a requirement for additional protection. Interviewees who suffer from a learning disability may not understand the significance of questions and the implications of their answers.

- *Physical and mental health of interviewee.* An interviewer should be alert to the signs and symptoms of health problems, especially in relation to people in detention. Detainees are entitled to medical assistance. Care should be taken not to interview people who are under the influence of alcohol or drugs.

- *Previous contact with the police.* Knowledge about any previous criminal behaviour may help to challenge his or her account of events. For many interviewees, the interview to be conducted is the first interview by police they will have experienced. When this is the case it is helpful if the interview process is explained to interviewees. They should also be told what happens after the interview; whom they should contact if they recall information later; and what support and assistance may be available for them.

- *Recent experiences of interviewees.* Victims, witnesses and suspects may have been through a traumatic experience that may affect their ability to recall from memory what happened.

In respect of all interviews it is important for an investigator to be aware of the legal requirements, including the points that need to be covered in order to prove an offence. The investigator should understand clearly the points to prove, and the exact requirements of any legal defence that may be offered in respect of the offence or offences under investigation. In respect of interviews of suspects, interviewers should bear in mind the right to presumption of innocence of accused people. The main areas to consider, in respect of all interviews, are:

- *Intent* – what was in the mind of the suspect at the time? Why may he or she have committed the crime?

- *Action* – what did the suspect actually do?

- *Method* – how was the crime committed?

A number of practical arrangements need to be considered for the preparation and planning stage. For example, visiting the scene of the crime can be helpful, especially if the interviewer has no previous knowledge of the location.

Deciding on the location of the interview, and the time it is to take place is also important. Whilst interviews of suspects are likely to be conducted in detention, victims and witnesses may be interviewed in their homes or places of work. This may mean that it is difficult to secure the best conditions in which to conduct an interview. It must be remembered that the type of concentration needed for recalling information from memory is enhanced when there is peace and quiet for the person engaged in that process. As far as the time is concerned, it is important to bear in mind such factors as the requirements of the investigation, the appropriateness of the time for the person being interviewed, and any rules or guidelines on this matter.

Another important point to be considered in relation to the practical arrangements is the role of each interviewer if there is to be more than one. The plan should allow the first interviewer to avoid the possibility of having the second interviewer interrupting or breaking planned silences, and it should provide an opportunity for the second interviewer to ask questions at an appropriate time or times. Furthermore, ensuring the availability and proper functioning of the necessary equipment if the interview is to be recorded, and the availability of exhibits if these are needed for the purposes of the interview, are also important elements of preparation and planning.

A written interview plan is also an important element in preparing for a professionally competent interview because it summarises the aims of the interview and provides a framework on which to base the questioning. Furthermore it gives interviewers confidence and flexibility. In particular, a written plan assists interviewers to keep track of what has been covered and what remains to be dealt with; to identify areas where the interviewee's account conflicts with what is already known or, has been suggested in other accounts; to identify new information whilst keeping track of the purpose of the interview; and to identify any issues that have not been covered.

(b) Engage and Explain

Engaging someone in conversation is not always an easy task. The most appropriate way to engage in conversation is not the same in every case, but it can be helpful to establish something that they have in common, for example being parents or liking sport. Co-operation may be affected by his or her first impressions of the interviewer and, as both parties in an interview may show signs of anxiety, it is important to plan for and manage the opening of an interview. This helps to create the right atmosphere and establish rapport.

In order to establish a good working relationship it is important to treat people as individuals. This is assisted by such means as personalising the conversation (for example through the way in which the interviewer addresses the interviewee); identifying the immediate needs and concerns of the interviewee; showing an interest in the interviewee and his or her individual circumstances; showing empathy as appropriate; and avoiding responding to the interviewee on the basis of a stereotyped image.

An interviewer must aim to create an atmosphere in which the interviewee will want to talk to him or her.

The purpose of the interview should be explained to the interviewee, including the reason for the interview, the routine to be adopted and the outline of the interview. This allows some ground rules to be established which both the interviewer and the interviewee should fully understand. These include the fact that interviewees should be encouraged to tell all they know without anything being edited anything out; that they can give their account of what happened in their own words; that they should give as much detail as possible; and that they must not fabricate or make up answers to please the interviewer or anyone else.

Furthermore an interviewee needs to concentrate. When the matter under investigation is painful, embarrassing, complicated or confusing, remembering things accurately and giving a truthful account can be difficult. Interviewees must be given time and encouragement to remember, and to provide their account. As far as people suspected of crime are concerned, they need to have their rights (for example to medical attention, legal advice, access to a third party) explained to them. This final point is an essential element of a lawful and ethical interview.

(c) **Account, Clarification and Challenge**

A person being interviewed must be given the opportunity to provide the fullest account that he or she is able or willing to provide. Three approaches that assist this process are allowing interviewees to provide their own uninterrupted accounts; encouraging interviewees to expand and clarify their accounts; and, where necessary, challenging interviewees' accounts.

Frequently interviewees attempt to recall events that they experienced days, weeks or even years previously. It is often difficult to recall specific details from these events easily and accurately. Psychologists have found that it helps to reinstate the context. For example if you have lost your wallet you may ask yourself the questions – 'Where was I when I last had it?' or 'What was I doing or thinking about when I last used it?' This process of recalling contextual information helps interviewees to recollect information that is relevant. It is extremely unlikely that everything available in interviewees' memories will be immediately recalled. They should be encouraged to concentrate and be allowed to make repeated attempts at recalling the information.

The first accounts of interviewees may be incomplete. The process of recall can be assisted if their accounts are broken down into manageable chunks. By breaking down accounts in this way, the interviewer can keep track of what has been covered; understand new information introduced by interviewees and fit this into the overall investigation; and assist the expansion of accounts by systematically examining each chunk of information.

It can be helpful to summarise what has been said before moving to the next topic. This gives an opportunity to check that interviewees' accounts have been understood correctly, and it may give rise to the need to clarify any ambiguities or inconsistencies in the accounts. In some cases it is necessary to challenge the accounts given. This can arise under two circumstances – when challenges are planned as a result of holding back information in order to test what may be said; or in response to interviewees' accounts that are contrary to other evidence in the investigators' possession. However it is important to note that inconsistency or evasiveness do not necessarily mean that an interviewee is lying or even mistaken.[247]

The timing of challenges should be carefully considered. It is not normally appropriate to challenge interviewees whilst they are actually giving their accounts. To do so might discourage them from continuing. It is helpful for interviewers to explain to interviewees that their persistent questioning is a form of problem solving to which both parties can contribute. In this way interviewees are not put on the defensive, and are better able to change their accounts or to add to them without embarrassment and without losing face. Interviewers should try not to give an explanation of why discrepancies have occurred (for example: 'you are lying'). They need to remember to give plenty of time for interviewees to respond to queries.

Once an interviewee has provided his or her account, and all necessary clarifications and challenges have been made as appropriate, the next stage is to bring the interview to a close.

---

[247] *Ibid.*

256

(d) Closing the Interview

When the interview is drawing to a close the interviewer should ensure that there is mutual understanding about what has been said; that the interviewee understands what the future stages of the process will be; that an atmosphere has been created in which the interviewee is disposed towards helping and providing accurate and reliable information in the future; and that all aspects of the investigation, in respect of which the interviewee can assist, have been sufficiently covered.

Before an interview is concluded the interviewer must be satisfied that all relevant questions have been asked, and that the interviewee has provided all the information he or she is able or willing to provide.

The interviewer should ensure that abrupt endings are avoided by allowing adequate time to close the interview properly, and explain the next stages of the process. In the case of suspects they should be left feeling that they have been dealt with fairly and in an approachable, professional manner. It must be remembered that there may be occasions in the future when their help may be needed. Such people can be an important source of information in future investigations. People frequently recall important information after the interview and they should be provided with a means of contacting the interviewer so that this information is not lost to the investigation.

Investigators should explain to victims and witnesses that they are likely to remember more information about the incident in the future, and that they should make a written record of any such further information. It is very important that there should be an efficient means for victims and witnesses to convey new information to the investigator. In appropriate cases the investigator should contact them a few days after an interview to see if they have remembered anything else, and to inform them of developments in the investigation.

The final stage of the PEACE model deals with Evaluation.

(e) Evaluation

The information obtained from an interview, the significance of that information to the whole investigation, and the performance of the interviewers should all be evaluated. Furthermore, it is necessary to consider whether the objectives for the interview were achieved.

It must be established whether or not information that is needed to prove the offence being investigated has been obtained. Any new information needs to be considered in the light of the evidence already obtained. It must be established whether or not

IV:3

there are any conflicts between different pieces of evidence, and what further inquiries need to be made to resolve those conflicts. It is also useful to re-evaluate the investigation in the light of the evidence obtained from each interviewee.

Finally, evaluating an interview is a good way of improving interviewing skills, learning from experience, and developing best practice. A good interviewer is always looking for ways to improve, and should consider which aspects of the interview were satisfactory; which aspects could be improved upon; and which particular skills need to be developed. Police agencies that have a commitment to cultivating good interviewers have introduced formal systems of evaluation and supervision in which trained supervisors analyse interviews, and give feedback and advice on how to develop interview skills.

One of the worrying aspects of the questioning of detainees is that it is generally conducted in conditions of privacy and, for a variety of reasons, has not been easy to supervise. This is why many police agencies are introducing technology (sound or video recording equipment, which can be either analogue or digital) to ensure that there is an accurate record of what is said and done during interviews. It is a means by which an assessment can be made about the evidence obtained and, specifically, whether verbal statements made during questioning are freely made and accurately recorded. The cost of this technology is falling rapidly bringing it within the reach of most agencies. The cost is insignificant compared to the cost of an investigation and subsequent trial, especially one that results in a wrongful conviction. This form of technology, and the training of interviewers are considered in the next chapter.

Chapter 4. Methods to Secure Good Practice – Supervision, Monitoring and Training

(A) CODES OF PRACTICE

Good behaviour in the investigative process, and specifically in the conduct of interviews, is one element that is essential to the delivery of a high quality, effective service to the community. The other element is the application of a high degree of expertise and skill in the craft of policing. It is important to reinforce the point made in previous chapters of this book that in the practice of this craft, no operation or activity can be judged independently of the means by which it is effected.

In order to provide guidance for police officials, and to promote good behaviour and best practice, codes of practice for the detention, treatment and questioning of people in detention have been developed in some countries.

These codes seek to ensure that all people in detention are dealt with expeditiously, lawfully, and humanely, and released as soon as the reasons for detention have ceased to apply. The codes of practice are usually made available for consultation by police officials, detained persons and members of the public, and are a means of providing reassurance that human rights are being respected.

The codes usually embody specific provisions to secure lawful and humane treatment of detainees who are vulnerable, such as juveniles, those who are suffering from mental illness or mental impairment, and detainees who need an interpreter. They differ from country to country to the extent that they reflect the requirements of national law and practice, but it is possible to identify basic elements of good practice – most of which are included in of codes of this nature.

(a) Basic Elements of Best Practice

(i) Records of Arrest and Detention

As soon as practicable after a person is brought to a police station on arrest or detention, a record should be opened. This record should show the personal details of the detainee together with the reasons and the authority for detention, and it should be signed by a supervisory police official responsible for authorising detention. That official should be independent from those officials who have made the arrest or who are conducting the investigation. The supervision of detention should be separate from the management of the investigation because problems can arise when these two roles are combined, where the guards in effect became subordinate to the intelligence function.

The record of detention should be a complete and accurate account of what has happened to the person being detained since the initial moments of arrest or detention, and should accompany the detained person if he or she is removed to another place of detention. The record should show the time and reason for any transfer, and the time the person is released from detention.

(ii) Explanation of Rights, Vulnerable Detainees, Physical Needs

The supervisory police official authorising detention should explain to the detainee the reason for detention, and the rights to which detained people are entitled. These should include the right to have a relative or friend informed of the arrest or detention; the right to legal advice; and the right to consult the codes of practice. All of this information should be readily available in all languages commonly in use in the locality.

In the case of a detainee who is a juvenile, or mentally handicapped, or suffering from a mental disorder a person with the authority and the ability to advise and assist the detainee should be called to the place of detention. Where the detainee is a juvenile such a person would be a parent or guardian, and where the detainee is mentally disordered or handicapped it should be someone who has experience in dealing with such people.

Detainees are, of course, entitled to reasonable standards of physical comfort which include the provision of adequate food and drink, access to toilets and washing facilities, clothing, writing and reading materials, and exercise. These entitlements are also set out in international human rights instruments.

(iii) Incommunicado Detention

A detained person has the right, subject to certain qualifications, not to be held incommunicado. For example there may be a temporary suspension of the right to have another person notified of the detention if there is a genuine belief that notification may cause interference with witnesses to crimes, or the loss of material evidence. If the right to notify another person of arrest and detention is suspended, the reasons should be noted in the record of detention. Any temporary suspension of the right to legal advice, usually on similar grounds, should also be recorded. An important safeguard is provided if a legal representative is allowed to inspect the record of detention when such temporary suspensions of rights do take place.

(iv) Use of Force

Rules expressing best practice on the use of force against detainees usually stipulate that reasonable force may be used only when strictly necessary for maintaining order within the place of detention, when personal safety is threatened, or in order to prevent damage to property or the destruction of evidence. Such rules should also prohibit the use of firearms against detainees except in self-defence or defence of others against the immediate threat of death or serious injury, or when strictly necessary to prevent the escape of a person presenting a grave threat to life.

(v) Complaints, Medical Treatment

If a complaint is made by or on behalf of a detained person it must be referred to a senior police official as soon as practicable, and that official should enquire into the matter, or cause it to be enquired into, immediately. It is good practice to have an independent organisation for investigating complaints and this may take the form of independent police complaints commissions, Ombudsmen, or Human Rights Commissions. These regulatory bodies are more effective when they have their own investigative resources and are established with investigative powers on a statutory basis. If the complaint is one of assault a medical practitioner should be called to examine and, if necessary, treat the detainee. A medical practitioner should also be called if a detainee appears to be suffering from physical illness or a mental disorder is injured; fails to respond normally to questions or conversation; or otherwise appears to be in need of medical attention.

It is important to remember that a person who appears to be behaving abnormally may be suffering from illness, or the effects of alcohol, drugs or injury (particularly head injury). A medical practitioner should advise whether further detention should be authorised, and, specifically, whether the detainee needs to be treated in a hospital.

(vi) Rules for Questioning: Judicial Supervision

It is clear from preceding chapters of this book that when detainees are interviewed, or indeed at any time, no form of duress, oppression or force may be used to try to obtain answers to questions. It is good practice to have a system whereby the record of detention shows the place of all interviews with a detainee, any breaks in the interview, and the names of all persons present. A record should also be made of what is said during the interview, either a verbatim account recorded contemporaneously or in the form of an accurate summary. It is good practice not to require people being questioned to stand. Short breaks for refreshment must also be provided at regular intervals. Furthermore, a detained person should be allowed a significant and continuous period of rest free from questioning within any period of twenty-four hours.

Most jurisdictions, in compliance with international standards, require judicial supervision of detainees and set a time limit within which a detained person is to be brought before a judicial authority. It is good practice to have these time limits clearly set out in codes of practice.

(vii) Intimate Body Searches

In exceptional circumstances, and when authorised by law, it may be necessary to conduct intimate and 'strip searches' of detainees. These involve the physical examination of a person's bodily orifices. It is good practice to ensure that such searches are only carried out by medical practitioners or nurses, and to ensure that they are conducted with regard to the sensitivity and vulnerability of the person in these circumstances. Intimate searches should be regulated so that they are necessary do not degenerate into a frequent 'punishment' and dehumanising of detainees.

Rules for such searches usually require that an official conducting the search should be of the same gender as the person being searched, and that the search should take place in an area from where the detainee cannot be seen by anyone who does not need to be present. Where necessary, to assist the search, the detainee may be required to hold his or her arms in the air or to stand with his or her legs apart and to bend forward so that a visual examination may be made of the genital and anal areas, provided that no contact is made with any bodily orifice. If during the search articles are found the person should be asked to hand them over. A strip search should be conducted expeditiously and the detainee allowed to dress immediately the procedure is complete.

(viii)   National Codes and International Standards

As indicated above, the basic elements of best practice for the treatment of detainees summarised here can be found in various national codes for the proper treatment of detainees. Furthermore, these national codes usually embody international standards as expressed in human rights treaties prohibiting arbitrary arrest and detention, and torture and ill-treatment, and in the more detailed provisions of non-treaty instruments. An example of such an instrument is the Body of Principles for the Protection of All Persons under Any Form of Detention or Imprisonment, which was summarised in Chapter 3 of Part III of this book.

(b) **Technology as a Means of Supervising, Monitoring and Training Interviewers**

(i)   Types of Systems and General Principles for Supervision and Monitoring

It is good practice to establish a system for the electronic recording of interviews. The cost of purchase and installation of this equipment is very low and as technology develops the costs continue to reduce.

One reason why the electronic recording of interviews is good practice is that it allows investigating officials to produce irrefutable evidence that during interrogation they acted fairly, and respected the human rights of the detainee. Furthermore the fact that an independent record of the questioning process is available turns what is normally a closed system, and therefore difficult to supervise, into an open system. Law enforcement agencies have also found that it enables them to assess the level of interviewing skill, or competence, of their officials and to respond to any observed skill deficit by providing training. The recording should not be carried out covertly as an open system instils confidence in the system as an impartial and accurate record of the interview.

Two kinds of equipment are currently available to law enforcement agencies for this purpose. The first relies on computer technology to digitally encode the time simultaneously with the recording of the interview. This is sometimes known as 'TPR' or tamper proof equipment. Less sophisticated and more widespread systems rely on the audio or video analogue recording together with procedures to ensure that the tape cannot be interfered with. These systems use two or more tapes operating simultaneously. One tape, which is referred to as the 'master tape', is sealed in the presence of the interviewee at the conclusion of the interview. The tape is then retained in a secure place. A second tape is referred to as the 'working copy'.

It is important to make clear to the suspect that there is no opportunity for the investigators to interfere with the recording. Sealing the master tape in the presence of the interviewee ensures that confidence in the integrity of the tape is preserved. The working copy of the tape can be used for making further copies, one of which can be given to the interviewee. In some jurisdictions all interviews are electronically recorded, whilst in others only interviews concerning serious offences are recorded.

Sometimes interviews concerning terrorist offences or those relating to national security are excluded from this process. This creates an anomaly in that the cases involving suspects at highest risk become those where their protection through an independent record of the interrogation is weak or virtually non-existent. It also enables groups involved in terrorist activity to make allegations of mistreatment of detainees, whether or not such mistreatment occurs, which are more difficult to refute because of the lack of any source of independent evidence of what occurred.

(ii) Good Practice in the Operation of a Supervision and Monitoring System

All interviews with a suspect should be recorded. Recording should not be confined, as is often the case in the USA, to a final interview which has been preceded by unrecorded interviews.[248] At the commencement of an electronically recorded interview the official conducting the interview should explain to the interviewee that the interview is being recorded. He or she should then identify all of the officials present and invite the interviewee to give his or her name together with that of any other party present on his or her behalf such as a lawyer. (It is helpful for the purposes of voice identification if all parties present identify themselves.) The interviewer should then pronounce the date, time of commencement and place of the interview. Finally the interviewer should explain what will happen to the tapes on which the interview is recorded at the conclusion of the interview.

Clearly the length of an interview depends on a number of factors such as the complexity or seriousness of the crime being investigated. However it is generally possible to conclude most interviews within the time span of a single tape, and the equipment usually has a facility for indicating when the tape is coming to an end. In the case of lengthy interviews, the interviewer should conclude the first part of the interview and proceed with a second set of tapes. The tapes should be marked with a sequential number so that there is no confusion about the identity of the tapes.

At the conclusion of the interview the suspect should be offered the opportunity to clarify anything said or to add anything. In some jurisdictions a written statement is obtained from the interviewee whilst the interview is being recorded. The master tape should be labelled and sealed. The signatures of those present during the interview should be obtained on the label.

Police officials should bear in mind that, during audio recording, if it is necessary to refer to any exhibits they should first be described (by stating, for example, 'I am showing the suspect a knife with a long blade which appears to be covered in blood stains'.). Similarly if interviewees use body language to respond to a question (for example by nodding or shaking the head) the interviewer should describe the body language and encourage the interviewee to express his or her response in words.

---

[248] *Ibid.*

In some jurisdictions the working copy of the tape is then used to compile a full written transcript of what was said during the interview. Sometimes a brief summary of what was said is acceptable with the relevant parts, for example denial or confession, being recorded verbatim. However no written record can convey as well as an audio or video record what was actually said and done, and best practice is for the authorities to rely on the primary evidence by playing the recording. This means that playing back the tape is preferable to a secondary source such as a transcript or summary.

It is vitally important for the integrity of the system that the master tapes should be kept in a secure place where they cannot be interfered with. If it becomes necessary to have to access a master tape, then the seal should be broken in the presence of an independent person who should also witness the tape being resealed after use.

The arrangements for the video taping of interviews are almost identical to those for sound recording, although in most jurisdictions videotaping is confined to the most serious cases in order to reduce costs.

Once tape recording has been introduced in a jurisdiction, it is important that investigators restrict their questioning of suspects without the use of electronic recording facilities to the absolute minimum. Should a suspect provide an explanation or admission to investigators prior to a recorded interview, a written record should be made at the time or as soon as possible afterwards. It is best practice for the suspect to countersign as accurate what has been written. At the start of the recorded interview the interviewee should then be invited to repeat what was said in the previous unrecorded conversation. It is also important to prevent any suggestion that what is said during a recording session was previously rehearsed or coerced. As previously noted it is best practice, therefore, for those responsible for detention to be independent from those conducting the inquiry and in particular, systems should be in place to prevent any unauthorised interviews prior to the one to be recorded, otherwise the integrity of the system will be compromised.

There is no doubt that the introduction of low cost technology to record what happens during questioning of detainees can go a long way towards creating a safe environment for the interview process. Furthermore, systems based on such technology provide a powerful means for governments and law enforcement agencies to show that international human rights obligations are being met. Once installed the agency has a duty to ensure that the equipment is kept in working order and that the interviewers cannot use the lack of availability of equipment as a reason for not recording their interviews with suspects.[249] Increasingly, interviews with

---

[249] *Ibid.*

victims in serious cases are also being recorded, and in some jurisdictions this can be accepted as their primary evidence.

(iii) Training of Interviewers

Such systems also provide a means for police agencies to assess the skills of their interviewers, and to assess the quality of the information they obtain during interviews. Following an assessment of this nature, training programs can be established to raise the level of skill within an agency to an acceptable minimum standard, and to identify officials who have displayed an aptitude for interviewing and who could, with further training, form a cadre of advanced interviewers to advise their colleagues in specific cases and promote best investigative practice. Many law enforcement agencies are creating behavioural science units and these have been at the forefront of introducing new scientifically sound methods of interviewing.

Interviewing is a skill that can be taught and learnt. Clearly some people have a particular aptitude for interviewing, but in respect of every person the basic skills can be learned. In the investigation of the most serious crimes, there is a need for interviews to be conducted by interviewers who are experienced and have been identified as possessing an aptitude for interviewing and who have been trained to a high level.

As far as training courses for interviewers are concerned, these need to meet the requirements of national legislation and rules and guidelines which, in turn, ought to be in compliance with the international standards described in this book – particularly in Chapters 3 and 4 of Part III herein. Training courses based on the system of interviewing described in Chapter 3 of this part, or on systems derived from the same principles, can equip police officials with the skills necessary to conduct interviews in accordance with those international human rights standards.

As has been indicated in this chapter, technology can be an important element in securing compliance with human rights standards in the process of interviewing. Furthermore it can assist in the Evaluation stage of the PEACE model that requires assessments of interviews to be made. There is no need for the interviewing of detainees to be routinely carried out unsupervised – with or without the assistance of technology, or for detainees to be subjected to the crime of torture or other inhumane treatment. Whilst there are international instruments that address custody and the use of force, there is as yet no instrument that specifically addresses how people should be interviewed in ways that respect their human rights. There is therefore a missing instrument in international human rights law and international humanitarian law. From time to time evidence of unlawful, inhumane and unprofessional interview techniques has emerged. Such cases demonstrate the urgent need for such an instrument. In its absence much depends on the quality of training, supervision and leadership displayed by states and individuals in the law enforcement and intelligence communities.

Supervision, monitoring and training of police officials are all responsibilities that belong to police leaders. The implications of international human rights standards for police leaders, and the challenge of implementing a style of policing that practices respect for human rights are matters considered in Part VI of this book.

PART V

POLICING CONFLICT, DISTURBANCE AND TENSION – PREVENTIVE AND REACTIVE RESPONSES

Chapter 1. Understanding Conflict, and Strategies for Prevention

(A) INTRODUCTION

International standards relevant to policing in times of conflict are discussed in Chapters 1 and 2 of Part II herein. The standards are those of international human rights law and international humanitarian law. Four categories of conflict are defined and discussed: international armed conflict, non-international armed conflict, internal disturbances and tensions, and terrorism. The purpose of this and the following two chapters is to examine police responses to situations of non-international armed conflict, and internal disturbance and tension. It will be recalled from Chapters 1 and 2 of Part II that the conduct of police and other security forces in situations of internal disturbance and tension is governed by international human rights law. However, whilst international humanitarian law comes into force only when armed conflict, international or non-international, breaks out, it is argued in those earlier chapters that the application of international humanitarian law, even in situations where this branch of law may not be legally applicable, amounts simply to good practice. As police have duties to protect life and property, and to restore and maintain peace and social order some of the principles of international humanitarian law should form an important element in the strategy and tactics of policing civil disturbances, especially when the disturbances are serious in terms of scale or intensity of violence.

(B) A HISTORY OF VICTIMS OF CONFLICT

The political scientist Rudolph Rummel's study of wars and conflicts between 1900 and 1987 revealed that governments murdered an estimated 169,198,000 persons compared to 38,000,000 combatants killed in war. In effect, during the 20th Century, governments murdered four times more people than were killed in combat. Rummel's study categorised the killing of victims as follows:

1. **Actions designed to kill or cause the death of people:**

- because of their religion, race, language, ethnicity, national origin, class, politics, speech, actions construed as opposing the government or wrecking social policy, or by virtue of their relationship to such people.
- in furtherance of a system of forced labour or enslavement.
- massacre.
- imposition of lethal living conditions.
- directly targeting non-combatants during a war or violent conflict.

V:1

2. **Causing death by virtue of an intentionally or knowingly reckless and depraved disregard for life as in:**

- deadly prison, concentration camp, forced labour, prisoner of war, or recruit camp conditions.
- fatal medical or scientific experiments on humans.
- torture or beatings.
- encouraged or condoned murder, or rape, looting, and pillage during which people are killed.
- a famine or epidemic during which government authorities withhold aid, or knowingly act in a way to make it more deadly.
- forced deportations and expulsions causing deaths.[250]

Most of the killings were committed by governments against their own citizens through the actions of government officials including police, military or secret service; or through nongovernmental action (e.g. by brigands, secret societies or death squads) with overt or clandestine support or approval from government.[251] The largest proportion of these murders is the consequence of the Nazi policies of extermination, and pogroms and purges in Stalinist Russia and communist China. Nevertheless, it is clear from historical evidence and truth commissions established after non-international armed conflict in all parts of the world that overall, police agencies operating independently or on behalf of the state or military have committed murder, torture, mutilation and all manner of atrocities against innocent civilians on an appalling scale. Additionally, police agencies have been complicit in, or facilitated murder and atrocities by the military.[252]

In a number of countries, not only have numerous police officials been the instruments of the state in the commission of human rights abuses, but they have

---

[250] R. J. Rummel, *Death by Government* (Transaction Publishers, New Brunswick, New Jersey, 1994).

[251] *Ibid.*

[252] *See e.g.*, Commission on the Truth for El Salvador, Report: *From Madness to Hope: The 12-Year war in El Salvador*, 15 March 1993, <www.usip.org/library/tc/doc/reports/el_salvador/tc_es_03151993_toc.html>, last visited September 2006.

Commission to Clarify Past Human Rights Violation and Acts of Violence That Have Caused the Guatemalan Population to Suffer, Report: *Guatemala: Memory of Silence*, 24 June 1994, <shr.aaas.org/guatemala/ceh/report/english/toc.html>, last visited September 2006.

V. Perera, *Unfinished Conquest: The Guatemalan Tragedy* (University of California Press, Berkeley, Los Angeles, California, 1993).

E. Cuya, *Las Comisiones de la Verdad en America Latina*, 1 March 1999, <www.derechos.org/koaga/iii/1/cuya.html>, last visited September 2006.

J. S. Abrams, *Accountability for Human Rights Atrocities in International Law: Beyond the Nuremberg Legacy* (Oxford University Press, Oxford, 2001).

also acted under their own motivation. Some of the most extreme cases of police violence have been a consequence of members of police agencies terrorising society, including kidnapping, torturing and murdering innocent civilians, for their own ends and advancement.[253]

The facts of history beg some fundamental questions of police officials. At what stage of escalating illegal state violence does a police official declare that he or she is no longer willing to participate? When does inflicting torture and death on the innocent become 'normal'? When does moral or social conscience or sense of sworn legal duty dictate 'no more'? When brought to account, would the platitude, 'My conscience is clear. I was simply doing my duty' amount to an expurgation of past actions?[254] These questions and the reasons for their being posed challenge police officials who declare with righteous indignation that there is no requirement for *them* to be sensitised to human rights. They fail to realise that they have an epic role and duty of protecting the human rights of the citizens they serve.

(C) CAUSES OF INTERNAL TENSION AND DISTURBANCE, AND NON-INTERNATIONAL ARMED CONFLICT

Tensions and disturbances are routine aspects of policing, for example neighbourhood disputes, street violence and antisocial behaviour including alcohol fuelled street disorder. Most experienced police officials can testify to the existence of criminals in the community who simply enjoy creating disorder and using violence against others. Much of this type of conflict is temporary and transient, and both the cause and the effect can be resolved through effective street policing.

Other causes of tension are much more problematic and can lead to disturbances, and non-international armed conflict. Causes are rooted in a sense of injustice emanating from historical, religious, cultural, political, and economic issues. They can become intractable. They remain unresolved for long periods of time and then become stuck at a high level of intensity and destructiveness.[255]

Tension based around intractable issues can lead to long term disorder, serious violence, riots and ultimately, non-international armed conflict. The issues that contribute to intractability can be characterised as follows:

---

[253] *See* W. Stanley, *The Protection Racket State: Elite Politics, Military Extortion and Civil War in El Salvador* (Temple University Press, Philadelphia, 1996).
[254] Words of Franz Stangl, former Austrian police official, who admitted killing 900,000 people whilst commanding the Nazi extermination camps in Sobibor and Treblinka between March 1942 and August 1943, <www.auschwitz.dk/sobibor/franzstangl.htm>, last visited September 2006.
[255] M. Maiese, *Underlying Causes of Intractable Conflict*, posted October 2003, <www.beyondintractability.org/essay/underlying_causes>, last visited September 2006.

V:1

- *Justice Issues.* Perceived injustice is a frequent source of tension. It is usually characterised by the denial of fundamental rights such as political rights, freedom of speech or religion, and neglect of economic rights such as access to food, housing and employment.

- *Moral or Value Issues.* Tensions around intractable moral issues tend to arise when one group believes the beliefs and actions of another group are so fundamentally wrong or evil that they exceed the bounds of tolerance. These conflicting views are often wholly intractable and can never be resolved because in the minds of the opposing parties, their fundamental beliefs are not only right, but can never be proven wrong.

- *Identity Issues.* Identity is the primary issue in racial, ethnic and religious tensions. Historically, these types of tensions and subsequent conflicts have been extremely intense and resulted in serious human rights abuses including acts of genocide.

- *High Stakes Distribution Issues.* These are similar to justice issues insofar as they are concerned with access to rights. Due to the fact that they centre on class and status, and issues of who gets what and how much they get, they have an extra dimension of the rift between rich and poor, unequal political and economic power and land distribution, and issues of rule by powerful minority elites. At the extreme level of intractability they are exemplified by non-international armed conflict characterised as 'class war'.

- *Human Rights Issues.* Abuses of human rights lead to tensions and disturbances that typically also result in further human rights violations. Human rights abuses are often at the centre of non-international armed conflicts. Hence, protection of human rights is central to reducing tensions and resolving conflict.[256]

Police leaders cannot be effective if they simply respond to the effects and consequences of tensions in society. Police leaders require the intellect and strategic vision to be aware of international and national affairs and events. Police leaders need to be strategic scanners. They need to study, read and monitor the media to gain an understanding of current affairs and to make themselves and their staff aware of the cultural diversities of the communities they serve. In particular, police leaders need to be aware that diasporas and migrations of people can result in immigrants bringing their political, ethnic and other forms of tension and conflict

---

[256] *Ibid.*

from their country of origin to their new homeland. The PESTEL model, described in Chapter 3 of Part VI herein, is a useful a tool for scanning and identifying the political, economic, social, technological, environmental and legal issues that could result in tension and conflict in society. Meanwhile, policing is only one means by which social order is maintained in a state. Governments and societies have a responsibility to adopt and implement social and political reform and policies to remove inequalities from society and thus reduce sources of tension and dissatisfaction that can lead to disorder and conflict.

(a) Situations that can lead to Disorder and Conflict

The following situations can lead to disorder and, eventually, to conflict:

- Industrial disputes and strikes.

- Marches, public demonstrations and single issue protests: for example, demands for democratic government, and protests about taxation or the environment.

- Official action by the state: for example, clearance of residents or traders from land or streets.

- Policing action: for example, lawful operations against criminal gangs.

- Disproportionate or insensitive policing.

- Neighbourhood or factional disputes between families, clans or gangs.

- Rivalry amongst factions at and around sporting events.

- Gatherings and public celebrations at holidays, festivals and fiestas.

- Tension in prisons and other correctional facilities can lead to serious disorder within those establishments. Inmates can also organise violence in the wider community from within prison: for example, violence by street gangs.

Whilst some of these situations are of a temporary or transient nature, or are associated with criminal behaviour, they may also be linked to deeper-rooted intractable causes that are not immediately apparent. Escalation of tension and disorder, especially when driven by intractable issues, can eventually lead to non-international armed conflict. Parties who have been involved in non-international

V:1

armed conflict have consistently informed the author that when this level of conflict is reached, the causes of tension and the reasons for the conflict often become clouded and forgotten. Violence, including kidnapping and murder, can become routine aspects of everyday life. They become reflexive responses to political and private disagreements, and a means of achieving ambitions that may have no direct connection to issues of intractability. Even after conflict has finished and formal peace has been restored, individuals and factions may continue for many years to seek revenge or reprisal against their former enemies for real or perceived past offences.

(b) The Dynamics of Disorder and Conflict

Tension does not necessarily have to result in disorder or conflict. Effective leadership and action by police officials can help to reduce tension and prevent disorder and conflict occurring. Police agencies have a duty to protect life and maintain public safety. They have a prime role in not only dealing with public disorder, but also preventing it. In situations where serious public disorder accompanied by extreme violence is threatened, preventing disorder and defusing tension may prevent loss of life, serious injury or serious damage to property. Additionally, in order to be able to continue to provide policing services, it is essential to prevent disorder and conflict, and if they do break out, to use all lawful measures to quell them. Unless dealt with effectively, situations of serious disorder can result in mobs or organised groups creating 'no-go' areas. This leads to the breakdown of governance, as the agents of law and order are prevented from entering territory occupied by some communities and thus are unable to provide protection and other services to citizens.

Police leaders need to have systems and plans for understanding and monitoring tension in the community, and preventing it from escalating into serious disorder or conflict. If disorder does break out, then police leaders need to be able to restore peace and tranquillity as quickly as possible. Produced below is a model that helps to illustrate the dynamics of disorder and conflict.

V:1

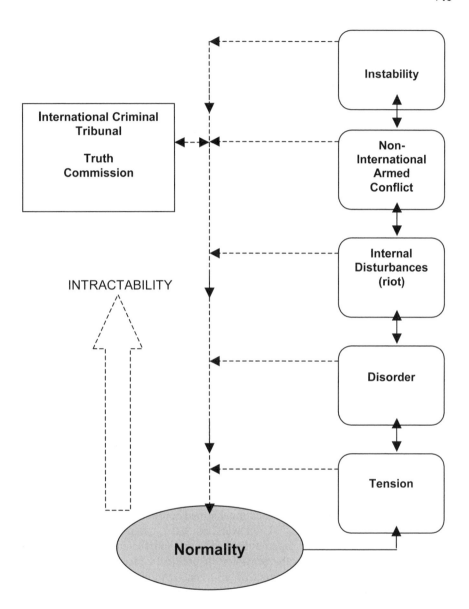

The Dynamics of Disorder

V:1

The levels of the model are examined as follows:

1. *Normality*. Normality is predicated upon crime and disorder being inevitable and ordinary phenomena in society. Therefore, all communities will have an existing level of crime and disorder. The extent to which it remains 'tolerable' to the community and controllable by the police determines its 'normality'. The concept of normality is subjective and will vary from one community or society to another.

2. *Tension*. When crime and disorder mounts or groups unusually begin to congregate in public places, a feeling of general public anxiety and heightened tension can occur. This is a critical period because the slightest action can cause the situation to become inflamed: for example, a speech by a politician, a rumour or a street arrest by the police.

3. *Disorder*. At this stage, spasmodic or sustained damage and violence breaks out. The disorder may ebb and flow with a series of trigger incidents. At this stage, police plans need to be implemented to increase police resources and to actively control and quell the disorder.

4. *Internal Disturbance*. This is the most serious level of public disorder commonly faced by police officials: for example, riot, arson, looting, serious criminal damage and destruction of buildings, vehicles and property; the use of weapons and the throwing of missiles and petrol bombs; violent attacks including homicidal attacks on individuals, groups of individuals and police

5. *Non-International Armed Conflict*. As defined in Chapter 2 of Part II herein, non-international armed conflict is generally understood to be a civil war in which an insurgent group seeks to displace the government by force of arms. On occasions more than one insurgent group is involved. Between 1946 and 2004, the numbers of non-international armed conflicts significantly exceeded international armed conflicts, reaching a peak during the Cold War period.[257] Civil wars can have a more complex dimension when they become 'internationalised' through the involvement of other states – for example, the provision of political education, military advice, aid and arms to government or insurgents. Additionally, training may be provided to police officials and military personnel.

---

[257] L. Harbom and P. Wallensteen, 'Armed Conflict and Its International Dimensions, 1946-2004', 42:5 *Journal of Peace Research* (2005) pp. 623–635.

It is during these types of conflict that police officials are most likely to commit the most serious forms of human rights abuses. The evidence from international war crimes tribunals and truth commissions indicates that, historically, governments and police agencies have not only been responsible for human rights abuses, but also have abrogated their responsibility and duty to investigate such crimes and prosecute offenders. All police leaders should actively defend the human rights of all citizens against illegal acts, whether by state forces or insurgents. Moreover, it is essential for governments and police agencies to be more active in invoking the criminal law and investigating and prosecuting those who commit international crimes.

In recent years, international criminal tribunals and truth commissions have been important processes for restoring peace to societies traumatised by war. International criminal tribunals provide opportunity for States and the international community to bring those responsible for human rights crimes to justice. Unlike courts, truth commissions do not seek punishment or retribution. Developed primarily in Latin America during the 1980s, truth commissions enable countries emerging from non-international armed conflict to set the historical record straight and attempt to reconcile the factions, but without the trials of those alleged to have committed human rights crimes.[258]

6. *Instability*. This level is similar to the tension period. During this period, there may be relative calm as protestors or rioters withdraw or armed conflict ceases. It provides opportunity to listen, to mediate, to communicate with community and political leaders, to resolve differences and grievances, and to gain commitment from the appropriate authorities to meet reasonable demands or compromise. Police leaders need to exhibit the most sensitive political and leadership skills, and avoid any precipitate action that may cause confrontation and a return to disturbances or more serious conflict.

Upward progression from one level of the model to the next is not necessarily inevitable. Timely and effective responses can prevent an escalation of tension and disorder. It is important for responses to be lawful, measured and proportionate. An over-reaction to a situation, for example by deploying an inordinately high number of personnel, rather than de-escalating it may in fact have the opposite effect and provoke even more violence. It is at times of post-disorder and post-conflict

---

[258] J. D. Tepperman 'Truth and Consequences', 81 *Foreign Affairs* (March/April, 2002) pp. 128-145.

instability that police leaders need to be at their most vigilant and active in preventing situations and incidents from progressing to less controllable and more volatile levels. Moreover, a police agency with a service ethos, that operates lawfully and protects and respects human rights, is more likely to succeed in deactivating tension and disorder than a police agency with a reputation for brutality and corruption.

(D) STRATEGIES FOR REDUCING TENSION AND PREVENTING INTERNAL DISTURBANCE AND NON-INTERNATIONAL ARMED CONFLICT

(a) Background

The strategies for reducing internal tension and preventing internal disturbance and non-international armed conflict examined in this chapter are:

- Collecting Community Information
- The Use of Intelligence
- Effective Briefing and Debriefing
- Threat and Risk Assessment

The same strategies will be necessary during the course of internal disturbances and even non-international armed conflict.

In recent years, demands from governments for increased accountability and performance have resulted in a prodigious range of new policing styles and methods being created and employed around the world. There has also been the emergence of a whole new academic body of knowledge on matters of citizen security, security sector reform and studies of crime and violence in society. New management approaches to policing emphasise the need for proactivity. Rather than waiting for things to happen, police managers are advised that they must identify and analyse problems, gain an understanding of the environment they police, and make informed decisions about how they are going to plan and deploy personnel and resources to deal with priorities. This is a constantly recurring theme, which is examined in more detail in Part VI herein. Policing has become intelligence led, and numerous models have been adopted to support the new styles and methods of policing. These include the SARA model, Problem Oriented Policing (POP) and the 5I's framework.[259]

---

[259] For models, *see* <www.crimereduction.gov.uk/ learningzone/sara.htm>, and <www.popcenter.org>, last visited September 2006.

In order to use many of these models effectively, there is a requirement for technology, computer programs and the availability of trained analysts. Consequently, for many police agencies in developing countries, the costs and necessary expertise for equipment and training may be prohibitive. Police leaders in these countries who witness the financial and technological advantages of their colleagues in more developed countries can become disconsolate in the knowledge that similar resources may never be available to them. It is the author's experience that a common reaction amongst police leaders from developing countries is to conclude that it is a waste of time to try to deal with some of the problems they face. In effect, they surrender to policing problems within their own demesne in the misconceived belief that, because they do not have the resources and technology they would wish, they cannot achieve anything. Rather than doing something they do nothing. This is a serious mistake that results in a disservice to the citizens they are supposed to help, and crushes the aspirations of their subordinates who wish to be active, valued and usefully engaged in serving their society. It is important for police leaders who lapse into this mind-set to understand that, notwithstanding a lack of finances and technology, they *can* be effective and creative. If they do not know already, they may find it reassuring to be advised that police officials can become too reliant on technology and complicated systems, instead of maximising the use of their own professional skills, experience, judgment, and material and human resources. The reality is that technology does not solve crimes or prevent disorder. Technology can be an important aid. However, ultimately, it is the inspiration, ingenuity, and sometimes luck, but mostly, the patient and painstaking hard work of ordinary police officials that achieves results.

Consequently, rather than attempting to re-educate those many police officials who are already skilled in technologically aided methods and styles of policing, this chapter is used to examine some basic principles and methods of planning for and managing the pre-disturbance or pre-conflict environment. It is intended that this approach will be of particular assistance to police officials in newly democratised states who, perhaps for the first time, have to resolve tensions and disturbances in accordance with principles of proportionality and the protection of human rights. Most importantly, the effective strategies and planning to be examined can be achieved with simple tools: namely, the innate creativity and energy of most competent police leaders and their staff, using basic manual paper-flow and written documentation and reporting systems.

(b) Collecting Community Information

Early intervention and interaction with the community can reduce tension. Regular meetings and communication with the community and its leaders can help to dispel

V:1

rumours and misinformation that so often cause or inflame tension. The police can also mediate and resolve disputes between parties and factions.

In democratic societies, most progressive police organisations are pro-active in routinely interacting with the public to address community concerns, to reduce crime and disorder and maintain good police-community relations. For example, the Office of the Deputy Commissioner of Community Affairs, City of New York Police Department (NYPD), USA deploys specially trained police officials for this purpose. One of their critical roles is reproduced here because it is so clearly and succinctly expressed: "the deployment of community affairs supervisors and officials to public events, areas of unrest, and crisis situations in order to establish open lines of communication, defuse tension, and disseminate timely and accurate information to community members."[260]

In developing good community relations, police leaders need to be aware of factors relating to members of society who are described as 'hard to reach'. These include:

- disabled people
- the elderly
- young people
- minorities, for example immigrants and transient people
- residents whose first language is not the national language
- single parents
- people with low literacy levels
- the poor

Poverty or simply being poor is perhaps the most common factor amongst the hard to reach of society. Attempting to live from day to day without sufficient means, and forced into a routine having no other purpose than subsisting and feeding one's self and immediate family precludes any wider interest or social interaction or role in the community. Life becomes a drudge. The plight of the hard to reach can be aggravated by multiple factors. For example, a young unemployed person who is poor and an immigrant with a low level of literacy may be even more isolated in society.

Without encouragement or incentive, the hard to reach and underprivileged are unlikely to attend meetings and public forums with other citizens and police officials to participate in debate on local matters of crime, disorder and other issues affecting their lives. Apathy and indifference then lead to communities becoming neglected

---

[260] New York Police Department, Deputy Commissioner of Community Affairs, <www.nyc.gov/html/nypd/html/dcca/dcca-page.html>, last visited September 2006.

and blighted by graffiti, litter and decay. The hard to reach can become a cause of social disorder as a combination of environmental, economic and other social factors provides the breeding ground for tension born out of resentment and lack of opportunity.

Sadly, communities like this are all too common in many parts of the world, particularly in inner cities. They provide a daunting challenge to police leaders who are faced with the effects and consequences of state economic and social policy outside of their control.

All police officials should have a proactive role in interacting with the community and developing good relations. Police leaders should encourage uniform patrol officials and their managers and supervisors to develop effective community liaison and policing partnerships[261] Operational beat patrol officials should be the 'antennae' of the service in collecting information about the community.

In addition to internal sources, police leaders need to monitor demographic and social trends, and work in partnership with a variety of external sources to monitor communities and gain as much information as possible that may impact on crime and disorder. Furthermore, these sources can provide a conduit for communicating with the hard to reach. External sources include:

- schools and education services
- social and welfare services
- health officials
- other criminal justice agencies (e.g. probation service and correction facilities)
- municipal housing officials
- religious leaders
- ethnic minority leaders and representatives
- local elected representatives
- women's groups
- youth groups
- local pressure groups and activists
- police community forums
- local trade and commerce groups
- the media

---

[261] *See e.g.*, Chapter 5 of Part VI herein.

V:1

Regular contact with these sources enables the gathering of information that may indicate tension in the community. Clues and indicators to impending disorder and conflict could include damage to property and transport systems, minor assaults and street disorder. Minor crime and disorder can escalate into major disorder, including personal violence or the throwing of missiles or petrol bombs, either between factions and/or directed against the police.

(i) Graffiti

Graffiti can be an important indicator of tensions and a fertile source of information and intelligence. Graffiti relating to political, racial, ethnic or other forms of tension may indicate rising hostility in the community. Graffiti is of special significance where street gangs operate. These types of gangs are found around the world and have become a serious national threat to peace, stability and security in some countries of Central America. Gang graffiti is usually intended to:

- identify their existence, reputation and notoriety
- mark a specific area as their territory or 'turf' – for example by writing on a wall or building
- make disrespectful pronouncements and challenges to rival gangs
- commemorate deaths of gang members[262]
- make provocative political comments where the gang is affiliated to a political faction

(c) The Use of Intelligence

Intelligence drives modern policing. It is central to criminal investigation and the maintenance of public safety. The adoption of community policing has resulted in progressive police organisations developing increasingly proactive approaches to crime and disorder. Rather than simply reacting to reports of crime or anti-social behaviour and providing temporary solutions, the police together with citizens and other agencies seek to identify and target the causes of problems and 'hot-spots' where and when problems are known to occur. Policing has become intelligence-led. In many countries that are in post-conflict situations or that are making the transition to democracy, the word 'intelligence' has sinister and threatening connotations. Consequently, the acceptance of criminal intelligence as a measure of citizen security has been slow to evolve in some post conflict societies. In such societies, intelligence was not used to maintain public safety but as a political weapon to persecute innocent citizens and deprive them of their rights. Under repressive

---

[262] W. B. Brown *et al.*, *Youth Gangs in American Society* (Wadsworth Publishing, California, 1997) p. 116.

regimes, police units, and regular and irregular militia are directed by the government to spy on the population and to encourage ordinary citizens to spy on their neighbours in order to identify any person who may be perceived as a potential opponent of the *status quo*.

A classic example of the misuse of intelligence was that of Malawi during the authoritarian regime of Dr Hastings Banda. Following independence in 1964, The Malawi Young Pioneers (MYP) and Youth League were recruited and deployed as tools of the ruling party to provide a law enforcement role throughout the country. Over 18,000 strong and highly politicised, they took precedence over the regular Malawi Police Force and the armed forces. The Malawi Police Force became almost irrelevant and could operate only with the authority and permission of the MYP – many of whom were illiterate, undisciplined and untrained in law enforcement. The MYP spied on civil society through a network of informers, and through their information and 'intelligence', gained favours to maintain the authority of the ruling elite.[263]

In democratic societies, intelligence has an important part to play in the policing of pre-conflict, conflict and post-conflict situations. The collection of information about unusual activity within the community, and the use of intelligence are essential strategies for preventing, reducing and tackling disorder and violence. The use of intelligence in all forms of tension, disturbance and armed conflict, including the fight against international terrorism, places a heavy responsibility on law enforcement officials. They have to provide a balance between the legitimate and effective use of intelligence to protect the security of the state and its citizens, whilst protecting, *inter alia*, the right to private and family life. Article 4 of the United Nations Code of Conduct for Law Enforcement Officials states that, "Matters of a confidential nature in the possession of law enforcement officials shall be kept confidential, unless the performance of duty or the needs of justice strictly require otherwise."[264] The following articles of the European Code of Police Ethics provide more specific guidance on police interventions and investigations, including the gathering and use of intelligence:

> 40. The police shall carry out their tasks in a fair manner, guided, in particular, by the principles of impartiality and non-discrimination.

> 41. The police shall only interfere with an individual's right to privacy when strictly necessary and only to obtain a legitimate objective.

---

[263] S. Cullen, *Field notes from the Malawi Police Training Project*, September 1995.
[264] United Nations Code of Conduct for Law Enforcement Officials, *supra* note 10.

V:1

42. The collection, storage, and use of personal data by the police shall be carried out in accordance with international data protection principles and, in particular, be limited to the extent necessary for the performance of lawful, legitimate and specific purposes.

43. The police, in carrying out their activities, shall always bear in mind everyone's fundamental rights, such as freedom of thought, conscience, religion, expression, peaceful assembly, movement and the peaceful enjoyment of possessions.[265]

Practical aspects of the ethical use of intelligence are incorporated in the following set of ten basic principles of intelligence work.

(i) Principles of Intelligence

1. **Centralised Control.** Centralised control avoids duplication of effort and enables resources to be used most efficiently. In a multi-tier organisation like the police, there should be a clear intelligence hierarchy within the chain of command. For the purposes of security and accountability, it is essential for intelligence files and records to be held centrally. A senior police official should be accountable for the safe custody and security of all intelligence files and, together with a designated tasking team, should decide target priorities, and how and to whom tasks should be directed and disseminated. The Head of Intelligence is accountable not only for performance, but legal and human rights implications of intelligence and its use.

2. **Timeliness.** Intelligence can only be effective if it reaches the person requiring it to deal with the operational incident. For it to be of any value, the whole intelligence process must be capable of responding to the timely need of the user.

3. **Systematic Exploitation.** Sources and agencies should be used systematically by methodical tasking.

4. **Objectivity.** As information is gathered and the intelligence picture emerges, it is possible to fall into the trap of making assumptions based on perceptions. A useful maxim is, '*if the information is not being questioned or challenged, then it is likely that assumptions are being made.*' It is essential to remain objective, look at the information and then ask the

---

[265] European Code of Police Ethics, *supra* note 13.

questions of it – how, why, when and where? Hence, fresh information is not distorted to fit preconceived ideas.

5. **Accessibility.** Relevant material must be available to intelligence staff and users within the limits of security (see 9 below).

6. **Responsiveness.** It is essential that the intelligence function of a police organisation does not merely exist for its own ends. Some highly sensitive intelligence will need to be kept to closely confined groups. However, other intelligence should be shared with investigators and commanders under a 'need to know' policy, thus enabling effective investigations and other operations. Intelligence staff must be responsive to the needs of operational police leaders.

7. **Source Protection.** All sources of protection must be adequately protected. The gathering of information for intelligence purposes must not put life at risk, for example the life of a police informant. Informants must have their identities protected at all times. It may be necessary to sanitise intelligence in such a form that the source or surveillance mechanism cannot be deduced. (Guidance on the use of informants is examined in Chapter 4 of Part VI herein).

8. **Continuous Review.** Intelligence must be constantly reviewed, taking account of all new information. Information or intelligence that proves unfounded or inaccurate should be weeded out of the system.

9. **Security.** Security is of the essence in an effective intelligence system. Perhaps the most important aspect of security is the protection of sources (see 7 above). However it is important to stop operations being frustrated or sources being fed false information. Organisations need to establish and comply with stringent security rules.

10. **Legality.** It is axiomatic that all intelligence work must be strictly within the law. National laws of confidentiality and privacy concerning telephone monitoring and data protection should always be observed (See for example, article 42 of the European Code of Police Ethics, above).[266]

---

[266] Colonel R. C. Bell, *Ten Principles of Intelligence*, Unpublished, Bramshill, England, May 1992.

V:1

(ii) The Intelligence Cycle

Intelligence is different from information. The latter is simply the acquiring and passing of knowledge from one source to another. Intelligence is the compiling of information, the checking of information and analysing and processing it into a form where it can be used for planning and decision-making. It can also help to provide the evidence for successful prosecution in criminal trials. The effective use of intelligence systems should be used at the pre-conflict, conflict and post-conflict stages. Effective intelligence enables the formulation of strategies and tactics, and informed decision-making by police leaders. Additionally it assists resource planning, for example identifying the number of personnel and equipment required and any training needs.

The intelligence cycle is a logical sequence of activities leading to the provision of intelligence to users. This cycle can be operated using manual and paper systems and without the use of technology.

The Intelligence Cycle

Note: Reassessment is a continuous process throughout.[267]

---

[267] *Ibid.*

The various stages of the cycle are explained as follows within the context of conflict:

Direction. This is the process of deciding the intelligence requirement, planning the collection effort, issuing orders and requests for its collection.

For example, beat patrol officials report that rumour in the community and graffiti suggest that an individual or group (the 'target') are intent on committing acts of violent public disorder. Following this information, the local police commander decides that a dedicated intelligence unit should be deployed to collect information about the target.

Collection. This is the use of information resources to meet intelligence requirements.

At this stage of the cycle, community information is invaluable. Collection resources could include police records and other agencies (for example criminal records, known modus operandi of criminals, immigration records, passport office, telephone records, motor vehicle licensing bureaux, municipal housing information) or human sources such as members of the community, arrested suspects or police informants in the community or in correctional facilities. Surveillance is also important. Information collected may include the identities of the targets and their associates, premises used or occupied, vehicles owned and driven and habits and movement of the targets.

Intelligence about the community should also include such information as population, historical development, demographic factors and profiles, and geography.

Processing. Following collection, the intelligence teams pass the information to analysts at a central point for processing. Processing comprises collation, evaluation and interpretation.

Collation. requires indexing for rapid retrieval. Also information gaps may be identified leading to asking for the collection of further information.

Evaluation. requires the validation of the accuracy, reliability, credibility and relevance of the information. This process leads to the interpretation and grading of credibility and reliability of the intelligence. There are many variations of intelligence evaluation; some use a five or six stage categorisation. The following provides a very simple model that can be maintained and managed using written systems.

V:1

Reliability of the intelligence source can be categorised and indexed alphabetically as follows:

A. *Completely reliable: the reliability of the source has always been consistent in the past. Official records and documents are seldom open to doubt.*

B. *Usually reliable. In the past, information provided has almost always proved reliable.*

C. *Unreliable. Previous reliability has not always been consistent and has sometimes been totally unreliable.*

D. *Reliability cannot be judged, perhaps because the source has never been used previously.*

Credibility of the content of intelligence can be categorised and indexed numerically as follows:

1. *Confirmed by other sources. The information has been corroborated by another police official or independent and reliable source.*

2. *Probably true. The information is consistent with other known facts or previous information.*

3. *Doubtful. The information is inconsistent with known facts or previous information.*

4. *Truth cannot be judged. The information cannot be corroborated by any source or by investigation.*

Interpretation. This stage takes information which has been collated and evaluated and asks questions of it to yield intelligence.

Dissemination. This is the provision of intelligence to the right person or persons for timely action. Intelligence should be provided in concise, unequivocal and coherent written format. The intelligence organisation must be fully aware of the needs of the users, and effective dissemination channels must exist.

After dissemination, police leaders can use this information for strategic and tactical decision-making. This might include the deployment of public order personnel, the arrest of targets or, on the basis of continuous cyclical reassessment, directions for surveillance and collection of information.[268]

It is important to emphasise that the above process is a cycle. As information is obtained and processed there is a continued need at any stage during the cycle to review the situation and to re-task sources and agencies.

(d) Effective Briefing and Debriefing

Effective briefing and debriefing are primary means for effective top-down and bottom-up communication within any police organisation. Effective briefing and debriefing is essential to the success not only of major operations, but also of day-to-day policing, including beat patrol duties. All operational police staff must be briefed daily before being deployed, and debriefed at the conclusion of their deployment. Information on crime and disorder and community information gleaned during briefings and debriefings may be critical and of special relevance during periods of tension. The information may require action as part of the intelligence cycle. For example it may confirm or corroborate the relevance or reliability of information, or new intelligence requirements may come to light that require direction and targeting. Briefings enable the dissemination of intelligence and the implementation of operation plans based on intelligence.

Police leaders should ensure that briefings and debriefings are not perfunctory. Briefings and debriefings provide opportunity for police leaders to be visible, inspirational and motivational – and *ethical*. They should also ensure that they and their managers and supervisors are trained to deliver effective briefings and debriefings, and that all briefings and debriefings are prepared, structured, and dynamic. Briefing and debriefing is about professionalism.

Before deploying personnel to major operations, for example, dealing with large scale and violent public disorder, police leaders should (subject to availability) use presentation aids such as overhead projectors, transparent slides, PowerPoint or flip charts.

Police leaders in charge of major operations should lead briefings and debriefings, but may wish to consider using other members of their staff of any rank who possess good communication, presentation and facilitation skills. Debriefing, in particular, is a special skill. An effective and experienced debriefer, who is able to ask the right questions and encourage people to respond to those questions, will be able to not only gain the most relevant information but also prioritise its importance.

---

[268] *Ibid.*

V:1

(i)   Briefing

Briefing of personnel is necessary for the following reasons:

- To ensure they are properly equipped, correctly dressed, and motivated to perform their duties in an efficient and effective way. In public order situations, police leaders have a duty of care to safeguard as far as possible the health, safety and welfare of their staff. They should ensure their staff are trained, equipped and *briefed* to deal with potential violent disorder.

- To familiarise personnel with their legal powers and constraints, and to reinforce the need for the observance of human rights standards and practices.

- To advise how force should be used only when absolutely necessary and be proportionate to the threat being faced.

- To disseminate the information and intelligence they need to perform their duties efficiently and effectively.

- To collate information, intelligence and evidence and to identify new intelligence requirements.

- To answer questions, including 'naïve' questions that help personnel to fully understand their duties and tasks. 'Personnel should not be made to feel inhibited or subject to ridicule for asking questions to which the answer may seem obvious. Personnel should be encouraged to ask any questions that assists understanding or clarification. Effective operations and avoiding mistakes require every person deployed to have a total understanding of their role and duties.

- To stimulate and encourage the sharing of ideas, information and intelligence.

- To encourage personnel to participate in solving problems and providing solutions.

- To enable personnel to understand policing goals and objectives.

- To update personnel with knowledge of law, procedures and policies.

- To provide personnel with the knowledge they require for special operations.

For briefings to be effective, it is important to remember the following:

- Be dynamic. Give the briefing in a clear and confident manner that will gain the total attention of personnel.

- Briefings should be out of earshot and sight of citizens.

- Briefings should preferably be delivered in a special briefing room. Try to use a separate room if a briefing room is not available.

- It is essential that briefings are not interrupted.

- Although resources may be scarce, try to obtain writing materials, maps or blackboard and chalk to be used as briefing aids. These will make briefings more interesting and effective.

- Personnel being briefed may stand or sit. For longer briefings, they may be more comfortable and attentive if allowed to sit.

- As far as possible, briefings should be short, sharp and impactive. Prioritise the most important information. Do not overload the briefing with too much information.

- Involve subordinates in the briefing. Encourage them to share information and knowledge, it may provide the solution to a problem. The briefing officer should not do all the talking.

- At briefings and team meetings always encourage subordinates to participate, and to brief their managers and colleagues about knowledge, information or ideas they may have. Involving them in briefings will develop their confidence and their skills as effective communicators.

(ii) Debriefing

Debriefing of personnel is necessary for the following reasons:

- To review the events of the day, the operation or period of duty.

V:1

- To ensure all tasks have been completed as far as possible.

- To collate information, intelligence and evidence and to identify new intelligence requirements.

- To disseminate information and intelligence.

- To analyse incidents and actions and identify reasons for success or failure.

- To identify ways of improving performance and professionalism.

- To learn from each other.

- To identify matters requiring the attention of others, for example specialist departments (criminal investigation and traffic police), senior police managers, other agencies.

- To identify and attend to matters of health safety and welfare.

For debriefings to be effective, it is important to remember the following:

- Direct the debriefing in a clear and confident manner that will gain the total attention of personnel.

- Encourage suggestions, comments and ideas from personnel being debriefed. Debriefing is about communicating, it is not a one-way process.

- Establish from those being debriefed what has occurred during their period of duty or at an operation. Those in charge of the briefing should gain an understanding of events from the perspective of those being briefed, and not their own.

- Analyse events and make an honest evaluation of whether the operation has been successful or not.

- If things went wrong or mistakes were made, a cool and dispassionate attempt should be made to find out why. It is important to be objective and encourage personnel to admit collective mistakes.

- Decide how improvements can be made for the future.

- At all times, the debriefing commander must keep control of the debriefing and not allow it to deteriorate into an exercise in blame. It is important not to not allow criticism or comments to be personalised or become potentially offensive.

- Debriefings should be used as opportunities to learn and to develop better policing practices and systems.

In the following chapter, briefing and debriefing is examined again within the context of planning for disorder and conflict, and the command and control of major incidents.

(e) Threat and Risk Assessment

Notwithstanding the best preventive efforts, including intervention and mediation of police leaders, a period of tension, perhaps accompanied by minor sporadic disorder, may escalate into large-scale internal disturbance or even non-international armed conflict. When disorder or conflict break out it is essential that plans are in place for an effective reaction to deal with the disorder or conflict, and to restore normality as quickly as possible.

At every stage, police leaders should make a threat and risk assessment of the vulnerability of and danger to citizens, police officials and property. The following provides some examples of the types of question that might be asked for a threat and risk assessment:

1. Who could cause harm?
Who are the individuals or groups who present the threat?
How many persons might be involved?

2. What could cause harm?
Would a hostile crowd have access to missiles, petrol or weapons?
Are materials available for barricades?

3. Who could be harmed?
Who are likely to be the innocent residents in the community?
Have the vulnerable been identified?

4. What could be harmed?
Is vulnerable property at risk?
Are there premises that might attract looting?

V:1

    5.   What are the risks or hazards to police officials?
Have threats been directed towards police officials?

    6.   Do plans and control measures exist to deal with the threats and risks?
If not, what new measures need to be introduced (for example, training and equipment) to deal with the threats and risks?
Are contingency plans and exit strategies available?

If police leaders and their teams have been diligent in acquiring the maximum amount of community information and operating an effective intelligence model, and have well-briefed and motivated personnel at their disposal, the likelihood is that they will be able to achieve an accurate threat and risk assessment and a successful plan to react to disorder. Hence, they are less likely to fall victim to the adage, *'To fail to plan is to plan to fail'*.

Chapter 2. Conflict – Command, Planning and Operations

(A) INTRODUCTION - AN INTERNATIONAL PERSPECTIVE

It is not the purpose of this chapter to recommend specific tactics for policing armed conflicts, disturbances and tensions. Dependent upon their specific experiences, culture and environment, police agencies around the world have developed their own styles, methods and tactics for policing in these circumstances. Consequently, there are some similarities, but there are also many differences. Methods vary considerably. Non-lethal methods can include a range of equipment from batons, water cannons, tear gas grenades, rubber bullets or bean-bag rounds. Some police agencies may deploy armoured vehicles, mounted police or dogs. Although ostensibly intended to be non-lethal, disproportionate force using any of these methods or equipment can lead to fatalities. A nation's history, traditions, religion and culture may determine that any of these methods or equipment may be unacceptable.

Culture is a very powerful influence. The following is an account given to the author by a professional police leader having a responsibility for dealing with major urban disorder affecting his nation.

> "Before the riot, the rioters line up in the street facing us and we line up facing them with our shields. We leave a space between us – they might be students – and then I walk towards the crowd and meet their organizer. Just me and him between the police and the crowd. Nobody else can hear us. We negotiate what time the riot should start and finish and he tells us what their targets are. He says, 'We're going to try and reach that building there (indicating a nearby building behind police lines) and set fire to your police cars'. We agree that the building and the police cars will be their targets but nothing else. We agree that the riot will last for an hour and a half then it must stop. We turn round and walk back to our lines. Someone blows a whistle and the riot starts. They try to break through our lines and throwing missiles. We go backwards and forwards. There's a lot of pushing. Our job is to push them back and stop them reaching the building or our cars. We keep them back. After an hour and a half exactly, someone blows a whistle again and the riot stops and we all turn round and go back to our lines. We take our injured away. They take their injured away. Nobody breaks the agreement. Then I meet the leader again and we agree to all go away and come back next day – at an agreed time – and start again. This is how we do it all the time. I have a very important job and everyone says I'm good at it."
>
> *Captain of the Mobile Reserve,*
> *Indonesian National Police, July 1999.*

V:2

The captain's account exemplifies a singular and almost ritualistic style of policing violent disorder at a time when serious rioting was commonplace in his country. It compares to the chivalry between confronting medieval armies. Looking more deeply into the account, it implies that within set bounds, the Indonesian National Police demonstrated admirable regard and respect for the democratic right of citizens to protest. The captain knows confrontation and violence is inevitable and so he successfully negotiates a confrontation that will limit levels of violence and damage. In terms of accountability, for any crimes that may be committed by demonstrators in the course of the protest and for any human rights violations that may be committed by police in responding to the situation, the orthodoxy of agreeing an acceptable level of violence may be questionable. Nevertheless, it works. The style and method of policing (and rioting) indicate (at least in Indonesia in 1999) a distinctive cultural setting for disorder with a twist of compromise that may seem very different to people of other nations and cultures.

Some countries have a tradition of violent public protest. A minor altercation or event can soon bring rioters onto the streets. Other countries are more pacific and street disorder or rioting is rare. The single most common feature of policing disorder which has evolved internationally is that described by the Indonesian police captain, namely the deployment of units comprising lines, cordons or phalanxes of uniformed police officials equipped with protective shields and clothing to deter or push back and disperse determined and organised protestors or rioters. The dynamics of this type situation may seem like a military battle where, however, rules on the use of force by police, rather than those for military, apply. The foremost strategy of the police is to retain power and control over the struggle, to maintain the upper hand, and not allow the protestors to gain the initiative, dominance or control. As the changing nature of the violence and strength of force applied against them increases and decreases, the police have to react proportionately, increasing or decreasing the level of counterforce necessary to maintain dominance and control. The ultimate goal is the dispersal of the protestors or rioters and the restoration of normality.[269]

(B) TACTICAL SUPPORT UNITS

Police organisations in different states have varying types of police agencies and paramilitary units for dealing with riots and other forms of public disorder. They are described variously, for example, as 'riot unit', 'mobile reserve', 'special reserve force', or 'special security division'. For the purpose of uniformity, the term

---

[269] For further reading, *see* P. A. J. Waddington, 'Policing Public Order and Political Contention', in T. Newburn (ed.), *Handbook of Policing* (Willan Publishing, Devon, England, 2005).

'tactical support unit' (TSU) is used in this chapter. Within the context of democratic policing, the word 'support' reflects what the role of these units should be. Their role should not be to operate arbitrarily and autonomously to quell protest or disorder. Their role is to support police leaders and wider society when efforts at defusing tensions within the community using ordinary policing methods have failed. As a consequence, strategic and tactical options have to be considered and implemented to deal with escalating violence and disorder.

Some states employ specialist or autonomous police agencies having a dedicated role in dealing with major disorder and other national emergencies. These include the emergency police units of the German States[270] the Mobile Gendarmerie and Central Service of the Companies of Republican Security (SCCRS) of France, [271] and the Mobile Reserve of Indonesia .[272]

In some states, specialist TSUs are a section of the main police agency and police officials are transferred to and from general policing duties, with periods of attachment to the TSU. Some police agencies maintain a special reserve of trained units to provide the first-line rapid emergency response to major disorder that are supplemented by officials from general police duties when disorder escalates. Highly decentralised police models with widespread, small and autonomous police agencies – for example, as found in the United States of America – have only a limited response capability to serious disorder.

Rather than examine the advantages or efficacy of any particular style or method, this chapter concentrates on examining some strategies for, and the principles of, effective command, planning and operations for the proportionate policing of conflicts, disturbances and tensions in accordance with human rights law and principles. Before doing so, it is important to understand the strategies and tactics of adversaries in conflict.

(C) THE WAR OF NERVES

Article 20 of the Universal Declaration of Human Rights declares the right to freedom of peaceful assembly and association. Democratic States put in place the measures necessary for this right to be enjoyed. Usually the right is respected, and the police facilitate lawful protest and the legitimate objectives of those who wish to exercise this right.

---

[270] L. Sullivan *et al.* (eds.), *Encyclopedia of Law Enforcement* (Sage Publications, Thousand Oaks, CA, 2005) p.1074.
[271] *Ibid.*, pp. 1067–1069.
[272] *Ibid.*, p. 1109.

V:2

Notwithstanding that the reasons for protest may be related to perfectly just and morally reasoned issues or causes, members of some protest groups wish to provoke violence for their own ends. They become militant. For them, the issue has become intractable and destructive. They may also commit acts of terrorism. No matter how just the cause may be, police officials have a duty to respond to such violence in order to protect life and maintain public safety. It is important for police leaders to understand the rationale and strategies of those who seek violent confrontation. The following provides a useful insight into the mind of the 'urban guerrilla'.

> "When the police designate certain of their men to go into the crowd and arrest a demonstrator, a larger group of urban guerrillas must surround the police group, disarming and beating them and at the same time allowing the prisoner to escape. This urban guerrilla operation is called 'the net within a net'.
>
> Street tactics have revealed a new type of urban guerrilla who participates in mass protests. This is the type we designate as the "urban guerrilla demonstrator", who joins the crowds and participates in marches with specific and definite aims in mind. The urban guerrilla demonstrator must initiate the "net within the net", ransacking government vehicles, official cars and police vehicles before turning them over or setting fire to them, to see if any of them have money or weapons.'"
>
> *C. Marighella,*
> *Minimanual of the Urban Guerrilla, Brazil, July 1969,*
> *www.marxists.org/ archive/marighella-carlos/1969/06/minimanual-urban-guerrilla.*

Although Marighella's tactics are designed to provoke revolution against repressive regimes in non-democratic states, they are tactics that are familiar to experienced police officials who face conflict and disturbance in all societies, including those having a democratic system of government.

Marighella's rationale for violence is that, by attacking the police as representatives of the government or elite, the regime will react with increasingly harsh and repressive measures that, over a period of time, will turn the citizens against them. To further their cause and to gain sympathy, they want the police to be (or appear to be) brutal and violent. Images broadcast around the world of police officials beating protestors are priceless political capital. Such images fuel the propaganda of militant protest groups and for some it results in them winning their cause. Many leaders of protest achieve their goals through the calculated use of violence. Police brutality and indiscipline help them to gain the power they seek through a calculated 'war of nerves.' Sometimes they can then evolve from radical firebrands to respected and urbane elder statesmen.

> "The objective of the war of nerves is to mislead, spreading lies among the authorities in which everyone can participate, thus creating an atmosphere of nervousness, discredit, insecurity, uncertainty and concern on the part of the government. Exploiting by every means possible the corruption, the mistakes and the failures of the government and its representatives, forcing them into demoralizing explanations and justifications . . ."
>
> *C. Marighella,*
> *Minimanual of the Urban Guerrilla, Brazil, July 1969,*
> *www.marxists.org/ archive/marighella-carlos/1969/06/minimanual-urban-guerrilla*

Marighella's tactics to win the war of nerves strongly imply that responses such as police brutality ('the mistakes') assist their purpose. He also reveals how the leaders of determined militant factions can use the police as a major pawn in conflict. Having achieved power, or having won their cause, the former urban guerrilla then basks in his newly found celebrity and status as moral victor. Meanwhile, the discredited and brutal police officials, having served their purpose as expendable actors in the process of the urban guerrilla gaining power or winning the cause, have long since been consigned to ignominy.

The following is another rationale of violence from a protagonist in a major late 20th Century non-international armed conflict rooted in an intractable high stakes distribution issue, amounting to a civil class war. Providing the converse of Marighella's reasoning, these words express most compellingly that those actors in conflict who exercise a measure of humanity by respecting humanitarian law will occupy the moral high ground. Thus, they are less likely to provoke violent reaction. For police officials, this is an important pragmatic insight and lesson from an honest and credible source.

V:2

> "Political violence can be thought of as a type of communication mechanism (or language) between two actors…[V]iolence is a real act and that the way it is used opens or closes spaces to ideas and possible understandings. An actor that has greater legitimacy and moral and political advantage is more inclined to use violence in a way that transmits messages so that the exchange becomes constructive. Terrorism, massacres and torture transmit messages that impede understanding, while noble acts and compassion transmit constructive messages. It is less a matter of which actor using force is materially stronger, but who has the moral advantage in the use of force. In the Salvadorean case, it was the insurgency that held greater legitimacy, not the authoritarian regime, which reacted disproportionately to resistance to its political model in a way that only escalated the violence. While it did make serious mistakes, the insurgency used violence as a political mechanism to consolidate its moral advantage. This translated into treating prisoners well, shunning revenge and respecting humanitarian law."
>
> *Joaquín Villalobos,*
> *former leader of the Farabundo Martí National Liberation Front (FMLN),*
> *El Salvador.*
> *J. Villalobos, 'The Salvadorean Insurgency; why choose peace?'*
> *Choosing to Engage: Armed groups and peace processes;*
> *R. Ricigliano (ed.), 2005,*
> *Retrieved 22 December 2005 from*
> *http://www.c-r.org/accord/engage/accord16/08.shtml.*

Villalobos also describes the struggle for the moral high ground as a 'war of nerves' in which the police are essential 'victims' of the conflict.[273] These examples demonstrate that those who plan disorder, internal disturbance and tension, and non-international armed conflict are highly motivated and committed. With limited resources, they aim to be more potent and organised than those they oppose. In consideration of the need for police officials to collect community information and the need for the use of intelligence as examined in the preceding chapter, Marighella's guidance to the urban guerrilla is very familiar.

---

[273] Interview by author with J. Villalobos, former leader of the FMLN, Oxford, England, 11 March 2006.

302

> "The revolutionary method of carrying out actions is strongly and forcefully based on the knowledge and use of the following elements:
>
> 1. Investigation and intelligence gathering
> 2. Observation and vigilance
> 3. Reconnaissance, or exploration of the terrain
> 4. Study and timing of routes
> 5. Mapping
> 6. Mechanization
> 7. Careful selection of personnel
> 8. Selection of firepower
> 9. Study and practice in success
> 10. Use of cover
> 11. Retreat
> 12. Dispersal
> 13. The liberation or transfer of prisoners
> 14. The elimination of evidence
> 15. The rescue of wounded"
>
> *C. Marighella,*
> *How to Carry Out the Action, Minimanual of the Urban Guerrilla, Brazil, July 1969,*
> *www.marxists.org/archive/marighella-carlos/1969/06/minimanual-urban-guerrilla/*

It is pointless for police officials to constantly complain that, in facing conflict, disturbance and tension, they are the brunt of hostile criticism and vulnerable to unreasonable, false and malicious complaints. Such feelings may in some circumstances reflect reality. However they can sometimes be unreasoned responses that are symptomatic of the paranoia found within some police subcultures.[274] The harsh reality for all police officials to understand is that those who promote conflict and violence and, in doing so, commit serious crimes of violence and, where there is armed conflict, violations of international humanitarian law, can sometimes escape the consequences of their actions. Yet police officials can never commit violations of human rights with impunity.

Consequently, rather than harbouring resentment at the perceived unfairness of the world, police officials could take a more positive approach by learning from Marighella and Villalobos. The lessons are not to fall into the trap set by those who seek confrontation with the police, not to lose the war of nerves, not to use disproportionate force and, most importantly, not to abuse human rights. Well-

---

[274] H. Goldstein, *Problem Oriented Policing* (McGraw-Hill Publishing Company, New York, 1990) pp. 29, 30. *See also* Part VI (Police Organisations – Management and Change), Chapter 3 (Managing the Process of Change) herein.

briefed, properly trained, competent and disciplined police personnel deployed by inspirational leaders who are confident in the ethicality and professionalism of their plans and strategies will hopefully confound the urban guerrilla and not be forced into making 'demoralising explanations and justifications'.

The inescapable fact is that disproportionate force is unlawful under all circumstances and all police officials are accountable for their actions. Consequently, all police leaders must ensure the highest standards of planning, preparation and training to deal lawfully with disorder, internal disturbance and tension, and non-international armed conflict.

(D) UNDERSTANDING PUBLIC RESPONSES

Policing internal disturbance and tension and, indeed, non-international armed conflict is a coercive activity. Although police officials are supposed to be politically neutral in the affairs of the nation, they are duty bound as protectors of public safety, to confront militant violent protest and armed insurgency, no matter how just and reasoned that protest may be. Consequently, the police may be perceived, *de facto,* as a reactionary force that supports the political views of the government. This creates difficulties in terms of community relations, as some sections of the population perceive the police as enemies of the people and not as their friends and protectors

Moreover, policing internal disturbances and tensions, in the form of riots and other violent forms of protest, requires a disciplined paramilitary style of policing that depends on obeying orders and commands rather than on using individual discretion. An individual police official may be deployed in anti-riot paramilitary mode in a community whose citizens know that official as their local neighbourhood patrol or community official. Herein lies a dichotomy. After the disturbance and tension are resolved and concluded, the neighbourhood patrol official then has to revert to his or her normal duties within the community. If citizens of that community harbour resentment consequent to real or perceived actions on the part of the police during the preceding situation, trust between police and citizens may be seriously damaged. The neighbourhood official is then perceived as a party to the source of the resentment and will have a difficult, if not impossible, task in rebuilding constructive and harmonious relations with the community. Such a situation can be highly detrimental to long-term police/public relations in times of both tension and normality. To avoid this occurring, it is preferable that police leaders avoid deploying neighbourhood police officials to this dual role within the community they routinely police. At times of internal disturbance and tension and non-international armed conflict, all police leaders should be sensitive to the needs and expectations of the wider community. Some damage to police/public relations may be inevitable in intractable conflicts. Nevertheless, *rapprochement* can be achieved if police leaders have demonstrated integrity and goodwill, and responded to disturbance and conflict in ways that are lawful, proportionate, transparent and humane.

(E) PROPORTIONALITY AND THE USE OF FORCE

The capability to respond effectively to major disorder, and the availability of tactical support and reinforcements are critical factors when examining issues of reasonable force and proportionality. Chapter 4 of Part II herein examines the Basic Principles on the Use of Force and Firearms by Law Enforcement Officials. Articles relating to the use of force are also examined in two other instruments, namely, the Code of Conduct for Law Enforcement Officials and the European Code of Police Ethics. It is important to reiterate these principles. In the first instance, peaceful means should be attempted to resolve conflict, disturbance and tension before force is applied. Further, in the use of force, proportionality should apply. Principle 5 on the Use of Force and Firearms by Law Enforcement Officials, states that whenever the use of force and firearms is unavoidable, law enforcement officials shall exercise restraint and act in proportion to the seriousness of the offence and the legitimate objectives to be achieved. They are required, *inter alia,* to minimise damage and injury, and respect and preserve human life.

A useful practical definition of proportionality within the context of policing conflict, disturbance and tension, and which encapsulates the articles and principles is "the amount of force which is reasonable in intensity, duration and magnitude, based on all known facts to the commander at the time, to decisively counter the hostile act or intention".[275]

Notwithstanding the immutability of these articles and principles, police officials are confronted with awesome difficulties and dilemmas in endeavouring to conform to them in situations where they may be facing their own imminent murder or life threatening injury. These difficulties and dilemmas need to be examined within the practicalities of police settings. They need to be understood not only by police officials, but also by government officials having a responsibility for policing, judges, lawyers, ombudsmen and commissioners for human rights, and members of non-governmental organisations and other groups who operate as guardians or scrutinisers of international human rights standards. This has already been touched upon in Chapter 3 of Part II, herein, concerning the right to life, where it is observed

---

[275] Organisation for Security and Cooperation in Europe, *Use of Force and Kosovo Police Service Policy, Kosovo Police Service School Training Notes*, May 2001, p. 4.

V:2

that, "it is almost inevitable that defects in training, equipment, planning and command and control of police operations have led to loss of police lives".

There has also been loss of civilian non-police lives, including those of rioters and innocent citizens, not necessarily through malicious or illegal acts on the part of police officials, but because of the very defects identified. The following two scenarios are presented to help illustrate the practical difficulties that can face operational police officials during times of conflict, disturbance and tension.

Scenario 1. In developed or small, highly centralised countries, with modern and efficient transport networks and communications systems, national policing arrangements generally ensure that police agencies have integrated radio networks and common standards of public order training. They also have coordinated mobilisation and support procedures, standardised protective clothing, defensive and offensive equipment, and practised public order strategies and tactics. In this setting, using lethal force by discharging firearms against a violent crowd throwing petrol bombs would unlikely to be regarded as a proportionate response. This is because the strategic commander would probably have at his or her disposal a range of non-lethal tactical options. In these circumstances, if outnumbered or under withering attack, the police commander may decide to make a tactical withdrawal in the knowledge that, within a reasonable period of time, adequate numbers of personnel, additional equipment and appropriate countermeasures could be quickly deployed or put in place to deal effectively with the situation with the minimum necessary force.

Scenario 2. By contrast, in countries with highly decentralised policing systems, the various small, autonomous police agencies with total strengths of, perhaps, no more than twenty personnel can experience considerable difficulties when having to deal with similar levels of mob violence. These same difficulties confront small police units deployed to isolated rural areas, or in developing countries, perhaps geographically large, and having limited communications and infrastructure. Operating under these conditions, police officials may have only limited experience in dealing with major public disorder and lack training and equipment. Their only defence may be a firearm or baton. Being geographically isolated, the nearest neighbouring police agencies may be many kilometres away and in different jurisdictions. These agencies may not have compatible communications and other equipment. There may be no system for mobilising assistance or support, and it could take many hours or days from making a request to receiving assistance and reinforcements.

In these settings, using lethal force by discharging firearms against a violent crowd throwing petrol bombs would probably be regarded as a proportionate response. It is highly likely that a lightly equipped and small group of police officials confronted and possibly outnumbered by a violent crowd, would be able to show that they were in imminent threat of death or serious injury. This is because the range of tactical options open to them would be severely limited, and may not include the possibility of tactical withdrawal or other non-lethal responses.

These scenarios point up a dilemma that police can face in some situations where they have to respond to violence. In each of the hypothetical situations described above the violence faced by the police is of the same nature and magnitude. However, in the second instance the threat and the danger to police are enhanced because of circumstances that include shortcomings in policing arrangements. This is clearly the case because it has been possible to posit the first scenario in which lethal force by police would not be justified against the same level of violence. In other words, the lives of police and public may be jeopardised because of policing failures. These are failures, at least, of training, equipment and planning, including contingency planning.

Clearly situations that could not have been foreseen can and do arise but, in the case of communal violence, it would be most unusual if signs of increasing tension, which should be monitored by police, were not apparent. Furthermore, there should be some level of contingency planning that takes into account such factors as geographical isolation and limited communications facilities and infrastructure.

Any enquiry into killings by State officials, as required by international standards,[276] that arose out of the circumstances described in the second scenario should take into account all of the circumstances of the case, including those that arose out of shortcomings in policing arrangements. This may well have the effect of removing accountability for any deaths from those that actually applied lethal force to those responsible for the wider policing arrangements. In a right to life case arising out of the use of lethal force, described in Chapter 3 of Part II herein,[277] the European Court of Human Rights deplored the lack of equipment, such as truncheons, riot shields, water cannon, rubber bullets or tear gas, that would have allowed a graduated and proportionate response to a riot.

Governments and police leaders can reduce, mitigate or eliminate the factors and inconsistencies that lead to the dilemma described above in the two contrasting scenarios. Training police officials in public order strategies and tactics and the

---

[276] *See e.g.*, articles 6, 11, and 22 of the Basic Principles on the Use of Force and Firearms by Law Enforcement Officials, and jurisprudence of human rights courts and bodies on this matter under the heading 'Investigations into Killings by State Officials' in Chapter3 of Part II herein.

[277] *Güleç* v. *Turkey, supra* note 123.

provision of all necessary protective equipment will save lives and reduce the risk of injury to both police and other citizens. Governments and police leaders who are accountable for the safety of the people they lead and the citizens they protect, should regard it as mandatory to ensure the highest possible standards of training and equipment to enable police officials to respond lawfully and *proportionately* in situations of conflict, disturbance and tension. Furthermore, effective command, planning and operations are central to standing the test of accountability.

(F) COMMAND, PLANNING AND OPERATIONS

(a) The Need for Operational, Emergency and Contingency Plans

Operational, emergency and contingency plans are required for reasons of effective command, control and accountability. The principles of planning for and managing events arising in the context of conflict, disturbance or tension, whether or not they are sudden and unexpected, apply equally to other types of situation, for example:

- natural disasters such as earthquakes, volcanic eruptions, forest fires, floods and hurricanes;
- man made disasters such as sporting events disasters, stampedes, train and aircraft crashes, and fire and industrial accidents such as leakages of noxious chemicals;
- pre-planned major events such as visits of heads of states, major international conferences, outdoor music concerts and sporting events.

Plans for all these types of situation are central to the primary goal of policing, namely, public safety. Effective plans can prevent or reduce casualties and provide the means to protect and save life and property.

Planning for natural and man-made disasters requires many of the same activities described in the previous chapter for policing in situations of conflict, disturbance and tension. There is a need for collecting community information and intelligence, for example identifying members of the community and other agencies who can provide rescue, specialist and logistical support. There is also a need for police leaders to make a risk and threat assessment by identifying natural, environmental or other factors that could cause or contribute to disaster. For example, is the area prone to flooding or earthquake? Is there a large plant in the area that produces dangerous chemicals? Is there a sports stadium where large crowds congregate? An affirmative answer to these and similar questions indicates a need for emergency and contingency planning and a need for constant review and revision of plans in the light of changing circumstances. Although none of these plans relate directly to dealing with planned or spontaneous acts of public disorder there are two important connections between them:

Plans for natural or man made disasters, and other major events will often require a contingency plan for policing disorder. For example, a natural disaster could lead to major disorder through looting or protest at government inaction. A visit of a head of state could lead to protests against the policies of that state - alleged human rights abuses are a common cause of protest.

The consequences in terms of accountability are the same. If plans for dealing with emergencies, disasters or other similar major events are lacking or defective and there is a consequent loss of police and civilian lives, then police leaders will be as liable to be brought to account as they would be for defective planning for policing events in situations of conflict, disturbance and tension. The practical considerations affecting the right to life and the legal implications in terms of liability and accountability are very similar.

(b) Command

A proven command structure for major events and emergencies, including those arising in situations of conflict, disturbance and tension, comprises the three levels of Gold, Silver and Bronze.

Gold: The strategic level. Strategy can be defined as assessing the situation and deciding what action will be taken. In short, 'what will be done'.[278] The gold commander, usually a senior ranking police official determines the overall strategy of operations, sets objectives and communicates those objectives to silver command. Located away from the event to prevent distraction by minutiae and immediate operational matters, the gold commander is responsible for providing all the necessary information, resources and logistical support to ground commanders.

Silver: The tactical command level responsible for achieving the strategy of the gold commander. Tactics can be defined as deciding how the strategy will be implemented. In short, 'how things will be done'.[279] The silver commander, usually a senior to middle ranking official determiners tactics in accordance with the overall strategy set by the gold commander. The silver commander makes the immediate operational decisions and arranges support for the bronze commanders. As the commander conducting operations, the silver commander needs to be located near to

---

[278] G. Markham and M. Punch, 'The Gemini Solution – Embracing Accountability', in M. Amir and S. Einstein (eds.), *Police Corruption: Challenges for Developed Countries* (OIJC, Huntsville, TX, 2004).
[279] *Ibid.*

V:2

the event where he or she can be accessible to bronze commanders. Proximity has the further advantage of assessing situations on the ground by visual observation.

Bronze: The tactical sector level. Bronze commanders, usually middle or junior ranks together with their serial or unit of police officials (TSUs), achieve the tactical objectives set by the silver commander. They take the immediate operational decisions within their sector and require mobility and flexibility. They command and deploy their TSUs who are equipped with the necessary defensive and offensive equipment to respond to operational needs. Any changes they require in resources to achieve their objectives can be communicated to silver command for action. Bronze commanders are also able to provide an assessment of the situation on the ground for communication to the silver commander.

There should be a single gold commander. For the purposes of continuity, it is also highly desirable that designated, competent police officials are deployed to the respective roles of silver and bronze command. Changing commanders at later stages of the operation will inevitably result in a loss of effectiveness. Deploying new commanders who may be unfamiliar with the ongoing nature and dynamics of events on the ground may lead to questions of accountability if they make mistakes, defective decisions or responses that lead to unnecessary use of force resulting in injury or loss of life. In protracted operations, changes of personnel may be unavoidable in order to avoid fatigue that could, in itself, cause defective decision-making, leading to mistakes and possible human rights abuses. In these circumstances, it is advisable to deploy a deputy silver commander to 'shadow' and relieve the silver commander. Additionally, sufficient numbers of briefed bronze commanders and TSUs should be held in reserve.

In many operations it will be necessary to have only one silver commander. However, where the operation involves a number of locations or venues some distance from each other, or which may require different strategic and tactical considerations, it may be necessary to deploy separate silver commanders for each location or venue. It is relatively straightforward to operate this principle in relation to pre-planned events, but in spontaneous unanticipated outbreaks of disorder or sudden emergencies such as natural disasters, then in the first instance, available personnel will have to be deployed to assume the respective levels of command. Thereafter, formal arrangements can be put in place to appoint dedicated personnel who can be deployed to assumed longer term command responsibilities for the operation.

In pre-planned events, gold and silver commanders should be responsible for preparing the plan they will have to implement. They should have total ownership of the plan and be accountable for its implementation. Ownership of the plan is more likely to result in its effective implementation, including strategies and tactics that will reduce endangerment of public safety. Ownership also provides a sharper focus on accountability. Hence, if mistakes are made, accountability cannot be shifted elsewhere.

The gold, silver, bronze command structure is discrete and separate from the main organisational hierarchy. Senior police officials, even those of more senior rank to the gold commander, or the local territorial commander responsible for the day-to-day policing of the area, should not interfere with the operation other than to respond to any request for support or resources which the gold commander decides are operationally necessary. There should be sufficient trust in the leadership, competence and technical skills of the commanders. Leadership in the command structure has an essential principle, namely pushing responsibility down to the appropriate level whilst drawing accountability upwards.[280]

The Gold, Silver, Bronze command structure demands effective 'top-down' and 'bottom up' communications involving regular conferences of the gold and silver commanders to constantly reassess the situation, to identify priorities and tasks and to examine resource implications. Regular briefing and debriefings are essential for identifying problems, effective problem-solving, decision-making prioritising tasks, tasking commanders and support staff, and intelligence collection, direction, processing and dissemination. The Gold, Silver, Bronze command structure and its various support functions and roles are shown in the following model:

---

[280] *Ibid.*

V:2

THE COMMAND STRUCTURE

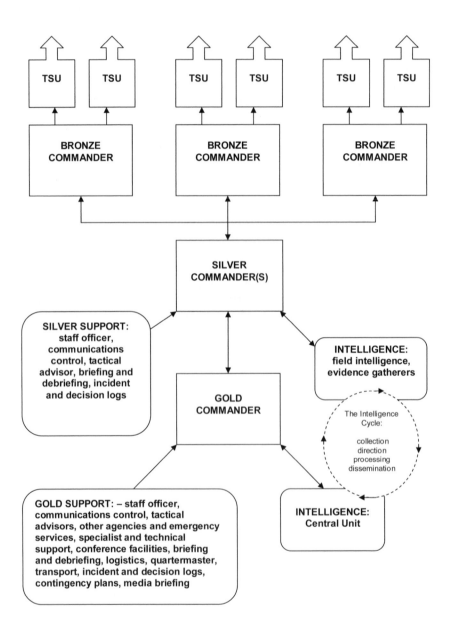

Although there is a hierarchy within the command structure, it will be noted that the arrows between the respective command levels are directed both upwards and downwards. This emphasises the flexible nature of the structure and is intended to reinforce the essential principle of having effective 'top-down' and 'bottom up' communications. The following provides an explanation of the various support functions.

- *Intelligence.* Success of the command and control of operations is dependent on operating the intelligence cycle examined in the previous chapter. Intelligence should be a dedicated and integral part of the structure. Intelligence operatives should provide intelligence for decision-making to the gold and silver levels whilst gaining information and intelligence from silver and bronze commanders for necessary direction, processing and dissemination. They can also have a proactive role in intelligence and evidence collection operating as overt or covert 'spotters' in the field, for example in identifying individuals or groups who are organising, encouraging, inciting, leading or committing violence or other crimes.

- *Communications.* Where available, secure and dedicated radio communications and operators are necessary for directing operations and receiving information from the field. At major incidents dedicated telephone landlines may be necessary.

- *Specialist and Technical Support.* Subject to the availability of technology, specialist and technical support, this could include a diverse range of technical equipment including air support, surveillance, scenes of crime, explosives detection, search equipment and listening devices. In some countries, it may be necessary to have a state lawyer, fiscal or judge available to authorise police operations and to issue search or arrest warrants.

- *Tactical Advisors.* It is impossible for operational commanders to be skilled in every aspect of police work. Consequently, they require specialist advisers on the tactical deployment of specialists, for example firearms teams, search specialists and bomb disposal personnel.

- *Other Agencies and Emergency Services.* In situations where it is anticipated they will be needed, whether they be situations of tension, disturbance or conflict or natural or man-made disasters, fire-fighting and ambulance crews should be on standby. A senior ambulance or fire officer may operate from the gold command centre to coordinate operations with the police. This may be necessary to avoid ambulance or fire personnel being put at risk.

- *Contingency Plans.* Contingency plans including all necessary maps should be held at the command centre.

- *Incident and Decision Logs.* For the purposes of accountability and post incident investigations, including complaints of police misconduct, it is essential to maintain incident logs and written records giving the rationale for the decisions made by the commander. In post incident situations, the availability of contemporaneous documented evidence can provide powerful rebuttal to allegations of human rights abuses. Documentation can provide evidence that the commander took all lawful and reasonable measures to follow the principle of proportionality and to protect life.

- *Quartermaster/Logistics.* Police officials or other suitably qualified personnel should have responsibility for the provision and maintenance of all necessary equipment

- *Transport.* Police officials or other suitably qualified personnel should have responsibility for the provision and maintenance of all motor vehicles and efficient management of transport arrangements.

- *Conference and Briefing Facilities.* Gold and silver commanders require suitably appointed conference and briefing facilities including presentation aids and maps. At major operations, it may be necessary to utilise dedicated briefing and debriefing teams.

- *Media Briefing.* Commanders should have an open and transparent relationship with the media. Media briefings are important for giving reassurance to citizens. At major incidents it is advisable to use specialist press or public relations staff having professional media skills. To avoid the media disrupting operations by making approaches to operational officials in the field, for example, bronze commanders and their TSUs, it is essential to have the media briefing facilities some distance away from the operations. The safety and security of journalists and other media is an additional important consideration in situations of violent disorder.

(c) **Planning**

Written plans should be structured and coherent. They provide all the necessary information for:

- Effective command and control.
- Briefings of the personnel responsible for managing and carrying out the plan.
- Instructions on the tasks necessary to realise the plan.

A useful mnemonic for preparing plans is **IIMAC**:

Information (the background to the event)
Intention (what the police will have to do)
Method (how the police will achieve the plan)
Administration (what the police will need to support the plan)
Communications (how the police will communicate)

Information. The information should comprise a very short statement describing the event (e.g. state visit of President X), the venue of the event, and the dates and times to be held. The information should also include a short and concise generic and local risk and threat assessment based on intelligence. For example, what is the international threat to the event and what is the more specific national or local threat of disruption or violence?

Intention. This part of the plan should include statements regarding the level of security to be imposed, any crime control, traffic or public order procedures that will have to be put into effect. Reference will also be made to contingency plans relating to other factors of public safety.

Method. This section of the plan contains the detail of the intention. It will list and identify commanders within the command structure, the numbers of staff involved and the tasks they will perform to achieve the plan. In large operations separate written orders will list the names of personnel and their tasks. Public order cordons and operating sectors should be delineated together with a breakdown of each phase of the event.

Administration. This will contain important information about rendezvous points, times and periods of duty, and briefing and debriefing arrangements. It will also include feeding arrangements (times and venues) and instructions on type of uniform or protective clothing to be worn, and the equipment to be carried. It is essential to communicate this information prior to the briefing to ensure personnel are properly dressed and equipped. Additionally, this section of the plan will include details of transportation and vehicles to be used and the hours of duty to be worked. Guidance on the basic procedure for the detention of prisoners following arrest should also be included

V:2

Communications. This section will identify the locality of communications centres and control posts, details of radio equipment and channels to be used. This section should provide guidance on policy for dealing with the press and media.

(i) Briefing and Debriefing

In addition to direct briefing and debriefing, all personnel should be issued with their own personal briefing booklet set out in accordance with the IIMAC model. In large scale-operations, with a number of sectors or functions under the command of separate silver commanders, the booklet need only pertain to their sphere of operations. Specifically, under the section on Method, it will detail the tasks and duties relating to their roles.

In countries where non-police personnel (for example, scouts, youth associations and pioneers) are used as marshals at major events involving large gatherings they, too, should be given appropriate briefings. Similarly, members of other emergency services should be briefed.

As examined in the previous chapter, effective briefing should be used to familiarise personnel with their legal powers and constraints and to reinforce the need for the observance of human rights standards and practices. Effective briefing and debriefing, together with relevant good practice, is the key to successful operations. Furthermore, in policing situations of conflict, disturbance and tension, police officials, especially those of junior rank who are at the front line of operations, work under conditions of danger, stress, confusion and uncertainty. Unless junior ranks know what they are supposed to do, the operation will fail. Without information, they will feel isolated and abandoned by their leaders. They are then more likely to vent their frustrations by over-reacting in situations of disorder, and use disproportionate force.

(ii) Morale, Health and Welfare

It is essential to maintain morale, health and welfare of personnel. Fatigue will affect personnel involved in protracted operations. Adequate periods for feeding and rest should be incorporated in the plan. In addition to briefing and debriefing personnel, commanders and their supervisors should exercise visible and inspirational leadership. They should walk around and talk to their subordinates to keep them informed of events. They should communicate with them and make them feel valued. Health and welfare matters, particularly where police officials are posted away from their homes for long periods, should be a management priority.

(d) **Operations**

As stated at the commencement of this chapter, because of worldwide variations in dealing with conflicts, disturbances and tensions, and because of resource constraints in some countries, it is impossible to recommend a definitive range of tactics for policing in these circumstances. Nonetheless, especially in relation to demonstrations and other forms of public protest, there are some generic principles and methods of good practice that can be applied at the tactical level to assist effective policing operations, to reduce or eliminate the potential for violence, and to secure greater levels of public safety. These are examined as follows.

(i)   Liaison and Negotiation

It is recommended that police commanders make early contact with the organisers or representatives of intended public demonstrations, rallies, marches or other events likely to involve large crowds or congregations of people. Organisers or representatives of these events can provide information on their intentions and may undertake to assist in ensuring that events are peaceful. No matter how militant they may be, it is important to endeavour to gain a rapport with them, both in the planning stages and throughout the course of the event. By gaining their trust and goodwill, organisers can often be persuaded to cooperate in agreeing to times, routes and locations that are less likely to cause disruption to the business community and the routine lives of ordinary citizens and residents. Consequently, it may be possible to reduce the level of resources to police the event, and the potential for conflict or violence can be reduced or eliminated.

The Internet and underground militant newssheets are a valuable source of information about forthcoming demonstrations or other forms of protest. Many protest groups have their own websites and increasingly use the internet to inflame opinion, rally support and to provide information of *rendezvous* points and times, dates and locations of intended events. The Internet can be especially useful if militant organisers of anti-authority extremist groups refuse to liase or cooperate with the police. Informants within these groups or undercover officials can also be important intelligence sources.

(ii)   Occupying the High Ground

Commanders should take the initiative and make early pre-emptive deployments of TSUs to vulnerable locations in order to prevent them from being occupied or overrun by demonstrators. For example, if intelligence reveals that they may attack commercial premises, it is essential to cordon off business or shopping districts, thereby gaining early control of the high ground and preventing access to, or assembly of, demonstrators at these locations. Demonstrators should also be

V:2

prevented from gaining access to locations where missiles are available or can be improvised – for example, bricks on building sites.

(iii) Dispersal

Notwithstanding the level of intense violence faced by the police in serious disturbances, they have an overriding priority to maintain public safety and the protection of life and property. The protection of life must be foremost over that of property.

In the event of the spontaneous dispersal of a violent or disorderly assembly, perhaps as the police gain dominance, panic may ensue and there is the possibility of stampede in which those participating and, indeed, other citizens may be at risk of serious or fatal injury. It is essential therefore, that in planning the location of major events, marches, rallies or protests, account is taken of the need for large numbers of people to disperse *en masse* from the area. For example, sports stadiums with confined entry and exit points are especially problematic. In preparing their plans, commanders should take account of this contingency and identify predetermined entry and exit routes and operational procedures for the dispersal of large numbers of people by the safest possible means.

(iv) Arrest

When people are arrested at any large-scale public event, it is essential that detention procedures take into account the need for accountability, continuity of evidence and identification. This is especially important when there are large numbers of detainees and in situations where there might be some confusion, for example unlawful or violent assemblies. A brief account justifying the arrest presented to the custody personnel, together with a photograph, which matches the arresting official with the suspect/offender will avoid confusion and aid in criminal prosecution.

Although arresting protagonists at the scene of an unlawful or violent assembly may be effective in depleting their numbers and gaining control, it may not always be the best tactic.

For the purposes of public safety and the safety of police personnel, it may be advisable and preferable to exercise a greater degree of discretion in arrest procedures than would be the case in conditions of normality. This is not to suggest a tolerance of criminality. For example, if individuals can be identified at the scene of an incident as being involved in criminal activity, or if intelligence leads to their identification, it may be unnecessary to pursue their immediate arrest. To do so may be counterproductive. It may unnecessarily endanger the arrest team, deplete police resources, and may inflame the situation. Consequently, it may be preferable to locate suspects at their homes, places of work or other places frequented by them and to arrest them after the event. Experienced police officials know that it is a salutary experience for offenders to be awakened from their beds in the early hours of the morning in order to be lawfully arrested for a crime for which they mistakenly believed they had evaded justice. This tactic for arrest reinforces the need for effective intelligence, and the deployment of overt or covert intelligence and evidence gatherers in the field. To secure successful prosecutions and convictions, video recording and observational notes by evidence gatherers are invaluable for providing evidence of identification and proof of criminal acts.

Gold and silver commanders should consider their strategic and tactical options in relation to arrest procedures according to prevailing circumstances, and provide guidance to bronze commanders and their TSUs.

(v)   Crowd Warnings

In some countries it is a legal requirement to make an audible warning to those participating in unlawful or violent assemblies of the impending use of force to disperse the protagonists. The use of a loudspeaker is the most effective means to make the warning. It also has to be born in mind that some of the crowd may be innocent non-participating bystanders. Whether or not required by law, it is always advisable to give such warning and a description of the force that is intended, for example use of CS gas (tear gas), baton charge, water cannon or mounted police.

All of the tactics described in this chapter, and the other information provided, are designed to achieve the objectives of effective resolution of conflicts, disturbances and tensions with the minimum amount of force and casualties. If successful, other measures can be considered for the restoration of normality and rebuilding effective community relations. This is not an easy process. The following chapter examines how police agencies can be proactive in helping to restore peace and security, thus enabling them to revert to their traditional role of citizen security.

Chapter 3. Post Conflict – Strategies for Peace and Security

(A) THE POLICE AND GOOD GOVERNANCE

Chapter 1 of Part VI herein, 'Policing, Democracy and Reform', examines the relationship between government, police agencies and citizens in democratic societies, and the need for police agencies to be, *inter alia*, separate from the military and to have a prime role in citizen security.

This chapter emphasises the important role of the police in effective peace-building and good governance following conflicts, disturbances and tensions:

> "What are the lessons of post conflict peace-building? [N]ever neglect security. This is the point closest to achieving consensus among experienced peace builders: most of the tasks that we call peace-building can only be carried out where there is already a reasonable level of physical security... [W]ithout security almost everything else is impossible; no return of refugees; no return to school; no elections."
>
> *Kofi Annan, United Nations Secretary General,*
> *'Learning the lessons of peace-building,' Tip O'Neill Lecture, Magee Campus,*
> *University of Ulster, United Kingdom, 18 October 2004*
> *http://www.un.org/News/Press/docs/2004/sgsm9549.doc.htm*

The creation of the National Civil Police (PNC) of the Republic of El Salvador provides an example of an effective peace-building model. During the twelve year civil war in El Salvador the various military forces, police and law enforcement agencies of that nation probably committed some of the worst abuses of human rights during any non-international armed conflict in the Western Hemisphere during the late 20th Century.[281] In El Salvador, former police agencies were one of the principal causes of a major non-international armed conflict based on high stakes issues.[282] Notwithstanding the role of police in the conflict, and the fear and bitter distrust of police agencies by the general population, the PNC was created to provide the lead role in the formation of a new democratic society. The PNC was also intended to become the role model for integrity and justice in society. This was achieved by disbanding all the former police agencies and creating the PNC,

---

[281] *See* M. Danner, *The Massacre at El Mozote* (Random House, New York, 1994).
[282] *See* Stanley, *supra* note 253.

comprised of 20 per cent former leftist combatants, 20 per cent former police and security force members, and 60 per cent newly recruited civilians having no recognised association with former factions in the war. Essentially, the PNC was created on a clean sheet of paper from a zero-base.

The example of the PNC is used here as a model of police reform because, despite continuing national problems of crime and endemic violence, the organisation has so far been successful in coalescing unity of purpose for democratic policing, and effectively addressing and attempting to resolve major issues of reconciliation, nation-building and citizen security. Experienced practitioners in the field of police reform generally agree that the reform of the El Salvador police is a model that can be strongly held up as exemplifying the most successful of international security sector reform programs.

However, no Salvadoran police official would pretend that it has been easy. In the early days of the formation of the PNC, there was some internal polarisation of factions, and resistance to change. Police leaders demonstrated their determination to maintain the highest standards. From 2001 to 2002, exceptional laws were used during a purge to dismiss some 1300 police officials responsible for crimes and other grave disciplinary matters.

Some resistance to change continues. But this negativity has been reduced through effective, strong political and police leadership, and through reconciliation and the goodwill of the members of the PNC and the citizens of El Salvador. All classes of society, both rich and poor, know that a return to the decades-long tradition of state brutality, violence and repression is something that could simply never be contemplated.[283] Importantly, the role of the PNC has enabled stability and, increasingly, a return to a level of normality and political and economic engagement in the international community.

(B) LESSONS FOR POLICE REFORM

Since 1989, there has been wide international donor support for police reform as a prerequisite for democratisation, peace-building, nation-building and effective citizen security in post conflict societies. Many United Nations (UN) agencies have been involved, including the Department of Peacekeeping Operations (DPKO), and the UN Civilian Police deployments (CIVPOL).[284] Other major international donors

---

[283] Personal communication and interviews by the author with state officials of the Republic of El Salvador, former guerrillas and members of the PNC, El Salvador and England, 1995 – 2006.

[284] W. G. O'Neill, *Police Reform in Post-Conflict Societies: What We Know and What We Still Need to Know*, International Peace Academy Policy Paper, April 2005, p.1.

include the United States of America, European Union, numerous other bilateral donor states and non-governmental organisations (NGOs). In addition to El Salvador, other police reform programs have included those in East Timor, Guatemala, Haiti, Kosovo, Mozambique, Namibia, Rwanda and Sierra Leone. Similarly, former communist Eastern European states not engaged in conflict have reformed their police agencies as part of the process of democratisation and, in many instances, as a requirement for accession to membership of the European Union.

Police reform is part of the process of healing fractured societies:

Before police reform in Guatemala:

"Community members recalled their fairly universal condemnation for the former police, the PN *(National Police)*. A 50 year old woman in Limoncito, San Marcos, commented that they were worse than the delinquents and robbers they were supposed to be catching. They drunkenly traversed the community firing their guns indiscriminately so that people had to hide...[I]t was the 'old police force' that destroyed the community."

After police reform in Guatemala:

"[T]he new PNC *(National Civil Police)* was generally held in higher regard than its predecessor... [V]iolence had declined when they arrived... [A]n elderly woman noted that they had intervened in domestic disputes, something that the old police would never have done... [A]nother woman commented, 'the police are good now that they're the civil force; they look after the community and when they're called they come and investigate'."

C. O. N. Moser and C. McIlwaine,
Encounters with Violence in Latin America: Urban poor perceptions from Colombia and Guatemala, pp. 83–84, Routledge, New York, 2004.

International assistance can be especially helpful in bringing pressure to bear on the new authorities for ensuring that new or reformed police agencies are representative of society and reflect its diversity. Women, indigenous people and other ethnic groups should be encouraged to join the police and have equality of opportunity. Results have been mixed. Some reform programs have been more effectively managed and successful than others. Lessons have been learned regarding good and bad practice. The following lessons have been learned by the author and other experienced practitioners in the sphere of international police reform programs:

V:3

Lesson 1: Engage the support of government leaders and elites

To achieve success, it is essential that members of national governments and state institutions have the political will, leadership, commitment to, and ownership of, the reform of their police agencies. It is important for national unity of purpose that members of elites, opposition parties and other stakeholders in citizen security achieve a consensus on their vision of the formation of a civilian police organisation operating in a democratic society on behalf of the citizenry. Donors should provide capacity-building assistance on citizen security to governments and policymakers in order to facilitate reform.[285] Reform will fail without the engagement of those who hold power (or, opposition parties who may hold power in the future).

Often, new governments will be comprised of former protagonists in the conflict. Some will be authoritarian figures and will not be accustomed to exercising the subtle political skills, awareness and nuances necessary for operating successfully within a democratic framework. Notwithstanding the reputation of these leaders, including their past involvement in state repression and possible human rights abuses, they cannot be ignored. They can be a potential force for good. They can be the new champions of human rights because, in response to public concerns, they know it is the right thing to do. It serves their interests and ambitions. However they may need help and persuasion. International reform practitioners must engage and influence political leaders and help them to recognise the purpose and value of change, and the potential (if they make the right choices) for improving their standing and status within society. Thus, the leaders will take ownership of the process and move from being 'warlords' to 'peacelords'.[286] Moreover, they will exercise their power and authority over the police leaders who are accountable to them, and compel them to change and to engage and cooperate in the process of reform.

This is the most important and overriding lesson of them all. Actors at the heart of power are the key to reform. If elites cannot be successfully engaged, reform programs will collapse and human rights abuses may continue.

Lesson 2: Personnel on peacekeeping and police reform deployments should hold the highest standards of professionalism, honesty and integrity

---

[285] R. Neild and M. Ziegler, *From Peace to Governance: Police Reform and the International Community*, a report from the November 2001 conference sponsored by the Washington Office on Latin America and the John Hopkins Nitze School of Advanced International Studies, 2002, p.3.
[286] M. Fitzduff *et al.*, *From Warlords to Peacelords: Local Leadership Capacity in Peace Processes*, report from INCORE, December 2004.

International deployments for peacekeeping and for reform of police agencies can flounder or fail because of inadequate preparation, planning and management. It is essential that personnel deployed on these missions are selected for:

- Honesty and integrity.
- Competence and experience in the field of operational policing.
- Motivation.
- Experience of operating as police officials in a democratic society.
- Experience of working in societies that respect human rights.
- Awareness of the principles of human rights and ethical policing.[287]

International donors should consider the advisability of monitoring the activities of members of international police missions in line with required professional standards.

Lesson 3*: Aid programs should be sustainable*

If recipient police agencies are simply provided with short term solutions, especially in training and organisational development needs, the program will fail. Recipient aided governments and their police leaders must be encouraged to take ownership of the reform program and the strategic tasks necessary for longer-term organisational change, development and training. Donors should not impose the solutions. These should be formulated in partnership with designated host police agency strategic management teams, responsible for identifying realistic aims and objectives. A senior leader from the recipient police agency, having power, executive authority, and commitment to the program, should be accountable for the delivery of the program. Strategic management teams should be trained in the necessary knowledge and skills and be equipped with the management tools to deliver the strategy.

Host training staff should be provided with the necessary management of training and trainer skills necessary to fulfil longer term training needs. Following withdrawal of donor trainers, they can then fully assume independent ownership and responsibility for all necessary new training programs, including organisational change and development training, management and supervision training, operational skills training and human rights training.

---

[287] S. Cullen and W. H. McDonald, 'Post Conflict Democratization of the Police: The Sierra Leone Experience.' in Y. Cerrah *et al.* (eds.), *Democratic Policing: Global Change from a Comparative Perspective* (Sage Publishing, Thousand Oaks, CA, 2006).

V:3

Donors and recipients should also consider the benefits of the intellectual investment and specialist management training skills available from in-country government departments, NGOs, independent consultants, universities, business management colleges and other higher education tertiary sources. They can provide significant support for reform programs and help to position them within the political, cultural and social setting.

Lesson 4: *Aid programs should have coherent leadership*

This lesson is strongly linked to lesson 3. Some aid programs lack coordination and continuity. For example, Country 'A' is contracted to provide aid to a recipient nation for twelve months. At the conclusion of the contract, the donor then contracts country 'B' to take over the program. Country 'B' may operate very different policing systems and methods to country 'A' and might give contradictory messages about policing practices. This confuses members of the recipient police agency, and undermines the credibility of the program. Collective and corporate expertise are good reasons for having multi-national deployments, but suitable donor nations or groups, including members of NGOs, having regard for the importance of human rights, should be identified and retained to provide a lead role in police reform programs.[288]

Lesson 5: *Be wary of recipient 'wish lists' for aid and reform*

Leaders of emergent donor aided police agencies often 'do not know what they do not know'. When asked what they need, they submit 'wish lists' of what they want or think they need. For example, they typically request the immediate provision of technology, and the capacity for money-laundering and high-tech crime investigations units. They want to form specialist elite police squads that they mistakenly believe are necessary for modernisation and reform. They ignore the fact that many of their police officials may be routinely incompetent in performing basic police tasks. The organisation may not have the legal framework, capacity or skills to operate technology. Leadership, management and supervision may be weak. However, given the opportunity to make bids, leaders of recipient police agencies often feel it necessary to compensate for their inadequacies. They believe that the only way to catch up with the police agencies of developed, democratic nations is to seek what they perceive as supporting the 'glamorous' side of policing. All bids should be thoroughly researched and assessed, and not accepted at face value. Albeit that some bids may be necessary for longer-term desirable or essential needs, and in some instances may be identified immediate priorities, they may ignore the needs of

---

[288] *See also* Neild and Ziegler, *supra* note 285, p. 5; and D. Helly, 'Developing an EU Strategy for Security Sector Reform,' 28 *European Security Review* (February 2006).

the foundations of policing. For example, the need for effective basic citizen security measures such as effective patrol policing and community engagement. Emerging from an authoritarian model, police leaders may lack awareness of the need for training and deploying police officials who are sensitised to acting lawfully, respecting human rights and developing the skills for providing a caring and effective service to citizens. Specifically they need the basic skills for the effective investigation of crime, and the lawful arrest, detention, interview and treatment of suspects.

Furthermore, bids are often made to finance recruitment to enhance the strength of a police agency. Police leaders believe that more personnel will create a more effective organisation. Although sometimes such bids are perfectly reasonable, for example where police strength has been significantly underfunded and is obviously below acceptable police to citizen ratios, they sometimes ignore the fact that the agency does not have the infrastructure or organisational capacity to train, equip, deploy and effectively manage and supervise additional personnel. If such bids are met, it is likely that more police officials will be deployed who lack the basic police competencies inherent within the organisation. Hence, problems will only be magnified and exacerbated. Such a situation is fraught with dangers relating to effective supervision, and ensuring the defence of, and respect for, human rights. It is better to aim for high quality, and high standards of integrity and professionalism of existing personnel, than to aim for quantity, and consequent dilution of professionalism, standards and integrity.

Donor practitioners should be good listeners. They should not appear unsympathetic, but help police leaders who make these bids understand why they may be unrealistic. They should help them to readjust their aspirations without disappointing them, and help them to formulate and take ownership of a new, more realistic and achievable vision. They should give hope and a new optimism. Moreover, it is essential that donors are wise and circumspect in considering these bids and that, in the first instance, efforts are directed at providing or enhancing the foundations for effective policing, and at the sensitisation of police officials to human rights. On condition that there is evidence that aid can be used to fulfil these purposes, further aid to support more specialist functions and the provision of technology and other equipment can be justified.

Lesson 6: *Validate and evaluate*

Following delivery of training to meet identified needs for effective reform, capacity building, and human rights, donors should follow up with some level of validation or evaluation of the training, to obtain evidence that it has been effective and, most

V:3

importantly, is being applied to enhance skills, knowledge and awareness in the workplace – and the humane treatment of citizens.

Too often, time and donor finances are wasted. Expensive training is not utilised by the recipients. Police officials from some democratising states have regularly confided to the author that, after receiving training abroad in donor states, they have not been allowed to utilise their newly acquired skills and knowledge for effective reform after returning to their home country. Their political masters and police leaders, often from the old guard, instruct them to continue to operate in the traditional way. They do not want change. Creativity, initiative and expression of new ideas are crushed in order to preserve centralisation of authority and decision-making. Aid has been accepted in accordance with externally imposed political and economic conditions, but the donor or donors have been deceived into believing that there is genuine commitment to reform.[289]

Often, no form of validation or evaluation is built into the program. Donors may consider the necessity of applying conditionality, and demanding evidence that recipient governments and police leaders have conformed to signed and binding agreements for the tangible outcomes of training and reform.

Lesson 7: *Ensure reform and training programs accord to the needs of local and national policing*

For effective reform, donor practitioners must ensure that measures for reform, including training, accord to the prevailing national and local political, cultural, religious and social environment.[290] Introducing 'off the shelf' programs simply based on the fact that they have previously been successfully delivered in other countries is likely to fail.[291] Local conditions must be professionally assessed in cooperation with recipient government and police officials, who should be encouraged to take ownership of the program. Bespoke training programs that meet the needs of individual nations must be designed, written and delivered. Account should also be taken of specific crime phenomena and trends, and local, regional, national and transnational factors contributing to crime.[292] Reform must have a strategic perspective and be positioned to address these issues.

---

[289] The author chooses not to identify nations in order to protect the human rights of his confidants.

[290] O'Neill, *supra* note 284, p. 5; *see also* Helly, supra note 288, p. 2.

[291] Cullen and McDonald, *supra* note 287.

[292] *See also* O'Neill, *supra* note 284, p.5.

Training should be a lead function in the change process. An example of good practice is the international police reform program in the Republic of Guatemala following the end of the civil war. From 1996 to 2004, the United Nations Verification Mission in Guatemala (MINUGUA) was deployed to verify compliance with the Peace Agreement. MINUGUA personnel designed and delivered human rights training to existing members and recruits to the National Civil Police (PNC). The training material was tailored to the specific needs of the citizens of Guatemala. In particular, it addressed the neglected special needs of the large and marginalized indigenous population.[293]

Lesson 8: *Always expect determined resistance to change*

Police practitioners from established, developed democratic nations involved in reform programs will find that reform and change can be a slow process. They may become frustrated at institutional resistance to change. In newly democratised states, it will take many years for some leaders of police agencies to readjust their thinking and to move from a military or paramilitary model intended, for example, to protect the interests of authoritarian ruling elites, to an accountable, civilian and service-oriented model. Until these leaders depart the organisation or can be skilfully persuaded and manoeuvred to realise the benefits and potential of their new role, they will prefer to stick to the comfort of the old ways. They are often charismatic leaders and powerful and influential opponents of change, and of human rights training, especially in societies where violence is endemic. They are conditioned in the belief that policing is purely a repressive activity. Most damagingly, they will continue to exert their influence on their subordinates to adhere to the old ways. That is why it is so important, as described in lesson 1 above, to engage the cooperation of their political masters to exert influence on police leaders for the political necessity of change; and again, for donors to enforce conditionality.

(C) THE ROLE OF THE POLICE IN PEACE-BUILDING

Following internal conflicts, tensions and disturbances up to the level of non-international armed conflicts, police agencies have a prime role in peace-building, engaging the citizenry and restoring society to normality. Others are typically involved. For example, United Nations international peacekeeping forces including contingents of civilian police units (CIVPOL), regional and bilateral donors, and NGOs. Post conflict peace-building is also concerned with prevention. Diplomatic missions and mediators are needed to prevent the collapse of peace, and to re-

---

[293] Personal communications by the author with MINUGUA personnel, Guatemala City, Republic of Guatemala, May-December 2001.

establish a stable political process between contending political leaders and elites[294] Capacity-building and development of national police agencies enables police officials of those agencies to engage in a range of key tasks for strategic peace-building. Most of these tasks cannot be achieved by police agencies alone. They have to be supported, and they need to cooperate with other agencies and actors within the peace-building process.

(a) **Demobilisation of Parties involved in Conflict and Restoring Civilian Police Primacy**

Following non-international armed conflict, police officials should be involved in mediation. Governments supported by international donors should implement strategies for the disarmament, demobilisation and peaceable reintegration of parties involved in the conflict into society.

Ordinary civilians and persons put out of action by injury, sickness, capture, or other cause must be respected and protected.[295] It is important that the special needs of children, including child soldiers (see below), females, the elderly and other vulnerable groups are attended to.

Demobilisation and withdrawal from conflict zones of armed groups enables the civilian police, as soon as they have the necessary capacity, to assume the prime role in law-enforcement and the provision of normal policing services to communities

(b) **Preventative Disarmament**

It is estimated that there are over 600 million small arms and light weapons in circulation worldwide.[296] Of 49 major conflicts in the 1990s, 47 were waged with small arms as the weapon of choice. Small arms are responsible for over half a million deaths per year, including 300,000 in armed conflicts and 200,000 from homicides and suicides.[297] It has been recognised that "small arms and light weapons destabilise regions; spark, fuel and prolong conflicts; undermine peace initiatives; exacerbate human rights abuses; hamper development; and foster a culture of

---

[294] United Nations Staff College, *Typology and Survey of Preventive Measures, Rolling EWPM Project Reference Document*, March 1999.

[295] Office of the United Nations High Commissioner for Human Rights, *Human Rights Standards and Practice for the Police*, HR/P/PT/5/Add.3, New York and Geneva, 2004.

[296] UNDP, *Small Arms and Light Weapons, UNDP Essentials*, No.9, October 2002, p.1, < www.undp.org/eo/documents/essentials/Small%20Arms30October2002.pdf#search=%22600 %20million%20small%20arms%20and%20light%20weapons%20un%20conference%22>, last visited September 2006.

[297] *Ibid.*

violence".[298] In African conflicts during the same period, thousands of children were recruited as armed soldiers and have been both the perpetrators and victims of death by firearms, and of other gross human rights abuses.[299]

The voluntary surrender of firearms, both legal and illegal, can be problematic. Firearms amnesties or donor funded 'buy-back' programs, whereby firearms owners are encouraged or paid to surrender their firearms, have had mixed results. Citizens will retain firearms unless they are confident that police agencies can protect them from violent crime.[300]

The United Nations Protocol against the Illicit Manufacturing of and Trafficking in Firearms, Their Parts and Components and Ammunition,[301] supplementing the United Nations Convention against Transnational Organized Crime[302] provides measures against the illicit transnational arms market that fuels conflict and violence associated with transnational crime, drug trafficking, terrorism and non-international armed conflicts. The Protocol was modelled on the Inter-American Convention Against the Illicit Manufacturing of and Trafficking in Firearms, Ammunition, Explosives and Other Related Materials.[303] As of 9 August 2006, the Inter-American Convention had been ratified or signed by 34 Member States.[304]

Based on the firearms laws and regulations of the United States of America, the key provisions of the OAS Convention provide a very concise, comprehensive and, practical guide for governments and law enforcement agencies, including police and customs officials. The provisions are summarised, as follows:

- *Export, Import and Transit Licenses*: To help ensure firearms are transferred only to legitimate users, parties to the Convention are required to maintain an effective licensing or authorisation system for the export, import and transit of firearms, ammunition, explosives and other related materials.

---

[298] *Ibid.*

[299] *See* R. Stohl, 'Under the Gun: Children and Small Arms,' 11:3 *African Security Review* (2002).

[300] Author's conversations with firearms holders in post-conflict societies.

[301] Adopted by UN General Assembly resolution 55/255 of 31 May 2001, entered into force on 3 July 2005.

[302] Adopted by General Assembly resolution 55/25 of 15 November 2000, entered into force 29 September 2003.

[303] Adopted by the Organization of American States in November 1997, entered into force in July 1998.

[304] United States Department of State, Bureau of Western Hemisphere Affairs, *Fact Sheet*, 9 August 2006, <www.state.gov/p/wha/rls/fs/2006/58645.htm>, last visited September 2006.

- *Marking of Firearms*: To improve the ability to trace illegal firearms, parties are obligated to require at the time of manufacture, the marking of firearms with the name of the manufacturer, place of manufacture and serial number. Similarly identifying markings are required for imported firearms.

- *Criminalisation of Illicit Manufacture and Trafficking*: Parties to the Convention are required to criminalise the illicit manufacturing and trafficking in firearms, ammunition, explosives and related materials.

- *Information Exchange*: Consistent with their national laws, parties will share information on legislative practices and other national measures to combat illicit trafficking; techniques to combat money laundering related to illicit transfers; routes customarily used by criminal organisations; and the means of concealment used and methods for detecting them.

- *International Coordination*: Parties agree to cooperate with one another in the effort to eradicate illicit arms trafficking through a single national point of contact that will act as the formal liaison with the other states.

- *Law Enforcement Cooperation*: The treaty provides for cooperation between the parties in the various fields of law enforcement such as extradition, mutual legal assistance, confiscation and forfeiture.

- *Technical Assistance and Training*: Parties agree to cooperate to ensure adequate training in such areas as identification and tracing; intelligence gathering and detection methods and search protocols at borders.

- *Consultative Committee*: Parties have agreed to meet each year to exchange information and facilitate implementation of the Convention.

In addition to the OAS, the majority of governments and regional groups support the United Nations Protocol and initiatives against the illicit manufacturing of and trafficking in firearms; for example, the European Union (EU), the African Union (AU), the Association of South East Asian Nations (ASEAN), the Economic Community of West African States (ECOWAS) and the Southern African Community.[305]

---

[305] N. E. W. Colton, *The United Nations Conference on the Illicit Trade in Small Arms and Light Weapons in all its Aspects*, summarized on the website of the Nuclear Age Peace

Notwithstanding this laudable international commitment, it is essential that the urgency for action against illicit manufacturing of and trafficking in firearms, and their possession and use, is communicated from regional and government level to law enforcement officials in the field. For effective enforcement there must be 'bottom up' as well as 'top down' responses. In post conflict societies where problems of violence, conflict and crime remain through the use of firearms, governments should require leaders of their police and other law enforcement agencies to design and implement national and local strategies and action plans that accord to the provisions exemplified in the UN Protocol and OAS Convention. Intelligence gathering should be the priority for effective pro-active enforcement, seizure and the reduction of firearms in societies.

(c) **Investigation of Crimes and Human Rights Abuses**

Chapter 1 of Part II herein referred to the duty of police to investigate genocide, crimes against humanity and war crimes so that perpetrators may be brought to justice.

The reality is that the scale of violence and resultant death in some non-international armed conflicts has been of such magnitude that it has been impossible to investigate every case. Therefore, only the most serious acts of violence were investigated. For example, those acts which caused the greatest outrage to society and were intended for its intimidation.[306] However, the fact remains that perpetrators of crimes such as murder and torture do need to be vigorously pursued and, to reiterate the concluding comment in Chapter 1 of Part II herein, "police officials should apply their skills and experience in the most energetic and dedicated manner to bring such appalling criminals to justice".

The requirements to protect and respect the right to life mean that there should be prompt, official and thorough investigations of deaths arising in the context of all conflicts, disturbances and tensions, including those falling short of non-international armed conflict (for example, public disorder or riot). Accountability demands the investigation of actual or alleged police criminality or misconduct, including violence or the disproportionate use of force resulting in death or injury. The UN International Human Rights Standards for Law Enforcement[307] state that "investigations into violations (of human rights) shall be prompt, competent, thorough and impartial", and "investigations shall seek to identify victims, recover

---

Foundation, <www.wagingpeace.org/articles/2001/07/09_colton_un-conference.htm>, last visited September 2006.
[306] Commission on the Truth for El Salvador, *supra* note 252.
[307] *Human Rights Standards and Practice for the Police, supra* note 295.

V:3

and preserve evidence, discover witnesses, discover cause, manner, location and time of the violation, and to identify and apprehend perpetrators". Furthermore, "superior officers shall be held responsible for abuses if they knew, or should have known of their occurrence, and did not take action".

The honesty and transparency of police leaders in admitting mistakes and in demonstrating their determination to investigate and bring to justice those police officials responsible for unlawful violence and abuses of human rights, are significant factors in preventing the escalation, continuation or recurrence of violence.

(d) **Exhumation of the Dead**

The following provides a powerful expression of the need for the exhumation of the remains of victims following a non-international armed conflict:

> "[T]he exhumation of the remains of the victims of the armed confrontation and the location of clandestine and hidden cemeteries, wherever they are found to be, is in itself an act of justice and reparation and is an important step on the path to reconciliation. It is an act of justice because it constitutes part of the right to know the truth and it contributes to the knowledge of the whereabouts of the disappeared. It is an act of reparation because it dignifies the victims and because the right to bury the dead and to carry out ceremonies for them according to each culture is inherent in all human beings."
>
> *Guatemala Memory of Silence,*
> *active policy of exhumation, Page 54,*
> *Report of the Commission for Historical Clarification:*
> *Conclusions and Recommendations, Guatemala, 1994.*

In addition to reconciliation, exhumation is essential for the investigation and prosecution of those responsible for kidnapping, homicides, massacres, torture and other gross human rights abuses. Police agencies should be proactive in searching for and tracing hidden cemeteries, clandestine graves and illegal burials.

Hidden cemeteries are created by the friends and relatives of the deceased victims who have died over a period of time as a consequence of several events, for example massacres, individual killings or death caused by illness or injury during hiding. Clandestine graves are burials resulting from a single event, usually a massacre, where the perpetrators, or others forced by the perpetrators, bury the dead in a mass grave. Illegal burials are defined as any burial that was not reported or authorised by law. They include burials in hidden cemeteries and clandestine graves – either individual or collective.[308]

Police agencies should preserve illegal burials sites as crime scenes, and assist forensic anthropologists in identifying the victims and determining the causes of death. Compassionate and caring involvement with the bereaved can be an important way of re-engaging police agencies with fractured communities.

Additionally, forensic anthropologists can suffer death, violence or threats of violence and intimidation from former protagonists in conflict who endeavour to prevent the evidence of their past crimes being revealed. Police officials should ensure the security and safety of members of forensic teams, and diligently investigate crimes or acts of intimidation against them.

(e) **Engaging Citizens**

Engaging citizens is the primary task of all police officials. However, to achieve a state of normality, engaging citizens is all the more critical following conflict.

The UN International Human Rights Standards for Law Enforcement[309] state under an umbrella heading of 'Community Policing' that the police should establish a partnership between police and law-abiding members of the community. In recent years, community policing has become the preferred style of policing in democratic nations. It has become axiomatic that community policing is democratic policing. However, community policing is practised differently in different countries. Meanwhile, a plethora of academic and police literature convey a sometimes confusing variety of meanings and definitions of what constitutes community policing.

Some practitioners believe that community policing involves no more than engagement and promoting harmony with the community. Police agencies in some societies already operate *de facto* a style of community policing. For example, it is customary for police officials to work closely with tribal leaders, chieftains or caciques in order to serve the needs of traditional communities.[310] Other versions of

---

[308] L. Peñados-Ceren, Presentation: *Truth and Justice: Forensic Sciences in a Post War Context*, Department of Forensic and Investigative Science, University of Central Lancashire, United Kingdom, 16 November 2005.

[309] *Human Rights Standards and Practices for the Police, supra* note 295.

[310] Interviews by the author with Claudio Rudy Perez Batui, Sub Inspector, National Civil Police, and Vincente Elias Lajpop, Maya Cacique, Momestenango, Guatemala, May 2001; and Morie Lengor, Assistant Commissioner of Police, Sierra Leone Police, April 2005.

community policing are more complex and demand rigorous accountability and measurement of organisational performance.

In an effort to define a universal model, the author has drawn together those features of community policing that appear to be most commonly understood and practised around the world. First, it is essential to dispel some common misunderstandings and misconceptions about the meaning of community policing. For example:

Misconception 1: Community policing is just about uniform patrol policing.

Reality: community policing must involve all ranks and departments of the police (e.g. traffic police and crime investigators) in coordinated strategies against crime and other problems affecting communities.

Misconception 2: Community policing is 'soft' or over-tolerant policing.

Reality: community policing demands better communication and understanding between police and citizens. It does not demand more liberal attitudes towards delinquency. The opposite is true. Proactive policing is more effective and can increase arrests and convictions of delinquents.

Misconception 3: Community Relations means the same as Community Policing.

Reality: this is a common misconception. 'Community relations' is an important discrete activity in building contact and communication with citizen groups, for example, schools, business and local community groups. It is essentially a one-way process but is important for supporting community policing by improving the image of the police.

(i)   The Characteristics of Community Policing

The following comprise the main elements of community policing:

Policing should be visible and accessible
- Some patrol officers are assigned permanently to community beats/areas/precincts and have specific responsibility for policing those beats/areas/precincts.
- Community patrols are high visibility, preferably patrolling on foot, interacting with citizens, gaining the cooperation of citizens, and developing local knowledge.
- Patrols should be preventive and give reassurance to citizens.

- All citizens should feel able to seek the assistance of the police.

Community policing involves consultation and cooperation with communities

- The police participate with citizens in identifying and prioritising the needs of the community.
- The police and the community form a partnership and devise agreed solutions to problems.

Community policing is proactive policing

- The underlying causes of crime, incidents and problems are analysed and identified.
- Instead of simply reacting to crimes, incidents and problems, the police adopt an intelligence-led problem-solving approach.
- All ranks and branches of the police are involved in problem-solving, contributing ideas and designing initiatives for more effective policing.

Community Policing is about providing quality of service

- The police develop a culture of service excellence.
- Standards of service delivery are measured.
- The defence and observance of human rights are central to all aspects of policing.

Community policing involves multi-agency cooperation

- The police liase and work together with citizens, other agencies and organisations in finding solutions to crime and other problems.

The police are accountable

- Police managers are open and accountable about matters affecting the community.
- Policing effectiveness is monitored, evaluated and open to scrutiny.
- Police officials of all ranks are accountable for their professional and personal standards and their treatment of citizens.

Centralisation militates against community policing. Community policing requires decentralisation of decision-making and resources. Police leaders operating at the local level should be empowered, and afforded the trust and discretion to make

V:3

competent decisions affecting the community they are responsible for policing. Hence, they can make timely and effective responses without reference to centralised authority.

Although engaging with the citizenry is the absolute priority in all post-conflict societies, the immediate introduction of formalised community policing systems may not always be possible. For example, a lack of resources may inhibit the mobility and effective communications necessary for effective community policing. Where a police agency is at an emergent stage of development, newly recruited police officials need time to practice and develop basic policing and patrol skills. For example, how to talk to citizens with courtesy, and how to deal with a crime or other incident reported to them. Importantly, in addition to proving their basic competence, they will need to prove their commitment to defending human rights and gaining the trust and respect of citizens. Thereafter, they can progress to a more formal model of community policing.

(D) THE CHALLENGE OF CRIME IN POST CONFLICT STATES

The forms of criminality considered under this subheading affect all humankind and all states. However, it is important and useful to consider them in the context of post conflict situations. States emerging from conflict, especially non-international armed conflict, are vulnerable to crimes of this nature which can undermine political, economic and social reforms being carried out in the wake of conflict. In current conflicts in nations such as Afghanistan and Colombia, crime in the form of narcotics production and trafficking provides both a source and driver of conflict.

The effects of globalisation demand that police agencies are alert to changing trends and patterns of crime. Police officials need to work closely with their counterparts, both regionally and internationally, in order to counter the crime and corruption that can threaten peace and citizen security.

Increase in crime in post conflict societies appears to be strongly related to transition from authoritarian rule to democracy.[311] Post-conflict societies and nations in transition are especially vulnerable to all forms of crime, including transnational and

---

[311] M. Shaw, *Crime and Policing in Transitional Societies: Conference Summary and Overview*, 2001, p. 9, <www.kas.org.za/publications/seminarreports/crimeandpolicingintran sitionalsocieties/shaw.pdf#search=%22Crime%20and%20Policing%20in%20Transitional%2 0Societies%20%E2%80%93%20Conference%20Summary%20and%20Overview%22>, last visited September 2006.

organised crime.[312] As exemplified in the Republic of South Africa during the apartheid regime and the former Yugoslavia, crime can also provide a means of avoiding international economic sanctions as criminal organisations operate illegal markets to fill the vacuum created by sanctions.[313] Furthermore, the escalation of crime following conflict is difficult to analyse and understand. Often, crime statistics relating to the pre-conflict environment are unavailable or unreliable.[314]

(a) **The Criminal Justice System**

In many post conflict societies, the criminal justice system is weak. Often, it may be corrupt. There are insufficient numbers of trained lawyers, and legal procedures are slow and inefficient. This situation can have a dilatory effect on the restoration of peace, justice and citizen security.

When citizens who do not understand the processes of the law feel that they are not receiving the redress to which they are entitled, they do not blame the law or the legal institutions. They blame the police whom they perceive as the face of the state, its law and authority. Thus, confidence in the police is undermined. Breakdown in trust can lead to communities taking their own initiatives against crime through vigilantism.[315] Vigilantism in parts of Africa and Latin America has resulted in the lynching of suspects for the most minor of crimes, and has also resulted in the lynching of innocent citizens, foreign tourists and legal officials.[316]

Chapter 3 of Part I herein examined the interdependence between democracy, human rights and the exercise of power by state officials. An important point is made that the police (and wider society) require respect for the rule of law. This principle is especially important in post-conflict societies where former protagonists responsible for human rights abuses may seek to use power or influence to flee justice, or invoke immunity, or manipulate a weak or corrupt judicial system to escape prosecution for their crimes. The police should not collaborate or acquiesce in this type of abuse of power. They should enforce the law and should have proportionate powers of arrest and search to investigate effectively crimes against all citizens, particularly violence and sexual abuse of women, children, and the vulnerable and poor of society. All citizens should be equally liable and answerable to the law.

---

[312] M. Shaw, Chief of Criminal Justice Reform Unit, Presentation: *The Global Picture of Organized Crime and the Strategy of UNODC*, International Faculty, Leadership Academy for Policing, Bramshill, England, 3 February 2006.

[313] *Ibid.*

[314] *Ibid.*

[315] Shaw, *supra* note 311, p. 13.

[316] Cullen and McDonald, *supra* note 287; Sullivan *et al.* (eds.), supra note 270, p. 1085.

V:3

The criminal justice system must support effective law enforcement, human rights and the rule of law. Capacity-building and reform of the criminal justice system should support measures for:

- enforceable laws that reflect the needs of citizens in a democratic society
- high ethical and professional standards for police officials, prosecutors and judges
- an efficient courts system that ensures judicial decisions are properly enforced

(b) Transnational Organised Crime

Transnational organised crime threatens the political, economic and social fabric of societies.[317] It is also a source of funding for terrorist groups. The United Nations Convention against Transnational Organized Crime[318] commits States parties to the Convention to criminalizing acts of participation in an organised criminal group, money laundering, corruption and the obstruction of justice. The Convention also includes provisions on extradition laws, administrative and regulatory controls, victim and witness protection and crime prevention measures.

The Convention is supplemented by three Protocols:

1. Protocol against the Illicit Manufacturing of and Trafficking in Firearms, Their Parts and Components and Ammunition.[319]
2. Protocol against the Smuggling of Migrants by Land, Air and Sea.[320]
3. Protocol to Prevent, Suppress and Punish Trafficking in Persons, Especially Women and Children.[321]

Some provisions of the Protocol against the Illicit Manufacturing of and Trafficking in Firearms, Their Parts and Components and Ammunition are examined above under the heading of 'Preventative Disarmament'. Some provisions of the Convention and the two latter protocols, on the smuggling of migrants and trafficking in persons, are examined below.

---

[317] United Nations Office on Drugs and Crime, *Organized Crime, UNODC Fact Sheet*, <www.unodc.org/unodc/en/organized_crime.html>, last visited September 2006.
[318] United Nations Convention against Transnational Organized Crime, *supra* note 302.
[319] Protocol against the Illicit Manufacturing of and Trafficking in Firearms, Their Parts and Components and Ammunition, *supra* note 301.
[320] Adopted by UN General Assembly resolution 55/25 of 15 November 2000, entered into force 28 January 2004.
[321] Adopted by UN General Assembly resolution 55/25 of 15 November 2000, entered into force 25 December 2003.

For the purposes of the Convention:

- 'Organised Criminal Group' means a structured group of three or more persons, existing for a period of time and acting in concert with the aim of committing one or more serious crimes or offences established in accordance with the Convention, in order to obtain, directly or indirectly, a financial or other material benefit.

- 'serious crime' means conduct constituting an offence punishable by at least four years imprisonment.

- 'structured group' means a group that is not randomly formed for the immediate commission of an offence and does not need to have formally defined roles for its members, continuity of its membership or a developed structure.

The UN terms provide a useful general guide. However, the first definition set out above is not particularly descriptive and could benefit from some elaboration. More typically, organised criminal groups can be defined as hierarchical mafia type gangs or a network of clustered groups of determined professional criminals who commit crime for high stakes and who will use intimidation and violence, including murder, to escape detection and to protect their crime operations from the intrusion of other criminal groups, the infiltration of informants, and the interdiction of law enforcement.

The following provides a typology of crimes by organised criminal groups:[322]

- Predatory crime: theft, robbery, kidnapping, blackmail, extortion, credit card fraud.
- Commercial crime: fraud through the medium of business.
- Money laundering.
- Corruption.
- The obstruction of investigations or prosecutions.
- Trafficking and smuggling of contraband, including pharmaceuticals, cigarettes and alcohol.
- Environmental crime: illegal logging.
- Theft and trafficking in art and cultural artefacts.
- Production and trafficking of narcotics.

---

[322] M. Levi, professor at the University of Cardiff, Presentation: *Typologies of Organized Crime Groups*, Leadership Academy for Policing, Bramshill, England, 9 February 2006.

V:3

- Production and trafficking of firearms.
- Trafficking of humans and smuggling of migrants.

(i)   A Case Study of an Organised Criminal Group – Youth Street Gangs

In December 2004, members of the Mara Salvatrucha youth street gang surrounded a public transport bus in Chamalecon, Honduras and with automatic weapons massacred 28 passengers. The victims were chosen at random. The massacre was a protest against government anti-gang laws.[323] Two main gangs, the Mara Salvatrucha and the 18th Street Gang, together with other smaller gangs, are now estimated to number up to 100,000 members in Central America, Mexico and Hispanic neighbourhoods in some cities of the United States of America.[324] A major transnational organised crime group, youth street gangs pose a serious threat to citizen security and the political, economic and social stability of a major region of the Western Hemisphere. Having access to all types of firearms leftover from non-international armed conflicts, and knives and other weapons, their crime activities include homicides, street robberies, robberies on public transport systems, the smuggling of migrants to the United States of America, kidnapping for ransom, extortion, gang rapes, narcotics trafficking and abuse, and the wholesale terrorising of neighbourhoods. They are also responsible for massacres and other atrocities at correctional facilities where they are interned. In El Salvador, 20 per cent of public transport operators are paying protection money to gangs.[325] The introduction of national anti-gang laws in Guatemala, Honduras and El Salvador has failed to stem escalating gang membership and their activities. As a consequence of gang violence, these three countries have some of the highest homicide rates in the world.[326]

Law enforcement measures alone are insufficient to deal with the youth street gang problem. The factors that contribute to young people joining street gangs need to be studied, analysed and understood in order for affected societies to develop social policies and strategies to combat the problem. The age profile of gang members (typically 15 to 25 years) demands that government agencies, educational authorities, NGOs, police and correctional agencies are proactive in developing educational and rehabilitation programs to prevent young people from joining gangs, and to encourage them to rejoin mainstream society as useful citizens.

---

[323] A. Arana, 'How the Street Gangs Took Central America', *Foreign Affairs* (May/June 2005) p. 98.
[324] *Ibid.*
[325] Interview by author with J. Villalobos, former leader of the FMLN, Oxford, England, 11 March 2006.
[326] *Ibid.*

(c) **The Smuggling of Migrants and Trafficking in Persons**

Smuggling of migrants is defined in the Protocol dealing with this matter as the procurement, in order to obtain, directly or indirectly, a financial or other material benefit, of the illegal entry of a person into a State Party of which the person is not a national or a permanent resident. The Protocol is intended to strengthen the international community's response in countering transnational organised crime groups and their highly sophisticated networks to smuggle migrants.[327]

Trafficking in persons is defined in the Protocol dealing with this matter as the recruitment, transportation, transfer, harbouring or receipt of persons, by means of the threat or use of force or other forms of coercion, of abduction, of fraud, of deception, of the abuse of power or of a position of vulnerability or of the giving or receiving of payments or benefits to achieve the consent of a person having control over another person, for the purpose of exploitation. Exploitation includes, at a minimum, the exploitation of the prostitution of others or other forms of sexual exploitation, forced labour or services, slavery or practices similar to slavery, servitude or the removal of organs.[328]

Dependent on the purpose, circumstances and consequences, smuggling of migrants and trafficking in persons can amount to, or result in, crimes against humanity as defined in article 7 of the Statute of the International Criminal Court.[329] The criminal acts listed in that article include acts that are sometimes perpetrated on smuggled migrants and trafficked persons, for example:

- Murder.
- Enslavement.
- Imprisonment or other severe deprivation of physical liberty.
- Torture.
- Rape, sexual slavery or enforced prostitution.
- Enforced disappearance of persons.
- Other inhumane acts of a similar character intentionally causing great suffering, or serious injury to body or to mental or physical health.

Post conflict societies are especially vulnerable to the activities of organised criminal groups who seek to exploit the misery of those attempting to escape

---

[327] Article 3, paragraph (a) Protocol against the Smuggling of Migrants by Land, Air and Sea.

[328] Article 3, paragraph (a) of the Protocol to Prevent, Suppress and Punish Trafficking in Persons, Especially Women and Children.

[329] The International Criminal Court is described in Chapter 1 of Part I herein, and the crimes over which it has jurisdiction are provided for in Chapter 1 of Part II.

economic deprivation.[330] Globalisation is likely to increase the scale of these crimes. It is estimated that trafficking in persons (essentially a form of modern day slavery) and migrant smuggling is generating income of USD 30-35 billion per year to organised criminal groups.[331] Yet currently, these crimes remain a low priority for the majority of most law enforcement agencies around the world; certainly, much lower than drugs trafficking.[332]

Police officials in post conflict countries with large numbers of refugee camps need to be aware that refugees are especially vulnerable to abduction for the illegal removal of body parts and organs. For example refugees, including children, are abducted from refugee camps in Afghanistan and taken to surgeries in other parts of South Asia for the illegal removal of organs and body parts. The victims are then left mutilated or dead.[333]

Trafficking in persons and the smuggling of migrants are predicted to become the major crime phenomena of the new millennium.[334] The Global Program against Trafficking in Human Beings (GPAT) designed by the UN Office on Drugs and Crime (UNODC) was launched in March 1999. GPAT assists Member States in their efforts to combat trafficking in human beings. The GPAT's objective is to bring to the foreground the involvement of organised criminal groups in human trafficking and to promote the development of effective criminal justice-related responses including the training of law enforcement officials, prosecutors and judges.[335]

Government, legal and police officials need to develop urgently an increased awareness of the problem of human trafficking, and cooperate with regional and international partners and NGOs in developing legislation and law enforcement strategies, including the collection and use of intelligence relating to the activities of organised criminal groups engaged in these activities. The also need to cooperate in identifying the smuggling and trafficking routes and methods of exploitation used. Moreover, governments, police officials and other agencies in transit and destination

---

[330] Dr. H. Konrad, Special Representative on Combating Trafficking in Human Beings, Organization for Security and Cooperation in Europe (OSCE), Presentation: *Trafficking in Human Beings*, Leadership Academy for Policing, Bramshill, England, 10 February 2006.
[331] *Ibid.*
[332] *Ibid.*
[333] Personal communication with Taimoor Shah Habibi, Ministry of Refugees and Repatriation, Islamic Republic of Afghanistan, 10 February 2006.
[334] Konrad, *supra* note 330.
[335] United Nations Office on Drugs and Crime, *Trafficking in Human Beings*, <www.unodc.org/unodc/en/trafficking_human_beings.html>, last visited September 2006.

countries should ensure measures for the humane reception, care, support and protection of victims and witnesses to these crimes.

(d) Corruption

Aspects of police corruption are examined in Chapter 4 of Part VI herein. Corruption undermines the economy of states and can create instability leading to conflict.[336] The United Nations Convention against Corruption[337] is the first legally binding global instrument designed to help Member States fight corruption in both the public and private sectors.[338] It requires Member States to establish criminal and other offences to cover a wide range of acts of corruption.

The Convention rests on four pillars: *prevention* and *criminalization* of corruption, *international cooperation* and *asset recovery*.[339] Many of the measures contained in the Convention against Transnational Organized Crime are mirrored in the United Nations Convention against Corruption, thereby providing law enforcement officials with the necessary tools and other measures for effective investigation and the seizure and confiscation of the proceeds of corruption.

(E) MEASURES AGAINST TRANSNATIONAL ORGANISED CRIME

The 41 Articles of the Convention against Transnational Organized Crime are too numerous to examine in detail within this volume. However, experienced practitioners currently engaged in the investigation of transnational organised crime identify five key Articles as paramount for the effective investigation and prosecution of crimes within the Convention and the Protocols:

1. **Special Investigative Techniques.** The use of electronic surveillance, telephone monitoring (wire taps [US]) and undercover operations are essential for effective intelligence and evidence gathering against members of organised criminal groups. (Article 20: Special investigative techniques).

2. **Transfer of Criminal Proceedings.** Where the activities of organised criminal groups have occurred in several jurisdictions, each State Party may consider the possibility of transferring to one another proceedings for the prosecution of an offence covered by the Convention in cases where such

---

[336] Cullen and McDonald, *supra* note 287.

[337] Adopted by UN General Assembly resolution 58/4 of 31 October 2003, entered into force 14 December 2005.

[338] United Nations Information Service, UNIS/CP/528, *Press Release*, 13 December 2005, <www.unis.unvienna.org/unis/pressrels/2005/uniscp528.html>, last visited September 2006.

[339] *Ibid.*

transfer is considered to be in the interests of the proper administration of justice. For example, if available evidence is primarily based on conversations recorded during telephone monitoring (wire taps [US]), then a successful lawful prosecution is more likely in a jurisdiction where such evidence is admissible rather than a jurisdiction where it is inadmissible. (Article 21: Transfer of criminal proceedings).

3. **Witness Protection.** Effective witness protection schemes should be in place to protect witnesses, their families, friends and associates from violence, retaliation or intimidation, and to ensure their availability to give evidence in a court of law. In terms of protecting human rights, this is an important provision. (Article 24: Protection of witnesses).

4. **Incentives for Law Enforcement Cooperation.** This provision recommends immunity from prosecution or mitigated penalties for members of organised crime groups who give information on the activities of organised criminal groups or provide evidence for the investigation and prosecution of members of organised criminal groups. This will encourage members of criminal groups to expose the activities of their associates (Article 26: Measures to enhance cooperation with law enforcement authorities).[340]

5. **Law Enforcement Cooperation.** State Parties shall cooperate closely with one another, consistent with their respective domestic, legal and administrative systems, to enhance the effectiveness of law enforcement action to combat the offences covered by the Convention. Cooperation is essential for the effective collection, exchange and use of information and intelligence to combat transnational organised crime, and should involve all competent law enforcement agencies and appropriate experts. Cooperation should include the identification and activities of suspects, the movement of proceeds of crime and the movement of property or equipment used in the commission of crime. Additionally, State Parties should consider entering into bilateral or multilateral agreements on direct cooperation between their law enforcement agencies and the posting of liaison officers. (Article 27: Law enforcement cooperation)

The investigative techniques encapsulated in Articles 20 and 21 are often subject of controversy and debate. They must be regulated. It is essential, therefore, that

---

[340] For further reading, *see* H. Hill and G. Russo, *Gangsters and Goodfellas: Wiseguys, Witness Protection and Life on the Run* (M Evans, New York, 2004).

legislation and procedures that permit special investigative techniques are accountable, and subject to stringent judicial oversight, and that police agencies are rigorous in restricting them to the purpose for which they were intended, namely, the determined investigation and prosecution of the most serious crimes. Moreover, the use of electronic surveillance and telephone monitoring should be seen to be proportionate methods of evidence gathering when other methods have been impossible or impracticable.

Chapters of this book have focused on police behaviours that amount to serious abuses of human rights and corruption. These behaviours are recorded historical facts and are the truth. However, police officials are not inherently wicked. Nor do they routinely engage in the inhumane treatment of humankind. For every single misdeed or mistake, police officials around the world perform countless acts of courage and selflessness in defence of the citizens they serve. They defend human rights. They also routinely help ordinary citizens and victims at their time of greatest need, danger and vulnerability. Characteristically, police officials perform these duties without any expectation of recognition or reward. They perform these duties because they are inherently compassionate and noble. This is the greater truth.

PART VI

POLICE ORGANISATIONS – STRATEGY FOR MANAGEMENT AND CHANGE

Chapter 1. Policing, Democracy and Reform

(A) NATIONS IN TRANSITION

United Nations General Assembly resolution 34/169 of 17 December 1979, as outlined at the beginning of Chapter 3 in Part I, recommends a Code of Conduct for Law Enforcement Officials (hereinafter referred to as the Code of Conduct). Notwithstanding that in 1979 less than half of United Nations member nations were democracies, the Code of Conduct was unequivocal in declaring that standards for policing were those expected of a *democratic society*. The following chapters examine and recommend a range of practical policing methods and styles, together with management practices and procedures to assist personnel in police organisations to fulfil their duties and responsibilities in accordance with human rights requirements and the provision of effective and accountable policing services.

Before moving on to these chapters it is necessary to recall the requirement on states, referred to in Chapter 2 of Part I, to secure respect for and observance of the human rights of people within their jurisdiction. The police being first line protectors of human rights, this requirement has direct linkages with the assertions in Chapter 3 of Part I that in a fundamental sense policing is a highly political activity and that the need for a policing function arises at an early stage in the development of a society. Knowledge of the relationship between police organisations, government and wider society is essential for all police officials in understanding how policing (an essentially authoritarian and restraining function) can operate effectively with the cooperation and consent of the citizenry in a free and democratic society.

It is axiomatic that the creation of civilian, service-oriented police organisations having a prime role in citizen security is a prerequisite for a stable and harmonious society in which political, social, and economic activity can flourish. Following recent conflicts in El Salvador, Guatemala, Bosnia, Kosovo, Sierra Leone, Rwanda, Afghanistan and Iraq, reform of the police and the timely training and deployment of adequately trained personnel to restore public safety have been the absolute priorities in terms of institutional reform and the democratisation process.

Since the adoption of the United Nations Code of Conduct in 1979, political upheaval and conflict around the world have led to the spread of democracy as the preferred choice of government in more than half of the world's nations and its peoples. The collapse of the Soviet Empire has led to countries in Eastern Europe and the Caucasus region commencing or completing the transition towards democracy. In 1979, only two Latin American states were true democracies. Most were authoritarian regimes bolstered by the military. Dramatically, by 2005, after a period of dynamic change, the majority of Latin American states had adopted free elections and a significant measure of democratic rule and liberalisation

There have also been failures. Following the early optimism of post-colonial independence and the creation of new democracies, the ruinous decline of many African nations and the oppression of its peoples by authoritarian kleptocracies has demonstrated the tenuous nature of democracy.

These events have had a dramatic and even traumatic effect on police officials from many of these nations. Often used as tools of the oppressors and the abusers of human rights, they now find themselves in a changed world in which they are the first to be the subject of scrutiny and reform. Many have operated in military and paramilitary mode, knowing little or nothing of the nature of civilian, service-oriented policing. Their duty has been to protect and serve the interests of elites as a priority over the needs of the ordinary citizenry. Various post conflict commissions and enquiries around the world have exposed some police officials as being the ultimate delinquents of society operating in violent organisations; their barbaric and murderous conduct, including the operating of death squads, amounting to the grossest excesses of human rights abuses. It behoves those police officials who scorn the need for training and awareness in human rights to remember the atrocities of the twentieth century that shame the name of policing.

As a consequence of the progress of democratisation, police reform has been undertaken in many countries around the world. Central to all reform has been the absolute imperative for police officials of all ranks to protect human rights. Human rights are not an adjunct to policing. They are not something that police officials simply need to know about or a set of rules to protect them from scrutiny or criticism. They are not something that police officials can simply pick up and put down as required. They are the foundation of professional effectiveness and ethical standards of behaviour at every level of policing activity.

(B) DEMOCRATIC POLICING

Democratic civilian policing is an essential component of good governance operating under a range of basic principles. In ensuring that a police organisation is civilian rather than military there must be separate government ministers having control and oversight over the police and military. Similarly, the commander or chief of police and senior police posts should not hold military rank or be associated with the national armed forces. Whereas the military have a primary role in the security of the state from external threat, the police should have a primary and accountable role in citizen security and serving the law. Extraordinary circumstances may demand military personnel having to assist the police in joint public safety operations (for example, in protecting the citizenry from terrorists or armed bandits). In these circumstances, it is essential for the police to have primacy in command and control of operations. Legislation or the constitution should prevent the police from being controlled by political parties or the military. For example, the Peace Agreement signed at Chapultepec, Mexico in 1991 following the civil war in El Salvador established a bill organising the National Civil Police (PNC), as follows:[341]

> "In accordance with…the Constitution, it is the responsibility of the President of the Republic: To command, organize and maintain the National Civil Police to preserve peace, tranquillity, order and public security, in both urban and rural areas, adhering strictly to respect for human rights and under the control of civilian authorities. The National Civil Police and the armed forces shall be independent and shall be placed under the authority of different ministries."

The police should be accountable to government, for example through a Minister of Citizen Security or Home or Internal Affairs, and to the citizens, for example through community consultative groups representing all sections of society. The police should be able to respond to community needs and expectations. This can be facilitated by the organisation of an independent civilian review board or commission comprising cross party political appointees and other non-partisan appointees. Their role is to oversee and monitor policing functions and senior police appointments, and to ensure matters of public concern are being addressed. Police reform is more likely to be effective if there is cross party political support and a shared vision of democratic policing, together with the support of other government departments, trade unions, commercial and business interests and community groups. If there is a change of government, it is important that the police continue to operate under politically neutral democratic principles and transparent policies agreed by all stakeholders. Similarly members of other sectors of the criminal justice system, such as judges and prosecutors, need to be in agreement and attuned to democratic policing.[342]

Chapter 4 of Part I outlined the important eight articles from the United Nations Code of Conduct for Law Enforcement Officials. To reiterate the articles in summary, they make recommendations relating to operating within the law, accountability and service to the community, respect for human rights, the use of

---

[341] The El Salvador Peace Agreement, Chapter 1(6): *Public security forces*, Chapultepec, Mexico, 1991.
[342] I. Clegg *et al.*, *Policy Guidance on Support to Policing in Developing Countries*, Centre for Development Studies Report, University of Wales, November 2000, pp. 72–74, < www.swan.ac.uk/cds/pdffiles/POLICE%20GUIDANCE.pdf#search=%22Guidance%20on%20Support%20to%20Policing%20in%20Developing%20%22>, last visited September 2006.

force including firearms, the need for confidentiality, the prohibition of torture, the treatment of detainees and the reporting of contraventions of the Code. Furthermore, in its resolution adopting the Code, the United Nations General Assembly recommended that, "favourable consideration should be given to its use within the framework of national legislation or practice as a body of principles for observance by law enforcement officials". The parties to the El Salvador Peace Agreement acted upon this recommendation by establishing it within the reformed constitution in the form of a doctrine that conforms to the eight articles of the Code. In addition to providing an existing example of the translation and incorporation of this recommendation into legislation, the doctrine provides a very powerful and coherent new vision of policing in a nation in which, historically, the police had been cruel oppressors of the people.[343]

Doctrine of the National Civil Police of El Salvador

A. The legal regime, staff training, organisational lines, operational guidelines and, in general, the institutional definition and operation of the National Civil Police shall accord with democratic principles; the concept of public security as a service provided by the State to its citizens, free from all considerations of politics, ideology or social position or any other discrimination; respect for human rights; the effort to prevent crime; and the subordination of the force to the constitutional authorities. Citizens' exercise of their political rights may not be impaired by police activities.

B. The National Civil Police shall be a professional body, independent of the armed forces and free from all partisan activity. Without prejudice to the right of its members to make, as citizens, their own political choices, they shall not be able to use their status for partisan purposes.

C. Members of the National Civil Police shall at all times observe the duties imposed on them by law, serving the community and protecting all persons from illegal acts, in keeping with the high degree of responsibility required by their profession.

D. In the performance of their tasks, members of the National Civil Police shall respect and protect human dignity and shall preserve and defend the human rights of all persons.

E. Members of the National Civil Police may use force only when strictly necessary and to the extent required for the fulfilment of their tasks.

---

[343] The El Salvador Peace Agreement, Chapter 2: National Civil Police, Chapultepec, Mexico, 1991.

F. Questions of a confidential nature of which members of the National Civil Police have knowledge shall be kept secret, unless compliance with duty or the needs of justice strictly demand otherwise.

G. No member of the National Civil Police may inflict, instigate or tolerate any act of torture or other cruel, inhuman or degrading treatment or punishment, nor invoke the orders of a superior or special circumstances, such as a state of war or threat of war, threats to national security, internal political instability or any other public emergency to justify torture or other cruel, inhuman or degrading treatment or punishment.

H. All orders from above shall be in keeping with the laws of the Republic. Obeying the orders of a superior is no justification for committing acts which are clearly punishable.

I. Members of the National Civil Police shall ensure full protection of the health of persons in their custody and, in particular, shall take immediate steps to provide medical care when necessary.

J. Members of the National Civil Police shall not commit any act of corruption. They shall also strongly oppose such acts and shall combat them.

K. Members of the National Civil Police who have reason to believe that a breach of these rules of conduct has occurred or is about to occur shall so inform their superiors and, if necessary, any authority or appropriate agency having powers of control or correction.

L. In the performance of their functions, members of the National Civil Police shall, as far as possible, utilise non-violent means before resorting to the use of force and firearms. They may use force and firearms only when other means prove ineffective or do not in any way guarantee the achievement of the legitimate anticipated result.

M. Members of the National Civil Police shall not use firearms against people except in self-defence or in defence of other people, or in case of imminent danger of death or serious injury, or with the intention of preventing the commission of a particularly serious crime involving a serious threat to life, or for the purpose of arresting a person who represents such a threat and resists their authority, and only where less extreme means prove insufficient to achieve such objectives. In any case, lethal weapons may be used intentionally only when strictly unavoidable for the protection of a life.

N. As part of the performance of their duty to safeguard the exercise of the rights of individuals, members of the National Civil Police shall protect the exercise of the right of assembly and demonstration. When, for legal reasons, they are compelled to break up a demonstration or a meeting, they shall use the least dangerous means and only to the minimum extent necessary. Members of the National Civil Police shall refrain from using

VI:1

firearms in such cases, save where the meetings are violent and other means have been exhausted, and only under the circumstances provided for in the preceding paragraph

(C) POLITICAL LEADERSHIP – A VISION OF POLICING

The importance of political investment in policing from the highest government level cannot be overstated. Strong and enlightened leadership from government is essential to the promotion of a police organisation that provides a lead role model for society and its citizens. Honesty, integrity and a strong service ethos should be the core values of the organisation.

High quality political leadership resulting in successful police reform in the most difficult of circumstances is exemplified in the experience of the Republic of Sierra Leone.

Sierra Leone gained its independence in 1961 following 150 years of rule as a British protectorate. The nation was established as a constitutional democracy and a member of the British Commonwealth. Within six years, the nation had degenerated into a one party state and the police were politicised to operate on behalf of the ruling clique and to oppress its rivals through violence and corruption. Between 1991 and 2001 a violent civil war ensued, causing tens of thousands of deaths, countless atrocities against the civilian population and the displacement of more than two million refugees to neighbouring countries. During the crisis, civil society, the rule of law and the criminal justice system were largely abandoned until the United Nations established a fragile peace in 1998.[344] The Sierra Leone Police systematically failed to react to the needs of citizens. Following the full restoration of democracy, the newly elected government of President Ahmed Kabbah determined its priority of restoring law and order and reforming the Sierra Leone Police. One of the first tasks was to address the corruption endemic in police ranks. In August 1998 President Kabbah penned his vision of policing through the Government Policing Charter reproduced below in Figure 1.[345]

---

[344] S. Cullen and W. McDonald, 'Sierra Leone', in L. Sullivan *et al.* (eds.), *Encyclopaedia of Law Enforcement* (vol. 3) (Sage Publications, Thousand Oaks, CA, 2004).
[345] Sierra Leone Police, Strategic document: *From Crisis to Confidence*, 1998.

THE SIERRA LEONE POLICE
Government Policing Charter

Introduction

My Government wants to create a police service which will be a credit to the Nation.

The Role of the Police

The Sierra Leone Police will assist in returning our communities to peace and prosperity by acting in a manner which will:

- eventually remove the need for the deployment of military and para-military forces in our villages, communities and city streets
- ensure the safety and security of all people and their property
- respect the human rights of all individuals
- prevent and detect crime by using the most effective methods which can be made available to them
- take account of local concerns through community consultation
- at all levels be free from corruption

Equal Opportunities

The personnel policies of the Sierra Leone Police will be the same for all members, regardless of sex or ethnic origin. All recruitment, training, postings, promotions and opportunities for development will be based on a published equal opportunities policy

The Role of My Government

The Government will do all in its power to ensure that the Sierra Leone Police is:

- directed and managed in accordance with The Constitution
- locally managed so as to ensure that community views are always taken into consideration
- adequately resourced and financed
- well equipped to undertake its duties
- professionally trained
- dynamically led and,
- that the terms and conditions of service for members of the Sierra Leone Police reflect the importance of the task they perform.

The Role of the People

In order that our police officers can successfully fulfil our expectations, it is essential that all people of Sierra Leone help and support them at all times.

Conclusion

Our aim is to see a reborn Sierra Leone Police, which will be a force for good in our Nation.

August 1998   His Excellency The President Alhaji Dr Ahmed Tejan-Kabbah

VI:1

The Charter was a vision of a truly service-oriented police organisation intended to provide a professional service to meet the needs and expectations of all citizens, and working in partnership with the citizenry. Moreover, the Charter was explicit in encouraging respect for human rights, proscribing corruption, and removing the existing culture of nepotism, tribalism and favouritism. The Charter promotes leadership, equal opportunities and wider positive values and ethical standards. Its keynote was that the Sierra Leone Police should be a 'Force for Good'.

The Charter provided the Inspector General of the Sierra Leone Police and his senior team with themes for a Mission Statement that conveyed the new values of the organisation, including respect for human rights, to all its members and to citizens. It also provided the foundation for the five year-strategic development program. The Mission Statement is reproduced as follows:[346]

SIERRA LEONE POLICE FORCE
A Force for Good

Our Duty   We will provide a professional and effective service which:

- Protects Life and Property
- Achieves a peaceful society
- Takes primacy in the maintenance of Law and Order

Our Values   We will respect Human Rights and the freedoms of the individual
We will be honest, impartial, caring and free from corruption

Our Priorities   We will respond to local needs
We will value our own people
We will involve all in developing our policing priorities

Our Aim   To win public confidence by offering reliable, caring and
accountable police services

August 1998

The Government Policing Charter combined with inspirational leadership, both political and within senior police ranks, has resulted in the Sierra Leone Police seeking to become and remain an enlightened and progressive police service. The Charter was a vanguard for human rights and ethical standards. Thus, governments and non-governmental bodies around the world could be convinced that Sierra

---

[346] *Ibid.*

358

Leone and its police were worthy of donor aid, training and logistical support. Similarly it provided the catalyst for business and commercial confidence and the return of much needed foreign investment. Crucially, having been written and endorsed by the President himself, the Charter was most unlikely to be challenged or obstructed by other political leaders or police officials.

The political masters and leaders of police organisations of all nations, including those with an existing tradition of democratic government and democratic policing, need to be continuously alert to a constantly changing environment. There are new challenges: the effects of globalisation, terrorism, transcontinental organised crime and drugs trafficking, cyber crime, people trafficking and the problems associated with migrations of people from war and poverty. These problems and issues affect police of all nations. Consequently, police leaders have to be strategically aware and have an understanding of the political, social and economic context of policing and the wider issues and sensitivities relating to human rights and ethical policing. Only then can they look inside their organisation with the wisdom to know how best to harness the talents and energy of their workforce.

Chapter 2. Managing People for Change

(A) HUMAN RESOURCE MANAGEMENT

There is a remarkable correlation in police organisations around the world in terms of the percentage of budgetary expenditure on wages, typically about 80 per cent, which is significantly higher than all other public sector services. Police organisations can operate with comparatively low budget expenditure on logistics and equipment. Policing is essentially about people and the deployment of a trained, effective and motivated workforce. It is personal interaction with citizens that determines the image and reputation of police organisations. Equipment, including vehicles and radio are essential in supporting policing effectiveness and provide the means and mobility to respond efficiently to the needs of citizens. However, citizens judge the effectiveness of police organisations by the quality of the service they receive from police personnel, not by the quality of police equipment or the technology they use.

Effectiveness depends to a great extent on human resource management systems that support the workforce and help to meet the goals of the organisation. The ability of police officials to maintain the highest standards of conduct and professionalism in meeting the needs and expectations of citizens is at the core of effective human resource management.

Article 2 of the Universal Declaration of Human Rights states that everyone is entitled to all the rights and freedoms set forth in the Declaration without distinction of any kind, such as race, colour, sex, language and religion. Article 23 states, *inter alia*, that everyone has the right to work, to free choice of employment, to just and favourable conditions of work and to protection against employment. Chapter 3 in Part I refers to the stipulation in the United Nations Code of Conduct for Law Enforcement Officials that police agencies should be representative of the community as a whole and its membership must be representative of that community according to such criteria as race, colour, sex, language and religion.

These requirements affect every element of human resource management and impose a range of responsibilities on not only human resource managers, but also all police managers and supervisors including civilian support staff. Human Resource Management has eight distinct elements:

1. Recruitment and selection
2. Equal opportunities
3. Performance and motivation
4. Pay and other benefits

5. Health, safety and welfare
6. Employee relations
7. Organisational development
8. Training and development

The eight elements are interlinked to provide a strategic approach to the management of people within an organisation, thus ensuring that the organisation obtains the greatest possible benefit from their abilities. The consequences of this process being effective are often described by the principle of having the right person for the right job at the right time.

It is not intended in this chapter to describe all the processes of human resource management. Describing the processes of designing job descriptions, for example, would occupy a major section of a book devoted to human resource management. Such skills are already available in most developed police organisations. Police organisations in democratising countries that are perhaps moving from a military model will probably not have human resource management systems and will need to develop them in the future. For police organisations in transition, there are likely to be experts in country, within public sector or government departments, universities, tertiary or business colleges who can provide the necessary expertise and advice.

(a) **Recruitment and Selection**

Recruitment and selection require marketing of the organisation in order to select the best people. Advertising through the press and other communications media will reach the widest range of suitable candidates and help to avoid discrimination. Internal information bulletins, memoranda and newspapers published by the organisation should be used to advertise vacancies for internal posts and opportunities for promotion.

Job descriptions, skills or competency profiles are required to match applicants to the job. There should be fair and transparent systems for testing, assessment and interviews including a written record of decisions made by the selection panel. In all recruitment and selection processes it is essential to identify, through structured tests and interviews, the qualities and aptitudes necessary for the role applied for. Recruits and candidates should be physically fit and psychologically able to withstand the rigors of working as a police official. They must possess honesty and integrity and display the ability to exercise their powers with fairness, conviction and discretion. Candidates who are tested and found to harbour bigotry or intolerance of minorities should be rejected. As well as honesty and integrity, recruitment tests should include questions that test tolerance of race, ethnicity, sexual orientation and gender.

In some countries, selection or promotion can be based on ties of kinship, friendship, tribal loyalty, bribery or patronage. Favouritism through tribalism has been particularly common in African countries, whilst patronage is common in many Latin American countries. It often results in personnel being appointed or promoted to posts and receiving remuneration which they do not deserve. As they are unqualified, the effectiveness of the organisation is adversely affected. Wholly unsuitable personnel may behave improperly, have a negative impact on colleagues and citizens, and jeopardise the image and reputation of the organisation. Notwithstanding that favouritism in its various forms is often cultural, it can be a major source of demoralisation and disaffection amongst personnel. Furthermore, it is corruption. Chiefs of police and all senior police managers should send a clear and unequivocal message that it has no place in a modern and progressive police organisation providing a role model for society

(i) Recruitment Centres

There is a direct relationship between recruitment and integrity. A police organisation that invests significant resources and qualified personnel to adequate facilities in its recruitment process sends a powerful message about its professional standards to potential applicants.[347] Recruitment centres are the 'shop front' of the organisation, and for most recruits attending them will be their first experience of the police organisation they wish to join. For this reason premises used for recruitment should be clean and inviting, and reflect a professional ethos. Recruitment centres should be adequately equipped with the necessary materials for testing and examination, for example, desks, writing materials and paper. Recruitment staff should be selected as having the necessary qualities and competencies for their role. Staff should be smart in bearing and appearance, have a thorough knowledge of their role, possess good interpersonal and communication skills, and importantly, be committed and motivated to their task.

Candidates attending recruitment centres that are situated in a squalid environment or where recruiting staff lack education or professionalism will be deterred from joining the organisation. Consequently, potential candidates having a good education and motivation for public service will not join the police service because of its poor image, status and reputation in society. Under these circumstances, the more talented and able of society's youth, and the sons and daughters of the elite, join the armed forces and other professions. Consequently, the police are consigned to the lower level of social status and desirable employment.

---

[347] M. R. Haberfeld, *Police Leadership* (Prentice Hall, New Jersey, 2006) p. 22.

VI:2

If they wish to attract the best candidates, police leaders having a strategic role in the recruitment of personnel should actively ensure that best practices are being operated in the recruitment processes. Police leaders and government officials responsible for ensuring the recruitment of personnel having the highest potential for both professional policing and protecting the human rights of citizens need to be aware of these factors when seeking finance, suitable premises, manning and logistical support for police recruiting centres.

Governments of poorer countries may not regard financial investment in police recruiting as a priority. However, investment in recruiting is essential if governments wish to have a progressive police service that will provide a professional response to the needs of citizens and be a role model for society.

(b) Equal Opportunities

Article 5 of the International Convention on the Elimination of All Forms of Racial Discrimination[348] requires States parties, in compliance with the fundamental obligations laid down in article 2 of the Convention, to undertake to prohibit and eliminate racial discrimination in all its forms and to guarantee the right of everyone, without distinction as to race, colour, or national or ethnic origin, to equality before the law, notably in the enjoyment of, *inter alia*, economic, social and cultural rights, and in particular the rights to work, to free choice of employment, to just and favourable conditions of work, to protection against unemployment, to equal pay for equal work, to just and favourable remuneration.

Article 1 of the Convention on the Elimination of All Forms of Discrimination against Women[349] defines the term 'discrimination against women' as meaning the distinction, exclusion or restriction made on the basis of sex which has the effect or purpose of impairing or nullifying the recognition, enjoyment or exercise by women, irrespective of their marital status, on a basis of equality of men and women, of human rights and fundamental freedoms in the political, economic, social, cultural, civil or any other field.

Article 2 requires States parties to condemn discrimination against women in all its forms, and to agree to pursue by all appropriate means and without delay a policy of eliminating discrimination against women. Measures against discrimination include applying the principle of equality between men and women, and adopting legislation

---

[348] International Convention on the Elimination of All Forms of Racial Discrimination, *supra* note 6.
[349] Convention on the Elimination of All Forms of Discrimination against Women, *supra* note 7.

364

that prohibits all discrimination against women and ensures that all public institutions and other organisations and persons eliminate discrimination.

Article 11 requires States parties to take all appropriate measures to eliminate discrimination against women in the field of employment in order to ensure equality of men and women. Furthermore, it requires that women shall have, *inter alia*, the right to work as an inalienable right of all human beings, and the same entitlements as men in relation to selection for employment, job selection, job security, pay and benefits, conditions of service, promotion, training, maternity rights and social security benefits.

All police organisations around the world are male dominated. Increasing the percentage of female officials can help to improve gender-awareness and allow the development of effective strategies to deal with female victimisation in society.

Fair and transparent recruitment and selections systems ensure selection of the best people for the job, irrespective of race, gender, religion or ethnicity. Women and people of racial or ethnic minorities must be encouraged to apply for posts. The organisation should ensure that its policies and procedures accord to human rights, and diversity and equal opportunities legislation. Most police organisations around the world have difficulty in recruiting sufficient females or members of minority groups to ensure that the organisation truly reflects the diversity of their societies. Reasons for this are complex and manifold. However, systems should be in place to monitor this aim, and positive efforts sustained to recruit more females and minority candidates. Importantly, an effective police organisation is one that has a healthy culture of camaraderie and teamwork, and as such should be a job that welcomes all.

(c) Performance and Motivation

It is important that any police organisation has a culture of service excellence. The culture should be supportive of human rights, ethical standards of behaviour, and valuing citizens and employees. If employees are not valued and are treated in a negative way by their leaders or managers, they are likely to treat citizens in a similar manner. Motivation should be encouraged together with controls for accountability. Participative management should stress the importance of making employees aware of what is happening in the organisation. It is important to ensure that jobs are interesting and challenging. The aims of the individual and the team should match those of the organisation. To avoid favouritism, regular staff appraisals or assessments of individual employees should be based solely on their professional performance in meeting organisational goals and objectives. Conduct should also be assessed.

VI:2

In 1998 the Independent Commission on Policing for Northern Ireland was established to lead the reform of the Royal Ulster Constabulary so that it could be transformed into the Police Service of Northern Ireland. The Commission made an important recommendation that awareness of human rights issues and respect for human rights in the performance of duty should be an important element in the appraisal of individuals in the police service.

A range of required competencies held by individuals makes them competent to perform their role and duties effectively. Competencies allow managers in organisations to be pro-active in assessing personnel against those competencies. Hence, they can be used in recruitment, selection and promotion, staff appraisal, effective supervision, and the monitoring of overall professional ability and performance. Importantly, they can also be devised to enable monitoring of behaviour.

In any appraisal/assessment system it is absolutely essential for supervisors and managers to be trained in their use, otherwise the system will fail to achieve its ends. Appraisals/assessment should be totally objective and provide an honest grading of the competencies being assessed. A narrative of evidence should support negative or positive appraisals. The system should be open, and the person being appraised should be allowed to read his or her assessment and grading before being invited to countersign them. There is a tendency for many managers and supervisors to be reluctant to make adverse comment or criticism of subordinate colleagues. Training should emphasise that this can be counterproductive to personal development and the overall effectiveness of the organisation. It militates against identifying training and development needs. The success of the system depends totally on honesty and objectivity.

In 2002, the United Kingdom Home Office published Circular 42/2002 entitled 'Implementing the National Competency Framework'. The Circular exhorted all chief officers of police in England and Wales to adopt the framework in their personnel functions. It is reproduced below:

Behavioural Framework	
Area	Behaviour
Leadership	*Strategic Perspective* Looks at issues with a broad view to achieve the organisation's goals. Thinks ahead and prepares for the future.
	Openness to Change Recognises and responds to the need for change, and uses it to improve organisational performance.
	Negotiation and Influencing Persuades and influences others using logic and reason. Sells the benefits of the position they are proposing, and negotiates to find solutions that everyone will accept.
	Maximising Potential Actively encourages and supports the development of people. Motivates others to achieve organisational goals
Working with Others	*Respect for Diversity* Considers and shows respect for the opinions, circumstances and feelings of colleagues and members of the public, no matter what their position, background, circumstances, status or appearance.
	Teamworking Develops strong working relationships inside and outside the team to achieve common goals. Breaks down barriers between groups and involves others in discussions and decisions.
	Community and Customer Focus Focuses on the customer and provides a high-quality service that is tailored to meet their individual needs. Understands the community that is served and shows an active commitment to policing in a diverse society.
	Effective Communication Communicates effectively, both verbally and in writing. Uses listening and questioning techniques to make sure that they and others understand what is going on and can effectively transfer ideas and information.

VI:2

	Problem solving Gather information from a range of sources. Analyses information to identify problems and issues, and makes effective decisions.
Achieving Results	*Planning and Organising* Plans, organises and supervises activities to make sure resources are used efficiently and effectively to achieve organisational goals.
	Personal Responsibility Takes personal responsibility for making things happen and achieving results. Displays motivation, commitment, perseverance and conscientiousness. Acts with a high degree of integrity.
	Resilience Show resilience, even in difficult circumstances. Prepared to make difficult decisions and has the confidence to see them through.

To quote from Circular 42/2002, the Framework "has been designed and developed from information and data gathered from over 400 Key Event and Repertory Grid interviews nationally of police officials and civil/support staff". The framework is generic and essentially values based. The behavioural competencies contained therein apply to all ranks and civilian grades. The framework can be used as a template to design competency frameworks for individual roles and ranks, taking account of variations in desired competencies. It provides a medium for assessing values that the Circular describes as effective human behaviour, and it contains competencies directly relevant to human rights, such as respect for diversity and community and customer focus.

Importantly, it assists and encourages motivation to change and to provide a quality service to all citizens. In this sense it is an excellent medium for identifying strengths and weaknesses, at the individual, group and organisational level. More importantly, it can enable an organisation to remedy weaknesses. The framework can be used to identify training needs. Again quoting from the circular, "competencies help in assessing the capability and potential of individuals, identifying their development needs and meeting them though targeted training and development".

(d) **Pay and Other Benefits**

Securing high police morale is important if governments wish to gain the support of the police and prevent corruption. Government should ensure that the status of police officials compares favourably to that of other public sector professionals. The police should feel they are valued by government and society and receive adequate pay, food and shelter. A useful indicator is that their wages, at least at junior rank level, are higher than corresponding ranks in the armed forces.

Benefits can also include non-financial rewards such as awards and citations and awards for good conduct. This should include awards for ethical standards and good work in support of human rights and community and race relations.

(e) Health, Safety and Welfare

Police leaders have a duty of care to all employees and must ensure that they are not exposed unnecessarily to danger or conditions that could adversely affect their physical or mental health. If police officials are exposed to danger in an operational environment, police leaders should take all necessary steps to ensure that they are trained and equipped with approved protection and defensive or other equipment to provide a proportionate response to the task facing them. This duty accords to the importance of securing the human rights of police officials as a desirable end in itself, as examined in the paragraph under 'Entitlement' in Chapter 2 of Part I.

Effective health, safety and welfare systems ensure the availability of officials for work and their ability to provide a professional service to citizens. Sickness monitoring and health and welfare counselling are key tasks for managers and supervisors. Selected managers should have skills in stress counselling and be familiar with the symptoms of post- traumatic stress disorder.

(f) Employee Relations

Effective employee relations are especially important in times of change. Change must be explained in advance to all employees and their trade unions or staff associations, which should also be included and consulted in change programmes. It is essential that there should be effective systems for sideways, top-down and bottom-up communications in police organisations. As well as receiving orders from above, subordinates should be encouraged and enabled to communicate their problems, ideas and comments to senior level. Hence, they can be active participants in the management process and the development of good practice. Staff associations can be important conduits for supporting, formulating and disseminating good practice in relation to all aspects of human resource management including human rights and equal opportunities. Good employee relations ensure that discipline and grievance procedures are operated fairly and consistently.

VI:2

(g) **Organisational Development**

Organisations need flexible values, style and structure to respond to both government and citizens' needs and expectations. A police organisation cannot remain static. It should be periodically reviewed to ensure it is able to respond to changing demands. For example, new legislation, and new or emerging crime trends or social problems may require new responses and the development and learning of new skills. Demographic changes may require adjustment of territorial command boundaries and the relocation of personnel in order to meet community needs and expectations, and to ensure that all citizens have equal access to policing services. Strategic development ensures that the organisation can avoid uncertainty and can accommodate change.

This latter comment reinforces the importance of the human resource management department of a police organisation having a strategy that links to training. The human resource management function of the organisation identifies training needs. The training function then designs and delivers the training. This is extremely difficult because, unlike the manufacturing industry, policing does not involve manufacturing a single or limited range of products. Police managers operate in a world of chaos. They are constantly endeavouring to identify training needs that respond to change, and to deliver relevant training to improve the performance of their staff. The following section, in the context of some general observations about training, examines ways in which training needs can be identified. It also proposes a model for human rights training where a distinction is made between 'education' and 'training' although it is acknowledged here that, generally, the process of equipping police officials with the knowledge, attitudes and skills to perform their functions is generally referred to as training.

(B) **TRAINING AND DEVELOPMENT**

Financial and resource constraints and operational demands dictate that no police organisation, 'even in the wealthiest of nations, can afford to deliver training for every single identified or perceived training need. Consequently, training must be prioritised according to the degree of importance to the strategies and needs of the organisation, the state and its citizens. Formal training should only be delivered when it is absolutely necessary. The design and delivery of training is not necessarily the most appropriate response on every occasion to a training need. A shortfall in performance of an individual or group my be remedied by on the job supervision, or by advice or counselling, either informally or at formal staff appraisal or counselling sessions. However, from the perspective of any police organisation, human rights should be a non-negotiable training requirement for all members of the organisation, for both police and civilian support staff of all

370

departments, grades and ranks. Training should meet the short, medium and long-term strategic aims of the organisation relating to human rights, diversity, equal opportunities and community and race relations.

Training is not an end in itself. Training must serve the organisation. All members of police organisations have responsibility for their own learning and keeping abreast of new knowledge and skills. Training is not just the responsibility of trainers or training departments. All supervisors and managers have a responsibility for the training and learning of others, thus ensuring that they can provide an effective and professional service to the public and are equipped to manage the challenges and uncertainty of change.

There are four components to the management and delivery of all police training: identifying training needs, training design, training delivery, and training validation and evaluation. The application of these components in a logical and structured way will result in cost-effective and relevant training and, hence, to more effective policing that provides better service to the public through improved police performance. Identifying training needs and training delivery, specifically of human rights programmes are considered in more detail below (under the sub-heading 'A Model for Human Rights Education and Training').

Training design should be structured and aimed towards meeting specific learning objectives. At the end of the training there should be some qualitative or quantitative improvement in the knowledge, skills and/or awareness of the learner. Training validation is required in order to establish whether or not the learning objectives have been achieved. For example, a reduction in the number of complaints about the unnecessary use of force may be interpreted as validation that training in arrest and restraint techniques has been effective; although, of course, such a reduction may have occurred because of other causes. Training evaluation includes validation but also assesses the cost benefits of training. It is a costly and time-consuming exercise and not all police organisations are able to afford to conduct evaluations or have personnel trained in the necessary skills. Validation and evaluation are another means of identifying training needs. If the training has not met the objectives achieved it may pose some additional questions. For example, was the training appropriate to the needs? Or were the trainers sufficiently skilled? A negative answer to either of these questions may indicate that there is a need for training of trainers.

(a) Identifying Training Needs

Identifying and prioritising training needs through training needs analysis enables training to be designed and delivered to fill the skills gap in the organisation, the shortfall of training from what exists to what is required. The following sources allow effective training needs analysis:

(i) Human Resource Management Systems

The monitoring of staff assessment/appraisals, self-assessments, discussions with manager, promotion assessments and competency framework can identify weaknesses in the competence of any individual or group of individuals within the workforce. At a basic level, the remedy may simply require additional supervision, counselling or advice. More serious shortcomings may require formal training.

(ii) Legislation

The introduction of new criminal laws, codes or procedures affecting law enforcement will require training of police officials to ensure that they have the necessary knowledge, skills and awareness to perform their duties efficiently and effectively. Police leaders, especially those having a role in human resource management and training should be regularly monitoring the parliament and its legislature, and the judiciary, in order to make themselves aware of any impending passing of laws or procedures that are likely to have implications for training. Considering the mandatory need for human rights and other associated training, police leaders need to make early budgetary provision to ensure sufficient finances and other resources are available for training. To this end, there requires to be close liaison with and support from both government and the civilian review board or committee having oversight of policing and police training matters.

(iii) Organisational Needs

Strategic plans and policing plans may reveal specific training needs for that particular organisation. For example, an objective to improve community and race relations may require awareness training relating to local minorities.

(iv) Effective Management and Supervision

All police leaders, especially those with territorial command responsibility, should be alert to the needs of the citizens and the communities they are responsible for policing. They should encourage their command team and supervisors to provide early warning of new and emerging issues, problems and needs affecting the communities. In addition to identifying timely resolutions, including predictions of financial and logistical needs, attention should be given to additional or new training requirements. Managers and supervisors should be cooperating with communities, partners and other agencies in designing and implementing action plans to deal with local policing problems. Again, this will focus the attention of managers and supervisors on the training needs of themselves and their personnel.

(v) Professional Standards

All police organisations should have a department for the investigation of crimes committed by police officials, investigation of complaints against the police from citizens, or breaches of internal administrative rules and procedures. These departments are called variously Internal Investigations, Department of Internal Affairs, Discipline and Complaint Department or Professional Standards. They are an important source of identifying training needs. For example, an inordinately high number of complaints of assault or unnecessary use of force may indicate there is a training need for efficient arrest and restraint techniques.

(vi) Inspectorate Departments

Most police organisations have a department responsible for inspecting the organisation's systems to ensure that all of its functions are being operated efficiently and effectively, and that service standards and performance are meeting government, organisational and citizens' expectations. The inspectorate department is an important source for identifying training needs. For example, it may be found that equal opportunities procedures do not match national legislation and are a potential cause of complaint from members of minorities working for the organisation.

(vii) Training User Groups

Formalised organisational groups comprising staff associations and members of all ranks and branches can form a training user group. Meeting at regular intervals, they can discuss problems and weaknesses in competence or performance they experience amongst themselves or their staff. Training needs can then be identified and communicated to the Human Resource Management Department for remedy.

(viii) Public Forums

Local police commanders and their managers should hold regular meetings with political representatives of the people and citizens at public forums or community consultative committees. Comments received at forums may reveal training needs. For example, comments about incivility of patrol officials may indicate a need for counselling or attitudinal training.

VI:2

(ix) Lay Visitors to Police Detention Facilities

In some countries, arrangements exist for appointed citizens to visit police detention facilities in order to monitor prisoners and detention conditions. Such arrangements can be a useful source of identifying training needs relating to detention. For example, a police gaoler may be found to lack sufficient knowledge of detention procedures. Other human rights issues may be identified that demonstrate a lack of awareness of police leaders responsible for detention facilities. For example, the facilities may lack poor ventilation and be overcrowded, thus putting the health and safety of prisoners and detention staff at risk.

(x) Media and Press

The media and press are often the first to receive reports from citizens of police misconduct. Criticism of police by the press or other media should not always be seen as a threat. It should be seen as an opportunity to examine procedures to see if there is a training need, and to redress matters that may be of public concern.

(b) **Media Training and Human Rights**

In view of the last point above about the media and the press, it may be helpful at this stage to make some observations about training for police in media matters, especially in the context of human rights. Serious investigative journalism can provide a valuable public service in exposing and monitoring police abuses of human rights, police misconduct and corruption. Many police officials around the world complain that they are the targets of unfounded or unfair criticism, and sometimes scurrilous comment from their national press and other news media. It is known also that in some countries journalists enjoy prosperous lifestyles beyond their legitimate means by operating as the paid spies and mouthpieces of unprincipled politicians, power cliques and other vested interest groups. Nevertheless, the press and media cannot be ignored or shunned by police leaders simply because they dislike or distrust them. If the police refuse to speak to, or avoid the media then the media will be more likely to publish or broadcast stories based on rumour or falsehood. Conversely, if the police cooperate with the media and provide them with the accurate information they require, negative publicity can be avoided or mitigated.

Reality has to be faced: the media and the police are dependent upon each other. The media need the police to gain information on crime and other matters of public interest; the police need the media to seek public support for crime prevention and detection, and to communicate information widely to the public. Police officials need to be professional in their dealings with the press and media. To enhance the relationship between police and the media, it is essential for police organisations to operate a professionally manned public relations department or press office that interacts with the media on a day-to-day basis. Training is essential to assist police officials to understand the role of the media, and to learn the skills necessary to deal more effectively with members of the press, television and radio. In terms of human rights, police leaders need to be open and transparent in engaging with the media and in gaining their trust and support. Media training, especially if held jointly with members of the media, can enhance this relationship. Simulated sessions at being a police spokesperson and being questioned and challenged by real press, television and radio journalists will assist police officials in improving the image of themselves and the organisation. Thus, they will be able better to communicate an objective and balanced perspective of policing issues, especially those relating to police conduct that may impact on the public's perceptions of police attitudes towards human rights.

(C) A MODEL FOR HUMAN RIGHTS EDUCATION AND TRAINING

It will be recalled from previous chapters that some international human rights instruments contain provisions requiring education and training of police. For example, article 10 of the Convention against Torture and Other Cruel, Inhuman or Degrading Treatment or Punishment[350] requires States parties to ensure that education and information regarding the prohibition against torture are fully included in the training of law enforcement personnel, civil or military, medical personnel, public officials and other persons who may be involved in the custody, interrogation or treatment of any individual subjected to any form of arrest, detention or imprisonment.[351]

The wording of article 10 of the Convention against Torture is an indication that, for the purposes of enlightening police on the subject of human rights, it is useful to distinguish between education, which is concerned with intellectual, moral and social instruction, and training, which is concerned with teaching and acquisition of specific skills. Informing police about human rights and convincing them of the need to respect and protect them can be considered to be an educational process. Equipping police officials with the technical skills necessary to enable them to carry out their duties in conformity with human rights standards is a training process.

---

[350] Convention against Torture and Other Cruel, Inhuman or Degrading Treatment or Punishment, *supra* note 8.

[351] *See also* principle 18, principle 19, and principle 20 of the Basic Principles on the Use of Force and Firearms by Law Enforcement Officials; rule 84 of the United Nations Rules for the Protection of Juveniles Deprived of Their Liberty; principle 16 of the Declaration of Basic Principles of Justice for Victims of Crime and Abuse of Power; article 4 (i) of the Declaration on the Elimination of Violence Against Women; and article 7 of the Inter-American Convention to Prevent and Punish Torture.

VI:2

Human rights programmes for police have been delivered regularly by a number of international organisations in recent years,[352] and best practice in this field has been developed and set out in manuals and other teaching resources produced by and for these organisations.[353] The following observations are based on best practice set out in the manuals and other teaching resources referred to above, from which it is possible to identify purposes and principles of human rights education for police

(a) **Purposes**

Clearly, human rights education for police should be designed and delivered to affect the attitudes and thence the behaviour of police officials so that they deliver effective, lawful and humane policing. Having set that as the primary purpose of human rights programmes for police, it is then necessary to acknowledge that the achievement of that objective is dependent upon a number of factors outside the influence or remit of educational programmes. These factors include the existence of the necessary political will to change police agencies; the realisation of cultural and organisational change within police agencies; and the enforcement of measures to secure the accountability of police to the communities they serve and to the law.

For this reason it is important to recognise that there are other objectives of human rights programmes for police, which can contribute to the achievement of the primary purpose to a greater or lesser degree depending upon the factors already referred to. These other objectives include simply making police officials aware of human rights norms and standards; providing a forum for police officials to discuss human rights and policing issues; providing an opportunity for police officials to consider policing from a human rights perspective; and providing a basis for continuing efforts within police agencies to deliver effective, lawful and humane policing.

---

[352] These include the Council of Europe, the International Committee of the Red Cross, the Raoul Wallenberg Institute of Human Rights and Humanitarian Law, and the United Nations Centre for Human Rights.

[353] *See e.g,* Office of the UN High Commisioner for Human Rights, *Human Rights and Law Enforcement: A Trainer's Guide on Human Rights for the Police, Polic Training Series No.5 Add.2,* 2002, for UN Centre for Human Rights; R. Crawshaw, *Police and Human Rights: A Manual for Teachers, Resource Persons, and Participants in Human Rights Programmes* (Kluwer Law International (Brill Academic Publishers), 1999, for RWI; International Committee of the Red Cross, *To Serve and Protect: Guide for Police Conduct and Behaviour,* Geneva, 2002; and Council of Europe, *Police and Human Rights Training and Awareness Material.*

This latter objective can be achieved by means of workshop activities of various kinds. For example operational police officials can be asked to work collectively in groups to identify all of the action they could take immediately on return to their places of duty, without any additional resources, to enhance respect for and protection of human rights by officials under their command.

(b) Principles

These objectives, and the workshop method given as an example, indicate that one of the principles of human rights education for police is that of participation. Police officials need to be given the opportunity to discuss any reservations and concerns they may have about the notion of human rights; they need to be challenged about assumptions they may have, for example that it is acceptable under some circumstances to break the law in order to enforce the law; they need to be presented with practical and theoretical case studies that enable them to discuss human rights issues arising out of various courses of police action.

Two other principles are centrality and continuity. Human rights must be central to police education and training programmes. Educational components should provide knowledge and develop or reinforce attitudes appropriate to policing in a democracy governed by the rule of law. These components are discussed below under the sub-heading 'A framework for best practice'. Training components should develop or reinforce skills appropriate to policing in a democracy governed by the rule of law, for example to communicate with people; to interview witnesses and suspects; and to adopt the most appropriate tactics in specific situations - in fact the entire range of technical policing skills.

The main point, however, is that these components should form one of the principal pillars of curricula. In educational programmes, human rights should be dealt with as a specific topic, and should be incorporated, where appropriate, into the subject matter of themes dealt with in other lessons. Human rights should also be incorporated into all sessions of training programmes in which policing skills are taught. Furthermore education and training in human rights should be continuous processes, taking into account the educational and training needs of officials as they are promoted through rank structures, or deployed in specialist police units. Human rights should be given due prominence and emphasis in instructional programmes that police officials follow throughout their entire careers.

A fourth principle is the principle of relevance. Police officials need to be convinced that awareness of, and compliance with, human rights standards are essential to the effective performance of the craft and profession of policing. They need to understand how, through the performance of their duties, they actually protect

VI:2

human rights. They need to be aware that their difficult and dangerous task gives them specific entitlements to human rights, and that securing these entitlements is a responsibility of governments and of police leaders.

(c) A Framework for Best Practice

The basic framework for human rights education of police described here is adapted from that developed in the manual *Police and Human Rights – a Manual for Teachers, Resource Persons and Participants in Human Rights Programmes*,[354] where comprehensive guidance on how to implement a full programme based on the Manual can be found. This manual was developed as a teaching resource for human rights programmes consisting of a seminar element in which international standards on human rights are presented and discussed, and a workshop element, exemplified above, designed to provide a basis for continuing efforts within police agencies to deliver effective, lawful and humane policing. The basic framework has four parts: context, police powers and respect for human rights, police functions and protection of human rights, and realisation of human rights through leadership.

The term context refers to a professional context, an international context and a democratic context. It is useful to provide these contexts before proceeding to the other, more substantive, parts of the framework in order that the substantive elements may be better understood. The purpose of the professional context is, by discussion, case studies and other participative means, to show the relevance of human rights to policing.

The international context is provided for two main reasons. Firstly, it is important to make police officials aware of the historical reasons for the development of the international system for the protection of human rights, and of the characteristics of human rights (e.g. inherent in every human being, universal, equal, and inalienable). Secondly, police officials need to understand that their acts or omissions could be scrutinised by courts and other bodies established for the protection of human rights. Discussions around these themes enable police officials to begin to reassess any reservations they may have about the notion of human rights. After all, the rationale for the development of the international system of human rights protection, and the all too evident need for its continuance, provide compelling reasons for officials who enforce the law to accept that it is essential "that human rights should be protected by the rule of law".[355]

---

[354] Crawshaw, *ibid.*

[355] Third preambular paragraph of the Universal Declaration of Human Rights.

The democratic context is provided so that police officials can better understand their role in a democracy governed by the rule of law, and can appreciate their duty to protect human rights essential to democracy and the rule of law. These rights and the interdependence of democracy, the rule of law and human rights are discussed in Chapter 3 of Part I herein.

Concerning the second part of the framework, police powers and respect for human rights, it is good practice to link an account of police powers with an account of the rights that regulate them and with a discussion on the significance of each of those rights. It is quite clear from preceding chapters of this book that essential police powers, for example to use force and to deprive people of their liberty, are limited by the need to respect fundamental human rights such as the right to life, the right to liberty and security of person, and the right to humane treatment as a detainee.

Concerning the third part of the framework, reference is made in chapter 2 of Part 1 to the ways in which police protect human rights. They create conditions for the enjoyment of all human rights by maintaining social order, and they protect specific rights in specific ways. In fact, it is argued, the protection of human rights can be seen as a distinct police function equal in importance to, and interconnected with, other police functions. Some human rights, such as the right to be presumed innocent until proved guilty and the right to a fair trial,[356] are particularly relevant to the investigation of crime and should be given due prominence in police education programmes, especially those for investigators. Other human rights, such as the right to freedom of peaceful assembly and association,[357] are particularly relevant to public order policing, as are international standards on the use of force and firearms when responding to unlawful or violent assemblies (discussed in Chapter 4 of Part II herein). In respect of police responses to conflict, it will be recalled from Chapter 1 of Part II that signatory States to the four Geneva Conventions of 1949 are obliged to disseminate provisions of these Conventions to police.

The final part of this basic framework for a human rights programme for police concerns the realisation of human rights through leadership. Clearly there are many aspects to the administration and management of complex organisations such as police agencies, but the aspect dealt with in this part of the book, the management of change, is particularly important for the realisation of human rights. Police leaders need to direct police agencies so that their responses to changes in society are effective, lawful and humane. Furthermore they need to manage change within police agencies so that a human rights culture replaces any culture that is inimical to human rights.

---

[356] *See e.g.*, articles 10 and 11 of the Universal Declaration of Human Rights.
[357] *See e.g.*, article 20 of the Universal Declaration of Human Rights.

VI:2

As indicated in previous chapters herein, provisions of international human rights instruments, and decisions and findings of human rights treaty bodies, place specific requirements on police leaders to supervise the routine activities of police officials; to command and control the actions of police officials during the conduct of police operations; and to ensure or facilitate prompt investigation of reports and complaints of human rights violations by police. Furthermore, police leaders have a duty of care towards their subordinates. The nature of police work, with its almost unique dangers and discomforts, places particular responsibilities on police leaders to secure the human rights of those under their command. Human rights education of police leaders should inform or remind them of all of these responsibilities and requirements, and indicate how they may be met. Training of police leaders should equip them with the necessary skills to fulfil their responsibilities. Committed, well-informed, and highly skilled police leaders are essential for the realisation of human rights by and through policing.

Realising human rights through leadership extends beyond the education of police leaders in this aspect of their duties. Police leaders should actively demonstrate their leadership and their commitment to human rights by strongly endorsing human rights education and training courses for all police. This can be done by various means including issuing public statements of support for human rights programmes and by formally opening human rights courses and interacting with course participants.

(D) HUMAN RIGHTS EDUCATION AND TRAINING AND WIDER SOCIETY

In order to reinforce the benefits of human rights education and training programmes for police, it is helpful to inform the wider society that police officials of all ranks are being provided with effective human rights training. For example government officials responsible for policing, members of police civilian review boards or committees, and the most senior police leaders could visit police human rights programmes. This type of sponsorship, accompanied by explanatory media publicity, can send a powerful message that government, citizens and police are committed to transparent and democratic policing.

Furthermore, members of police liaison forums and other community groups comprising ordinary citizens could be informed about and invited to human rights training. Citizens can provide important perspectives on how they see the relationship between police and citizenry. Efforts could be made to facilitate their making presentations to police groups. It has been convincingly argued that traditional police training methods create problems derived from the closed nature of police training institutions, the lack of community involvement in training design and delivery, the discrepancy between the theory taught to a new recruit and the practice on the street, and the failure to integrate human rights and cultural awareness training across all courses.[358] Training in an institutional environment isolates the recruit from the wider environment and the reality of policing in the real world. "The closed academy model tends to encourage a siege mentality; it may be the nursery of many of the dysfunctional aspects of police culture; and, it is an integral part of the closed organisational structure which encourages an organisational orientation rather than a community and practice orientation."[359]

The academic community could also be involved in human rights programmes for police, and in police education and training generally to the mutual benefit of both police and scholars. Intellectual investment and participation in police human rights education by members of universities, colleges and international and national academic bodies can enhance human rights programmes whilst, at the same time, members of the academic community can benefit from interaction with police students. Furthermore, awarding certificates or diplomas for the successful completion of human rights programmes can add value to the whole process, especially if a police organisation can gain accreditation for its human rights courses from universities or other academic institutions.

(E) EDUCATORS AND TRAINERS OF POLICE

In order to successfully implement human rights programmes for police, teachers and trainers must have expertise in policing, the education or training of police officials, and in the international standards relevant to policing. Teaching manuals referred to above[360] are some of the means by which teachers or resource persons with expertise in policing can develop expertise in international human rights and humanitarian standards relevant to policing.

---

[358] *See e.g.*, and Dr. L. Moore and M. O'Rawe, Report: *Human Rights on Duty - Principles for Better Policing: International Lessons for Northern Ireland*, The Committee on the Administration of Justice, 1997, p. 66, quoting Chief Superintendent Cioccarelli, New South Wales Police.
[359] *Ibid.*, p. 67.
[360] *Supra* note 353.

VI:2

However, the delivery of human rights programmes for police demands more of teachers and trainers than simply conveying information. It requires that they convince participants of the overriding need to comply with human rights standards. It would be fatal to the purposes of a human rights course if a teacher or trainer were to agree that there may be some circumstances in which it is permissible to violate human rights in the processes of policing. Occasionally a teacher or trainer may come under intense peer group pressure from participants to agree to such a proposition. This is especially the case when participants express deeply held prejudices about, for example, ethnic minority groups which are perceived to be causing problems in their country or on such matters as sexual orientation. Teachers and trainers need to believe in what they are doing and to show that compliance with human rights standards is an essential element of effective policing. They need to insist that unlawful and abusive behaviour by police has no place in a police agency that values and supports democracy and the rule of law.

Chapter 3. Managing the Process of Change

To be successful, any organisation has to be in a constant state of change. Change is especially problematic for police leaders. Whilst elected governments and police organisations are accountable to society, only governments have a mandate to introduce or amend laws, or implement or encourage social change by other means. Police, who are the servants of both government and people, must operate only within the law and enforce it with fairness and discretion. Furthermore, they must be aware of, and respond sensitively and intelligently to, various aspects of social change. They need to be tolerant of diverse radical and alternative causes and lifestyles that challenge the values of the majority of mainstream society. As society and its values and laws change, the police must respond appropriately. In management terms this puts the police at a disadvantage, because they have to respond to social phenomena whilst having little control over them or the direction they take. They are always a step behind.

Consequently, an effective police leader is one who has the skills and awareness to predict or anticipate future events that are likely to affect policing and cause change. Thus, he or she is able to overcome uncertainty by developing strategies that will meet the challenges of a changing world.

(A) THE CAUSES OF CHANGE

Change is one of the most critical aspects of effective management. Apart from its frequency in most organisations, the nature of change is becoming more complex and the impact of change is often more extensive. Many of the change situations in which a police manager can be involved are incremental rather than fundamental, and although there is some commonality there are also differences in how these types of situations should be managed. It is important therefore, to be aware that as change situations differ considerably, the response should vary with the situation. There is no single formula that will be successful in all situations.

To remain successful, the structure of the organisation and the way it operates must reflect the nature of the environment in which it is operating.[361] Furthermore, change also operates within the organisation. For example, existing technology may not be capable of being adapted to modern methods of criminal investigation or higher workloads. The skills of the workforce may be outdated and not capable of addressing changing crime trends.

---

[361] L. J. Mullins, *Management and Organizational Behaviour* (4th edition) (Pitman Publishing, London, 1996).

VI:3

As an open system, any police organisation is open to change stimuli from political, economic, social, technological, environmental and legal factors arising around the organisation's activities.[362] These factors, known collectively by the acronym PESTEL, provide a useful environmental scanning tool for predicting events and outcomes that may affect the organisation. An example of how scanning can be effected is demonstrated as follows:

> **Political:** A new government may declare a change in its relationship with police. It may demand more centralised/decentralised control. This may affect the authority and role of police leaders.
>
> A change of government or policy may cause protest and tensions resulting in public demonstrations and disorder. For example, a common cause of violence and unrest in parts of Africa and Latin America has been caused through national and local government forcibly removing street traders from city centres.
>
> **Economic:** Financial restraints on public sector services may limit resources available to the police. For example, the purchase of new vehicles may have to be delayed, or training may have to be cancelled or deferred. The government may demand greater output and improved service from existing resources.
>
> There are also social implications. For example, wealthier minority groups having a monopoly on retailing and sale of food and other essential items at the expense of poorer indigenous people is a common economic destabilising factor in many countries, particularly in Africa.
>
> **Sociological:** Community expectations may change owing to social change or increasing demands for individual rights. For example there may be greater demands for women's rights, or for more effective police responses to domestic violence, or for the relaxing of enforcement against certain classes of controlled drugs.
>
> **Technological:** Technological changes may render police equipment obsolete. This may limit the quantity and quality of management information and adversely affect quality of service to citizens. Police organisations cannot ignore developments that give them an advantage in improving quality of service or investigating crime. Additionally, it is only very rarely that a new

---

[362] J. M. Hart, *The Management of Change in Police Organizations*, p. 5, <www.ncjrs.gov/policing/man199.htm>, last visited September 2006.

development can be substituted for an old one without causing changes to skills requirements, jobs, the structure and often the culture of the organisation.

Environmental: This could be viewed from a community perspective. 'Greening' and the newfound sensitivity expressed by environmental pressure groups and citizens can cause tensions with government and business interests over the use of land or natural resources.

Legal: One of the most powerful drivers of change. It impacts not only on law enforcement, but also police styles and methods. For example a law requiring mandatory tape recording of interviews with suspects impacts on technology and the use of police detention facilities.

Changes in legislation may affect employee relations and have significant impact on human resource management systems and the duty of care of police leaders towards their employees. This may include ensuring that they are properly trained to deal with conflict and violence.

PESTEL also enables police managers to identify training needs and the personnel and resources needed to meet future challenges. The analysis should be a regular management process involving key members of the organisation including the executive, operational territorial commanders and departmental commanders. Specialists in financial management, human resource management and information technology and other experts should participate. In large and modern police organisations, the corporate development function has a day-to-day role in environmental scanning and the provision of relevant management information to senior leaders. Organisational analysis and environmental scanning is especially important during the budgetary cycle when preparing estimates and making bids to the police financial authority.

(B) RESISTANCE TO CHANGE

(a) The Culture

Culture is often defined as 'the way we do things around here'. A more detailed definition is, "the collection of traditions, values, policies, beliefs and attitudes that constitute a pervasive context for everything we do and think in an organisation".[363]

According to Schein, culture emanates from three sources:

---

[363] P. E. Atkinson, 'Creating Cultural Change,' 34:7 *Management Service* (1990) pp. 6–10.

VI:3

1. The beliefs, values and founders of organisations.
2. The learning experiences of group members as their organisation evolves.
3. New beliefs, values and assumptions brought in by new members and leaders.[364]

Police cultures appear generally to be inherited and passed on through the workforce. They are not created consciously. The roots of culture become lost with the progression of time, but in police organisations they seem strongly connected to tradition. Perhaps a powerful, charismatic leader or group of leaders has, in the past, established their own preferred values that have become the values and foundation of the culture. Those leaders and their acolytes become the role models for those who wish to become accepted and successful in the organisation, or a group within the organisation. Eventually, the people within the organisation become socialised to its culture. They may even go so far as to consciously or unconsciously adopt the mannerisms and style of speech of the dominant role models. Eventually the role models leave, they may even be forgotten, but their influence lingers in the culture and can pervade for generations later. If a role model establishes negative behaviour, for example a senior detective encouraging routine ill treatment of suspects to obtain confessions, that behaviour may become part of the culture and custom of the organisation or the group for years to come. It becomes normal unless events occur to modify the culture. Culture is very powerful and strikingly similar in police organisations around the world.

Whereas police organisations can appear to harbour healthy and positive cultures, they can also conceal beleaguered workforces that believe they are not appreciated by society – a culture within a culture. It is within this culture within a culture that unhealthy responses can result in a rejection of ethical values, abuse of authority, corruption and abuses of human rights. Additionally, the subculture can be a stubborn obstacle to change. Goldstein comments on the characteristics of police subculture as follows:

> "The strength of the subculture grows out of the peculiar characteristics and conflicting pressures of the job: the ever-present physical danger; the hostility directed at the police because of their controlling role; the vulnerability of police officers to allegations of wrongdoing; unreasonable demands and conflicting expectations; uncertainty as to the function and authority of officers; a prevalent feeling that the public does not really understand what the police 'have to put up with' in dealing with citizens; a stifling working

---

[364] E. H. Schein, *Organizational Culture and Leadership* (2nd Edition) (Jossey Bass, San Francisco, 1997) p. 211.

environment; the dependence that officers place on each other to get the job done and provide for their personal safety; and the shared sense of awareness, within a police department, that it is not always possible to act in ways in which the public would expect one to act."[365]

It is the last phrase of Goldstein's characterisation that represents the challenge to police leaders - ensuring that they lead, manage and supervise a service or department in which everyone knows clearly and unequivocally how they must act and what the public rightly expects of them.

According the Schein, "the ability (for leaders) to perceive the limitations of one's own culture and to develop the culture adaptively is the essence and ultimate challenge of leadership".[366] Schein reminds us that to understand the culture is to understand the organisation. The culture (or subculture) has its own rituals, traditions, language and customs. Although it is a private world, some police officials delude themselves into thinking that outsiders cannot comprehend it. Yet travelling to any part of the world and watching the behaviour and listening to the speech of police officials can lead to the revelation of a negative culture, uncaring to the needs of citizens. Officials patrolling in view of the public or working in the public areas of police stations provide some clues by the following behaviours:

- Dirty or untidy dress and appearance revealing a lack of pride in appearance and corporate image.
- Macho 'Rambo' style posturing in public place. For example the ostentatious wielding of firearms (especially heavy calibre weapons), chewing gum, or wearing mirrored sunglasses.
- Avoiding eye contact or failing to acknowledge citizens seeking their assistance, never smiling, adopting a 'deadpan' image.
- Inequitable policing. Ignoring the needs of poor citizens and treating them with disregard or contempt, whilst deferring to the needs of the wealthier citizens.
- Rudeness and unhelpfulness to citizens' enquiries. Responding with comments such as, 'What are you telling me for?' or 'What am I supposed to do about it?' or commonly, 'It's got nothing to do with me'.
- Failing to help citizens in a professional manner. For example, by writing names, addresses and details of victims or complainants on torn strips of scrap paper instead of official documents.

---

[365] Goldenstein, *supra* note 274, pp. 29–30.
[366] Schein, *supra* note 364, p. 2.

VI:3

Viewed in isolation, any one of these behaviours may be interpreted as a simple lapse of discipline, temporary impatience, or lack of effective supervision. However, if these are typical and collective patterns of behaviour, they demonstrate an organisational culture in which the police see the public as the enemy, as an irritant. Police officials with these types of attitude treat everyone, criminals and honest citizens, with disregard and disrespect. They are displaying the symptoms of an unethical and unhealthy police culture without service standards. If officials behave like this towards their fellow citizens, it is likely that they pay scant regard to human rights.

It is important for police leaders who are committed to operating in a healthy and ethical policing environment (or think they already operate in such an environment) to stand back occasionally from their organisation and try to look at it afresh. Likewise it is important to look at the people who work for them and observe them in action. Or ask some citizens what they think about their police. They may not like what they see and learn, and decide it has to be changed.

(b) Individual and Group Resistance

Change can have a psychologically traumatising effect on sections of the workforce. Change can cause fear, uncertainty and anxiety as employees may feel that their jobs or role are under threat. They may believe that organisational change will lead to disruption and upheaval and their having to move from their workplace or even their place of residence. Typically, at times of impending change, rumours and speculation of negative consequences can exacerbate any prevailing fear or uncertainty. Employees may resist change for the following reasons:

- **Selective perception.** People create their own reality in which they may selectively impose their own myths and biases. For example, they may choose to believe that managers are not to be trusted and that change is intended to exploit the workforce to the advantage of management but to the detriment of ordinary employees.
- **Habit.** People may feel at ease and secure in their job and are accustomed to their surroundings and routines. They feel comfortable with their routine and making decisions in their working environment.
- **Inconvenience or loss of freedom.** The change may make life more difficult or reduce freedom of action or increase control and supervision.
- **Economic implications**. Employees may perceive a likely reduction in pay or other rewards as a consequence of change.
- **Security in the past**. At times of change, employees find a sense of security in the past. This tendency is especially strong in police cultures,

where officials place a strong emphasis on tradition and sentimentalise on 'how it was better in the old days.'
- **Fear of the unknown.** Change can create uncertainty and fear of the unknown, particularly new technology or working practices.[367]

Resistance to change is variable throughout the organisation. Some will resist change, others will not. Others will be undecided as to whether or not they wish to board the ship of change and sail into new waters. The following model of the attitude bell curve helps to illustrate some of the human dynamics of change:

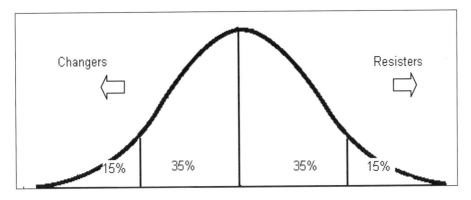

The Attitude Bell Curve

The bell curve, or curve of normal distribution, is based on the theory that human behaviour is predictable to the degree that it will produce a symmetrical normal curve of distribution or bell curve. Thus, using a simple example, 50 per cent of humans are of above average intelligence, with the most intelligent represented at one extreme end of the bell curve. The least intelligent appear increasingly at the opposite end of the bell curve. The majority of humans are of around average intelligence and appear in the largest area towards the centre of the bell curve.

Likewise, there is a similar probability of attitude to change within an organisation. A small percentage of perhaps five per cent will accept change immediately. A further ten per cent will quickly follow. These are the natural changers or innovators. The remaining 35 per cent of changers may require some persuasion to change but quickly rationalise that it is worth trying, or there is nothing to be gained by resisting change, or they may feel that it is own their career interests to do so.

---

[367] Mullins, *supra* note 361, pp. 732–733.

VI:3

The resisters are those who display some of the scepticism exemplified in various parts of the Mullins typology above. Eventually, the majority of resisters, perhaps 35 per cent will agree to change. Some of the 15 per cent of hard-core resisters may change. Other resisters will never change. It is the experience of many police managers that the total resisters may even leave the organisation rather than change.

The views of resisters should not be ignored. It is important that the organisation is open to all points of view and opinion. The real enemies of change programmes are those who dishonestly state that they support change but who, in reality and out of sight and hearing of managers, are secretly subverting the process. It is important for police leaders to identify subversives and counter their effects within the organisation.

(C) EFFECTIVE CHANGE MANAGEMENT

In times of impending crisis when members of the workforce lack direction, it is necessary for leaders to give orders and apply discipline to effect change and direction. This is wholly appropriate in a disciplined organisation when dealing with emergencies or crises, for example in situations of major public disorder where the police are compelled to use semi-military training and tactics to deal with violence from rioters. In less critical incidents, a coercive approach may also be necessary in order to provide a united front. For example, police officials cannot choose to disobey a lawful and ethical order simply because they prefer an alternative choice for action.

The real test of effective leadership is in situations of fundamental change, such as during the review and reform of a police organisation. If change is to be successful, strong and inspirational leadership is required, involving the participation of all members of the organisation. Strategies and methods to be used include:

- **Effective Communication.** An effective change programme requires the winning of hearts and minds. To win hearts, leaders need to be charismatic and appeal to the emotions of their workforce to increase their commitment and motivation.[368] To win minds, leaders must inform and educate members of the workforce of the details of proposed or impending change, and make them understand the purpose.[369] The process requires face-to-face meetings and briefing in which leaders address groups of employees and answer their questions in an open, honest and transparent way. All available forms of communication should be used including internal news bulletins,

---

[368] Haberfeld, *supra* note 347.
[369] *Ibid.*, p. 165.

390

newspapers and video. Language used should be simple and have impact. Management language should be avoided. Formal group briefings should be arranged at critical stages during the change process to keep employees informed of progress and to apprise them of developments.

- **Participation.** Employees of all ranks and grades should be involved and consulted during the change process. They should be invited to offer their own ideas at meetings, and a system should enable them to make written suggestions that should always be personally acknowledged. Leaders should 'walk and talk' – informally interacting with groups of employees to learn their ideas and gain their support for change. Irrespective of the outcome, all employees should be thanked for making suggestions and contributing ideas. Leaders should be seen to be participative and valuing the contributions of subordinates.

- **Support systems.** Leaders should have systems in place to assist employees who are likely to encounter or suffer difficulties as a consequence of change, for example having to move work or residential location. Effective human resource management systems, including the involvement of staff associations, can clarify uncertainty and provide solutions such as redeployment to a more favourable role or location.

- **Rewards systems**. Rewards systems such as promotion should recognise those who manifestly support change designed to meet the goals of the organisation.

(D) STRATEGIC PLANNING

Strategic planning is part of the continuum of change. It is a process that is undertaken in most modern and progressive police organisations around the world.

Strategic planning determines the direction of the police organisation to meet community needs and expectations. There are wider political and economic implications. In a financially straitened world, no government can allow police organisations to operate without being accountable for expenditure of public funds. Hence, in most developed countries, accountable police managers have to prove that they are able to deploy personnel and resources efficiently, effectively and economically in providing police services that satisfy the needs and expectations of both their political masters and the communities they serve. Policing performance and results have to be measured quantitatively and qualitatively, and not assessed on the basis of professional judgment alone. Accountability means that failure to meet agreed targets without any satisfactory excuse or explanation can result in censure or

VI:3

punishment. Ineffective leaders may find themselves moved to peripheral roles and replaced by individuals who are more dynamic and likely to succeed.

However, it is difficult to hold police leaders accountable for the results demanded of them if they are not provided with sufficient finances and resources. In some countries the government retains the police budget and senior police managers have no access to funds or control over expenditure. Poverty, state mismanagement and corruption blight many nations. Police leaders cannot be held fully accountable for failing to deliver policing services if the government will not or cannot provide finances to buy petrol or repair broken down patrol vehicles. In some countries in sub-Saharan Africa, sickness and mortality from the HIV/AIDS pandemic have resulted in police organizations being unable to recruit and train sufficient numbers of personnel to replace those dying of AIDS.[370] The consequence of being unable to provide efficient policing services must inevitably reduce the capacity to protect human rights, a role for which police officials are held accountable. It is for this reason that it remains essential for governments and international donors to prioritise policing as a component of good governance and protecting human rights.

Knowledge of strategic planning requires the study of specialist organisational management theory and practice. Space prevents it from being fully addressed in this volume. The practice of strategic planning requires experienced guidance from management practitioners or consultants. If none are available within a police organisation they can be located at universities, business management schools and tertiary colleges. A large private sector consultancy service exists, although police organisations that cannot afford consultancy services from the private sector may find that national or local government and non-governmental organisations can lend suitable members of their staff who are experienced practitioners in this field.

Police organisations around the world are organised in different ways according to historical development, social and cultural traditions, and legal and political systems. An increasing number of police organisations have routinely adopted the strategic planning process. Numerous examples include large national and metropolitan police organisations, and small police departments of just a few officials. Developing nations and post-conflict nations, as a consequence of support from donors, have been assisted in producing strategic plans as a requirement of good governance and the protection of human rights. Some police organisations have a degree of independence in preparing their strategic plans. Others are compelled to link plans to government policing goals. In other countries having more centralised, corporate styles of government it is government that may direct policing strategy and policy. Varying terminology is used and there are different

---

[370] L. Garrett, 'The Lesson of HIV Aids', *Foreign Affairs* (July/August 2005) p. 55.

approaches to strategic planning. Some strategic plans are referred to as policing plans or corporate plans. Notwithstanding these differences, the following provides a practical guide to some of the key tasks of strategic planning.

(a) Identifying the Issues

The chief of police (chief constable, director general, commissioner) should appoint a member of his top team (assistant chief constable, sub-director, assistant commissioner) to be the strategic coordinator of a strategic management team. The strategic coordinator's role is to chair strategic management team meetings, assign and coordinate tasks and actions, and set time deadlines for action. Importantly, the strategic coordinator should be accountable for the production and publishing of the overall plan and ensuring tasks and time deadlines are met.

There are advantages in including an external specialist consultant as a guide and facilitator on a strategic planning project. As they are independent and neutral, external consultants can view the organisation without bias or preconceived ideas. Additionally, because the consultant is not a member of any internal clique or under the discipline of the organisation, he or she can be honest and objective in their findings. This prevents the powerful leader, or the one who shouts loudest, from unfairly gaining an advantage over his or her peers.

The strategic management team should comprise middle and senior ranking police officials having specific operational or organisational skills. Each team member will be chairperson of a sub-committee or group that is tasked with examining or reviewing a specific department or activity of the organisation. These may include patrol policing, criminal investigation, traffic policing, community policing, human resources department, training department, finance department, and professional standards.

The groups should comprise six to ten members, including rank and file officials and civilian support staff, to ensure participation of every level of the organisation in the strategic review process. Innovation, creativity and the best ideas are not the preserve of senior rank. Involvement of all branches, ranks and grades of the organisation will reveal new ideas and solutions to problems. Additionally, members of staff associations should be included.

The PESTEL model can be used to scan the environment. External consultation should include the following:

- National government.

VI:3

- Local government or municipalities.

- Local political representatives/members of parliament elected to national government.

- Political representatives elected to local or regional government, for example mayors or councillors.

- Ordinary citizens, through police and community consultative groups or forums.

- Police officials and civilian support staff of all ranks and grades through direct communication and questionnaires.

- Other agencies and representative groups including women's and youth groups and members of the trades and business community.

- Monitoring the press and media.

A **SWOT** analysis is also an effective way of identifying the organisation's internal Strength and Weaknesses and the external Opportunities and Threats. A SWOT analysis can be achieved by answering the following questions:

Strengths:
What advantages does the organisation have?
Example situation: Excellent community relations.

What does the organisation do well?
Example situation: Training of personnel.

What relevant resources does the organisation have access to?
Example situation: Good communications network.

What do government and citizens see as the organisation's strengths?
Example situation: Effective leadership.

Weaknesses:
What could the organisation do to improve?
Example situation: Improve crime detection rates.

Where is the organisation not succeeding?

Example situation: Low percentage of recruits from ethnic minority communities.

What do government and citizens perceive as the organisation's weaknesses? Example situation: Failing to reduce public disorder.

Opportunities:
Where are the good opportunities facing the organisation?
Example situation: A new government having a strong law and order policy that is supportive of the police.

What technology, legislation or ideas could be used to the advantage of the organisation?
Example situation: New laws will increase powers of arrest for public disorder.

Threats:
What obstacles does the organisation face?
Example situation: The employment market is resulting in a shortfall of suitable recruits.

Is changing technology threatening the efficiency of the organisation?
Example situation: Computer technology is advancing to the extent that the organisation is facing technological obsolescence.[371]

(b) Creating a Mission Statement

The work of the various groups through consultation and analysis will identify the issues, and indicate the direction in which the organisation should be moving. Matters that are of greatest concern to the citizens will emerge and these should form the priorities of the mission statement and the strategic aims. Additionally, the desired values of the organisation (for example, its service ethos) will emerge. The mission statement of the Sierra Leone Police was examined in Chapter 1 of this part. Reproduced below is the mission statement and values of the New Zealand Police:

Police Mission
To serve the community by reducing the incidence and effects of crime, detecting and apprehending offenders, maintaining law and order and enhancing public safety.

---

[371] Mindtools, *SWOT Analysis*,
<www.mindtools.com/pages/article/newTMC_05.htm>, last visited September 2006.

VI:3

Police Values
- Maintain the highest level of integrity and professionalism.
- Respect individual rights and freedoms.
- Consult with, and be responsive to, the needs of the community.
- Uphold the rule of law.
- Consult with, and be responsive to, the needs, welfare and aspirations of all Police staff.
- Be culturally sensitive.
- Integrate Treaty of Waitangi principles and Maori values into policing.

The mission statement is short, concise and has impact. Its states succinctly what the organisation intends to do and what it can provide to citizens. Moreover, the values reflect the reality of the environment with regard to cultural sensitivity and the needs of indigenous people.[372]

(c) Setting Objectives and Strategies

The next phase of strategic planning is the setting of strategic aims or objectives and the strategies that will be adopted to attain those objectives. Objectives must be Specific, Measurable, Achievable, Relevant, and have a Timescale (**SMART**). The SMART model is explained as follows:

> **S**pecific: objectives should specify what it is intended to achieve. For example, to reduce offences of burglary.
> **M**easurable: objectives should include measurable targets. For example, to reduce burglary by 10%.
> **A**chievable: objectives must be achievable. For example, to reduce burglary by 100% would be unachievable.
> **R**ealistic: objectives must be realistic and relevant. For example it would not be realistic to expect to achieve objectives without sufficient resources.
> **T**ime: there must be a set timescale to achieve the measurable results. The timescale may be days, weeks, or months.

(d) Implementing the Plan

It is essential that strategies identify the number of personnel and resources required. In some instances, the police operational commander or departmental head may not

---

[372] New Zealand Police, *Police Strategic Plan to 2006*, <www.police.govt.nz/resources/2002/strategic-plan-to-2006/strategic-plan-to-2006.html>, last visited September 2006.

have sufficient resources to implement a plan. He or she may have to make a bid to the strategic management team for additional resources to be deployed from elsewhere. There may be competing bids from other police managers in which case the strategic management team will arbitrate on the allocation of additional resources. The plan is implemented by a series of strategies. Taking the example of burglary in the SMART model above, prevention and detection strategies could include:

- Analysing burglary offences and identifying 'hot spots' - places where they are most likely to occur and when they occur.

- Encouraging property owners to be more diligent in securing their premises and making then more difficult to break into.

- Increasing the number of police patrols at times when burglaries are known to occur.

- Intelligence gathering and targeting offenders.

Each objective must have a manager who is responsible for implementing the plan, monitoring its progress and ensuring it is measured and evaluated.

Due to the fact that all communities are different, they may have quite specific or localised problems that are not necessarily of national concern. It is important for police leaders to formulate and implement shorter-term local annual plans, that reflect the needs and expectations of the local communities they are responsible for policing. These should be formulated and measured in exactly the same way as national or regional plans.

(e) Measurement and Evaluation

The strategies must be measured to see if the desired results have been achieved. This can be a simple measure of results, for example, by the number of crimes detected or the percentage decrease in a particular classification of crime. The measure of performance can also be quantitative, using performance indicators. Performance indicators are more than statistics. They can reflect how the organisation is performing. For example they can indicate the annual numbers of arrests per 100 police officials, or the annual ratio of burglaries per 1000 houses, or crimes per 10,000 citizens. Within the human rights and ethical policing context performance indicators can provide a much more meaningful picture, for example the annual number of complaints from citizens per 100 police officials and the annual number of substantiated complaints per 100 police officials.

VI:3

Qualitative indicators such as public satisfaction surveys or questionnaires can provide information about the public perception of police performance. For example, is it very good, good, satisfactory or less than satisfactory?

Evaluation can assist organisations to learn. If the strategies have not been as successful as predicted then lessons have to be learned for the improvement of future plans and strategies. Plans must be debriefed in an open and honest way if learning is to be effective.

Finally, the need to set objectives that are realistic and achievable cannot be over-emphasised. The most common causes of failure are attempting to achieve too much without consideration of time and resource constraints, or setting targets that are too ambitious. When embarking on the strategic planning process for the first time, it is better to take a step at a time and set simple objectives and modest targets. All ranks should be involved in the planning process. Patrol officials and their supervisors should be encouraged to develop simple neighbourhood action plans designed to reduce or detect crime and other problems in communities. Thus personnel will gain confidence in practicing planning skills as they see the success of their efforts.

(f) Strategic Planning and Human Rights

Strategic planning has so far concentrated on examining the classical overall objectives of the police. These are described, for example, in the Objectives of the Police in the European Code of Police Ethics:

> "The main purposes of the police in a democratic society governed by the rule of law are:
> to maintain public tranquillity and law and order in society;
> to protect and respect the individual's fundamental rights and freedoms as enshrined, in particular, in the European Convention on Human Rights;
> to prevent and combat crime;
> to detect crime;
> to provide and service functions to the public."[373]

Quite properly, police strategic plans are always explicit in addressing crimes and other problems affecting communities. They usually contain a values based comment about being a 'caring' organisation and alluding to other such values. However, they are essentially about the practicalities of policing and police performance.

---

[373] European Code of Police Ethics, *supra* note 13.

Other strategies are required: namely, strategies that are concerned about ethical standards, conduct and behaviour – ensuring that policing standards are strengthened within the context of human rights. In December 1997, the Council of Europe's Directorate General of Human Rights launched a pan-European programme, 'Police and Human Rights 1997–2000'. During the programme a workshop of European police officials and representatives of governments and non-governmental organisations was convened. This produced a guide entitled 'Policing in a Democratic Society: Is your police service a human rights champion?'[374]

The guide provides a benchmark for auditing the organisation's performance in relation to human rights. It describes seven components of policing:

1. Basic values
2. Staff
3. Training
4. Management practice
5. Operational policing
6. Structure
7. Accountability

A statement that reflects what are generally agreed to be the principles of professional policing in a democratic society describes each component. The description is then followed by a set of tests that can determine whether or not a police organisation conforms to the principles. Finally, a set of performance indicators offers a means of checking or measuring each test. Thus, the organisation can be evaluated against the indicators. If the standards are not achieved, the various components of the guide could provide a ready made set of strategic objectives and indicators for change and training. A specimen example of each component description of principle, followed by samples of tests and relevant indicators is reproduced from the guide as follows:

---

[374] Council of Europe, Joint Informal Working Group on Police and Human Rights, *Policing in a Democratic Society: Is Your Police Service a Human Rights Champion?*, 2000.

Component 1: Basic Values		
Description	**Test**	**Indicators**
1. The Police Service should work to a service ethic which respects and promotes fundamental Human Rights	How are Human Rights made relevant to police work? To which extent are you and your officers aware of basic human rights?	a) -Human Rights are mentioned in: National police legislation Official policy statements Mission statements Codes of conduct behaviour Operational documents -Profile given in teaching/training -Line managers provide oral and effective commitment -Human Rights awareness is a performance criterion for promotion

Component 2: Staff		
Description	**Test**	**Indicators**
2. The Composition of an effective police service reflects the diversity of the population	How do recruitment practices take into consideration the various groups represented in society? What measures are in place to avoid discrimination?	a) Population/ethnic/gender representation Recruitment opportunities for various minority groups Percentage of diverse groups represented in the force Proactive recruitment and existence of outreach policies

Component 3: Training		
Description	**Test**	**Indicators**
2. Training integrates theory and practice	What importance is given to Human Rights during training?	a) Number of hours spent on national law and Human Rights Delivery of Human Rights modules, and included in wider training
	What kind of Human Rights law is included in the curriculum?	b) International and Regional Human Rights instruments
	How are community awareness, knowledge of other agencies and their attitudes to police work, and knowledge of the press integrated into training?	c) Profiles given to community awareness training Frequency of formal discussions between police officers and an identified community Joint training sessions between police and other agencies Human Rights considerations included in police logs Attitude of the police towards other public agencies such as press noted through stereotyping and comments

Component 4: Management Practice		
Description	**Test**	**Indicators**
4. Management practices must allow senior leaders to be aware of both good and poor practice through early warning systems, and be prepared to make changes quickly	What are the early warning benchmarks? How are they used?	a) Follow up the number and type of claims against the police Analysis of trends Negative and positive press and NGO reports breaches of discipline Internal reviews and investigations; incidents, type by type analysis of breaches of discipline Systematic feedback to line managers on accomplishment of operational objectives Incidence of stress indicators (in the community) Use of good and bad examples in initial and ongoing training and evaluation System of rewarding good practices

Component 5: Operational Policing		
Description	**Test**	**Indicators**
1. Consideration of the principles of Human Rights legislation should be contained within policy logs, operational procedures and reports, as well as tactical briefing and debriefing	To what extent are the principles of Human Rights incorporated in key operational documents and procedures. Are they used to ensure effective operational policing? How are the dilemmas and potential conflict situations addressed in the policy documents?	a) Inclusion of relevant documents Documents supervised Number of claims against police Successful defence of such claims Number of guilty pleas Incidence of persons detained subject to judicial disposal Incidents of deaths in custody Regular review of logs

Component 6: Structure		
Description	**Test**	**Indicators**
3. The structure integrates the police as part of society, government and the criminal justice system	In which ways is cooperation between the service and other agencies institutionalised?	a) Number of operational protocols Numbers of participation in public events Information campaigns Existence of a press and public relations service Protocol for information sharing Benchmarking against other services and partners

VI:3

Component 7: Accountability		
Description	**Test**	**Indicators**
1. Police accountability and transparency can be measured through internal and external review; through public, political and legal measures and can be reinforced through restitution or damages against the Service and individual officers. In terms of police activities.	To identify and constantly monitor professional and ethical standards, what independent means of monitoring police activities exist, other than those associated with formal complaints systems?	a) Audit trail of sensitive operations Lay visits to police stations Intrusive supervision in place Audit by data protection authorities

As the guide was formulated and written by operational police officials having years of practical policing experience from all parts of Europe, the guide has credibility amongst police practitioners. All the tests and indicators are realistic and achievable in any environment. Albeit the guide was produced by European police officials, it could be applied anywhere. There are many police organisations around the world that, for various reasons, are attempting to reform and improve their image and reputation, particularly following conflict. It is not easy for members of these organisations to change. Many are under a great deal of pressure as a consequence of scrutiny from national and international observers. Their conduct and behaviour in relation to human rights practices is being closely monitored. The guide is recommended to police leaders of these nations as a means of increasing knowledge of human rights and their application in everyday, operational policing. The guide can provide a benchmark for change, and can assist police leaders in making the successful transition towards becoming their nation's most effective defenders and champions of human rights.

Chapter 4. Professional Standards

Chapter 4 of Part I herein examined general aspects of police ethics and the provisions of two codes of behaviour, the United Nations Code of Conduct for Law Enforcement Officials and the European Code of Police Ethics. The purpose of this chapter is to define corruption within a police setting and examine how corruption, indiscipline and unethical conduct can manifest itself within police organisations. The chapter also examines ways of addressing corruption and maintaining ethical standards. Solutions include not only strategies, policies and procedures, but also leadership and supervision.

There is nothing within the Universal Declaration of Human Rights that directly expresses the right to live in a society free from corruption, although the delivery of the whole range of rights in the Declaration is dependent on the fact that government and other State agencies will be competent, not abuse their power and not engage in corrupt practices. Furthermore, article 28 states that: "Everyone is entitled to a social and international order in which the rights and freedoms set forth in this declaration can be fully realised." Police agencies that operate effectively, lawfully and humanely are essential elements in securing a social order for all human rights to be realised.

Article 5 of the United Nations Convention against Corruption[375] enjoins each State party to establish and promote effective practices aimed at the prevention of corruption. Further, the Convention requires countries to establish criminal and other offences to cover a wide range of acts of corruption, if these are not already crimes under domestic law. The Convention goes beyond previous instruments of this kind, criminalizing not only basic forms of corruption such as bribery and the embezzlement of public funds, but also trading in influence and the concealment and laundering of the proceeds of corruption. Offences committed in support of corruption, including money-laundering and obstructing justice are also dealt with.[376]

Article 7 of the Code of Conduct for Law Enforcement Officials requires that law enforcement officials shall not commit any act of corruption and that they shall rigorously oppose and combat all such acts. It further states that any act of corruption, in the same way as any other abuse of authority, is incompatible with the profession of law enforcement officials, and requires the law to be enforced fully

---

[375] United Nations Convention against Corruption, *supra* note 337.
[376] United Nations Office on Drugs and Crime, *United Nations Convention against Corruption*, <www.unodc.org/unodc/en/crime_convention_corruption.html>, last visited September 2006.

VI:4

with respect to any law enforcement official who commits an act of corruption. Article 21 of the European Code of Police Ethics requires effective measures to prevent and combat police corruption to be established in the police organisation at all levels. The commentary to this article describes a common understanding of police corruption as an abuse of being a police official.

Article 46 of the European Code of Police Ethics requires police personnel to oppose all forms of corruption within the police, and to inform superiors and other appropriate bodies of corruption within the police. The commentary to this article places a positive obligation upon a police official to avoid corrupt behaviour as an individual and to discourage it amongst colleagues. Furthermore, it requires police officials to carry out their duties in accordance with the law in an honest and impartial way, and not to allow their private interests to conflict with their position in the police.

(A) THE EFFECTS OF CORRUPTION

Transparency International is a leading non-governmental organisation researching corruption worldwide. Out of a total of 146 countries appearing in the 2005 Transparency International Perceptions Index, sixty were scored as suffering 'rampant' corruption.[377]

Corruption of police and other public officials has never been of greater concern. Organised crime, including international drug trafficking and people trafficking, now generates levels of wealth equivalent to national budgets. One authority estimates that of the eighty world's largest aggregate concentrations of wealth, ten are criminal enterprises.[378] In order to insure that their operations remain free from interference, crime enterprises have vast amounts of wealth at their disposal to make corrupt payments to law enforcement officials and members of the criminal justice system. Arguably corruption may be of such magnitude and sophistication that it may be impossible to detect fully, and to measure its actual presence within police organisations and other criminal justice institutions.

The findings of the 11th International Anti-Corruption Conference held in Seoul in May 2003 also identified customs administrations as being particularly vulnerable to

---

[377] Transparency International, *Transparency International Corruption Perceptions Index 2005*, *Press Release*, <www.transparency.org/cpi/2005/cpi2005_infocus.html>, last visited September 2006.
[378] Professor B. Rider, Presentation: *How to Define Corruption and the Functions of Corruption*, Conference on Combating Corruption, Goodenough College, London, November 2004.

corruption. The corrupt activities of customs officials damage legitimacy and the image of a nation, and are a major obstacle to international trade and development.

There is a link between corruption and human rights abuse, and there is little distinction between them. A police official abusing human rights is also likely to indulge in corruption. Police corruption is likely to prevent the effective investigation of abuses of human rights. Corruption has a corrosive effect on society. International donors and commercial organisations will not make loans or invest in countries with a reputation for corruption, thus adversely affecting the right to work of the poor and the economic development of nation states. According to the Transparency International Corruption Perceptions Index 2005, extensive research shows that foreign investment is lower in countries perceived to be corrupt, which further thwarts their chance to prosper. When countries improve governance and reduce corruption, they reap a 'development dividend' that, according to the World Bank Institute, can include improved child mortality rates, higher per capita income and greater literacy. [379]

(B) DEFINING POLICE CORRUPTION

McMullan's widely quoted definition of corruption of a public official, applicable to police, is that a public official is corrupt if he accepts money or money's worth for doing something he is under a duty to do anyway, that he is under a duty not to do, or to exercise a legitimate discretion for improper reasons.[380] Another definition, specifically of police corruption, is that of Kleinig who avers that police officials act corruptly when, in exercising or failing to exercise their authority, they act with the primary intention of furthering private or departmental/divisional advantage.[381]

Perhaps more than any other public servants, police officials have the opportunity to indulge in corrupt activities by the very nature of their work, their discretion and the authority they carry. Interacting with citizens, often unsupervised, provides opportunities for officials to betray the trust of their office and authority. In some countries the police are poorly paid and can rank as having the lowest status of any workers in society. Dealing regularly with criminal groups and feeling unappreciated by society as a whole can lead to a culture of cynicism and disregard of moral norms. Officials engaged in criminal investigation duties, particularly those having regular contact with informants, are especially vulnerable.

---

[379] Transparency International, *supra* note 377.
[380] M. McMullan, 'A Theory of Corruption', 9 *Sociological Review* (1961) pp. 183, 4.
[381] Kleinig, *supra* note 56, pp. 165, 6.

VI:4

Corruption, the breakdown of honesty, integrity and professional standards, can manifest itself in many ways. In literature on police corruption, a useful typology of corruption is that provided by Roebuck and Barker (1974). They identify nine types of police corruption.[382]

Type	Dimensions
Corruption of authority	When an officer receives some form of material gain by virtue of their position as a police officer without violating the law per se (e.g. free drinks, meals, services).
'Kickbacks'	Receipt of goods, services or money for referring business to particular individuals or companies.
Opportunistic theft	Stealing from arrestees (sometimes referred to as 'rolling'), from traffic accident victims, crime victims and the bodies or property of dead citizens.
'Shakedowns'	Acceptance of a bribe for not following through a criminal violation i.e. not making an arrest, filing a complaint or impounding property.
Protection of illegal activities	Police protection of those engaged in illegal activities (prostitution, drugs, pornography) enabling the business to continue operating.
'The fix'	Undermining criminal investigations or proceedings, or the 'loss' of traffic tickets.
Direct criminal activities	A police officer commits a crime against a person or property for personal gain.
Internal payoffs	Prerogatives available to police officers (holidays, shift allocations, promotion) are bought, bartered and sold.
'Flaking' or 'padding'	Planting of or adding to evidence.

Some observers attempt to distinguish between 'corruption' and 'crime'. In the former there may not be a victim. In the latter there usually is – for example the victim of a theft or assault. Nevertheless the effects and consequences are the same, the corrosion of the moral foundations, legitimacy and image of a police organisation.

---

[382] T. Newburn, *Understanding and Preventing Police Corruption: Lessons from the Literature*, *Police Research Series*, Paper 110, 1999, p.4, <www.homeoffice.gov.uk/rds/prgpdfs/fprs110.pdf#search=%22Understanding%20and%20Preventing%20Police%20Corruption%3A%20Lessons%20from%20the%20Literature%22>, last visited September 2006.

'Noble cause corruption' is examined in Part I, Chapter 4. It is useful here to re-examine this type of corruption within the context of police culture, and to consider how it manifests itself in practice. 'Noble cause corruption' is committed by police officials because they perceive that the rights of suspects are favoured over those of the police or the victims of crime. The criminal justice process is seen as an unreasonable obstacle to justice. Thus, police officials may use force to gain confessions, or fabricate evidence or confessions to ensure the conviction of those they believe to be guilty. This form of corruption is not normally committed for personal gain, but is based on the misguided assumption that police, even though they are using unlawful and corrupt means, are protecting citizens by taking criminals out of circulation. Although interpreted as crime rather than corruption, the operation of police death squads to eliminate 'troublesome' criminals, including street children, is an extreme manifestation of this phenomenon.

'Noble cause corruption' creates a policing paradox of crime. Intended to reduce crime, it actually increases crime. For example, a person suspected of one crime may become a victim of four serious crimes committed by police seeking to secure his or her conviction, namely unlawful imprisonment, assault to elicit a confession, perverting the course of justice by fabricating evidence, and perjury by giving false evidence under oath in court. All of these crimes are abuses of human rights.

Corruption often involves the engagement of two parties, the corruptor and the corrupted. The level of corruption in a nation's police is likely to be proportionate to the level of corruption within the wider society, its government and other institutions including other law enforcement agencies. Corruption can also occur within the judiciary, the legal profession and the wider criminal justice system. Levels of corruption may confirm the adages: 'the police reflect the standards of society as a whole,' and 'we deserve the police we get'. If corruption is endemic in society it is likely to be endemic in its police.

Ethical standards, especially those expressed in legal instruments, are self-evident to most police officials. Those standards derive from a moral base. As children, police officials were almost certainly taught the difference between right and wrong by their parents and teachers. Where police officials may encounter difficulty is in dealing with the moral dilemmas that confront them during the course of their work. Sometimes there are clear issues of right or wrong and a police official may knowingly choose to act wrongly. He or she may choose, sometimes through peer pressure, to act criminally, corruptly or unethically because he or she has been socialised in an organisation or group that either actively encourages or fails to discourage unethical or unacceptable standards of conduct and behaviour. For example, police managers and supervisors may not give clear guidance to their

VI:4

subordinates on ethical standards, or they may choose to ignore malpractices, or perhaps worse, encourage them either expressly or tacitly.

On occasions, police officials, having to make immediate and critical decisions in dangerous or uncertain situations, can only act reasonably and in good faith, and then hope that their decisions are later judged to be correct.

(C) ORGANISATIONAL RESPONSES AND IMAGE

The image of any police organisation has a powerful effect on the perceptions of citizens. Citizens can only have confidence in a police organisation that maintains high standards of integrity and conduct, and is free from corruption. Citizens of all classes and backgrounds should have equal access to policing. Furthermore they should have access to an effective and sympathetic response and redress if police standards fall short of their expectations.

In some traditional police organisations, particularly those having a military ethos, strong discipline is intended to secure obedience to orders and compliance with bureaucratic rules and regulations. Managers and supervisors generally rule by fear. Censures and punishments are directed essentially towards internal transgressions. Attitudes to the external environment, however, can be different. Although straightforward criminal acts of dishonesty such as theft or burglary by police officials may be dealt with expeditiously, complaints from citizens about other aspects of police officials' conduct can be seen by police leaders as a threat. Such complaints could bring the organisation into disrepute, a situation that police leaders seek to avoid. Complainants may be perceived as enemies of the police who only complain because they harbour anti-police attitudes. Therefore, rather than investigating a complaint, energy is focused on dissuading a victim or complainant from pursuing the matter. Consequently, a culture exists in which the real sin is not in the commission of an act of misconduct but in getting caught. It is felt that concealment is preferable to revealing the truth of what actually happened. A code of silence exists in which 'whistle-blowing' or cooperating with an investigation into police misconduct can lead to ostracism by work colleagues. In this type of organisational culture, police officials become highly skilled and proficient in not getting caught. Some supervisors ignore situations that they fear having to act upon. Others become so distanced and aloof from the lower ranks that they genuinely do not know what is happening at the operational level. In the latter circumstances small informal power groups can emerge, usually led by charismatic junior ranking police officials who create and impose the rules of their own subculture over those of the organisation.

Occasionally in police organisations, powerful and insidious delinquent subcultures emerge that are conducive to serious human rights abuses. Human rights abuses of this nature, for example the torture or ill-treatment of detainees to gain confessions, may become routine and remain undetected for many years. 'Noble cause corruption' is especially common in such circumstances. It is somewhat paradoxical that highly disciplined and authoritarian police organisations can harbour subcultures that are corrupt or brutal. These, if allowed to continue unrestrained or undetected, can lead to systematic human rights abuses and can ultimately bring the police and the whole of the authority and credibility of the criminal justice system into disrepute.

By contrast, leaders of progressive police organisations see complaints against police officials as opportunities to eliminate or alleviate the grievances of complainants, to provide redress to them, and to ensure that steps are taken to reduce the likelihood of cause for similar complaint occurring in the future. The paramount consideration is the complainant. As far as is reasonably possible, the police should ensure that the complainant is satisfied with the investigation, action and outcome resulting from their complaint. Awareness among the public that a police organisation responds promptly and effectively to complaints is more likely to enhance the image of that organisation. The complainant's perception of the police may actually improve following the resolution of his or her complaint. It may lead to that person recounting his or her positive experience to friends and contacts. Conversely, a grievance concerning treatment by the police, genuine or otherwise, may not be resolved because a citizen may feel that it is not worth making a complaint. The complainant may then harbour resentment, and in recounting their experience to friends and contacts is likely to damage the image of the police purely on the basis of hearsay. Hence, it is better for the police to receive a complaint, deal with it effectively, and have the opportunity to stop or limit any potential damage.

Interestingly, the transition of a police agency from a traditional organisational model to a more open, accountable and progressive model can result in an increase of reported and recorded complaints from citizens. This is because reporting and recording procedures become more efficient, and citizens develop greater confidence in police complaints and discipline systems and the responses of the police.

(D) STRATEGIES, SYSTEMS, POLICIES AND PRACTICES FOR SECURING AND MAINTAINING POLICE INTEGRITY

Progressive and ethical police agencies adopt a variety of means to prevent and respond to misconduct and corruption, and to investigate and resolve complaints against police officials. In other words, they put in place measures to secure

VI:4

effective, lawful, ethical and humane policing. Furthermore, pressures and influences are exerted from sources outside police agencies to the same ends. Herewith are some examples describing and calling for the foregoing.

(a) Donor Conditionality

Where donor aid is given to developing countries having poor human rights records or known for corruption, conditions can be imposed on the recipient governments. Although viewed as neo-colonialism in some quarters, it is essential that loans or aid should be conditional on the recipient governments' commitment to good governance, the protection of human rights and the eradication of corruption.

(b) Strong Leadership from Government

There must be strong leadership from government in committing itself to promoting a police organisation that provides a lead role model for society and its citizens. The protection of human rights of all citizens, honesty, integrity, fairness, equality and a strong service ethos should be the core values of the organisation.

The comments made under the section 'Pay and Conditions' in Chapter 2 of this part are reiterated here. Governments should ensure that the status of police officials compares favourably to other public sector professionals. The police should feel they are valued by society and receive adequate pay, food and shelter. As previously stated, a useful indicator is that their wages, at least at junior rank level, are higher than corresponding ranks in the armed forces.

(c) Strong Police Leadership

There must be firm commitments from police leaders to eradicate corruption and protect human rights. Police leaders must send out a corporate message that they demand and expect the highest levels of honesty, integrity and behaviour from all members of the organisation. They should encourage and develop a strong service ethos and a culture of excellence. Leaders should be transparent in demonstrating a preparedness to admit mistakes, and publicly reassure citizens of their determination to root out wrongdoing. Police leaders should have an 'open door' policy with the media in exposing corruption and police misconduct.

(d) An Oath of Allegiance

All police officials should be required to swear an oath of allegiance to protect human rights and to serve all citizens, regardless of economic status. These values should also be reflected in a public mission statement or vision of the police.

(e) **Independent Oversight of Policing**

There should be an independent civilian review board or commission comprising cross party political appointees and other non-partisan appointees to oversee and monitor policing functions and senior police appointments. They should ensure that matters of public concern are being addressed, and monitor professional standards including human rights and equal opportunities. The police should submit regular reports to the review board, providing details of the numbers of complaints against police made by citizens and the manner of investigation and disposal. Statistics and analyses of complaints and professional standards should be published on a regular basis for the information of the general public. Any trends showing improvement or deterioration of professional standards should be brought within the public domain. Measures should be taken to correct and improve professional standards including the design and delivery of training solutions.

(f) **Independent Investigation of Complaints Against the Police**

There should be a complaints investigation system independent of the police, for example an Inspector General function or an Independent Police Complaints Commission. There should be a coherent and fair system for hearing discipline charges against police officials and a flexible range of fair punishments, censures and remedies that may range from dismissal to counselling and training. Similarly, there should be a fair appeals system. As examined previously in Part I, Chapter 2, it is important that the rights of police officials are respected and that they are afforded a fair hearing as required in, for example, article 10 of the Universal Declaration of Human Rights.

There must be a coherent, effective and accessible system for citizens to make complaints against police. The system should be communicated to the citizenry, and police officials should be trained in how to receive and effectively process complaints for investigation. It must be possible for complaints to be made to a responsible police supervisor at all main police stations. Members of minority groups should have equal access to complaints systems and, if necessary, information on how to make complaints should be published in different languages to reflect the diversity of society.

In establishing police complaints and investigation systems to deal with corruption and other forms of indiscipline and misconduct it is important to recognise the need for balance. Some suspects make false or malicious complaints as a distraction to undermine the prosecution against them and to evade justice. Care must be taken to avoid the creation of a blame culture that results in 'police paranoia' and inhibits or deters officials from carrying out their lawful duties effectively. It is essential that

VI:4

corrupt officials are rooted out and punished. However, it also has to be recognised that policing, more than any other occupation, brings its practitioners into conflict with citizens. Unlike lawyers or judges, police officials who may be young and inexperienced, do not always have the luxury of time to deliberate on the legal niceties of their actions in dangerous or conflict situations. In making quick decisions, they inevitably make mistakes that result in complaints from citizens. It is essential to have transparent systems in place that correct mistakes promptly, ensure redress for citizens, provide reassurance and regain public trust.

Where, after investigation, it is established that allegations made against police officials are unfounded the European Code of Police Ethics states that public authorities shall support police personnel so affected.[383] The recommendation is not specific, but can be seen to imply that police officials may be supported in taking legal action against malicious and vexatious accusations.

Police officials suspected of human rights abuses, crime or corruption should be investigated and prosecuted in exactly the same way as ordinary citizens. When there is sufficient evidence, they should be prosecuted in the courts and not merely dismissed. Furthermore, aggrieved citizens should be able to seek redress from the police through the civil courts.

The reasons for complaints against the police should be analysed, and efforts should be made to reduce or eradicate them by, for example, effective supervision or training. This will lead to improved professional standards.

(g) Reducing the Burden of Proof in Discipline Cases

There can be difficulties in investigating and prosecuting police discipline cases involving wrongdoing that breaches internal discipline codes but, nevertheless, does not amount to a crime. Consideration can be given to reducing the burden of proof required to reach findings of guilt and conviction in such cases. For example, in countries that follow the Anglo-American legal rules, it may be possible to reduce the burden of proof from 'beyond reasonable doubt' that is required in criminal prosecutions to 'on the balance of probability' or the 'preponderance of the evidence' used in civil cases. Any decision to reduce the burden of proof has to be balanced against the rights of the accused and the nature of the charges.

---

[383] European Code of Police Ethics, *supra* note 13.

(h) A Code of Conduct

A code of conduct is a values-based, short, concise document written in simple language. It provides guidance on the ethical standards expected of all officials within the organisation. A code of conduct may operate independently or in parallel with national police laws and regulations. The latter are often concerned primarily with rules and serving the organisation rather than the citizen. They are seldom concerned with guidance about human rights or the provision of policing services to citizens. They are occasionally highly militaristic in style and content and resonant of a blame culture, whereas a code of conduct should promote a service culture. A busy operational official engaged on many tasks cannot reasonably be expected to remember all the discipline laws and regulations whereas a code of conduct is easier to learn and remember.

(i) Human Resource Management Systems

Human resource management systems, including reward and promotion systems, should assess police employees on the basis of effective performance, honesty, integrity and service to citizens. This enables the development and promotion of exemplary role models and high quality, ethical leadership.

(j) Training

Training in human rights and ethical policing should be thematic throughout the career of police officials, not just at the recruit training level. Newly trained police recruits should possess honesty and integrity, and have a strong sense of altruism and commitment to public service. Managers and supervisors should ensure that these values are maintained and not sullied by the negative values of others within the organisation. Newly trained recruits may be exposed to the 'canteen culture' to which the impressionable, or those wishing to conform to the norms of the group, are especially vulnerable during the early part of their career. Canteen culture is a symptom of Goldstein's sub-culture described in Chapter 3 of this part. It can be characterised by uninhibited macho banter between rank and file police officials when out of the earshot of the public and senior ranks. Participants use cynical or tasteless language and dark humour, expressing contempt for ordinary citizens and senior ranks. At worst, it is scornful of mainstream ethical standards and rules (for example the rights of suspects), and expresses language that may be sexist, homophobic, racist or violent. To prevent newly trained recruits from being exposed to this kind of behaviour, supervisors should closely monitor training in the workplace and confront inappropriate behaviour and language.

In some parts of the United Kingdom, strategies have been adopted to address the problem of the effects of canteen culture. Newly trained recruits are taught

VI:4

operational beat duties in the company of an assigned tutor who is an experienced patrol official selected not only for his or her professional ability, but also high standards of conduct and behaviour. The tutor system is intended to reduce the likelihood of recruits being drawn into the canteen culture. Over a period of time, it may help to improve and maintain individual and collective integrity within the organisation.

(k) Rights of Suspects and Detention Procedures

Managers and supervisors should ensure strict compliance with legal safeguards and procedures for the arrest and detention of suspects, including specified reasonable periods of detention for questioning and access to free legal advice. These safeguards and procedures were examined more closely in Parts III and IV herein.

(l) Supporting Victims and Witnesses

Successful prosecution of deviant police officials depends on victims, complainants and witnesses being available and willing to testify in court. Complaints systems should ensure that victims, complainants and witnesses are protected from threats or retribution from police officials or their associates. The police need to be supportive of the victims of police misconduct or crime, and keep them informed of the progress of investigations and prosecutions. Every assistance and reassurance should be afforded to complainants, victims and witnesses in the prosecution of police officials. It is essential that witnesses feel able to give evidence without fear of retribution. If witnesses or their relatives, friends, or associates are under threat of violence or intimidation, measures should be taken to ensure their protection, including removal to a safe environment under witness protection arrangements. The police should ensure that victims' rights are recognised and observed, and they should facilitate appropriate restitution, compensation or redress.

(m) Monitoring of Prosecution Files

Senior investigators and prosecutors should monitor prosecution files, and be satisfied that accused persons have been dealt with fairly and in accordance with the law and legal procedures. Police misconduct during investigations can not only affect accused people and suspects adversely and lead to miscarriages of justice; it can undermine the successful prosecution of those who should be found guilty of their crimes.

(n) Confidential Informant Handling Procedures

Confidential informants are an essential tool for effective crime prevention and investigation. However, informants are often not trustworthy or reliable. For example, they may operate as agent provocateurs in order to gain payment for information about crimes they have incited. Police officials are also in danger of being corrupted through their involvement with informants. For example, they may encourage informants to incite crime that would otherwise not have been committed, or they may become corrupted by procuring or retaining monies intended for the payment of informants.

In addition to ethical issues relating to the use of informants, there is another overriding human rights issue relating to the protection of life of informants who may be at risk if their activities are exposed. For all these reasons, it is essential for police leaders to establish and enforce clear and rigorous policy, rules and procedures for the engaging and managing of confidential informants. The United Nations human rights training manual for law enforcement recommends the following:

a. Only one police official should be responsible for 'handling' a confidential informant - i.e. conducting the relationship with the informant and carrying out all transactions with him or her. This arrangement makes one identifiable police official accountable for all transactions with the informant.

b. While the identity of a confidential informant must remain generally secret, for the protection of the police official dealing with the informant and for the protection of the informant, an official record should be kept showing the identity of the informant and the police official responsible for liasing with him or her. The record should be accessible to only one specific individual in the command structure of the police agency.

c. The activities of a confidential informant should be strictly monitored. It is often the case that, not only is the informant aware of the planning of a proposed crime, but he or she may also be involved in that planning and be regarded as a potential participant in its execution. The general rule should be that this is not acceptable, because it will mean, almost inevitably, that the informant will be committing a criminal act.

d. Very occasionally, the proposed criminal activity is of such a magnitude, and the non-participation of the informant will create such a danger to him or her, that the informant may have to take part in the criminal activity. Condoning any criminal activity, including that of confidential informants, raises very serious legal and ethical issues. Any decision to do so should be taken at the highest level within a police organisation, and only after full consultation with prosecuting authorities. Such decisions and consultation can take place on a case-by-case basis. No general immunity must ever be granted.

VI:4

    e.   Financial rewards to confidential informants for the information they provide should not be excessive. Payments should not constitute a big inducement to provide information otherwise they may tempt informants to encourage people to commit crime.

    f.   Payments to confidential informants should be strictly controlled through rigorous accounting procedures and supervision. The official making the decision on payment should be unaware of the identity of the informant. The decision maker does need to know the details of the crime and the nature of the information provided.[384]

The effective operation of these procedures may be critical to effective prosecutions. Consequently, lawyers and members of the judiciary must be aware of police procedures for handling confidential informants. They should also be aware of their responsibility for the safety of informants and ensuring that the identity of informants remains confidential.

(o) Gratuities and Gifts

All personnel should be made aware of what is acceptable in terms of gifts, gratuities and discounts, access to places of public entertainment and sporting venues, and free use of public transport systems. Some totally honest police officials may regard modest 'perks' as being perfectly legitimate. However, such practices can be insidiously corrupt. It is not just the duty of individual police officials to avoid corruption resulting from gratuities and gifts, but for leaders of police organisations to set an example and lay down firm guidelines as to what is acceptable.

A report on police integrity published in the United Kingdom by the Inspectorate of Constabulary opposes and actively discourages the acceptance of gratuities and gifts.[385] The Report summarises four convincing arguments against accepting such favours:

    1.   Even the smallest gift inevitably creates a sense of obligation if it becomes regularised.

    2.   Those who accept gratuities find themselves on a 'slippery slope' where the temptation often becomes imperceptibly greater and where refusal is increasingly difficult.

---

[384] Office of the United Nations High Commissioner for Human Rights, *supra* note 353.

[385] Her Majesty's Inspectorate of Constabulary, Report: *Police Integrity*, London, 1999, p. 4.

3. Although many officers may be able to exercise proper judgement about what it is reasonable to accept, not all can. It is more sensible for a police agency, therefore, to remove temptation altogether.
4. Businesses which offer gratuities to police officers do so because they wish either to encourage a greater police presence in the vicinity of their business, or they wish to maximise the chance that they will receive a positive response should they require a police presence. They are, in essence, purchasing preferential treatment.

(p) Integrity Testing

In addition to the rigorous investigation of police officials suspected of crime or corruption, there should be other proactive measures to prevent or investigate corruption. This may include integrity testing and the use of a confidential reporting system such as a special telephone line. Integrity testing can include dip-sampling of bank accounts, particularly of organised crime investigators and informant handlers who may be exposed to the temptation of receiving corrupt payments from criminals. The report on police integrity by the Inspectorate of Constabulary, referred to under the previous subheading, endorses the use of non-targeted or random testing. This would entail, for example, an undercover police official posing as a member of the public and handing over valuable property or drugs that it is unlawful to possess to a police official on the pretext that these items had been found. Whether or not the police official deals with such items in accordance with proper procedures is then monitored. Similarly an undercover police official can be used to request confidential information from a police official for payment of a financial reward.[386]

It is important to emphasise here that officials who are prepared to provide information about corrupt activities of colleagues should not be left isolated, but should receive proper support and counselling services from the organisation. Staff associations also have an important part to play in the counselling process.

(q) Special Anti-corruption Measures

Where high levels of corruption exist, an independent specialist police and legal team should be established to investigate, detect and prosecute offenders. Hong Kong provides an example. The Independent Commission against Corruption in Hong Kong was established in 1974. At that time corruption was widespread in the public sector and government. It was particularly serious in the Royal Hong Kong Police. Corrupt police officials covered up vice, gambling and drug activities. Social

---

[386] *Ibid.*, p. 58.

VI:4

law and order was under threat, and many in the community had fallen victims to corruption. The Commission adopted a three-pronged approach of investigation, prevention and education to fight corruption.[387]

(r) **Effective Supervision**

Experienced officials who investigate police corruption and other forms of police misbehaviour insist that effective supervision is the best guarantee of preventing misconduct and lapses in professional standards. Unfortunately, whereas senior managers may receive expensive command training, supervisor training in many police agencies is seriously neglected. Junior managers and supervisors do not always receive the levels of training they require and yet they carry the brunt of blame when problems occur. To be held truly responsible, junior managers and supervisors must be given the necessary training and support. They are at the front line of policing, and as role models they can ensure the professionalism and standards of behaviour expected of themselves and their subordinates.

The following chapter examines how the structure, roles and responsibilities of police organisations can be clearly delineated and defined to assist managers and supervisors to be more effective in maintaining professional and ethical standards.

---

[387] Independent Commission against Corruption, *Information*, <www.icac.org.hk/eng/main/>, last visited September 2006.

Chapter 5. The Effective Organisation

(A) INTRODUCTION

The previous chapters have examined how staff development, managing the process of change, and establishing effective strategies for preventing and dealing with corruption and police misconduct can create the foundations of an accountable police organisation able to protect human rights and promote an ethos of service excellence. However, effective management practices and a competent workforce alone cannot provide for maximum organisational effectiveness. The organisation should have a clearly defined structure and be able to direct and deliver effective services in accordance with a strategic vision. It should have clear and direct lines of communication and coherent systems of command and control. The structure of the organisation and the defined roles and responsibilities of managers and supervisors need to be integrated so that all functions and departments cooperate with each other and provide a unity of purpose that serves the needs of the state and its citizens.

In promoting the need for accountability, the European Code of Police Ethics recommends that, "the police organisation shall provide for a clear chain of command within the police. It should always be possible to determine which superior is ultimately responsibly for the acts or omissions of police personnel."[388] The following sections of this chapter examine how this can be achieved. First it is helpful to examine the effects and consequences of management neglect, lack of direction and lack of clarity of purpose.

(B) ORGANISATIONS IN CRISIS

The author's involvement in police reform and development projects around the world has provided the opportunity to engage with police officials from many nations. These include nations in transition following the collapse of communism, nations attempting to achieve peace and security following civil war, and developing countries attempting to reform and modernise their police organisations. Observation and research, including discussions with operational police officials of all ranks, has revealed that inefficient practices and wasteful use of resources are widespread in some countries. It is often in the less wealthy nations where government finances are limited and the need for careful expenditure is critical that these inefficient and wasteful practices appear to be most prevalent. The most common are characterised as follows:

---

[388] European Code of Police Ethics, *supra* note 13.

VI:5

(a) Lack of integration of personnel engaged on general uniform patrol duties

Some police leaders fail to recognise and promote the value and worth of police officials deployed to general uniform patrol duties who represent the majority of personnel in most police organisations. Some senior officials will not even communicate directly with a lower rank except through a supervisor. Patrol officials are the front-line of policing, having routine day-to-day contact with citizens at every level of society. Notwithstanding the importance of this role, in many organisations it is represented or perceived as the lowest level of policing, and of lesser importance and status when compared with specialist roles such as criminal investigation or traffic policing. General patrol policing is not seen as exciting or glamorous. Consequently, more able officials are quickly transferred to specialist branches or other elite units. Managers use redeployment to general patrol duties as a form of punishment, and as a 'dumping ground' for the less able. Patrol officials become demoralised and complain that they are the forgotten members of the organisation.

A demoralised and marginalized section of the workforce that believes it is neglected and has little status is more likely to have an uncaring attitude towards citizens, behave corruptly and abuse human rights. Police leaders should recognise and praise general uniform police patrol duties as having the highest value and worth. Police leaders should declare that general uniform police duties represent the foundation of policing and carry the image of the organisation. They fulfil the most important role of providing a high quality service to citizens. Most other policing functions are there to support professional patrol officials in their important tasks. The climate should be such that more able officials will aspire to become effective patrol officials as an essential part of their career development.

(b) Lack of direction and purpose

Police managers and supervisors fail to deploy uniform general patrol officials in stimulating and interesting work that addresses the problems affecting the community. Whilst managers and supervisors complain about lack of resources, junior ranking police officials including patrol officials are to be found idling around police stations or at fixed roadblocks without any direction or purpose. Unnecessarily large groups of officials are posted to static points outside the entrances to police stations, ostensibly on forms of security duty.

Many officials are not tasked before being deployed, and patrol in an aimless and undirected way. Managers and supervisors should brief patrol officials, and allocate them tasks and duties that improve the policing of the community and the quality of life of its citizens.

(c) **Resistance to change**

The reasons for resistance to change were examined in Chapter 3 of this part. It is especially common in police organisations making the transition from a military or paramilitary model to a civilian model. Moving from a relatively comfortable environment of maintaining the status quo into a performance culture where managers are accountable is a difficult transition and one that many are reluctant to make. Change must be led from the very top of the organisation. The executive leaders of a police organisation should stimulate, inspire and lead change. Senior managers will then do likewise.

(d) **Managers failing to manage**

In many countries, middle and senior managers neglect management tasks and concentrate most of their time and effort on supervising junior ranks. For example, by working in company with patrol officials and attending minor incidents, and bypassing the supervisory level when giving instructions or decisions. When asked why they do this, they explain that they have no confidence in the competence of supervisory ranks. There may be some justification in this belief if supervisors have not been trained to perform their duties. Alternatively, it is possible that another reason for this practice is an inability to delegate. At the individual level, delegation is the process of entrusting authority and responsibility to others.[389] Furthermore, it is apparent that many police leaders have no concept of managing personnel and resources. They see themselves as having only a role in operational policing. When they take on the role of supervisors, the actual supervisors fail to develop in competence, levels of performance decline and police leaders find themselves with a dearth of talent.

A consequence of inadequate training, inefficient management and supervision practices, and resistance to change is that the organisation eventually reaches crisis. Managers who are involving themselves in the minutiae of operational police work are dissipating their energy in so many directions that management tasks are neglected or left incomplete. For example, very commonly, the vehicle fleet is not managed and maintained. As vehicles and other equipment break down, the organisation is unable to provide an efficient service. Meanwhile, with no further funding available because of limited budgets, police leaders try to improvise, cannibalising vehicles for spare parts and begging resources from the community. Lethargy sets in. Eventually, a dispirited and demoralised organisation reaches a point of inertia.

---

[389] Mullins, *supra* note 361, p. 249.

VI:5

The scenario of the organisation in crisis has serious implications for human rights. An inert organisation is unlikely to have the necessary checks in place to prevent corruption, and to ensure ethical conduct and the effective protection of the human rights of citizens.

(C) CREATING THE EFFECTIVE ORGANISATION

(a) An International Perspective

There are a variety of structures of police organisations and styles and methods of policing around the world. Some are highly centralised and military in style. Classic models of this style include the Gendarmerie of France, the Carabineros of Chile and the Civil Guard of Spain. These types of national police organisations typically operate under the direct control of the minister of interior or (as in France) minister of defence, and have a primary role in maintaining national security. Some provide a military reserve.

In many countries, multi-tiered policing has evolved with national, local and municipal police organisations, each having their own separate structure and organisation. Sometimes, separate police organisations are responsible solely for public order, criminal investigation or financial crime. Municipalities may employ mayor's police with limited authority, for example, for the enforcement of local ordnances and minor offences.

Other policing systems are less centralised. For example, the United Kingdom does not have a national police force. It has a number of geographically based semi-autonomous forces, each governed by means of a power sharing arrangement between national and local government. There is a significant degree of community involvement and civic oversight. During its early history, the United States of America adopted aspects of the British police and legal systems but later became even more decentralised in policing terms. In addition to federal and state law enforcement organisations, numerous autonomous law enforcement agencies of diverse size and organisation serve the citizens of cities, towns and individual communities throughout that country.

The structure and style of law enforcement agencies may be linked to the culture and historical development of nation states. Some countries have strong military traditions that are reflected in the organisation of the police, its rank structure, discipline and drill. Police officials may be accommodated in barracks. Other nations prefer police officials to be less military in style and appearance. They may be unarmed whilst on routine patrol. The police are more understated, less intimidating and more approachable in image, residing amongst the community they work in. They operate within a service ethos.

It would be unrealistic to expect all police organisations to be the same. Nor should they be. Police structures may be appropriate and measured responses to the environment. An armed police having a military structure and style may better serve a nation during periods when it is confronted with internal armed conflict, terrorism or banditry. In societies where violence is endemic, this style of policing may be totally congruent with the wishes and expectations of the citizens.

(b) The Traditional Structure

The traditional police organisation is that of a steep pyramid shaped hierarchy employing uniformed, often armed personnel, with military or military style ranks and insignias. Senior police officials hold a high degree of authority over subordinates. Communication is exclusively 'top-down' by way of commands or orders passed down the chain of command. Orders must be obeyed. There is little interaction between the ranks. The institutional ethos is that of resistance to change and suspicion of new ideas or creativity. Subordinates are not expected to be creative or challenging.[390] They are not trusted to act independently. There is an assumption that knowledge is the sole preserve of rank. The style of policing is essentially reactive, only responding to incidents when they occur, with little effort devoted to prevention or problem solving. The organisation is essentially self-serving, the focus and energy being internal and directed towards maintaining the status quo, and the needs of the organisation. This type of police organisation still exists in many parts of the world.

(c) A Structure for Change

In many countries there has been a significant shift in direction from the traditional model. Even in police agencies that have a military structure and ranks and an authoritarian tradition, police leaders are increasingly delivering service-oriented policing. The realities of the global economy have forced governments to impose greater demands on police leaders for increased financial accountability and performance. The traditional organisational police model, with its rigid structures and inflexible management systems, is unable to respond to the demands for change. Consequently police leaders have been required to restructure and reform their organisations into progressive models that are able to respond.

---

[390] L. S. Miller and K. M. Hess, *The Police in the Community: Strategies for the 21st Century* (3rd Edition) (Wadsworth, California, 2002) p. 29.

VI:5

There has been a move away from the military model and an adoption of systems and practices from the business world. As is seen in many commercial organisations there has been a flattening of organisational structures, reducing layers of bureaucracy, and eliminating and/or reducing the number of senior ranks. Consequently, levels of responsibility and decision-making are pushed downwards. Middle managers and supervisors are trusted to carry out a wider range of management responsibilities without being controlled and supervised from above.[391] Patrol officials and other junior ranks are similarly trusted, and expected, to work with the minimum of supervision. Organisational flattening has been accompanied by decentralisation to local geographical command level. The empowerment of local commanders and the movement of the decision-making process from the centre to the local level are intended to enable better informed decisions that can be implemented more promptly in response to the identified needs of the community.

Flattening the organisational structure and reducing the numbers of senior ranks provides additional finances that allow the deployment of more operational officials to enhance service provision to citizens. Police posts that do not require police skills (for example, those of typists or telephone switchboard operators) can be filled with non-police support personnel on lesser remuneration, thus releasing police personnel for operational deployment.

An example of the flattening process is that adopted during the reform of the Sierra Leone Police following the end of the civil war. The Sierra Leone Police had become a top-heavy, steeply pyramidal bureaucracy overloaded with twenty-one ranks. Consequently, supervisors and managers habitually abrogated their responsibilities, passing everything upwards for decision-making. The decision-making and communications processes became blocked. Corruption was rife. Further inefficiencies existed because of duplication of roles and responsibilities. For example, identical duties were performed by the five ranks of constable, corporal, sergeant, sergeant major and sub-inspector. By 2003 the numbers of ranks had been reduced to nine, and modern police management methods introduced. An important lesson learned during the reform of the Sierra Leone Police was the need to consider the morale of personnel who may resent loss of rank and consequent perceived loss of status. It is better, as far as possible, to eliminate and reduce police ranks gradually and incrementally through natural wastage (i.e. resignations and retirements).[392]

---

[391] *Ibid.*, pp. 30–32.
[392] Interview with Keith Biddle, Inspector General of Police, Sierra Leone Police, 1999-2003, Cheshire, England, 13 April 2005.

Organisational flattening, decentralisation and pushing the decision making processes downwards has resulted in more interaction between ranks and enabled 'bottom-up' as well as 'top-down' communication of ideas and solutions. Sharing ideas has resulted in a strategic problem-solving approach towards decision-making. The need for greater professionalism has reduced the importance and status of rank. Role is increasingly more important, and the intrinsic skills, knowledge and professionalism of the individual holding that role. Unlike the traditional model, the focus has become external and has shifted from the needs of the organisation to the needs and expectations of the citizen.

(d) A Structure for Service

As the traditional policing model is essentially reactive, operational rank and file officials are often deployed without any clear direction or tasks. This type of work has the potential for extreme boredom. The more industrious will direct their energy towards performing tasks that they enjoy. For example, they may derive work satisfaction from issuing traffic tickets; therefore choosing to ignore the real concerns of citizens, they concentrate on traffic violations and ignore other types of offences. This type of behaviour is very common in traditional police organisations. It exemplifies an unaccountable organisation in which police officials choose to perform only the tasks they enjoy, or that they themselves think or believe the public require. They do not direct their main energies to the tasks that they should be doing, meeting the real needs and expectations of the citizens or the community. Without motivation from supervisors, others will choose to idle their time and do nothing. It is within this milieu that freedom allows the bored or the idle to turn to corruption.

There is a further problem with the reactive model of policing. In directing personnel and resources, some police leaders may be blind to the needs of the citizens and decide that they know what is best for communities. This can lead to conflict between police and community as police leaders fail to identify or misinterpret the needs and expectations of citizens. In England in the early 1980s, policing that did not take account of the sensitivities of citizens from minority groups led to major rioting and devastation in many cities.

In contrast to those operating in accordance with the traditional model, modern progressive police organisations are pro-active. As indicated in Chapter 3 of this part, strategic planning takes account of the needs and expectations of citizens. Community policing, considered in Chapter 3 of Part V herein, employs proactive styles and methods. Community policing is directed towards the problems and issues that are identified as being of prime concern to citizens, doing what needs to be done. Unlike the case with traditional policing, energy and creativity are concentrated on problem solving and effective and targeted policing. The energies of

VI:5

operational police officials are focused on meeting objectives and time deadlines. Consequently, they have little spare or undirected time to become idle or bored, or tempted into bad habits that can lead to misconduct.

Progressive police organisations should have a strong service ethos that can undermine the possible emergence of negative sub-cultures, misconduct or unethical behaviour. As indicated in Chapter 2 of this part, human resource management systems should not only assess and reward individuals on the basis of professional performance, but also on their integrity and ethical standards. The more participative style of management and supervision in progressive police organisations results in managers and supervisors being closer to operational policing and working more closely with subordinates. This style of management, and more effective communication, enables problems of discipline, either internally or affecting citizens, to be more quickly identified and resolved.

A clearly defined organisational structure facilitates more effective service delivery and police operations. It also enables clarity of functions, roles and responsibilities. The Council of Europe guidance document, 'Policing in a Democratic Society: Is your police service a human rights champion?' examined in Chapter 3 of this part, advises that the service structure should support the objectives of the service in accordance with the fundamental principles of human rights legislation. By this means, good police practice can be encouraged within an environment where delivery of policing can be constantly improved. Furthermore, the structure should be tested against its ability to encourage better practice at each level of the service. Both internal and external bodies need to be established to evaluate the quality of policing delivered.[393]

The following organisational chart provides a structure that is able to meet the objectives of the service:

---

[393] Council of Europe, Joint Informal Working Group on Police and Human Rights, *supra* note 374, p. 39.

428

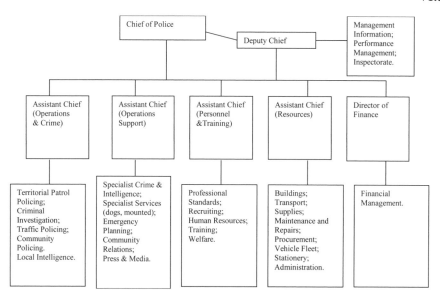

(e) Analysing the Structure

In the above model, there is a clear division of functions, roles and responsibilities. Each group of related roles is under the command of an assistant chief of police (equating to an assistant commissioner, assistant chief constable or sub-director). There is a clear rationale behind the structure. As indicated in Chapter 2 of Part I herein, the main functions of a police organisation are not only to prevent and detect crime but also to assist people who are experiencing some kind of personal emergency. General uniform patrol officials probably spend most of their time on the latter activity. Hence, policing is seen not only as law enforcement but also as the provision of a diverse range of activities that are described collectively as 'service'. In order to reflect more accurately the role and image of the police it is increasingly becoming practice in many parts of the world to abandon the terminology 'police force' in favour of 'police service'.

Service is delivered predominantly to citizens at the territorial or area command level. The territorial command area may be referred to variously around the world in such terms as department, delegation, division, precinct or basic command unit. The majority of police officials are deployed to the operational level to fulfil the mainstream roles of general uniform patrol duties, attending to emergencies, crimes and other incidents, responding to calls for assistance from the public, community policing, criminal investigation and traffic policing. These personnel are the 'deliverers'.

429

VI:5

The Operations Support function provides organisation-wide support for operational policing and special operations. These are the 'supporters' of operational policing. Some operational support functions are so specialised or so small that they have a limited scale of operations. It would be inefficient to deploy them to territorial command areas, as their effect would become fragmented. Therefore, they are held at the central level and if required can provide support to the territorial level. Examples of these types of functions might include VIP protection or commercial fraud investigations.

Finally, any police organisation requires equipment, financial management, human resource management, training, procurement and maintenance of vehicles and buildings. These are the 'providers' for operational policing and ancillary functions.

The benefit of this structure is that there is clarity of functions and roles. Importantly, the structure enables police leaders in command of territorial policing to provide policing services without being diverted by unnecessary involvement in the bureaucracy of support or procurement functions. They are able to focus all their energy on their strategic role of managing their personnel and resources efficiently and effectively. As and when required, they are able to bid for specialist services, equipment and finance through the planning and budget processes.

All members of the organisation must protect human rights and comply with equal opportunities legislation and procedures. Police leaders should be held accountable for ensuring that their subordinates are aware of these responsibilities, and that they comply with them. The Inspectorate function, which is aligned alongside the office of the deputy chief of police, fulfils an important role in regularly inspecting to ensure that members of the workforce are operating efficiently and effectively in support of organisational goals. The deputy chief of police should task the inspectorate team with making regular inspections of all functions and departments within the organisation to ensure compliance with human rights and equal opportunities standards, all relevant legislation, and good practice for policing diversity.

The positioning of the inspectorate function under the direction of the deputy chief of police and not under direct line command of other functional assistant chiefs of police helps to ensure that the inspectorate team can operate under a higher authority than functional heads. Therefore, members of the inspectorate team, who will be of junior rank to functional heads, are less likely to be put under pressure by senior police officials. They can maintain independence and produce inspection reports that are honest, accurate and objective without the fear of threat or repercussion from senior officials who may disagree with their findings. In addition to identifying weaknesses, the inspectorate role is able to identify and promote examples of good practice in relation to human rights, equal opportunities and policing diversity.

(D) LEADERSHIP, MANAGEMENT AND SUPERVISION

(a) Defining Leadership

Police officials perhaps have a clearer understanding of the concept and context of 'leader' and 'leadership' than workers in the business or commercial world. Leadership is not necessarily about rank. Policing is heroic. It is an occupation whose practitioners are faced routinely with physical danger and sometimes the tragic sacrifice of life for the protection of citizens. Policing is about fighting crime. It is about good versus evil, the themes of fiction, dramatic films and the lifeblood of the media. Policing is also about responding to emergencies and disasters where police officials unhesitatingly and unselfishly risk their own life and limb for others. It is hardly surprising, therefore, that leaders emerge from this kind of occupation. It has nothing to do with rank. Holders of subordinate ranks often operate as leaders. It is the junior ranking official who, without concern for his or her own safety, disarms a dangerous armed criminal or, whilst others merely watch helplessly, takes the initiative to rescue a person from drowning. A definition of police leadership that describes these kinds of actions is, "the ability to make a split-second decision and take control of a potentially high-voltage situation that evolves on the street".[394]

(b) The Manager as a Leader

The words 'manager' and 'leader' are used interchangeably throughout these chapters. They are intended to have the same meaning. A police manager should not only possess competent technical skills, but also the attributes of leadership. It is not appropriate to explore theories of leadership in any great detail in this book and, in any event, they are dealt with expertly elsewhere. [Ref Footnote: *E.g. ibid.*] However, some management and academic references and models have a resonance for policing. For example, management may arguably be viewed more in terms of the technical processes of planning, organising, directing and controlling the activities of subordinate staff. Leadership, however, is more concerned with attention to communicating with, motivating, encouraging and involving people.[395] Another way of expressing the distinction is through the notion that leaders create and change cultures, whilst managers and administrators live within them.[396]

---

[394] Haberfeld, *supra* note 347, p. 6.
[395] Mullins, *supra* note 361, p. 248.
[396] Schein, *supra* note 364, p. 5.

VI:5

Importantly, where a police official aspires to be a leader, he or she must have the confidence and charisma to inspire others to follow. However, as examined in Chapter 4 of this part, corrupt and unethical leaders can also be charismatic and create an unhealthy organisational culture. Additionally, informal leaders can arise and create and sustain sub-cultures that are corrupt and result in police officials abusing human rights. Therefore, effective leadership must have moral and ethical dimensions. Leaders must be able to guide subordinates who are confronted not only with technical and legal problems, but also with behavioural issues and moral dilemmas. Leaders can test themselves and others against a model that incorporates five character traits of leadership known as the five I's:

1. *Integrity* refers to being able to do the right thing without anybody telling you what to do, and being able to judge right from wrong, good from bad. Leaders with integrity are more competent to judge others fairly and impartially.
2. *Intellect* is often compared to credibility, since it is important that the public understand that the role of a police leader has become increasingly complex and challenging. It is important to develop a strong intellect for leadership.
3. *Industry* is an important trait for a police leader to possess since it sets an example of how the organisation is supposed to be run and at what pace.
4. *Initiative* refers to people who make things happen. Action is an important component of this character trait.
5. *Impact* is when an official shows confidence, competence, and a positive attitude, and makes a difference when he or she arrives at the scene of an incident. A leader with positive impact influences others in a good way and thereby makes the organisation stronger. [397]

As indicated in Chapter 3 of this part, leadership is required to motivate and drive the change process. Leaders need to be able to create and communicate vision. It is arguably a fallacy to maintain the adage that leaders are born and not made. This was the view in the traditional and authoritarian police model, where, irrespective of intellect and ability, subordinates were expected to 'know their place'. According to Kotter, "highly controlled organisations often destroy leadership by not allowing people to blossom, test themselves, and grow. In stiff bureaucracies, young men and women with potential typically see few good role models, are not encouraged to lead, and may even be punished if they go out of bounds, challenge the status quo and take risks. (They) tend to repel people with leadership potential."[398]

---

[397] N.C. Griffin, 'The 5 I's of Professionalism: A Model for Front Line Leadership' 65 *Police Chief* No.11 (November 1998) pp. 24, 26, 29 and 31.
[398] J. P. Kotter, *Leading Change* (Harvard Business School Press, Boston, 1996) p. 166.

In flatter organisations employees are empowered and tasks are delegated. Consequently an atmosphere of trust evolves, as more people are involved in the management and change processes. The organisation becomes a learning organisation, where staff can meet new challenges and be allowed to practice leadership. Members should be encouraged to be creative, and praised and rewarded for success. Failure should not always be seen as an occasion to be confrontational and point the finger of blame. Rather, it should be used as an opportunity for improvement by analysing mistakes and learning from them.

Organisations can be proactive in promoting leadership and standards. One police agency has endeavoured to do so by issuing a booklet to all of its members setting out expectations for inspirational leadership. It calls on leaders to:

- Give clear direction.
- Reward and recognise staff.
- Act with honesty and integrity.
- Focus on achievement and accountability.
- Lead by example.

Furthermore, the booklet sets out standards of expected behaviour for all ranks as follows:

- Act within the law at all times.
- Perform duties with honesty, integrity and objectivity.
- Put community interests first
- Be courteous, polite and respectful when dealing with the public or colleagues.
- Be accountable for their decisions or actions and be open to scrutiny
- Challenge unacceptable behaviour, disinterest or activity that undermines the reputation of the Constabulary.[399]

Promoting leadership and standards in this way defines the vision, ethos and image of the organisation and helps to develop an ethical bond that transmits to respecting the rights and freedoms of citizens and society.

(c) **Management Roles and Responsibilities**

The modern flatter, decentralised police organisation typically works with four levels of management. Any more than this number can lead to blockages of

---

[399] Lancashire Constabulary, England, Internal booklet: *Leadership and Standards*, 2004.

VI:5

communication and decision making. Any less can lead to a reduction in the motivation of the workforce, as there are fewer opportunities for promotion. Gaining promotion and meeting aspirations are important for members of any organisation. Employees seek to achieve higher level needs after lower level ones have been fulfilled.[400]

Before defining the four levels of management, it is useful to consider how these relate to the command and control of day-to-day policing. The following diagram demonstrates how the key roles of each level of management support the complexities of modern policing and quality service delivery:

---

[400] A. H. Maslow, 'Theory of Needs', in H. T. Graham and R. Bennet, *Human Resources Management* (8th Edition) (Pitman Publishing, 1995) p. 10.

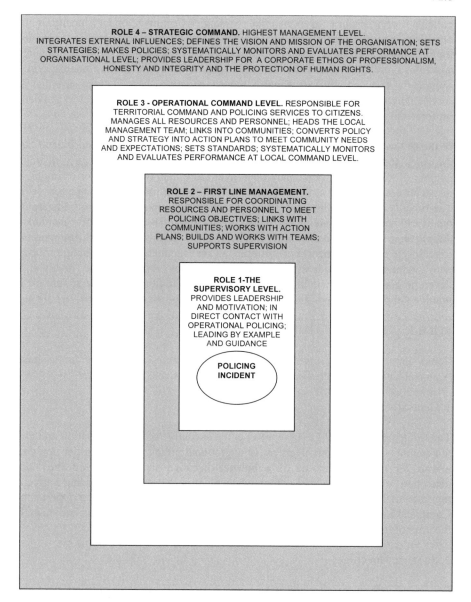

ROLE 4 – STRATEGIC COMMAND. HIGHEST MANAGEMENT LEVEL. INTEGRATES EXTERNAL INFLUENCES; DEFINES THE VISION AND MISSION OF THE ORGANISATION; SETS STRATEGIES; MAKES POLICIES; SYSTEMATICALLY MONITORS AND EVALUATES PERFORMANCE AT ORGANISATIONAL LEVEL; PROVIDES LEADERSHIP FOR A CORPORATE ETHOS OF PROFESSIONALISM, HONESTY AND INTEGRITY AND THE PROTECTION OF HUMAN RIGHTS.

ROLE 3 - OPERATIONAL COMMAND LEVEL. RESPONSIBLE FOR TERRITORIAL COMMAND AND POLICING SERVICES TO CITIZENS. MANAGES ALL RESOURCES AND PERSONNEL; HEADS THE LOCAL MANAGEMENT TEAM; LINKS INTO COMMUNITIES; CONVERTS POLICY AND STRATEGY INTO ACTION PLANS TO MEET COMMUNITY NEEDS AND EXPECTATIONS; SETS STANDARDS; SYSTEMATICALLY MONITORS AND EVALUATES PERFORMANCE AT LOCAL COMMAND LEVEL.

ROLE 2 – FIRST LINE MANAGEMENT. RESPONSIBLE FOR COORDINATING RESOURCES AND PERSONNEL TO MEET POLICING OBJECTIVES; LINKS WITH COMMUNITIES; WORKS WITH ACTION PLANS; BUILDS AND WORKS WITH TEAMS; SUPPORTS SUPERVISION

ROLE 1-THE SUPERVISORY LEVEL. PROVIDES LEADERSHIP AND MOTIVATION; IN DIRECT CONTACT WITH OPERATIONAL POLICING; LEADING BY EXAMPLE AND GUIDANCE

POLICING INCIDENT

The diagram indicates how each role has a set of tasks and responsibilities that supports and adds value to day-to-day command, management and supervision of

VI:5

policing services. For example, the Strategic Command Level positions the organisation to provide the services. The Operational Command Level is responsible for ensuring that all the key policing processes are in place and operating efficiently and effectively. The First Line Manager ensures the resources are coordinated to support the service deliverers. Finally, the Supervisor is there to make sure that the service deliverers (for example, the patrol official or criminal investigator) provide a professional, courteous and caring service to citizens.[401]

In the following section, each level of management is examined in more detail and the roles and responsibilities defined. Each level of management may include a number of ranks. Some ranks may operate at more than one level. For example, an inspector could operate at the supervisory level or the first line management level. The broadly corresponding rank titles used in different police organisations around the world are listed under each management level. They cannot be regarded as definitive and are intended only as a general guide. Many responsibilities appertain to all levels of management. For example, all management levels should be meeting with communities to identify problems, and they should all be involved in developing staff and attending to welfare matters. Additionally, they should all be involved in problem-solving and contributing ideas towards more effective policing.

ROLE 1: STRATEGIC COMMAND LEVEL

Ranks may include: Commissioner, Chief Constable, Assistant Commissioner, Assistant Chief Constable, Director General, Director, and Sub-Director,

1. General

The Strategic Command Level represents the executive of the organisation and does not routinely have any involvement in operational policing. This two-tier approach allows for the achievement of a balance between 'corporacy' and the 'local discretion' of the operational command level. It is the strategic, steering nature of the role that distinguishes the Strategic Command Level from the Operational Command Level. The Strategic Command Level will fulfil their role as laid down by the laws of the state.

2. Strategic Direction

Police officials at the Strategic Command Level will maintain political neutrality whilst remaining accountable for the operational performance of the organisation.

---

[401] B. Devlin *et. al.*, *Human Rights and Policing: Standards for Good Behaviour and a Strategy for Change* (Kluwer Law International, The Hague, 1998) pp. 259 and 260.

Police officials at this level will determine the vision and strategic direction of the organisation in accordance with the needs of the state and its citizens. They will prepare strategic plans and meet with senior leaders at the operational command level to determine the strategic direction, policy and procedures. The Strategic Command Level is responsible for developing a service culture and is ultimately accountable for the results achieved.

The Strategic Command Level should provide leadership for a corporate ethos of professionalism, honesty and integrity and the protection of human rights.

3. Command Role

The chief of police and his executive team are responsible for the management and performance of the organisation and its personnel, ensuring that all financial systems, policies, procedures and support systems and practices are in place. Each member of the Strategic Command Level should be responsible for a policy portfolio for the improvement of organisational practices. This should include a member responsible for human rights issues and professional standards.

These same members will be accountable for results achieved and will ensure that they are fully appraised about the current state of affairs relating to matters of national and public concern. Management information including qualitative and quantitative reports will be required from the Inspectorate Function.

4. External Consultation

- meeting with and reporting to members of national government to whom they are accountable for matters of citizen security.

- bidding to the government for finances for the efficient and effective provision of services.

- meeting with members of regional or local government having a role or interest in citizen security.

- maintaining regular contact and liaison with elected representatives of the people and other agencies to obtain information about areas of concern and provide reassurance that matters of citizen security are attended to.

- reporting to the independent civilian review board or commission on key issues of public concern or interest, including performance in relation to human rights and professional standards.

VI:5

- representing the organisation through the media and other forums and maintaining contacts and liaison with key members of other organisations, agencies and professions (e.g. the legal profession).

- maintaining liaison at the international level with police counterparts and other key agencies.

5. Internal Consultation

- meeting with commanders from the Operational Command Level to disseminate policy, procedure and best practice and to receive feedback on matters of concern at the operational level.

- promoting effective 'top-down' and 'bottom-up' lines of communication.

- 'management by walkabout'. Periodically visiting police stations, providing visible and inspirational leadership and motivating staff of all ranks and grades. Promoting morale by enquiring about the health and welfare and staff, and in the event of death or serious injury to a member of the organisation, ensuring that all welfare assistance is available for family, bereaved and colleagues.

ROLE 2: THE OPERATIONAL COMMAND LEVEL

Ranks may include: Regional Commissioner, Chief Superintendent, Superintendent, Sub-Commissioner, Colonel, and Major.

1. Strategic Coordination Role

They will provide information and project findings relating to their area of command to the Strategic Command Level. This information will assist the Strategic Command Level in identifying and prioritising issues of greatest public concern and the creation of national strategic initiatives to address them. In consultation with the community and staff, the Operational Command Level will identify and prioritise issues of local concern and will develop local plans to address them.

2. Line Management Role

Police leaders at the Operational Command Level are accountable to the Strategic Command Level for providing quality service delivery to the citizens residing within their area of command. The ultimate measure of their performance will be their competence in providing policing that matches community needs and expectations.

The line command role will include the following responsibilities:-

- ensuring that the organisation's priorities and plans are clearly disseminated, understood and actively pursued.
- ensuring that staff under their command have clearly defined roles and understand their duties.
- providing leadership in a way that is visible and inspiring, endeavouring to promote the image of the organisation, the motivation of its members and ethical standards.
- maintaining an operational oversight of his/her area of command - advising, intervening and coordinating as necessary.
- ensuring sufficient human and material/financial resources are available to enable effective policing services and to support proactive operations.
- measuring operational effectiveness of their staff, developing staff and assessing their performance against personnel systems and organisational objectives.

3. External Consultation

- assessing and identifying community needs and expectations through the development of formal and informal community contacts, ensuring regular meetings are held with community groups, their representatives, and other agencies.
- ensuring his/her staff, particularly supervisors and patrol officials with special responsibility for community policing, are actively engaged in community contact and liaison, including, where appropriate, attendance at meetings with community groups and their representatives.
- cooperating and liasing with other agencies in solving policing and community problems (multi-agency approach).

4. Internal Consultation

The Operational Command Level should hold regular local meeting of his/her staff for the purpose of:

- effective 'top-down' and 'bottom-up' communications.
- disseminating policy, procedures and good practice.

VI:5

- identifying problems relating to policing, and formulating and prioritising objectives to address them.
- measuring the results of objectives.
- problem-solving, including communicating ideas, innovation and creativity of their own, and of their staff, and ensuring that praise is given for the contribution of junior ranks.
- resolving welfare, personnel and training matters.

THE OPERATIONAL COMMAND LEVEL AND UNIFIED COMMAND

A common debate amongst police officials is whether police leaders at the Operational Command Level and their subordinate managers and supervisors should have unified command. Unified command means that every employee, including crime investigators, traffic patrol officials and other specialists, should be under the direct control of the operational commander and his first line managers and supervisors. It is useful to recall here the wording of the European Code of Police Ethics set out in the introduction to this chapter, "it should always be possible to determine which superior is ultimately responsibly for the acts or omissions of police personnel". Fragmented command can cause confusion as different police managers and supervisors who may be of equal rank or lesser rank may give different orders. Some subordinates, being aware of weaknesses or inconsistencies in the chain of command, may exploit this situation to undermine the credibility and authority of supervisors.

Fragmented command results in supervisors of specialist branches not always being available. It can also result in unhealthy elitism as officials from different departments pursue different goals. Unified command provides for a manager or supervisor always being available at any time to deal with an incident and give instructions and advice to any members of staff. Consequently, there is a more coherent process for decision-making. Situations are resolved more promptly and there is less likelihood of mistakes being made and shortfalls in performance, including abuses of human rights or other misconduct.

To be held truly accountable, police leaders at the Operational Command Level should have direct access to and command and control of all necessary personnel and resources. Hence, both in terms of policing performance and human rights, unified command is desirable.

ROLE 3: THE FIRST LINE MANAGER

Ranks may include: Assistant Superintendent, Chief Inspector, Inspector, Captain, and Lieutenant.

1. Management Tier

First Line Managers are the key link in the chain of command between the Operational Command Level and the Supervision Level. It is critical that they establish and maintain levels of discipline and yet establish and maintain open and effective 'top-down', 'bottom-up' and sideways lines of communication between all levels of the organisation.

In addition to being managers, they are front-line team leaders. They are also role-models for effective leadership and ethical standards of conduct and behaviour.

2. Line Management Role

Police officials at this level are accountable to the Operational Command Level for the effective deployment and direction of personnel and resources to support policing. They should have a unified command role by advising and supporting members of other branches of the organisation. The measure of their performance will be their competence in achieving results and realising objectives in support of local policing.

Their line management role will include the following responsibilities:

- ensuring that the organisation's priorities, policy and procedures, and local plans are clearly communicated to supervisors and other ranks.
- ensuring pro-active policing, coordinating and deploying resources intelligently to address crime and traffic problems and other incidents, in accordance with identified community needs and expectations.
- ensuring that supervisors and patrol officials do not remain for unnecessary long periods in police stations, and that patrolling is directed.
- ensuring supervisors and patrol officials are fully briefed and debriefed before and after being deployed to patrol duties.
- providing leadership, supervising and supporting at incidents, and monitoring the performance of staff.
- ensuring the general welfare and safety of staff during their duties.
- promoting the image of the organisation, motivating and ensuring high standards of appearance and behaviour, and the highest ethical standards.

3. External Consultation

- interacting with the community, and attending meetings with community groups.

VI:5

- ensuring supervisors and patrol officials are developing contact with the community.
- participating in multi-agency approaches to policing.

4. Internal Consultation

First Line Managers should hold regular meetings with their staff for the purpose of:

- promoting effective 'top-down' and 'bottom-up' lines of communication.
- familiarising themselves and their staff with policy, procedure and good practice, and disseminating it to supervisors and constables.
- participating in formulating local community/policing plans.
- reporting on the progress and results of action plans and objectives.
- problem-solving, including communicating ideas, innovation and creativity of their own, and of their staff, and ensuring that praise is given for the contribution of junior ranks.
- resolving welfare, personnel and training matters.

ROLE 4: THE SUPERVISORY LEVEL

Ranks may include Inspector, Sub-inspector, Lieutenant, Sergeant, and Corporal.

1. Supervision Tier

Supervisors are responsible for ensuring that they and their subordinates provide an effective high quality service to the citizens of the communities they serve. They are also responsible for discipline and maintaining ethical standards of themselves and their staff. Supervisors are operational staff and should assist in general policing,

Their effectiveness as supervisors will determine the image of the police and the conduct and attitude of constables.

2. Line Management Role

The line management role will include:

- briefing patrol officials prior to their being deployed to patrols.
- debriefing patrol officials following deployment to patrols.
- ensuring patrol officials do not remain for unnecessary long periods in police stations, or patrol in an aimless or undirected way.

442

- ensure that patrolling is pro-active and directed to community needs and identified priorities.
- devising and implementing action-plans in support of local policing.
- supporting subordinates in dealing with incidents, monitoring their performance and identifying any training needs.
- developing staff, guiding, counselling, advising, mentoring, coaching; assessing their performance in an honest and objective way, and ensuring they are provided with on the job training.
- ensuring the highest ethical standards and the protection of human rights.
- ensuring high standards of appearance, courtesy and behaviour of staff.
- ensuring staff treat all citizens equally.
- promoting the good image of the police at all times.
- ensuring all calls for assistance from citizens are responded to in an efficient way.
- ensuring that as far as possible, citizens feel reassured and are receiving a good service from the police.
- attending to all administrative tasks.
- ensuring the correct treatment of detained person in accordance with their human rights.
- promoting a service culture.

3. External Consultation

- interacting with the community, and attending meetings with community groups.
- ensuring patrol officials are developing contact with the community.
- participating in multi-agency approaches to policing.

4. Internal Consultation

Supervisors should hold regular meetings with their staff for the purpose of:

- promoting effective 'top-down' and 'bottom-up' lines of communication.
- familiarising themselves and their staff with policy, procedure and good practice.
- problem-solving, including communicating ideas, innovation and creativity of their own, and of their staff, and ensuring that praise is given for the contribution of junior ranks.
- participating with staff in identifying problems relating to local policing.
- assisting in measuring the results of objectives and action plans.

VI:5

- resolving welfare, personnel and training matters.

SUPERVISION AND SPAN OF CONTROL

Operational policing at the street level brings police officials into conflict with citizens. The work of a patrol official is very demanding, and tests patience and tolerance as well as judgment and decision-making skills. Patrol officials are often the youngest and less experienced members of the organisation. It is essential, therefore, that experienced supervisors are available and proactive in providing guidance, training and support. Operating at the front line of policing, supervisors are in a position to ensure that their staff is acting lawfully, humanely and professionally in their dealings with citizens.

Effective supervision is essential to the protection of human rights. In order to achieve effective supervision, it is important that supervisors have an optimum number of personnel to supervise. The 'span of control' refers to the number of subordinates who report directly to a given supervisor.[402] If a supervisor is allocated too many subordinates he or she will not be able to supervise them all effectively. Conversely, too few subordinates can lead to too close a level of supervision. Subordinates can then suffer loss of morale and initiative. Other factors can influence the span of control in police organisations, including:[403]

- *The geographical location and distance between supervisor and subordinate.* If a supervisor has to travel long distances to see or monitor subordinates this can reduce the number of personnel it is possible to supervise. It is easier to supervise subordinates at a single location.

- *The times of working of supervisor and subordinate.* As police organisations provide a service for twenty-four hours, they work shifts and flexible hours. If there is a wide disparity of periods of duty worked between a supervisor and subordinates, this can reduce the numbers of personnel it is possible to supervise. It is easier to supervise when the supervisor and subordinates work the same hours of duty.

- *The ability and competence of subordinate staff.* Less experienced subordinates, recruits for example, require more supervision, guidance and training. Highly competent specialists such as scene of crime officials require only the minimum of supervision.

---

[402] Mullins, *supra* note 361, p. 346.
[403] *Ibid.*, p. 347.

444

- *The work performed by subordinates.* The simpler the task, the less need for close supervision. The more complex the task, the greater need for supervision.

- *Willingness to delegate.* The extent of a supervisor's confidence in the competence of subordinates dictates the degree of delegation and span of control that is possible.

- *The range of non-supervisory responsibilities of the supervisor.* The more non-supervisory responsibilities a supervisor holds, the fewer opportunities there will be to supervise, thus reducing the span of control.

- *The effectiveness of communications systems.* Effective radio and telephone systems make it easier to contact subordinates and monitor their work. Where there is a paucity of resources and poor communications systems, supervision is more difficult.

Police leaders should be aware of these factors when deciding the number of subordinates allocated to managers and supervisors under their command. Due to the unpredictable nature of police work it is difficult to calculate the most efficient ratio of subordinates to supervisor. However, a general consensus amongst experienced police officials is that at the operational patrol policing level, the maximum number of subordinates allocated to the direct supervision of an experienced and competent supervisor should not exceed twelve. A number closer to six is preferable.

Finally, some comments are necessary about the people who are supervised – the subordinates. The word 'subordinates' has been used primarily in the context of patrol officials and others of the most junior rank in a police organisation. It is unfortunate that the word 'subordinates' can sometimes imply something of lesser worth. The reality is that subordinates, particularly the ordinary patrolmen and women are the most important people in the chain of command of any police organisation. They are the most important resource, performing the most important tasks. It behoves all managers and supervisors to remember this, and never to leave them isolated or unsupported when they are performing their difficult and dangerous duties, and protecting the rights of the citizens they serve.

Index

461

List of References

Books

J. S. Abrams, Accountability for Human Rights Atrocities in International Law: Beyond the Nuremberg Legacy (Oxford University Press, Oxford, 2001).

J. Amery, *At the Mind's Limits: Contemplations by a Survivor of Auschwitz and Its Realities* (S. and S. P. Rosenfeld (trans.)) (Indiana University Press, Bloomington, 1980).

M. Amir and S. Einstein (eds.), *Police Corruption: Challenges for Developed Countries* (OIJC, Huntsville, TX, 2004).

Archdiocese of Sao Paulo, *Torture in Brazil* (Vintage, New York, 1998).

H. Arendt, *Eichmann in Jerusalem: A Report on the Banality of Evil* (Viking Press, New York, 1963).

E. Bittner, *Aspects of Police Work* (Northeastern University Press, Boston, 1990).

T. Blass (ed.), *Obedience to Authority: Current Perspectives on the Milgram Paradigm* (Erlbaum, Mahwah, New Jersey, 2000).

W. B. Brown *et al.*, *Youth Gangs in American Society* (Wadsworth Publishing, California, 1997).

Y. Cerrah *et al.* (eds.), *Democratic Policing: Global Change from a Comparative Perspective* (Sage Publishing, Thousand Oaks, CA, 2006).

R. Crawshaw, *Police and Human Rights: A Manual for Teachers, Resource Persons, and Participants in Human Rights Programmes* (Kluwer Law International (Brill Academic Publishers), The Hague, 1999).

M. Danner, *The Massacre at El Mozote* (Random House, New York, 1994).

B. Devlin *et. al.*, *Human Rights and Policing: Standards for Good Behaviour and a Strategy for Change* (Kluwer Law International, The Hague, 1998).

J. L. Dratel and K. J. Greenberg (eds.), *The Torture Papers: The Road to Abu Ghraib* (Cambridge University Press, Cambridge, 2005).

J. Dwyer *et al.*, *Actual Innocence: Five Days to Execution and Other Dispatches From the Wrongly Convicted* (Doubleday, New York, 2000).

R. P. Fisher and R. E. Geiselman, *Memory Enhancing Techniques for Investigative Interviewing: The Cognitive Interview* (Thomas, Springfield, Illinois, 1992).

H. Goldstein, *Problem Oriented Policing* (McGraw-Hill Publishing Company, New York, 1990).

H. T. Graham and R. Bennet, *Human Resources Management* (8th Edition) (Pitman Publishing, 1995).

M. R. Haberfeld, *Police Leadership* (Prentice Hall, New Jersey, 2006).

M. Haritos-Fatouros, *The Psychological Origins of Institutionalized Torture* (Routledge, New York, London, 2002).

H. Hill and G. Russo, *Gangsters and Goodfellas: Wiseguys, Witness Protection and Life on the Run* (M Evans, New York, 2004).

M. K. Huggins *et al.*, *Violence Workers: Police Torturers and Murderers Reconstruct Brazilian Atrocities* (University of California Press, London, 2002).

J. Kleinig, *The Ethics of Policing* (Cambridge University Press, Cambridge, 1996).

J. P. Kotter, *Leading Change* (Harvard Business School Press, Boston, 1996).

J.-L. Loubet Del Blayle, *La Police dans le Systeme Politique* (*Centre d'Études et de Recherches sur la Police*, Toulouse, 1981).

C. Mackey and G. Miller, *The Interrogator's War* (John Murray (Publishers), London, 2004).

M. Mann, *The Dark Side of Democracy: Explaining Ethnic Cleansing* (Cambridge University Press, Cambridge, 2005).

S. Milgram, *Obedience to Authority: An Experimental View* (Harper & Row, New York, 1974).

470

L. S. Miller and K. M. Hess, *The Police in the Community: Strategies for the 21st Century* (3rd Edition) (Wadsworth, California, 2002)

A. Mulcahy, *Policing Northern Ireland: Conflict, Legitimacy and Reform* (Willan Press, Cullompton, Devon, England, 1999).

L. J. Mullins, *Management and Organizational Behaviour* (4th edition) (Pitman Publishing, London, 1996).

T. Newburn (ed.), *Handbook of Policing* (Willan Publishing, Devon, England, 2005).

V. Perera, *Unfinished Conquest: The Guatemalan Tragedy* (University of California Press, Berkeley, Los Angeles, California, 1993).

N. S. Rodley, *The Treatment of Prisoners under International Law* (Oxford University Press, Oxford, 1999).

R. J. Rummel, *Death by Government* (Transaction Publishers, New Brunswick, New Jersey, 1994).

E. H. Schein, *Organizational Culture and Leadership* (2nd Edition) (Jossey Bass, San Francisco, 1997).

W. Stanley, *The Protection Racket State: Elite Politics, Military Extortion and Civil War in El Salvador* (Temple University Press, Philadelphia, 1996).

L. Sullivan *et al.* (eds.), *Encyclopedia of Law Enforcement* (Sage Publications, Thousand Oaks, CA, 2005).

T. Todorov, *Hope and Memory – Reflections on the Twentieth Century* (Atlantic Books, London, 2003).

T. Williamson (ed.), *Investigative Interviewing: Rights, Research and Regulation* (Willan Press, Cullompton, Devon, England, 2006).

A. Wright, *Policing: An Introduction to Concepts and Practice* (Willan Press, Cullompton, Devon, England, 2002).

Chapters in Books

J. P. Buckley, 'The Reid Technique of Interviewing and Interrogation', in T. Williamson (ed.), *Investigative Interviewing: Rights, Research and Regulation*, (Willan Press, Cullompton, Devon, England, 2006).

S. Cullen and W. McDonald, 'Sierra Leone', in L. Sullivan *et al.* (eds.), *Encyclopaedia of Law Enforcement* (vol. 3) (Sage Publications, Thousand Oaks, CA, 2004).

S. Cullen and W. H. McDonald, 'Post Conflict Democratization of the Police: The Sierra Leone Experience.' in Y. Cerrah *et al.* (eds.), *Democratic Policing: Global Change from a Comparative Perspective* (Sage Publishing, Thousand Oaks, CA, 2006).

D. Dixon, 'Regulating Police Interrogation', in T. Williamson (ed.), *Investigative Interviewing: Rights, Research and Regulation* (Willan Press, Cullompton, Devon, England, 2006).

P. Ekman *et al.*, 'Investigative Interviewing and the Detection of Deception', in T. Williamson (ed.), *Investigative Interviewing: Rights, Research and Regulation* (Willan Press, Cullompton, Devon, England, 2006).

M. G. Gelles *et al.*, 'Al-Qaeda-Related Subjects: A Law Enforcement Perspective', in T. Williamson (ed.), *Investigative Interviewing: Rights, Research and Regulation* (Willan Press, Cullompton, Devin, England, 2006).

G. H. Gudjonsson, 'The Psychology of Interrogations and Confessions', in T. Williamson (ed.), *Investigative Interviewing: Rights, Research and Regulation*, (Willan Press, Cullompton, Devon, England, 2006).

S. Kassin, 'A Critical Appraisal of the Reid Technique', in T. Williamson (ed.), *Investigative Interviewing: Rights, Research and Regulation*, (Willan Press, Cullompton, Devon, England, 2006).

G. Markham and M. Punch, 'The Gemini Solution – Embracing Accountability', in M. Amir and S. Einstein (eds.), *Police Corruption: Challenges for Developed Countries* (OIJC, Huntsville, TX, 2004).

A. H. Maslow, 'Theory of Needs', in H. T. Graham and R. Bennet, *Human Resources Management* (8th Edition) (Pitman Publishing, 1995).

J. Pearse, 'The Interrogation of Terrorist Suspects: The Banality of Torture', in T. Williamson (ed.), *Investigative Interviewing: Rights, Research and Regulation* (Willan Press, Cullompton, Devon, England, 2006).

D. Rose, 'American Interrogation Methods in the War on Terror', in T. Williamson (ed.), *Investigative Interviewing: Rights, Research and Regulation* (Willan Press, Cullompton, Devin, England, 2006).

M. St-Yves, 'The Psychology of Rapport: Five Basic Rules', in T. Williamson (ed.), *Investigative Interviewing: Rights, Research and Regulation* (Willan Press, Cullompton, Devon, England, 2006).

P. A. J. Waddington, 'Policing Public Order and Political Contention', in T. Newburn (ed.), *Handbook of Policing* (Willan Publishing, Devon, England, 2005).

T. Williamson, 'Investigative Interviewing and Human Rights in the War on Terrorism', in T. Williamson (ed.), *Investigative Interviewing: Rights, Research and Regulation* (Willan Press, Cullompton, Devon, England, 2006).

P. G. Zimbardo *et al.*, 'Reflections on the Stanford Prison Experiment: Genesis, Transformations, Consequences', in T. Blass (ed.), *Obedience to Authority: Current Perspectives on the Milgram Paradigm* (Erlbaum, Mahwah, New Jersey, 2000).

Articles

A. Arana, 'How the Street Gangs Took Central America', *Foreign Affairs* (May/June 2005).

P. E. Atkinson, 'Creating Cultural Change,' 34:7 *Management Service* (1990) pp. 6–10.

A. Bandura, 'Moral Disengagement in the Perpetration of Inhumanities', 3:3 *Personality and Social Psychology Review* (1999) pp. 193–209.

I. Charny, 'Genocide and Mass Destruction: Doing Harm to Others as a Missing Dimension in Psychopathology', 49 *Psychiatry* (1986) pp.144-157.

A. M. Dershowitz, 'The Torture Warrant: A Response to Professor Strauss', 48 *New York Law School Law Review* (2003) pp. 275-94.

L. Garrett, 'The Lesson of HIV Aids', *Foreign Affairs* (July/August 2005).

N.C. Griffin, 'The 5 I's of Professionalism: A Model for Front Line Leadership' 65 *Police Chief* No.11 (November 1998).

G. H. Gudjonsson and S. Kassin, 'The Psychology of Confessions: A Review of the Literature and Issues', 5:2 *Psychological Science in the Public Interest* (November 2004).

L. Harbom and P. Wallensteen, 'Armed Conflict and Its International Dimensions, 1946-2004', 42:5 *Journal of Peace Research* (2005) pp. 623–635.

D. Helly, 'Developing an EU Strategy for Security Sector Reform,' 28 *European Security Review* (February 2006).

M. McMullan, 'A Theory of Corruption', 9 *Sociological Review* (1961).

S. Milgram, 'Behavioral Study of Obedience', 67 *Journal of Abnormal and Social Psychology* (1963) pp. 371-378.

L. Ross, 'The intuitive psychologist and his shortcomings: distortions in the attribution process', 10 *Advances in Experimental Social Psychology* (1977).

R. Stohl, 'Under the Gun: Children and Small Arms,' 11:3 *African Security Review* (2002).

J. D. Tepperman 'Truth and Consequences', 81 *Foreign Affairs* (March/April, 2002) pp. 128-145.

P. G. Zimbardo, 'The Human Choice: Individuation, Reason, and Order Versus Deindividuation, Impulse, and Chaos', 17 *Nebraska Symposium on Motivation* (1969) pp. 237-307.

P. G. Zimbardo, 'Pathology of Imprisonment', 9 *Society* (1972) pp. 4-8.

P. G. Zimbardo *et al.*, 'The Mind is a Formidable Jailer: A Pirandellian Prison', *New York Times Magazine,* 8 April 1973, p. *38 et seq.*

Internet

I. Clegg *et al.*, *Policy Guidance on Support to Policing in Developing Countries, Centre for Development Studies Report*, University of Wales, November 2000, < www.swan.ac.uk/cds/pdffiles/POLICE%20GUIDANCE.pdf#search=%22Guidance %20on%20Support%20to%20Policing%20in%20Developing%20%22>, last visited September 2006.

N. E. W. Colton, *The United Nations Conference on the Illicit Trade in Small Arms and Light Weapons in all its Aspects*, summarized on the website of the Nuclear Age Peace Foundation, <www.wagingpeace.org/articles/2001/07/09_colton_un-conference.htm>, last visited September 2006.

Commission on the Truth for El Salvador, Report: *From Madness to Hope: The 12-Year war in El Salvador*, 15 March 1993, <www.usip.org/library/tc/doc/reports/el_salvador/tc_es_03151993_toc.html>, last visited September 2006.

Commission to Clarify Past Human Rights Violation and Acts of Violence That Have Caused the Guatemalan Population to Suffer, Report: *Guatemala: Memory of Silence*, 24 June 1994, <shr.aaas.org/guatemala/ceh/report/english/toc.html>, last visited September 2006.

E. Cuya, *Las Comisiones de la Verdad en America Latina*, 1 March 1999, <www.derechos.org/koaga/iii/1/cuya.html>, last visited September 2006.

J. M. Hart, *The Management of Change in Police Organizations*, <www.ncjrs.gov/policing/man199.htm>, last visited September 2006.

U. Holmberg, *Police Interviews with Victims and Suspects of Violent and Sexual Crimes: Interviewees' Experiences and Interview Outcomes'*, Stockholm University, Department of Psychology, Stockholm, Sweden, 2004, <www.diva-portal.org/su/abstract.xsql?dbid=64>, last visited September 2006.

Independent Commission against Corruption, *Information*, <www.icac.org.hk/eng/main/>, last visited September 2006.

M. Maiese, *Underlying Causes of Intractable Conflict*, posted October 2003, <www.beyondintractability.org/essay/underlying_causes>, last visited September 2006.

Mindtools, *SWOT Analysis*, <www.mindtools.com/pages/article/newTMC_05.htm>, last visited September 2006.

New York Police Department, Deputy Commissioner of Community Affairs, <www.nyc.gov/html/nypd/html/dcca/dcca-page.html>, last visited September 2006.

New Zealand Police, *Police Strategic Plan to 2006*, <www.police.govt.nz/resources/2002/strategic-plan-to-2006/strategic-plan-to-2006.html>, last visited September 2006.

T. Newburn, *Understanding and Preventing Police Corruption: Lessons from the Literature, Police Research Series*, Paper 110, 1999, <www.homeoffice.gov.uk/rds/prgpdfs/fprs110.pdf#search=%22Understanding%20and%20Preventing%20Police%20Corruption%3A%20Lessons%20from%20the%20Literature%22>, last visited September 2006.

Professor B. Rider, Presentation: *How to Define Corruption and the Functions of Corruption*, Conference on Combating Corruption, Goodenough College, London, November 2004.

M. Shaw, *Crime and Policing in Transitional Societies: Conference Summary and Overview*, 2001, <www.kas.org.za/publications/seminarreports/crimeandpolicingin transitionalsocieties/shaw.pdf#search=%22Crime%20and%20Policing%20in%20Tr ansitional%20Societies%20%E2%80%93%20Conference%20Summary%20and%2 0Overview%22>, last visited September 2006.

Transparency International, *Transparency International Corruption Perceptions Index 2005, Press Release*, <www.transparency.org/cpi/2005/cpi2005_infocus. html>, last visited September 2006.

United Nations Information Service, UNIS/CP/528, *Press Release*, 13 December 2005, <www.unis.unvienna.org/unis/pressrels/2005/uniscp528.html>, last visited September 2006.

United Nations Office on Drugs and Crime, *Organized Crime, UNODC Fact Sheet*, <www.unodc.org/unodc/en/organized_crime.html>, last visited September 2006.

United Nations Office on Drugs and Crime, *Trafficking in Human Beings*, <www.unodc.org/unodc/en/trafficking_human_beings.html>, last visited September 2006.

United Nations Office on Drugs and Crime, *United Nations Convention against Corruption*, <www.unodc.org/unodc/en/crime_convention_corruption.html>, last visited September 2006.

UNDP, *Small Arms and Light Weapons, UNDP Essentials*, No.9, October 2002, < www.undp.org/eo/documents/essentials/Small%20Arms3October2002.pdf#search =%22600%20million%20small%20arms%20and%20light%20weapons%20un%20c onference%22>, last visited September 2006.

United States Department of State, Bureau of Western Hemisphere Affairs, *Fact Sheet*, 9 August 2006, <www.state.gov/p/wha/rls/fs/2006/58645.htm>, last visited September 2006.

476

<www.auschwitz.dk/sobibor/franzstangl.htm>, last visited September 2006.

<www.crimereduction.gov.uk/ learningzone/sara.htm>, last visited September 2006.

<www.popcenter.org>, last visited September 2006.

Other References (Interviews, Presentations, Reports, Etc.)

Amnesty International, *Torture Survey*, 2000.

Author's conversations with firearms holders in post-conflict societies.

J. Baldwin, *Video Taping Police Interviews with Suspects: An Evaluation, Police Research Series*, Paper 1, Home Office Police Department, London, 1992

Colonel R. C. Bell, *Ten Principles of Intelligence*, Unpublished, Bramshill, England, May 1992.

Committee on International Human Rights of the Association of the Bar of the City of New York and Center for Human Rights and Global Justice, *Torture by Proxy: International and Domestic Law Applicable to 'Extraordinary Renditions'*, New York, 2004.

Council of Europe, *Police and Human Rights Training and Awareness Material.*

Council of Europe, Joint Informal Working Group on Police and Human Rights, *Policing in a Democratic Society: Is Your Police Service a Human Rights Champion?*, 2000.

S. Cullen, *Field notes from the Malawi Police Training Project*, September 1995.

B. Denmark, *Ethical Investigation: Practical Guide for Police Officers*, Foreign and Commonwealth Office, London, 2005.

M. Fitzduff *et al.*, *From Warlords to Peacelords: Local Leadership Capacity in Peace Processes*, report from INCORE, December 2004.

Her Majesty's Inspectorate of Constabulary, Report: *Police Integrity*, London, 1999. Independent Commission on Policing for Northern Ireland, Report: *A New Beginning: Policing in Northern Ireland*, 1999.

477

List of References

International Committee of the Red Cross, *To Serve and Protect: Guide for Police Conduct and Behaviour*, Geneva, 2002.

International Review of the Red Cross, No. 262 (Jan – Feb 1988).

Interview by author with J. Villalobos, former leader of the FMLN, Oxford, England, 11 March 2006.

Interview with Keith Biddle, Inspector General of Police, Sierra Leone Police, 1999-2003, Cheshire, England, 13 April 2005.

Interviews by the author with Claudio Rudy Perez Batui, Sub Inspector, National Civil Police, and Vincente Elias Lajpop, Maya Cacique, Momestenango, Guatemala, May 2001; and Morie Lengor, Assistant Commissioner of Police, Sierra Leone Police, April 2005.

Dr. H. Konrad, Special Representative on Combating Trafficking in Human Beings, Organization for Security and Cooperation in Europe (OSCE), Presentation: *Trafficking in Human Beings*, Leadership Academy for Policing, Bramshill, England, 10 February 2006.

Lancashire Constabulary, England, Internal booklet: *Leadership and Standards*, 2004.

Landau Commission (named after Justice Mann Landau), *Report of the Commission of Inquiry into the Methods of Investigation of the General Security Service with Respect to Hostile Terrorist Activity*, Jerusalem, 1987.

M. Levi, professor at the University of Cardiff, Presentation: *Typologies of Organized Crime Groups* , Leadership Academy for Policing, Bramshill, England, 9 February 2006.

Dr. L. Moore and M. O'Rawe, Report: *Human Rights on Duty - Principles for Better Policing: International Lessons for Northern Ireland*, The Committee on the Administration of Justice, 1997.

R. Neild and M. Ziegler, *From Peace to Governance: Police Reform and the International Community*, a report from the November 2001 conference sponsored by the Washington Office on Latin America and the John Hopkins Nitze School of Advanced International Studies, 2002.

Office of the UN High Commissioner for Human Rights, *Human Rights and Law Enforcement: A Trainer's Guide on Human Rights for the Police, Police Training Series No.5 Add.2,* 2002.

Office of the United Nations High Commissioner for Human Rights, *Human Rights Standards and Practice for the Police,* HR/P/PT/5/Add.3, New York and Geneva, 2004.

W. G. O'Neill, *Police Reform in Post-Conflict Societies: What We Know and What We Still Need to Know, International Peace Academy Policy Paper,* April 2005.

Organisation for Security and Cooperation in Europe, *Use of Force and Kosovo Police Service Policy, Kosovo Police Service School Training Notes,* May 2001.

L. Peñados-Ceren, Presentation: *Truth and Justice: Forensic Sciences in a Post War Context,* Department of Forensic and Investigative Science, University of Central Lancashire, United Kingdom, 16 November 2005.

Personal communication and interviews by the author with state officials of the Republic of El Salvador, former guerrillas and members of the PNC, El Salvador and England, 1995 – 2006.

Personal communication with Taimoor Shah Habibi, Ministry of Refugees and Repatriation, Islamic Republic of Afghanistan, 10 February 2006.

Personal communications by the author with MINUGUA personnel, Guatemala City, Republic of Guatemala, May-December 2001.

Secretary General's statement at the UN Security Council meeting on counterterrorism on 18 January 2002.

M. Shaw, Chief of Criminal Justice Reform Unit, Presentation: *The Global Picture of Organized Crime and the Strategy of UNODC,* International Faculty, Leadership Academy for Policing, Bramshill, England, 3 February 2006.

Sierra Leone Police, Strategic document: *From Crisis to Confidence,* 1998.

United Nations Staff College, *Typology and Survey of Preventive Measures, Rolling EWPM Project Reference Document,* March 1999.

List of UN Documents and Legislation (UN and Regional)

UN Documents

E/CN.4/1985/SR.55.

E/CN.4/1986/15.

E/CN.4/1987/13.

E/CN.4/1988/17.

E/CN.4/1995/116.

E/CN.4/1998/87/Add.1.

E/CN.4/1999/92.

A/54/42.

E/CN.4/2000/94.

E/CN.4/2001/91.

A/59/324.

E/CN.4/2004/56.

E/CN.4/2005/62/Add.1.

E/CN.4/2006/87.

Legislation (UN and Regional)

Forced Labour Convention, 1930 (No. 29).

Freedom of Association and Protection of the Right to Organise Convention, 1948 (No. 87).

Convention on the Prevention and Punishment of the Crime of Genocide, approved by General Assembly resolution 260 A (III) of 9 December 1948.

Universal Declaration of Human Rights, adopted under General Assembly resolution 217 A (III) of 10 December 1948.

Right to Organise and Collective Bargaining Convention, 1949 (No. 98).

1949 Geneva Convention I for the Amelioration of the Condition of Wounded and Sick in Armed forces in the Field.

1949 Geneva Convention II for the Amelioration of the Condition of Wounded, Sick and Shipwrecked Members of Armed Forces at Sea.

1949 Geneva Convention III Relative to the Treatment of Prisoners of War.

1949 Geneva Convention IV Relative to the Protection of Civilian Persons in Time of War.

Equal Remuneration Convention, 1950 (No. 100).

Convention for the Protection of Human Rights and Fundamental Freedoms (European Convention on Human Rights), signed by Member States of the Council of Europe, at Rome, on 4 November 1950.

Convention relating to the Status of Refugees, signed by Member States of the United Nations and other States invited, at Geneva, on 28 July 1951.

Standard Minimum Rules for the Treatment of Prisoners, adopted by the First United Nations Congress on the Prevention of Crime and the Treatment of Offenders held at Geneva in 1955, (approved by the Economic and Social Council by its resolution 663 C (XXIV) of 31 July 1957 and 2076 (LXII) of 13 May 1977).

Abolition of Forced Labour Convention, 1957 (No. 105).

Discrimination (Employment and Occupation) Convention, 1958 (No. 111).

International Convention on the Elimination of All Forms of Racial Discrimination, adopted by General Assembly resolution 2106 A (XX) of 21 December 1965.

First Optional Protocol to the International Covenant on Civil and Political Rights, adopted by General Assembly resolution 2200 A (XXI) of 16 December 1966.

List of References

International Covenant on Civil and Political Rights, adopted under General Assembly resolution 2200 A (XXI) of 16 December 1966.

International Covenant on Economic, Social and Cultural Rights, adopted under General Assembly resolution 2200 A (XXI) of 16 December 1966.

Protocol relating to the Status of Refugees, signed by the President of the General Assembly and the Secretary General of the United Nations, at New York, on 31 January 1967.

American Convention on Human Rights, signed by Member States of the Organisation of American States, at San José, Costa Rica, on 22 November 1969.

Minimum Age Convention, 1973 (No. 138).

1977 Geneva Additional Protocol I to the Geneva Conventions of 12 August 1949, and Relating to the Protection of Victims of International Armed Conflicts.

1977 Geneva Additional Protocol II to the Geneva Conventions of 12 August 1949, and Relating to the Protection of Victims of Non-international Armed Conflicts.

European Convention on the Suppression of Terrorism, at Strasbourg, on 27 January 1977.

Code of Conduct for Law Enforcement Officials, adopted by General Assembly resolution 34/169 of 17 December 1979.

Convention on the Elimination of All Forms of Discrimination against Women, adopted by General Assembly resolution 34/180 of 18 December 1979.

African Charter on Human and Peoples' Rights, adopted by the Assembly of Heads of State and Government of the Organisation of African Unity, at Nairobi, on 27 June 1981.

General Comment No. 6 (16), adopted by the Human Rights Committee, at its 378th meeting (16th session), on 27 July 1982.

Convention against Torture and Other Cruel, Inhuman or Degrading Treatment or Punishment, adopted by General Assembly resolution 39/46 of 10 December 1984.

Declaration of Basic Principles of Justice for Victims of Crime and Abuse of Power, adopted by General Assembly resolution 40/34 of 29 November 1985.

UN Standard Minimum Rules for the Administration of Juvenile Justice (also know as the Beijing Rules), adopted by General Assembly resolution 40/33 of 29 November 1985.

Inter-American Torture Convention, signed by Member States of the OAS on 9 December 1985, entered into force 28 February 1987.

Convention for the Prevention of Torture and Inhuman or Degrading Treatment or Punishment, signed by Member States of the Council of Europe on 26 November 1987, (entered into force on 1 February 1989).

Body of Principles for the Protection of All Persons under Any form of Detention or Imprisonment, approved by General Assembly resolution 43/173 of 9 December 1988.

Principles on the Effective Prevention and Investigation of Extra-legal, Arbitrary and Summary Executions, recommended by Economic and Social Council resolution 1989/65 of 24 May 1989, (endorsed by General Assembly resolution 44/162 of 1 December 1989).

Convention on the Rights of the Child, adopted by General Assembly resolution 44/25 of 20 November 1989.

Second Optional Protocol to the International Covenant on Civil and Political Rights, adopted by General Assembly resolution 44/128 of 15 December 1989.

Basic Principles on the Use of Force and Firearms by Law Enforcement Officials, adopted by the Eighth United Nations Congress on the Prevention of Crime and the Treatment of Offenders, Havana, Cuba, 27 August to 7 September 1990.

Recommendations on international co-operation for crime prevention and criminal justice in the context of development, adopted under United Nations General Assembly resolution 45/107 of 14 December 1990.

UN Rules for the Protection of Juveniles Deprived of their Liberty, adopted by General Assembly resolution 45/113 of 14 December 1990.

The El Salvador Peace Agreement, Chapultepec, Mexico, 1991.

Turku (Abo) Declaration of Minimum Humanitarian Standards, first published in the *International Review of the Red Cross*, No. 282 (May–June 1991).

General Comment No. 20 (44), adopted by the Human Rights Committee, at its 1138th meeting (44th session), on 3 April 1992.

General Comment No. 21(44), adopted by the Human Rights Committee, at its 44th session, on 6 April 1992.

Declaration on the Protection of All Persons from Enforced Disappearances, proclaimed by the General Assembly of the United Nations on 18 December 1992.

Commission on Human Rights resolution 1997/21, 11 April 1997.

Inter-American Convention Against the Illicit Manufacturing of and Trafficking in Firearms, Ammunition, Explosives and Other Related Materials, adopted by the Organization of American States in November 1997, (entered into force in July 1998).

Commission on Human Rights resolution 1998/29, 17 April 1998.

Arab Convention on the Suppression of Terrorism, signed at a meeting held at the General Secretariat of the League of Arab States, at Cairo, on 22 April 1998.

Worst Forms of Child Labour Convention, 1999 (No. 182).

International Convention for the Suppression of the Financing of Terrorism, adopted by the General Assembly of the United Nations on 9 December 1999.

United Nations Convention against Transnational Organized Crime, adopted by General Assembly resolution 55/25 of 15 November 2000, (entered into force 29 September 2003).

Protocol against the Smuggling of Migrants by Land, Air and Sea, adopted by UN General Assembly resolution 55/25 of 15 November 2000, (entered into force 28 January 2004).

Protocol to Prevent, Suppress and Punish Trafficking in Persons, Especially Women and Children, adopted by UN General Assembly resolution 55/25 of 15 November 2000, (entered into force 25 December 2003).

United Nations Protocol against the Illicit Manufacturing of and Trafficking in Firearms, Their Parts and Components and Ammunition, adopted by UN General Assembly resolution 55/255 of 31 May 2001, (entered into force on 3 July 2005).

General Comment No.29 (72), adopted by the Human Rights Committee, at its 1950th meeting (72nd session), on 24 July 2001.

European Code of Police Ethics, Recommendation Rec. (2001) 10, adopted by the Committee of Ministers of the Council of Europe on 19 September 2001.
Security Council resolution 1373 (2001), 28 September 2001.

CPT Standards, CPT/inf/E (2002)1- Rev 2004.

United Nations Convention against Corruption, adopted by UN General Assembly resolution 58/4 of 31 October 2003, (entered into force 14 December 2005).

Commission on Human Rights decision 2004/118.

International Convention for the Suppression of Acts of Nuclear Terrorism, adopted by the General Assembly of the United Nations, at New York, on 13 April 2005.

Security Council resolution 1617 of 29 July 2005.

Additional Protocol III Relating to the Adoption of an Additional Distinctive Emblem, adopted on 8 December 2005.

General Assembly resolution 60/251 of 15 March 2006, establishing the Human Rights Council, which replaces the Commission on Human Rights.

List of Cases

The *Greek* case, *Yearbook of the European Convention on Human Rights, 1969* [vol. 12 *bis*], applications Nos. 3321/67 to 3323/67 and 3344/67, European Commission of Human Rights report adopted on 5 November 1969, Committee of Ministers of the Council of Europe resolution DH (70) 1 adopted on 15 April 1970.

Ireland v. *the United Kingdom, Publications of the European Court of Human Rights*, Series A: *Judgments and Decisions*, vol. 25 (1978), judgment of 18 January 1978.

López Burgos v. *Uruguay*, United Nations, *Official Records of the General Assembly, Thirty-sixth Session, Supplement No. 40* (A/36/40), annex XIX, communication No. 52/1979, views adopted on 29 July 1981.

Report on Case No. 1014 (*Dominican Republic*), International Labour Office, *Official Bulletin*, vol. LXIV, Series B, No. 3 (1981), p. 130, interim report of 13 November 1981.

María Fanny Suárez de Guerrero v. *Colombia*, United Nations, *Official Records of the General Assembly, Thirty-seventh Session, Supplement No. 40* (A/37/40), annex XI, communication No. 45/1979, views adopted on 31 March 1982.

Caldas v. *Uruguay*, United Nations, *Official Records of the General Assembly, Thirty-eighth Session, Supplement No 40* (A/38/40), annex XVIII, communication No. 43/1979, views adopted on 21 July 1983.

Quinteros and Almeida de Quinteros v. *Uruguay*, United Nations, *Official Records of the General Assembly, Thirty-eighth Session, Supplement No. 40* (A/38/40), annex XXII, communication No. 107/1981, views adopted on 21 July 1983.

Stewart v. *the United Kingdom*, European Commission of Human Rights, *Decisions and Reports*, No. 39 (1984), p. 162, application No. 10044/82, decision of 10 July 1984.

John Khemraadi Baboeram et al. v. *Suriname*, United Nations, *Official Records of the General Assembly, Fortieth Session, Supplement No. 40* (A/40/40), annex X, communications No. 146/ 1983, No.148/1983, No. 149/1983, No. 150/1983, No. 151/1983, No. 152/1983, No. 153/1983 and No. 154/1983, views adopted on 4 April 1985.

486

Report on Case No.1285 (*Chile*), International Labour Office, *Official Bulletin*, vol. LXVIII, Series B, No. 3 (1985), p. 115, definitive report of 7 November 1985.

Herrera Rubio v. *Colombia*, United Nations, *Official Records of the General Assembly, Forty-third Session, Supplement No. 40* (A/43/40), annex VII, sect. B, communication No. 161/1983, views adopted on 2 November 1987.

Plattform "Ärzte für das Leben" v. *Austria, Publications of the European Court of Human Rights*, Series A: *Judgments and Decisions*, vol. 139 (1988), application No. 10126/82, judgment of 21 June 1988.

Velásquez Rodríguez v. *Honduras*, Inter-American Court of Human Rights, Series C: *Decisions and Judgments*, No. 4 (1988), petition No. 7920, judgment of 29 July 1988.

Munoz Hermoza v. *Peru*, United Nations, *Official Records of the General Assembly, Forty-fourth Session, Supplement No. 40* (A/44/40), annex X, sect. D, communication No. 203/1986, views adopted on 4 November 1988.

Brogan et al. v. *the United Kingdom, Publications of the European Court of Human Rights*, Series A: *Judgments and Decisions*, vol. 145-B (1989), judgment of 29 November 1988.

Delgado Páez v. *Colombia*, United Nations, *Official Records of the General Assembly, Forty-fifth Session, Supplement No. 40* (A/45/40), vol. II, annex IX, sect. D, communication No. 195/1985, views adopted on 12 July 1990.

van Alphen v. *the Netherlands*, United Nations, *Official Records of the General Assembly, Forty-fifth Session, Supplement No. 40* (A/45/40), vol. II, annex IX, sect. M, communication No. 305/1988, views adopted on 23 July 1990.

Cases against Malawi, Case Nos. 64/92, 68/92 and 78/92.

Kokkinakis v. *Greece, Publications of the European Court of Human Rights*, Series A: *Judgments and Decisions*, vol. 260-A (1993), application No. 14307/88, judgment of 24 June 1993.

Mukong v. *Cameroon*, United Nations, *Official Records of the General Assembly, Forty-ninth Session, Supplement No. 40* (A/49/40), vol. II, annex IX, sect. AA, communication No. 458/1991, views adopted on 21 July 1994.

Decision No. 59/1993 (*Kuwait*), United Nations document E/CN.4/1995/31/Add.1, p. 22, decision adopted on 9 December 1994.

Neira Allegría et al. v. *Peru*, Inter-American Court of Human Rights, Series C: *Decisions and Judgments*, No. 20 (1995), judgment of 19 January 1995.

Report on Case No. 1598 (*Peru*), International Labour Office, *Official Bulletin*, vol. LXXVIII, Series B, No. 1 (1995), p. 38, request report of 27 March 1995.

McCann and Others v. *the United Kingdom, Publications of the European Court of Human Rights*, Series A: *Judgments and Decisions*, vol. 324 (1996), application No. 18984/91, judgment of 27 September 1995.

Bautista de Arellana v. *Colombia*, United Nations, *Official Records of the General Assembly, Fifty-first Session, Supplement No. 40* (A/51/40), vol. II, annex VIII, sect. S, communication No. 563/1993, views adopted on 27 October 1995.

Celis Laureano v. *Peru*, United Nations, *Official Records of the General Assembly, Fifty-first Session, Supplement No. 40* (A/51/40), vol. II, annex VIII, sect. P, communication No. 540/1993, views adopted on 25 March 1996.

Aduayom, Diasso and Dobou v. *Togo Ibidem, Fifty-first Session, Supplement No. 40* (A/51/40), vol. II, annex VIII, sect. C, communications No. 422/1990, No. 423/1990 and No. 424/1990, views adopted on 12 July 1996.

Ricky Burrell v. *Jamaica*, United Nations, *Official Records of the General Assembly, Fifty-first Session, Supplement No. 40* (A/51/40), vol. II, annex VIII, sect. R, communication No. 546/1993, views adopted on 18 July 1996.

Aksoy v. *Turkey*, European Court of Human Rights, *Reports of Judgments and Decisions*, 1996-VI, p. 2260, judgment of 18 December 1996.

Halford v. *the United Kingdom*, European Court of Human Rights, *Reports of Judgments and Decisions*, 1997-III, p. 1004, judgment of 25 June 1997.

Zana v. *Turkey*, European Court of Human Rights, *Reports of Judgments and Decisions*, 1997-VII, p. 2533, application No. 18954/91, judgment of 25 November 1997.

Domukovsky v. *Georgia*, United Nations, *Official Records of the General Assembly, Fifty-third Session, Supplement No. 40* (A/53/40), vol. II, annex XI, sect. M, communication No. 623/1995, views adopted on 6 April 1998.

Güleç v. *Turkey*, European Court of Human Rights, *Reports of Judgments and Decisions*, 1998-IV, p. 1698, application No. 21593/93, judgment of 27 July 1998.

Osman v. *the United Kingdom*, European Court of Human Rights, *Reports of Judgments and Decisions*, 1998-VIII, p. 3124, application No. 23452/94, judgment of 28 October 1998.

Suarez Rosero v. *Ecuador*, Inter-American Court of Human Rights, Series C: *Decisions and Judgments*, No. 35 (1999), judgment of 12 November 1999.

Prosecutor v. *Zejnil Delalic, Zdravko Mucic, Hazim Delic and Esad Landzo*, Case No. IT-96-21-T, judgment of 16 November 1998 (Trial Chamber), (*see also* Case No. IT-96-21-A, judgment of 20 February 2001 (Appeals Chamber)).

Prosecutor v. *Anto Furundzija*, Case No. IT-95-17/1-T, judgment of 10 December 1998 (Trial Chamber), (*see also* Case No. IT-95-17/1-A, judgment of 21 July 2000 (Appeals Chamber)).

Selmouni v. *France*, European Court of Human Rights, *Reports of Judgments and Decisions*, 1999-V, p. 149, judgment of 28 July 1999.

Villagrán Morales et al. v. *Guatemala* (the *"Street Children"* case), Inter-American Court of Human Rights, Series C: *Decisions and Judgments*, No. 63 (2000), petition No. 11383, judgment of 19 November 1999.

Kaya v. *Turkey*, European Court of Human Rights, *Reports of Judgments and Decisions*, 2000-III, p. 149, application No. 22535/93, judgment of 28 March 2000.

Chongwe v. *Zambia*, United Nations, *Official Records of the General Assembly, Fifty-sixth Session, Supplement No. 40* (A/56/40), vol. II, annex X, sect. K, communication No. 821/1998, views adopted on 25 October 2000.

Bámaca Velásquez v. *Guatemala*, Inter-American Court of Human Rights, Series C: *Decisions and Judgments*, No. 70 (2001), petition No. 11129, judgment of 25 November 2000.

Rafael Rojas García et al. v. *Colombia*, United Nations, *Official Records of the General Assembly Fifty-sixth Session, Supplement No. 40* (A/56/40), vol. II, annex X, sect. D, communication No. 687/1996, views adopted on 3 April 2001.

McKerr v. *United Kingdom*, European Court of Human Rights, *Reports of Judgements and Decisions*, 2001-III, p. 475 application No. 28883/95, judgment of 4 May 2001.

The *Ivcher Bronstein* case (*Peru*), Inter-American Court of Human Rights, Series C: *Decisions and Judgments,* No. 74 (2002), petition No. 11762, judgment of 6 February 2001.

Borisenko v. *Hungary*, United Nations, *Official Records of the General Assembly Fifty-eighth Session, Supplement No. 40* (A/58/40), vol. II, annex VI, sect. J, communication No. 852/1999, views adopted on 14 October 2002.

Report on Case No. 2189 (*China*), International Labour Office, *Official Bulletin*, vol. LXXXVI, Series B, No. 1 (2003), p. 101, interim report of 21 March 2003.

Khashiyev and Akayeva v. *Russia*, applications 57924/00 and 57945/00, judgment in Strasbourg on 24 February 2005.

Nachova and Others v. *Bulgaria*, European Court of Human Rights, applications No. 43577/98 and No. 43579/98, judgment 6 July 2005.

TABLE OF CASES

(*a*) Human Rights Committee

(*b*) Working Group on Arbitrary Detention

(*c*) International Tribunal for the former Yugoslavia

(*d*) Committee on Freedom of Association

(*e*) Inter-American Court of Human Rights

(*f*) European Court of Human Rights

TABLE OF INSTRUMENTS*

(*a*) Universal Declaration of Human Rights and universal human rights treaties

Universal Declaration of Human Rights

Adopted by the General Assembly of the United Nations
on 10 December 1948[1]

International Covenant on Economic, Social and Cultural Rights

Adopted by the General Assembly of the United Nations
on 16 December 1966[2]

---

* In the notes, *Essential Texts* refers to *Essential Texts on Human Rights for the Police: A Compilation of International Instruments*, edited by Ralph Crawshaw and Leif Holmström (The Hague/London/Boston, Kluwer Law International, 2001), and *RWI Compilation* refers to *The Raoul Wallenberg Institute Compilation of Human Rights Instru-ments*, edited by Göran Melander, Gudmundur Alfredsson and Leif Holmström, second, re-vised edition (Leiden/Boston, Martinus Nijhoff Publishers, 2004).
[1] See General Assembly resolution 217 A (III) of 10 December 1948; *Essential Texts*, p. 17; and *RWI Compilation*, p. 1.

---

[2] See General Assembly resolution 2200 A (XXI) of 16 December 1966; United Nations, *Treaty Series*, vol. 993, No. I-14531; *Essential Texts*, p. 25; and *RWI Compilation*, p. 9. The Covenant entered into force on 3 January 1976.

[3] See General Assembly resolution 2200 A (XXI) of 16 December 1966; United Nations, *Treaty Series*, vols. 999, No. I-14668, and 1059, No. A-14668 (corrigendum); *Essential Texts*, p. 37; and *RWI Compilation*, p. 21. The Covenant entered into force on 23 March 1976.

[4] See General Assembly resolution 2200 A (XXI) of 16 December 1966; United Nations, *Treaty Series*, vols. 999, No. I-14668, and 1059, No. A-14668 (corrigendum); *Essential Texts*, p. 59; and *RWI Compilation*, p. 43. This Optional Protocol entered into force on 23 March 1976.

---

[5] See General Assembly resolution 44/128 of 15 December 1989; United Nations, *Treaty Series*, vol. 1642, No. A-14668; and *RWI Compilation*, p. 49. This Optional Protocol entered into force on 11 July 1991.

[6] See General Assembly resolution 2106 A (XX) of 21 December 1965; United Nations, *Treaty Series*, vol. 660, No. I-9464; *Essential Texts*, p. 65; and *RWI Compilation*, p. 207. The Convention entered into force on 4 January 1969.

[7] See General Assembly resolution 34/180 of 18 December 1979; United Nations, *Treaty Series*, vol. 1249, No. I-20378; and *RWI Compilation*, p. 223. The Convention entered into force on 3 September 1981.

---

[8] See General Assembly resolution 54/4 of 6 October 1999; United Nations, *Treaty Series*, vol. 2131, No. A-20378; and *RWI Compilation*, p. 239. The Optional Protocol entered into force on 22 December 2000.

[9] See General Assembly resolution 39/46 of 10 December 1984; United Nations, *Treaty Series*, vol. 1465, No. I-24841; *Essential Texts*, p. 81; and *RWI Compilation*, p. 445. The Convention entered into force on 26 June 1987.

[10] See General Assembly resolution 57/199 of 18 December 2002; and *RWI Compilation*, p. 461. At present, the Optional Protocol has not entered into force.

Convention on the Rights of the Child

Adopted by the General Assembly of the United Nations
on 20 November 1989[11]

Rome Statute of the International Criminal Court

Adopted by the United Nations Diplomatic Conference
of Plenipotentiaries on the Establishment
of an International Criminal Court,
at Rome, on 17 July 1998[12]

United Nations Convention against Corruption

Adopted by the United Nations General Assembly
on 31 October 2003[13]

United Nations Convention against Transnational Organized Crime

Adopted by the united Nations General Assembly
on 15 November 2000.[14]

---

[11] See General Assembly resolution 44/25 of 20 November 1989; United Nations, *Treaty Series*, vol. 1557, No. I-27531, and, as amended by General Assembly resolution 50/155 of 21 December 1995, vol. 2199, No. A-27531; *Essential Texts*, p. 97; and *RWI Compilation*, p. 261. The Convention entered into force on 2 September 1990 and, as amended by General Assembly resolution 50/155, on 18 November 2002.

[12] See United Nations, *Treaty Series*, vol. 2187, No. I-38544; and *RWI Compilation*, p. 551. The Statute entered into force on 1 July 2002.

[13] See General Assembly resolution 58/4 of 31 October 2003, No. 42146, Doc. A/58/422. The Convention entered into force on 14 December 2005.

[14] See General Assembly resolution 55/25 of 15 November 2000. The Convention entered into force 29 September 2003.

Table of Instruments

---

[15] See General Assembly resolution 55/255 of 31 May 2001, entered into force on 3 July 2005.
[16] See General Assembly resolution 55/25 of 15 November 2000, entered into force 28 January 2004.
[17] See General Assembly resolution 55/25 of 15 November 2000, entered into force 25 December 2003.

498

---

[18] See United Nations, *Treaty Series*, vol. 75, No. I-970 (Geneva Convention for the Amelioration of the Condition of the Wounded and Sick in Armed Forces in the Field), No. I-971 (Geneva Convention for the Amelioration of the Condition of the Wounded, Sick and Shipwrecked Members of Armed Forces at Sea), No. I-972 (Geneva Convention relative to the Treatment of Prisoners of War) and No. I-973 (Geneva Convention relative to the Protection of Civilian Persons in Time of War); and for article 3 common to the Geneva Conventions of 12 August 1949, *Essential Texts*, p. 121. The four Geneva Conventions entered into force on 21 October 1950.

---

[19] See United Nations, *Treaty Series*, vol. 1125, No. I-17512 (Protocol Additional to the Geneva Conventions of 12 August 1949, and relating to the Protection of Victims of International Armed Conflicts) and No. I-17513 (Protocol Additional to the Geneva Conventions of 12 August 1949, and relating to the Protection of Victims of Non-International Armed Conflicts). The two Protocols entered into force on 7 December 1978.

500

*Protocol Additional to the Geneva Conventions
of 12 August 1949, and relating to the Protection
of Victims of Non-International Armed Conflicts
(Protocol II)*

(b) Regional human rights treaties

African Charter on Human and Peoples' Rights

Adopted by the Assembly of Heads of State and Government
of the Organization of African Unity, at Nairobi,
on 27 June 1981[20]

---

[20] See United Nations, *Treaty Series*, vol. 1520, No. I-26363; *Essential Texts*, p. 147; and *RWI Compilation*, p. 189. The Charter entered into force on 21 October 1986.

Protocol to the African Charter on Human and
Peoples' Rights on the Establishment of an African
Court on Human and Peoples' Rights

Adopted by the Assembly of Heads of State and Government
of the Organization of African Unity, at Ouagadougou,
on 9 June 1998[21]

American Convention on Human Rights
"Pact of San José, Costa Rica"

Signed by States Members of the Organization
of American States, at San José, Costa Rica,
on 22 November 1969[22]

---

[21] Visit http://www.africa-union.org; see *African Journal of International and Comparative Law*, vol. 12 (2000), p. 187. This Protocol entered into force on 25 January 2004.
[22] See OAS, *Treaty Series*, No. 36; United Nations, *Treaty Series*, vol. 1144, No. I-17955; *Essential Texts*, p. 165; and *RWI Compilation*, p. 145. The Convention entered into force on 18 July 1978.

---

[23] See OAS, *Treaty Series*, No. 67; and *Essential Texts*, p. 195. The Convention entered into force on 28 February 1987.

[24] The Convention entered into force in July 1998.

[25] See Council of Europe, *European Treaty Series*, No. 5 and, as amended by Protocol No. 11 to the Convention for the Protection of Human Rights and Fundamental Freedoms, restructuring the control machinery established thereby, No. 155; United Nations, *Treaty Series*, vols. 213, No. I-2889, and 2061, No. A-2889, respectively; *Essential Texts*, p. 203; and *RWI Compilation*, p. 61. The Convention entered into force on 3 September 1953 and, as amended by Protocol No. 11, on 1 November 1998.

Protocol to the Convention for the Protection
of Human Rights and Fundamental Freedoms

Signed by States Members of the Council of Europe,
at Paris, on 20 March 1952[26]

Protocol No. 6 to the Convention for the Protection
of Human Rights and Fundamental Freedoms,
concerning the abolition of the death penalty

Signed by States Members of the Council of Europe,
at Strasbourg, on 28 April 1983[27]

Protocol No. 11 to the Convention for the Protection
of Human Rights and Fundamental Freedoms,
restructuring the control machinery established thereby

Signed by States Members of the Council of Europe,
at Strasbourg, on 11 May 1994[28]

---

[26] See Council of Europe, *European Treaty Series*, No. 9 and, as amended by Protocol No. 11 to the Convention for the Protection of Human Rights and Fundamental Freedoms, restructuring the control machinery established thereby, No. 155; United Nations, *Treaty Series*, vols. 213, No. I-2889, and 2061, No. A-2889, respectively; and *RWI Compilation*, p. 79. The present Protocol entered into force on 18 May 1954 and, as amended by Protocol No. 11, on 1 November 1998.

[27] See Council of Europe, *European Treaty Series*, No. 114 and, as amended by Protocol No. (*continued*) 11 to the Convention for the Protection of Human Rights and Fundamental Freedoms, restructuring the control machinery established thereby, No. 155; United Nations, *Treaty Series*, vols. 1496, No. A-2889, and 2061, No. A-2889, respectively; and *RWI Compilation*, p. 87. Protocol No. 6 entered into force on 1 March 1985 and, as amended by Protocol No. 11, on 1 November 1998.

(*c*) Non-treaty human rights instruments

---

[28] See Council of Europe, *European Treaty Series*, No. 155; United Nations, *Treaty Series*, vol. 2061, No. A-2889. Protocol No. 11 entered into force on 1 November 1998.

[29] See Council of Europe, *European Treaty Series*, No. 187; United Nations, *Treaty Series*, vol. 2246, No. A-2889; and *RWI Compilation*, p. 101. Protocol No. 13 entered into force on 1 July 2003.

[30] See Council of Europe, *European Treaty Series*, No. 126 and, as amended by Protocols No. 1 and No. 2 to the European Convention for the Prevention of Torture and Inhuman or Degrading Treatment or Punishment, Nos. 151 and 152; United Nations, *Treaty Series*, vols. (*continued*)
1561, No. I-27161, and 2206, No. A-27161; *Essential Texts*, p. 221 (original text); and *RWI Compilation*, p. 477. The Convention entered into force on 1 February 1989 and, as amended by Protocols No. 1 and No. 2, on 1 March 2002.

[31] See Economic and Social Council resolution 663 C (XXIV) of 31 July 1957.

Declaration on the Protection of All Persons from
Being Subjected to Torture and Other Cruel, Inhuman
or Degrading Treatment or Punishment

Adopted by the General Assembly of the United Nations
on 9 December 1975[32]

Code of Conduct for Law Enforcement Officials

Adopted by the General Assembly of the United Nations
on 17 December 1979[33]

United Nations Standard Minimum Rules
for the Administration of Juvenile Justice
(The Beijing Rules)

Adopted by the General Assembly of the United Nations
on 29 November 1985[34]

---

[32] See General Assembly resolution 3452 (XXX) of 9 December 1975.
[33] See General Assembly resolution 34/169 of 17 December 1979; *Essential Texts*, p. 247; and *RWI Compilation*, p. 487.
[34] See General Assembly resolution 40/33 of 29 November 1985.

506

---

[35] See General Assembly resolution 43/173 of 9 December 1988; *Essential Texts*, p. 265; and *RWI Compilation*, p. 503.

[36] See Economic and Social Council resolution 1989/65 of 24 May 1989; and *Essential Texts*, p. 293.

[37] See *Eighth United Nations Congress on the Prevention of Crime and the Treatment of Offenders, Havana, 27 August - 7 September 1990: report prepared by the Secretariat* (United Nations publication, Sales No. E.91.IV.2), chap. I, sect. B.2; and *Essential Texts*, p. 257.

United Nations Rules for the Protection of Juveniles Deprived of their Liberty

Adopted by the General Assembly of the United Nations on 14 December 1990[38]

Declaration on the Protection of All Persons from Enforced Disappearance

Proclaimed by the General Assembly of the United Nations on 18 December 1992[39]

---

[38] See General Assembly resolution 45/113 of 14 December 1990; and *Essential Texts*, p. 277.
[39] See General Assembly resolution 47/133 of 18 December 1992; and *Essential Texts*, p. 299.

European Code of Police Ethics

Adopted by the Committee of Ministers of the Council
of Europe on 19 September 2001[40]

---

[40] See *The European Code of Police Ethics: Recommendation Rec(2001)10 adopted by the Committee of Ministers of the Council of Europe on 19 September 2001 and explanatory memorandum* (Strasbourg, Council of Europe Publishing, 2002).

(*d*) Other international instruments

Charter of the United Nations

Signed by States original Members of the United Nations
on 26 June 1945[41]

General   4, 8, 43

*Statute of the International
Tribunal for the former Yugoslavia*

Adopted by the Security Council of the United Nations
on 25 May 1993[42]

General   9, 10, 86, 87, 88,
                                            89, 153, 184, 194, 195, 221

*Statute of the International Criminal Tribunal
for Rwanda*

Adopted by the Security Council of the United Nations
on 8 November 1994[43]

General   9, 10, 87, 153, 194, 195

---

[41] See *Yearbook of the United Nations, 1947-48* (United Nations publication, Sales No. 49.I. 13) and, as amended by General Assembly resolutions 1991 A and B (XVIII) of 17 December 1963, 2101 (XX) of 20 December 1965 and 2847 (XXVI) of 20 December 1971, United Nations, *Treaty Series*, vols. 557, No. I-8132, 638, No. A-8132 and 892, No. A-8132, respectively; and *RWI Compilation*, p. 653. The Charter entered into force on 24 October 1945 and, as amended by General Assembly resolutions 1991 A and B (XVIII), 2101 (XX) and 2847 (XXVI), on 31 August 1965, 12 June 1968 and 24 September 1973, respectively.
[42] See Security Council resolution 827 (1993) of 25 May 1993 and, as amended, resolutions 1166 (1998) of 13 May 1998, 1329 (2000) of 30 November 2000, 1411 (2002) of 17 May 2002, 1431 (2002) of 14 August 2002, 1481 (2003) of 19 May 2003 and 1597 (2005) of 20 April 2005.
[43] See Security Council resolution 955 (1994) of 8 November 1994 and, as amended, resolutions 1165 (1998) of 30 April 1998, 1329 (2000) of 30 November 2000, 1411 (2002) of 17 May 2002, 1431 (2002) of 14 August 2002, 1503 (2003) of 28 August 2003 and 1512 (2003) of 27 October 2003.

(*d*) Other international instruments

Charter of the United Nations

Signed by States original Members of the United Nations
on 26 June 1945[41]

General   4, 8, 43

Statute of the International
Tribunal for the former Yugoslavia

Adopted by the Security Council of the United Nations
on 25 May 1993[42]

General   9, 10, 86, 87, 88,
                                                        89, 153, 184, 194, 195, 221

Statute of the International Criminal Tribunal
for Rwanda

Adopted by the Security Council of the United Nations
on 8 November 1994[43]

General   9, 10, 87, 153, 194, 195

---

[41] See *Yearbook of the United Nations, 1947-48* (United Nations publication, Sales No. 49.I.
13) and, as amended by General Assembly resolutions 1991 A and B (XVIII) of 17 December
1963, 2101 (XX) of 20 December 1965 and 2847 (XXVI) of 20 December 1971, United Nations, *Treaty Series*, vols. 557, No. I-8132, 638, No. A-8132 and 892, No. A-8132, respectively; and *RWI Compilation*, p. 653. The Charter entered into force on 24 October 1945 and, as
amended by General Assembly resolutions 1991 A and B (XVIII), 2101 (XX) and 2847
(XXVI), on 31 August 1965, 12 June 1968 and 24 September 1973, respectively.
[42] See Security Council resolution 827 (1993) of 25 May 1993 and, as amended, resolutions
1166 (1998) of 13 May 1998, 1329 (2000) of 30 November 2000, 1411 (2002) of 17 May
2002, 1431 (2002) of 14 August 2002, 1481 (2003) of 19 May 2003 and 1597 (2005) of 20
April 2005.
[43] See Security Council resolution 955 (1994) of 8 November 1994 and, as amended, resolutions 1165 (1998) of 30 April 1998, 1329 (2000) of 30 November 2000, 1411 (2002) of 17
May 2002, 1431 (2002) of 14 August 2002, 1503 (2003) of 28 August 2003 and 1512 (2003)
of 27 October 2003.

The Raoul Wallenberg Institute
Professional Guides to Human Rights

1. Barry Devlin, Ralph Crawshaw and Tom Williamson. *Human Rights and Policing*. Standards for Good Behaviour and a Strategy for Change. 1998.
    ISBN-13: 978-90-411-1015-2 ISBN-10: 90-411-1015-1
2. Ralph Crawshaw and Leif Holmström (eds). *Essential Texts on Human Rights for the Police*. A Compilation of International Instruments. 2001.
    ISBN-13: 978-90-411-1557-7 ISBN-10: 90-411-1557-9
3. Ralph Crawshaw. *Police and Human Rights*. A Manual for Teachers, Resource Persons and Participants in Human Rights Programmes. 1999.
    ISBN-13: 978-90-411-1209-5 ISBN-10: 90-411-1209-X
4. Ralph Crawshaw and Leif Holmström. *Essential Cases on Human Rights for the Police*. Reviews and Summaries of International Cases. 2006.
    ISBN-13: 978-90-04-13978-7 ISBN-10: 90-04-13978-8
5. Ralph Crawshaw, Stuart Cullen and Tom Williamson. *Human Rights and Policing*. Second Revised Edition. 2006.
    ISBN-13: 978-90-04-15437-7 ISBN-10: 90-04-15437-X
6. Judith Asher. *The Right to Health: A Resource Manual for NGOs*.
    ISBN-13: 978-90-04-15438-4 ISBN-10: 90-04-15438-8